SEXUAL BEHAVIOR
IN THE 1970s

SEXUAL

BEHAVIOR

IN THE 1970s

by Morton Hunt

P▾P

A PLAYBOY PRESS BOOK

Published simultaneously in the United States and Canada by Playboy Press, Chicago, Illinois. Printed in the United States of America. Library of Congress Catalog Card Number: 73–91653. ISBN #87223-393-6. First edition.

PLAYBOY and Rabbit Head design are trademarks of Playboy, 919 North Michigan Avenue, Chicago, Illinois 60611 (U.S.A.), Reg. U.S. Pat. Off., marca registrada, marque déposée.

Contents

Acknowledgments

The debt this book owes to the late Dr. Alfred C. Kinsey is beyond the scope of acknowledgment; he was the giant on whose shoulders all sex researchers since his time have stood. Those who participated in the present project used his data, his thoughts and his words every day until we supposed them our own. I hereby make restitution.

Dr. Paul Gebhard, director of the Institute for Sex Research, was helpful in a number of ways as the project was being designed, as was Dr. Wardell Pomeroy, formerly of the Institute staff. Among the persons who answered my queries, offered suggestions or provided information, were Mr. Robert Bell, Dr. Irving Bieber, Dr. William J. Goode, Mrs. Virginia Johnson, Mr. Roger Libby, Dr. William Masters, Dr. Ira L. Reiss and Dr. Robert N. Whitehurst. Hugh Edwards, director of the Research Guild, Inc. of Chicago, was responsible for conducting the survey and for much of the basic handling of the raw data.

Joseph S. Ruben, director of research for Playboy Enterprises, Inc., gave me invaluable assistance with statistical problems, and Ellen Goldsmith and Barbara Don did painstaking fact-checking and supplemental research. Laurence G. Ferleger gave me considerable help with bibliographical materials. Violet Serwin was, as always, a splendid amanuensis.

My wife, Bernice Hunt, set aside her own writing for months to aid in the depth interviews (she dealt with all the females), a job at which she proved outstandingly successful. But this was only one of her contributions; she also offered valuable editorial suggestions, research assistance, encouragement, food and drink. And her love, without which all else would have been worthless.

Note: A few of the data presented in this report differ slightly from those which have appeared in advance excerpts published in PLAYBOY from October 1973 to March 1974. The data as presented here represent a final rechecking of statistical procedures and calculations, and supersede any which have appeared previously.

A Word from, and About,
the Author

When *Sexual Behavior in the Human Male* appeared in 1948, the public was morbidly curious about Alfred Kinsey's personal life and his motives for doing research of that nature. Although the nation had come a long way by 1966, when William Masters and Virginia Johnson published *Human Sexual Response,* there was still no end of speculation as to what kind of people would, in the name of science, spend their days watching other people perform sexual acts, and as to how this kind of research affected their own performance. But in this more blasé year of 1974, I doubt that many readers will care about my sexual behavior, which is fortunate, since I regard it as my own business. I do think, though, that most readers will want to know—and deserve to know—something of my motives for undertaking this work and of my qualifications, since these things have a direct bearing upon the credibility of the conclusions I have reached from the data gathered by the Playboy Foundation's national sex survey.

First, my qualifications: I have been writing about various aspects of sex, love and marriage for 20 years (four of my books and over 80 of my articles are in this field). Part of this output consists of popularizations of psychological and sociological research done by professional behavioral scientists. The rest consists of my own original research (I have learned a fair amount from the professionals) and of reportage of contemporary behavior patterns.

Second, my motives: They stem from my qualifications. When representatives of the Playboy Foundation invited me to take part in the survey, interpret the findings and present them in book form, I regarded it as a *job*—a professional opportunity, decently remunerated, to do the very sort of thing I have been doing all along.

"Aha!" you may say, "but why have you been doing that sort of thing all along? What is the skeleton in your psychic closet?" It's nothing more fascinating, I suspect, than a somewhat too

Victorian upbringing (I use the term loosely—I grew up not in the Victorian era, but in the 1920s), which made me, as a child, deeply troubled and unappeasably curious about those subjects that were unmentioned and unmentionable in my home. That childish hunger to know was probably the origin of the professional desires that motivate me as an adult—the intellectual curiosity that makes me want to investigate hidden areas of human behavior and to share my discoveries with my equally curious fellow men and women. There, that's my secret, and I'm sorry if it disappoints you.

But could I expect this present project to be an objective and unbiased exploration? A number of friends and acquaintances have asked me whether I have been able to resist the pressures put upon me to make my interpretations consistent with the editorial outlook of PLAYBOY—that is, with the well-known "Playboy Philosophy." I *have* been able to—not because I have fought valiantly, but because no such pressures have been put upon me. But I had known this would be the case. I had previously written a number of psychological and sociological articles for PLAYBOY and had never encountered editorial interference when my views ran counter, as they sometimes did, to attitudes expressed in the magazine's editorial pages. No one at the Foundation, and no editor at the magazine or at Playboy Press, has attemped to influence the conclusions I have drawn from the data in this book, even though I suspect that many would have preferred those conclusions to sound more revolutionary than they do.

Some readers may wonder why the Playboy Foundation did not entrust this comparison of sexual behavior in our time with that in Kinsey's time to Kinsey's own research organization, the Institute for Sex Research at Indiana University. That had, indeed, been the original intention, but the Institute, preoccupied with other projects and other problems, made it clear that a survey and research report such as the Playboy Foundation wanted would be a long time in the making. The officers of the Foundation therefore decided to turn elsewhere, employing a private research organization to design the questionnaire and do the field work, and myself to analyze and write up the results. (The research procedures are described in more detail in Chapter 1).

The entire project has been fascinating to me—not only because the questionnaire data have been an endless source of surprise and enlightenment, but because in the supplemental depth interviews I have had the rare opportunity of sharing the experiences of many different kinds of people and, through them, coming to perceive the emotional realities behind the statistics. So much so, indeed, that for the time being my intellectual curiosity is sated; I have had my fill. I hope my readers will find that this book as thoroughly satisfies their own hunger to know as it has mine.

MORTON HUNT
East Hampton, N.Y.
January 1974

SEXUAL BEHAVIOR
IN THE 1970s

MALE, 25, SINGLE, A SEXUAL CONSERVATIVE: *I don't find it very exciting to play with a woman down there. I even tried eating it a few times, not because I liked it so much but because it seemed to excite her. But the reverse thing grosses me out—she was down there sucking me one time, and it felt good, but when I looked down and saw her doing it, it made me sick.*

FEMALE, 31, MARRIED, A SEXUAL CONSERVATIVE: *Sometimes I have a strong physical thing, but mostly not. But even when I don't, I'm pleased that he is experiencing strong things. . . . And I don't want him to do any more of this or that for my sake, because actually I don't enjoy a lot of foreplay. . . .*

MALE, 45, DIVORCED, A SEXUAL RADICAL: *[Swinging] is a real dilemma. How do you reconcile the fact that you want to have a physical ball with people you don't care for? You have to cut off a part of your own personality in order to use another part. But still, it's fantastic. You have five or six girls in one evening, and perform for hours on end. . . .*

FEMALE, 36, MARRIED, A SEXUAL RADICAL: *We've met dozens of couples who swing, and who would like to swing with us, but Duncan may be very turned on by the woman while I'm not attracted to the man, or vice versa. And even if both of us are turned on sexually, Duncan may find the man a pain, or maybe I can't stand the woman. . . . It's really terribly difficult.*

MALE, 40, MARRIED, A SEXUAL LIBERAL: *We stopped going to Mass and joined a nonsectarian People's Church, and went to meetings of a discussion group on contraception and sexual problems. . . . Bridgit started using the pill, and I bought books for us on sex techniques, and after a few months we began to feel changes taking place. In fact, we couldn't believe what was happening. . . .*

FEMALE, 26, SEPARATED, A SEXUAL LIBERAL: *I feel wide open to new people and new experiences, which I wasn't before. Not that I sleep all around—I have to really feel something about a man, I have to be totally absorbed by him, to go to bed with him. But it can happen fast. Just last week I looked into someone's eyes in a bookstore, and I knew at once that I wanted to know that person. . . .*

CHAPTER

1

Sexual Liberation:

A Generation of Change

Introduction

This is a report on a national survey of American sexual attitudes and behavior as they were in the early 70s, at the end of a generation of change of unprecedented scope and rapidity. The change has indeed been so swift and so great as to have often been referred to as the "Sexual Revolution"; for reasons which will become apparent later, the author of this report and his research colleagues prefer to call it the "sexual-liberation movement," or, more simply, "sexual liberation."

The monumental first two volumes by Dr. Alfred C. Kinsey and his associates—*Sexual Behavior in the Human Male* (1948) and *Sexual Behavior in the Human Female* (1953)—are landmarks, recording how matters stood a generation ago, some years before the present wave of sexual liberation got under way. But no measurements of behavior as comprehensive as his have been made since then. To be sure, a number of sex surveys have been conducted, and some of them have proven valuable, but only within limits. Some have measured change solely within the college student population, or special segments of it. National polls by public-opinion corporations have been limited to a few elementary questions. A major national survey of adults in 1963 yielded much significant information about changing attitudes (Reiss, 1967), but not about actual behavior. A 1971 national sample (Zelnik and Kantner) did deal with behavior, but only of unwed teen-aged girls, and another (Sorenson) dealt with behavior of both sexes, but only between the ages of 13 and 19. Until now, in sum, there has existed no body of recent survey data on the sexual behavior of the adult (18 and over) national population on which to base estimations of the magnitude of the changes since Kinsey's time.*

Uninhibited by the lack of reliable information, many people have taken strong positions about the value and extent of sexual liberation. Sexual radicals, while exuberant, feel that it has not gone far enough, and that it has only begun to yield some of the good that will eventually accrue to all when it goes much further. Sexual conservatives feel that it has already led America far down that same road to ruin that was taken long ago by Sodom and Gomorrah. Many of the young, proud of their sexual rebelliousness, are confident of its rightness, while many of their parents, horrified but powerless, are equally confident of its wrongness. Lobbyists and pressure groups, ranging from the John Birch Society at one extreme to the Gay Activists Alliance at the other, strive either to shore up or to break down the legal bulwarks against the tide of change.

But while so many people have firm opinions about the impact of sexual liberation, none of them has much in the way of hard data on which to base an opinion. There is little precise information available regarding the extent to which Americans have changed their attitudes about the sexual behavior of other people; still less exact information regarding the extent to which Americans have changed their own patterns of sexual behavior, or how widely or frequently various sexual practices have been adopted; and virtually no information at all regarding the extent to which sexual liberation has changed the central meaning of sexuality for Americans, the part it plays in their overall emotional life, or its relationship to love, marriage and family life. And if there is little or no precise and scientifically gathered information about these things, it is possible that much of what we believe to be true about sexual liberation is not true at all.

---

*The results of a 1970 national survey by Albert Klassen had not been published as of this writing; a few attitude data from that survey, however, appear in Reiss (1967).

It would hardly be the first time in human history that nearly everyone believed things that were not so.

This report, we believe, is a significant addition to the existing body of information, offering a series of measurements, on a national scale, of sexual liberation upon American life and of the present state of American sexual attitudes and practices, and providing a sounder basis than has hitherto existed for judging the influence of sexual liberation upon American life.

The Sweep of Change

Yet some will undoubtedly ask why any of this is necessary. After all, have we not all been bombarded with evidence enough, in the past few years, to prove that the changes summed up by the term "sexual liberation" have been vast, profound, unprecedented and revolutionary? Those who live in large cities have been confronted with such evidence face-to-face, but even those in remote country villages have surely been made aware of the remarkable developments through newspapers and magazines, and the unabashed conversations of guests on late-night television talk shows. Consider only these few examples:

—Although Kinsey's first volume was immediately acclaimed a major contribution to knowledge, much of the public and even many academic people regarded Kinsey and his associates as unwholesome and somewhat unclean. Among social conservatives, such hostility was engendered by the book that by 1954 the Rockefeller Foundation withdrew its aid to Kinsey's Institute for Sex Research, nearly wrecking its work.[1] By the end of the 1960s, however, sex research had become so respectable that any number of wholesome, clean doctoral candidates were engaged in it, foundation and government funds were being handed out for projects studying even such shady phenomena as prostitution and homosexuality, and little resistance existed to such research except among extreme rightists.[2]

—Even Kinsey, for all his courage, knew the limits of the possible. Along with his many thousands of interviews, he had also actually witnessed and filmed some sexual acts, but prudently said nothing about this in print.[3] For as anthropologist John J. Honigmann wrote in 1944 in the *Journal of Criminal Psychopathology*, sexual interaction in the presence of a third party would unquestionably be considered obscene in our society and, indeed, "our cultural norms would scarcely tolerate such a situation [even] in the scientific laboratory."[4] Yet hardly a decade later Dr. William Masters and Mrs. Virginia Johnson were closely scrutinizing couples having coitus in the laboratory and inspecting and recording the condition of their organs and tissues at every stage of the process. When the resultant data were published in 1966, under the title *Human Sexual Response,* medical men and the general public alike hailed their work, and it was considered obscene by only a few intellectual troglodytes. Emboldened by this, professional journals of sexology and sociology soon followed suit, even publishing articles by researchers who had attended group-sex parties and had been participant observers at pickup bars and at homosexual public-toilet encounters.

—Despite the rear-guard defenses of police, prosecutors and decency legions, the borderline between the showable and the unshowable has moved very far in the direction of total freedom in the past decade. The nude female breast, formerly portrayed only in trashy or arty magazines, has become an everyday sight in family, fashion and men's magazines, and the hairy female pubis, which had always been rigorously hidden even in nudist literature, made its mass-circulation debut in the January 1972 issue of PLAYBOY. Other magazines have followed suit and gone on to male frontal nudity.

Even earlier, female and male nudity had made the grade in X-rated films, and in on- and off-Broadway shows. In the mid-1960s the crotch remained in shadows, but during the next few years the lighting grew ever brighter, and the organs came into play—at least in simulated fashion—with copulation being very explicitly represented in *Oh, Calcutta!,* cunnilingus in the off-Broadway *The Beard* and homosexual rape in *Fortune and Men's Eyes.* In "soft-core" X-rated films, virtually every sort of sexual act was openly portrayed, though erection, intromission and orgasm were simulated or suggested rather than pictured in actuality; in "hard-core" blue movies, however, full-color close-ups of erect penises penetrating every available orifice, and freely spurting semen, were being exhibited publicly in erotic-movie houses not just in New York, Los Angeles, Chicago and San Francisco, but in Des Moines, Kansas City, Nashville, Dallas, Denver and a number of other cities.

—In virtually every city, meanwhile, many of the famous works of published erotica that had long been "caged" (locked away) in public libraries and brought out only for "qualified researchers" appeared openly in every bookstore. After the 1959 federal court decision permitting D. H. Lawrence's *Lady Chatterley's Lover* to be sent through the mails in this country, an ever-growing list of erotic classics such as the anonymous *My Secret Life* and the works of de Sade became available to anyone with the price of a paperback. At the bottom of the literary ladder, low-grade, hard-core pornography of no discernible literary or artistic merit, but of great explicitness and infinite perversity, became freely available by the late 1960s; many millions of copies of illustrated hard-core magazines and paperback books were sold annually in some 850 bookstores that specialized in erotica and even, to some extent, were to be found in a number of more conventional bookstores throughout the country.[5]

Even in respectable literary works, descriptions of sex acts ceased to be indirect and poetically allusive, and became clinically graphic. Writers such as Philip Roth, John Updike and Jean Gênet included scenes of masturbation, fellatio, cunnilingus, buggery—oh yes, and intercourse—of such explicitness that Lady Chatterley seemed second cousin to Heidi. Such historically unprintable words as "fuck," "cock," "cunt," "prick" and the like were, by 1970, being freely used in respectable books and even in some respectable magazines, and in late 1972 the unthinkable happened—the magisterial *Oxford English Dictionary,* for nearly 90 years the ultimate authority on the English language, included the word "fuck" in its long-awaited supplement. Yet how exceedingly daring we all thought Norman Mailer, in 1948, for repeatedly using the euphemism "fug" in *The Naked and the Dead,* and how bold we all thought that rock group in the mid-1960s for calling itself the Fugs.

—In the 1930s, the most advanced and liberal marriage manual in print was Theodoor Van de Velde's *Ideal Marriage.* Dr. Van de Velde advised the use of various types of foreplay—including (daringly, for that time) oral-genital stimulation—and described a number of alternative positions for intercourse and their various advantages. But he did all this in a refined and uplifting manner, as witness the following description of the woman-astride position:

> In the astride attitude, there is no possibility of mutual embrace or kisses. On the other hand, the full unimpeded view of each other's bodies . . . has a strongly stimulant effect. And the opportunity, often missing in other attitudes, of gazing face to face, into one another's eyes, of beholding, in the reciprocal play of expression, the rising tide of excitement to its ecstatic culmination, greatly enhances all the other stimuli of this attitude.[6]

And while he recommended the "genital kiss," if needed, he warned the husband to use it with "the *greatest gentleness, the most delicate reverence,*" and cautioned the wife, in employing fellatio, to exercise utmost *"aesthetic delicacy and discretion"* in order not to cross "that treacherous frontier between supreme beauty and base ugliness." (Presumably, this meant that she should not carry it through to the point of ejaculation; he regarded oral stimulation to orgasm as a species of perversion.)

By the 1960s, marriage-and-sex manuals had become less poetic and more abandoned. Most of them dropped the cautionary tone and took a lustier, earthier approach. Many urged their readers to make all sorts of efforts to attain maximum sensations, and some recommended not only all kinds of coital positions but simultaneous oral-genital stimulation to orgasm, anal play with the finger or tongue, anal intercourse, the use of vibrators, mirrors, crushed ice (a handful of which, jammed into the crotch at the moment of orgasm, immensely heightens the experience, according to Dr. John Eichenlaub) and so on. And by the end of the decade the tone of the prose employed in such books had changed radically from that of Van de Velde, as witness these words about "69" from the top seller of them all, Dr. David Reuben's *Everything You Always Wanted to Know About Sex:*

> She feels the insistent throbbing of the organ against her lips and experiences a slightly salty taste, as well as the characteristic but not unpleasant odor of the sudoriferous glands of the area. Because the penis is much larger in comparison to the clitoris she can also see the male genitals as she proceeds. By simultaneous cunnilingus and fellatio every possible sense is brought to a fever pitch and a mutual orgasm occurs rapidly unless the couple switches to a penis-vagina position. The most presumably undersexed man or woman will be brought to an explosive orgasm by using this technique providing they are willing to do it.[7]

Indeed, the immensely popular sex manuals written by "J" (*The Sensuous Woman*) and "M" (*The Sensuous Man*) employed a palpitating, salivating eroticism unlike anything previously available except in hard-core pornography:

> Put your girl in a soft, upholstered chair and kneel in front of her so your head comes about to the level of her breasts. . . . Now slide her off the chair and right onto that beautiful erect shaft. The feeling is dizzying. She is wet and very, very hot; you are face to face and in about as deep as you can be. . . . You lean back with your hands on the floor and raise your pelvis to plunge into her for a few moments, and then she should take over the action by moving her pelvic area up and down on your penis—faster and faster. . . . [It's] an exciting way to come. When you do explode, you'll find yourself in each other's arms—exhausted, wet, beautiful— a total state of A.F.O.—all fucked out.[8]

> . . . He may wish to investigate you anally with his mouth and tongue and expect you to reciprocate. Now don't freeze. If you have washed in this area, it is *not* dirty and, if you'll stop wailing like a banshee or playing Purity Raped for a moment, you will notice the beginning of a curious, warm and divinely demanding sensation and be secretly hoping he'll go on to the next step. . . .[9]

So much for the media. But what of actual behavior? Here, too, we are surrounded by evidence that many people are now openly doing things that were unthinkable a generation ago, or that at least were among the most closely guarded of all personal secrets. A few examples:

—While millions are reading the newer kind of sex manual, hundreds or perhaps thousands of couples are actually getting direct instruction at any one of scores of sex-therapy clinics and nude encounter groups. In some of the latter both married couples and single persons are taught, in groups, to touch, feel and explore each other's bodies, and in some "sexual development" groups surrogate coital partners are provided for those who need complete coital experience under expert supervision.[10]

—Premarital sex, formerly furtive and carefully hidden, especially from one's parents, has recently achieved something close to acceptance in certain parts of our society. On four-fifths of

U.S. coed college campuses, dorms are going coed; at some colleges all rules governing intersex visiting in dorm rooms have been dropped; and at a few, sex-information bureaus have been established for the benefit of the students.[11] Only half a dozen years ago it was big news that, here and there, a few daring undergraduate couples were secretly rooming together, even though unwed. Today, many such couples openly room together on a number of campuses, and college administrators and parents have all but given up trying to fight the trend.

—A remarkable degree of candor has lately marked the search for sexual partners: In many large cities a growing number of single men and women (or married people on the loose) go in search of sexual pickups to cocktail lounges and other public places, and make only a minimal pretense at socializing; indeed, in San Francisco such places are often jokingly called "body-exchange bars." In many cities entrepreneurs operate paid-admission parties for the same purpose, though sometimes a pretense at social decorum is maintained. No pretense, however, is involved in the advertisements placed in a growing number of underground newspapers and magazines by people seeking sexual partners, mate-swapping couples, group-sex parties and partners for deviant sex acts. Clubs and services introducing marital swingers to each other have multiplied; such swinging is practiced not just by druggies, hippies and far-out types but has been at least tried out by about one to two million largely middle-class, married, socially conventional Americans.[12]

—While most swingers still keep their unorthodox sexual behavior secret, a great many other people are far more willing to tell all than was the case until the last few years. In magazine interviews, author Gay Talese has spoken freely about his sexual exploits and open infidelity; film star Jack Nicholson has discussed his potency and his conquest of premature ejaculation; feminist author Germaine Greer has boasted of her sexual appetite and her one-night stands; women's liberationist Kate Millett and writer Merle Miller have both come out of the closet and spoken candidly (and in Millett's case proudly) of their homosexuality. A young Washington defense lawyer, Philip Bailley, was arrested in mid-1972 and charged in federal court with 22 morals offenses, including procurement, after FBI agents found 164 photographs of nude women, plus four address books and various sexual devices, in his apartment. Totally unabashed,

Bailley told a reporter, "Women get a thrill out of having their pictures taken in the nude. You take them up to your apartment, make love to them, take their picture, make love to them again. It sure as hell beats watching television." As for the sexual devices, "Hell, anybody who digs sex has stuff like that around his apartment. . . . Those Justice Department bureaucrats just don't understand my life-style, which is the life-style of half the people in America my age." (A federal court, ignoring the issue of life-style, convicted Bailley of transporting a woman into Washington, D.C., for purposes of prostitution, and sentenced him to five years in federal prison.)

—Gays have done far more than merely come out of the closet: They have organized—at least 600 homosexual organizations and publications now exist in this country—and grown strong enough and bold enough to launch a serious liberation movement. In the last few years we have seen things that would have been inconceivable a decade ago: thousands of homosexuals marching in parades and demonstrations, gay spokesmen appearing on national television shows to explain their cause, representatives of gay liberation writing protest letters to magazines and lobbying at political conventions, gay students demanding lounges and meeting rooms of their own on campuses, gay lovers filing court suits in an effort to establish the legality of homosexual marriage, ministers holding church services for homosexual congregations.

—By the end of 1973 an estimated 1500 persons had undergone radical surgery and made the transsexual leap from one identity to another. It was becoming a commonplace rather than a fascinating rarity, and in 1973 a few psychiatrists were even beginning to publish papers on patients who had married such transsexuals and were having emotional difficulties in those marriages.[13]

—Kinky types, who used to exhibit their peculiarities only in sheltered settings, now do so openly: drag queens, transvestites and other flagrantly deviant persons now show up en masse at the premieres of blue movies and rock concerts, and openly congregate at gay bars, beaches and parks.

(Rock concerts, incidentally, seem to induce exhibitionism even in straights; it is at such events that America in the last several years has witnessed the unprecedented spectacle of sexually normal young people stripping off their clothes and having intercourse out in the open, in front of thousands of other people, including representatives of the news media.)

—Sexual services have come out in the open: "Massage parlors" and "body rub" emporia—with girl "models" offering whatever kind of manual stimulation one wants—flourish in some cities; prostitutes who used to remain in defined "red-light" areas now roam the downtown streets freely; dildoes and other assorted sexual devices (including a number used in sadomasochistic activities) are offered for sale in sex magazines and by direct mail, and in New York and a few other cities are displayed in shops specializing in such equipment; gay baths, frankly functioning as places for quick sexual encounters, flourish in New York and elsewhere.

—A variety of individuals and groups have begun to openly advocate and practice alternatives to monogamous marriage, although most of these alternatives are technically against the law as well as against traditional morals. Some women's-liberation leaders are opposed to marriage altogether, favoring informal male-female relationships (a few endorse lesbian alliances). The more moderate women's liberationists still believe in marriage, but with drastic modifications of the traditional roles and duties of husband and wife—and of their sexual obligations to each other; fidelity, they argue, should be a matter of choice, decided between the marital partners, rather than a legal requirement. "Open marriage" and "flexible monogamy" have been advocated by a number of best-selling authors (anthropologists George and Nena O'Neill, for instance), and group marriages, idealized by novelist Robert Rimmer, have become a reality, there being anywhere from hundreds to thousands of them in existence, according to various estimates. Although sexual sharing in group marriages is illegal in nearly all states, hundreds of such marriages are openly listed in published directories of communes. Meanwhile, old-fashioned unwed alliances have either grown in number, come out in the open or both. One reads every day of actors and actresses, jet-setters and other celebrities who openly live or travel with some other-sex friend, or who even have and raise children out of wedlock, by choice. Living together unwed is, indeed, now so common, at least in larger and more sophisticated cities, as to have become a subject for self-help articles. New York magazine, in 1973, published an article full of practical advice on how to handle decorating, money, food, insurance and other such matters when living together without, as the saying used to go, benefit of clergy.

Several states, moving toward the model penal code adopted by the American Law Institute in 1962, have recently revised their sex laws, dropping most or all private sex acts between consenting adults from the list of crimes. Illinois, in 1961, and Connecticut, Colorado, Oregon, Ohio, North Dakota, Delaware and Hawaii more recently, have wiped out their long-standing penalties against private consensual sodomy, both heterosexual and homosexual. In most states the old laws against fornication, cohabitation, adultery and sodomy still stand, but with a few notable exceptions such laws are generally unenforced.[14] And in January 1973, even as moves were under way in a handful of states to liberalize their antiabortion laws, the Supreme Court handed down its stunning and epochal decision recognizing the constitutional right of women—as part of the right of privacy—to decide for themselves whether or not to terminate pregnancy by abortion. The only limitation the states could place upon this right, the Court held, was that in the final trimester, when the fetus was viable, the state could proscribe abortion except where it was necessary to preserve the life or health of the mother. Ten years ago, legal, safe and easy abortion in the United States had been unthinkable; five years ago, it had been thinkable but nonexistent; in 1972 it was legal, subject to certain limitations, in half a dozen states; and in 1973 it was legal, if not easily obtainable, everywhere.

Auspices and Methodology of the Present Survey

Thus, things unseen and unheard-of a generation ago or even a decade ago are now to be seen and heard of all around us. Why this should be so is a question the full answer to which lies outside the scope of this book, though many of the components of the answer are well known. They include the emancipation of women, the decreasing influence of religion, the development of effective birth-control methods, the diffusion of psychological knowledge throughout society, the revolt of youth against adult values and so on.

But the causes of sexual liberation interest the average person less than its meaning for his own life and the lives of the people he is directly involved with. If he resents the new freedoms or fears that they mean the impending collapse of our civilization, he will resist letting them alter his own behavior and may even support political and social backlash movements; if he regards the new freedoms as emancipating and as bringing about a healthier and more joyous life, he will try to incorporate them into his own behavior, and may lend his support to publications and organizations promoting sexual liberation. Even now we see people choosing sides and joining the battle. Women's liberationists are prodding state legislators and medical groups to implement the Supreme Court ruling on abortion via rewritten laws and abortion clinics; Catholics and other antiabortionists are delaying its implementation and seeking legal ways to circumvent the Court's ruling. Publishers and civil-rights groups are organizing to defend their right to print and to exhibit explicit sexual material, but the Supreme Court, stuffed with Nixon conservatives, clamped down on pornography in its bewildering and intentionally vague ruling of June 21, 1973. This gave local judges the power to decide whether a work violates "community" standards, rather than those of the nation as a whole, and whether, "taken as a whole, [the work does] not have serious literary, artistic, political or scientific value." In the wake of that ruling, many prosecutors have begun taking action against distributors of hard-core films and publications and, in some places, against distributors of soft-core works which were deemed beyond the bounds of local taste.*

Sex-education courses, advocated by SIECUS (Sex Information and Education Council of the United States), have been adopted in recent years by a number of public school systems, but in the last three years or so a backlash movement, headed in some areas by the John Birch Society, has forced some of those systems to drop the courses. And while Idaho, like the other states mentioned above, recently modernized and liberalized its sex laws, within a year the legislature, under massive

---

*It is too early to know what the ultimate impact of the Court's ruling will be. Many noted writers, publishers and film-makers are deeply troubled, but early indications are that it is primarily hard-core material that will be subject to attack in many areas of the country. One may legitimately doubt, however, that anything like a rollback to the general publishing and entertainment standards of a generation ago, or even a decade ago, is possible.

pressure from the predominantly Mormon population, reinstated a number of archaic statutes against adultery, fornication and nonconventional sex acts.

One's judgment as to the scope and impact of sexual liberation is, however, only as sound as the information on which it is based—and for all the barrage of words and the welter of strange new phenomena around us, adequate information has simply not been available. Lacking a major census of American sexual behavior, we have had no good way to judge whether that behavior has changed radically or merely come out in the open; whether such changes as have taken place are affecting only a highly visible minority or the large unseen majority; whether the increase in freedom, whatever its scope, has strengthened love relationships and marriage among the sexually liberated or weakened them; whether sexual liberation is bringing the liberated greater satisfaction or only a frenetic quest for stronger sensations and new kicks; and whether America is becoming a dissolute and degenerate nation or a sensuous and healthy one.

The present survey attempts to provide a body of information from which such judgments can be soundly derived. In effect, it seeks to resurvey the territory mapped out in 1948 and 1953 (though not in such ambitious and exhaustive detail as the Kinsey studies) and thereby to measure the dimensions of the changes that have taken place. As the reader will see, many of the measurements we made yielded astonishing results—some because they revealed change greater than any we had expected, but some because they thoroughly refuted certain widely accepted beliefs about the scope and meaning of sexual liberation.

Before inspecting our findings, however, the reader may wish to know how the information was gathered, so as to judge its trustworthiness for himself. (If not, he may pass over this brief summary of the survey procedure and turn to the next section of this chapter.)

The survey was commissioned by the Playboy Foundation as part of its continuing program of sponsoring research in sexual behavior and sex education. (The Foundation's other areas of activity are the protection and extension of civil rights and liberties and the modernization of laws pertaining to sex, drugs, contraception, censorship and, until 1973, abortion.) The Foundation asked the Research Guild, Inc., an independent market-survey and behavioral-research organization with headquarters in Chicago, to design and administer a questionnaire to a representative sample of adults throughout the nation and to process and analyze the data collected. The staff of the Research Guild developed a basic questionnaire, with four variant versions applicable to males and females, married and unmarried. The several versions asked for some 1000 to 1200 items of information covering the individual's background, sex education, attitudes toward sexual practices and complete sex history. As far as it was feasible, the questionnaire explored all the major areas investigated by the Kinsey researchers, and in a few important instances went beyond them. For example, there is little or no information in Kinsey on anal erotic practices, sadomasochism, mate-swapping and group sex, and nothing at all on incest, perhaps because in his time these things were too far beyond the pale, while we were able to explore all of them in some detail, and to gather some valuable data.

In the first half of 1972 the Research Guild gathered 2026 completed questionnaires, filled out by persons in 24 cities around the country. This sample closely parallels the American population of persons 18 years old and over. It consists of 982 males and 1044 females, is 90 percent white and 10 percent black, and includes 71 percent currently married, 25 percent never-married, and 4 percent previously married but still unremarried persons. Such other major characteristics as age, educational attainment, occupational status, and urban-rural background are all represented in about the same proportions as in the adult American population. On the other hand, the survey did not reach illiterates, members of the poverty culture, or inmates of prisons and other institutions, and only minimally reached strongly deviant groups such as commune-dwellers.

As balanced as the sample is, in the jargon of the professionals it is not a true "probability sample" (a scientifically randomized selection), and we cannot unequivocally assert that it is representative of the national population. But considerable effort was expended to guard against bias due to self-selecting factors, and it is our belief that the sample is, in fact, a reasonably good representation of American adult society.

The bulk of the sample was gathered by professional public-opinion survey teams in 24 cities. Using random selection of names, they initiated contact by telephone. Persons so reached were not told about the questionnaire, but were merely asked to participate anonymously in small, private, panel discussions of present trends in American sexual behavior, for the benefit of a group of behavioral researchers. About one out of five agreed, a rate considered normal for opinion surveys using this technique. Respondents met in groups of 16, under the informal chairmanship of staff members of the Research Guild. Only after extensive discussion were the members of each group asked to complete their contribution to research by filling in anonymous questionnaires, then and there. Motivated by the discussion, and unwilling to walk out on the group, virtually 100 percent of the discussants completed usable questionnaires.

To see whether these precautions had eliminated perceptible bias, the questionnaire included over a score of questions about the respondent's attitudes and practices in such nonsexual areas as the use of tobacco, alcohol and drugs, friendship and socializing patterns, stance on women's rights and consumer boycotts, and the like. By all these tests, the sample appears to be essentially a normal subsample of the national adult population.

Because the method did not adequately reach the youngest age groups, an additional subsample of several hundred persons was gathered by individual solicitation in a number of areas. Certainly, this group was not a national probability sample; nonetheless, aside from the factor of age, it appeared by all other internal criteria to be without discernible bias, and was therefore merged with the basic sample.

We comfort ourselves with the thought that Professor Reiss, as knowledgeable a person about sex surveys as there is, recently commented that "one can fault [Kinsey] on the level of not having a random sample of the nation, but using that yardstick we would throw out almost all sociological research."

The completed questionnaires were handled by standard data-processing methods, the answers being punched onto IBM cards from which an IBM computer produced data print-outs in accordance with programed instructions. These print-outs revealed the present-day relationship between each and every sexual attitude or sexual act investigated and the parameters of age, marital status, race, education, occupational level, religious preference, frequency of attendance at religious services and political self-rating.

Data, however, do not necessarily reveal the motives underlying, or the emotional content of, any particular kind of experience. One might, for example, find that young men were having more sexual partners, and using more varied sexual procedures before marriage, than young men a generation ago, but how could one know whether this betokened greater joyousness, or only a greater need to exhibit *machismo* in a time when sexual prowess is so greatly emphasized? One might find that wives were masturbating more often than formerly, but how could one know whether this was the result of increased discontent with their husbands' performance or merely a feeling of greater freedom to seek relief when necessary?

Accordingly, we supplemented the questionnaire data with a series of in-depth, tape-recorded interviews to seek clues to the meanings of trends showing up in the data and to gather illustrative first-person materials. The author of this volume, aided by some of the same recruiters who worked on the questionnaire-survey sample, assembled an interview sample similar in character to the survey sample but much smaller in size, consisting of 200 persons, half males, half females. The males were interviewed by the author, and the females by his wife, Bernice Hunt.* In about a fifth of all cases, both spouses of a marriage were interviewed (separately, however); this gave the interviewers an opportunity to evaluate the credibility of the answers elicited by the interview technique used. Although the comparisons indicated that the interviews had yielded highly reliable and credible answers, we chose not to contaminate the questionnaire data by merging the two samples; all figures given in this report, therefore, unless otherwise identified, refer only to the questionnaire survey, while all illustrative case histories, anecdotes and first-person quotations, unless otherwise identified, come from the interview sample.

Again, this study is not, strictly speaking, a replication of the Kinsey surveys, for it is much less detailed, it used a different sampling procedure and a self-administered questionnaire, and the questions used were worded differently from Kinsey's. We believe, however, that in many important areas our data can be directly compared with his, and that elsewhere, though not directly comparable, they provide useful indications of the direction and magnitude of change.

Finally, a modest disclaimer: As is true of almost all surveys,

---

*Mrs. Hunt, an author in her own right, is known professionally as Bernice Kohn.

ours did not directly examine what people did, but only what they *said* they did. Undoubtedly, the fading of memory, the magnifications of wishful thinking, the obscurations of prudery and other similar factors introduced some distortions, but there was no way to overcome this. Masters and Johnson (and a few others before and after them) have observed coitus directly, but they used a very carefully selected population functioning under very special conditions; this was acceptable, since Masters and Johnson were gathering only physiological information. But in studying the broad range of everyday sexual experiences from a behavioral standpoint, one would have to be invisibly present in thousands of bedrooms, automobiles and motel rooms observing millions of sex acts while they are occurring—an impossible program, albeit an intriguing fantasy. One can only rely on what people say, and on good questionnaire design and professional skill, to pinpoint and exclude data of low reliability and credibility.

An Overview of Changes in Sexual Attitudes in the Past Generation

In both the questionnaires and the interviews we sought to examine sexual attitudes before investigating overt behavior. The Kinsey team did so, too, but attached little value to the answers and reported very little attitudinal material except in the form of broad, impressionistic comments. They reasoned that an individual's acts show what his attitudes really are, while the things he says are "little more than reflections of the attitudes which prevail in the particular culture in which he was raised."[15] Kinsey himself had originally been a biologist dealing with infrahuman creatures—wasps, in fact—which may account for his antiverbal bias. It is not, however, shared by most sociologists or psychologists. For one thing, sociologist Ira Reiss, a leading investigator of contemporary sexual mores, compared the expressed standards of a group of 248 unmarried college students with their own actual behavior and concluded that "in the great majority of cases belief and action do coincide."[16] But even when what a person says is not the same as what he does, his expressed attitudes indicate some of his feelings about his own behavior, sometimes revealing self-disapproval, sometimes wishful thinking and unsatisfied hungers, and so on. And even if what he says sometimes reflects not his own feelings but the views that he thinks of as socially acceptable, this yields important information as to the probable direction of behavioral change in the future, for it is well established that when attitudes change, behavioral change follows suit.

Because attitudes were so sparsely reported in the first and second Kinsey volumes, we could make only a few direct comparisons to those works. But even without a firm statistical base line, it is abundantly clear to anyone who is reasonably acquainted with the state of sexual attitudes a generation ago that in many particulars our data show a dramatic shift toward permissiveness (by which we mean tolerant or liberal attitudes toward sexual ideas and acts, especially those held and practiced by other people), and more generally toward sexual liberalism (by which we mean both attitudinal permissiveness and freedom to include certain formerly forbidden acts in one's own behavioral repertoire). The new permissiveness and liberalism are not, of course, homogeneously distributed throughout the population, and in a little while we will see which segments of American society are the more permissive and liberal, and which are the opposite. But even taking the sample as a whole, and assuming it to be reasonably indicative of the society as a whole, we find a remarkably large proportion holding far more permissive attitudes than those which were dominant a generation ago. A few examples:

—Three-quarters of all males and more than three-quarters of all females feel that schools should teach sex education, and by far the largest number of these feel strongly about the matter. (In investigating attitudes, we offered a number of statements to which the questionnaire respondent could make any one of five answers—"Agree strongly," "Agree somewhat," "Disagree somewhat," "Disagree strongly" and "No opinion.")

—Should the man always be the one to initiate sexual intercourse? Over four-fifths of all males and of all females said no, and most of them took the strong position on the matter. Only 1 out of every 20 males and 1 out of every 40 females took a strong position against female initiative. There is nothing comparable in Kinsey, but it is worth pointing out that in marriage manuals written or still being sold as late as the 1940s, authors carefully assured their readers that it was permissible and even desirable for the woman to initiate sexual activity on occasion, a reassurance that would hardly have been necessary if this were not a point on which most men and women needed education.[17]

—Attitudes toward premarital intercourse have definitely swung strongly toward the permissive and approving end of the spectrum. While Kinsey offers nothing directly useful concerning attitudes in this area, the Roper polling agency asked national samples, in 1937 and again in 1959, "Do you think it is all right for either or both parties to a marriage to have had previous sexual intercourse?" There was virtually no change over that long span of years: Both in 1937 and 1959, 22 percent said it was all right for both men and women, 8 percent said it was all right for men only, and somewhat over half said it was all right for neither.[18] But samples taken in the 1960s by various sociologists, including Ira Reiss, Harold Christensen and Robert Bell, suggested that attitudes on this issue were changing markedly, particulary among the younger part of the population.[19] Our own survey provides evidence of a very considerable shift toward permissiveness: Depending on the degree of affection or emotional involvement between the partners, anywhere from 60 to 84 percent of our males felt that premarital sex was acceptable for men, and anywhere from 44 to 81 percent felt it was acceptable for women. The females in our sample were somewhat less permissive, but even so, anywhere from 37 to 73 percent felt that it was all right for men, and anywhere from 20 to 68 percent felt that it was acceptable for women. Similarly, when we asked our respondents what they thought of the statement "People who have sex before marriage are more likely to have happy and stable marriages later on," 59 percent of the males and 43 percent of all females agreed with the statement, a definite indication of a major shift in the direction of permissiveness. (A 1973 Gallup poll, made after our own survey, showed a quite comparable shift over a very short period: In 1969, 68 percent of a national sample had said premarital sex was wrong, but in 1973 only 48 percent said so. While older persons were more conservative than younger ones, the shift was as great among them as among the young.[20] And one more indication: In the early 1940s, the Roper agency found that from

64 percent to 72 percent of a national sample, depending on social class, felt that men should require virginity in a girl for marriage.[21] We did not ask this, but did offer the statement "Most men want to marry a virgin"—and found that only half of our total sample agreed, a sharp drop from the Roper figures. Moreover, well over two-thirds of the women and three-quarters of the men did not agree that a woman who goes to bed with a man before marriage loses his respect.

—Our questionnaire offered the simplistic proposition "Homosexuality is wrong," representing the unequivocal moral norm on this matter that has existed in our culture since early Christian times. But over half of all women and close to half of all men in our survey disagreed. Nearly half of all men and women, in fact, indicated in response to another item that homosexuality should be legal; slightly smaller proportions felt it should not; and the rest had no opinion.

—We asked respondents for their reactions to the statement "Masturbation is wrong." Fewer than 8 percent of the men and a little over 8 percent of the women agreed strongly, while roughly five times as many of each sex disagreed strongly. Even lumping together the "strongly" and "somewhat" responses, we find only a fifth of all men and women viewing masturbation as wrong, and well over two-thirds viewing it as not wrong. The general population has evidently adopted an attitude toward masturbation held only by the enlightened and psychologically sophisticated a generation or so ago.

—On a number of issues that have long been thought to run counter to majority opinion, we found near-majorities or even large majorities of our total sample taking the supposedly un-popular or avant-garde view. We had distinct majorities, for instance, favoring the legalization of prostitution, the legaliza-tion of abortion and the adoption of divorce laws that eliminate the need to offer reasons to the court.

—Mate-swapping, virtually unmentionable until recently, and violative of our most deeply entrenched ideas about sex and marriage, is wrong in the eyes of a majority—but, surprisingly, not an overwhelming one: Only 62 percent of men and 75 per-cent of women agreed that it was wrong, while a sizable minority —nearly a third of the men and a fifth of the women—felt that it was not.

—Although no specific data on attitudes toward the use of the mouth upon the sexual organs exist in Kinsey (he does, however, give data on actual behavior of this kind), we can judge the attitudes of a generation ago by the circumspection with which both fellatio and cunnilingus were treated even in so daring a marriage manual as that of Van de Velde. (Most other authors of marriage manuals at that time either avoided the subject altogether or mentioned it only in passing, noncommittally observing that psychiatrists and other experts did not necessarily consider these acts perversions, if used occasionally and only as foreplay.) But when we offered the statement "It is wrong for a man to stimulate a woman's genitals with his lips or tongue," three-quarters of all men and four-fifths of all women disagreed, most of them strongly. An even larger majority of men, and very nearly as large a majority of women, also refused to characterize as wrong the woman's stimulating of the male genitals with her lips or tongue.

—In contrast to the ancient Greeks and Romans, and to many other peoples, Christian civilization has always held anal intercourse to be among the vilest of perversions and the blackest of sins. We expected to find some measure of tolerance for it appearing as part of the general liberal trend, but were unprepared for the results that came out of the computer: Only a little over a quarter of all men and of all women agreed with the statement "Anal intercourse between a man and a woman is wrong," while well over half of each sex disagreed. The data are so remarkable that it is worth giving them here in detail (see Table 1).

Table 1

Anal Intercourse Is Wrong:
Total Sample, Percents Agreeing and Disagreeing

	Males	Females
Agree strongly	17	18
Agree somewhat	10	9
Disagree somewhat	26	25
Disagree strongly	33	32
No opinion	14	16

The explicit permissiveness of the "Disagree" replies is, if anything, understated by this table, since the unusually large proportion of "No opinion" replies may represent noncriticism of the practice. This is not to say that the majority of our sample considers anal intercourse appealing, exciting or mutually satisfying, but the majority clearly no longer accepts the historical evaluation of the act.

—Both the Gallup and the Harris polls have reported in recent years that very large majorities of Americans want pornography to be controlled by stricter laws, or even outlawed.[22] But the congressionally authorized Commission on Obscenity and Pornography sponsored its own rather deeper-probing survey and concluded that while only a third of all Americans feel that adults should be allowed to read or see any sexual material they wish, over half indicated that they would feel this way if it were proven that such material does no harm.[23] Our own data indicate a similar admixture of restrictive and permissive feelings, and of traditional and liberal responses to encounters with erotic materials: Four-tenths of all men and of all women reported that pictures, drawings, movies and writings showing or describing sexual acts either disgust them or cause a mixture of disgust and delight; yet anywhere from half to over nine-tenths also admit to being sexually aroused by various material of this sort. The latter figures are up to four times as large as the comparable figures reported for women by Kinsey, and up to twice as large as his figures for men.[24] In some part, the greater arousability probably has to do with greater opportunity; undoubtedly, a larger number of women today see erotic materials with some frequency than did a generation ago. But apart from opportunity, it is obvious that a substantially larger part of the population than formerly, especially of the female population, not only sees erotic materials anywhere from occasionally to often but has become sufficiently uninhibited to be aroused by it, even though continuing to feel an admixture of revulsion or guilt due to cultural conditioning.

Thus, taking the sample as a whole, there is ample evidence of a marked shift toward permissiveness in sexual attitudes. Putting it another way, the average American now holds many opinions about sex that a generation ago were rarely held by any but highly educated big-city sophisticates and bohemians. Here, for instance, are typical comments by some of our interviewees whom one might reasonably have expected to hold only conservative and conventional sexual attitudes:

A 40-YEAR-OLD SHOP FOREMAN, MARRIED, A LAPSED CATHO-
LIC: I think a lot of the pornography is a good thing,
though it's gone too far and will probably swing back.
But it's better to have it out in the open than secret,
and for people to know what's going on. . . . [*On
premarital sexual experience*]: Our wedding night was kind
of rough, because she was a virgin and I wasn't much
better off. I've only seen in the last few years how many
hang-ups I had due to the way I was brought up. I'm
changing my mind about a lot of things. Don't get me
wrong, I wouldn't want to see everyone running around
and screwing before marrying, but I think a certain
amount of premarital sex is a good thing for both sexes,
especially between people who have some commitment
to each other.

A 38-YEAR-OLD BUSINESSWOMAN, MARRIED, A CONVERT TO
CATHOLICISM: We have married friends who've had to be
apart all summer, and they both go off and whoop-de-doo!
—have a marvelous time, and then get together again afterward. I couldn't do that—I couldn't go to bed with ten
different men while my husband was away for two months,
and then right back in bed with him again. That's not me.
But I no longer look at that with disdain and disapproval,
as I used to. If that's their way of coping with life, and if it
suits them, that's fine with me.

A 50-YEAR-OLD DIVORCÉE, SALESLADY, A MODERATELY DEVOUT
JEW: Ten years ago I would have wanted my daughter to go
with a fellow, fall in love, have a courtship and get married.
Now, I only want to get across to her that what's important
is to know when she's ready to handle sex, ready to take
care of herself physically and emotionally. I want her to feel
that the important thing is to have a real experience with
someone, and not to think she has to marry some guy just
because she's slept with him.

A 26-YEAR-OLD AUTO MECHANIC, MARRIED, A NONATTENDING
CATHOLIC: [*On group-sex participants*]: They're crippled. *Crippled!* But no, I wouldn't say they should be prosecuted. I go
along with the idea that if they're consenting adults, that's
their business. Same goes for homosexuals—I wouldn't
want to see them prosecuted, because if they're over

twenty-one and not mentally deranged, well, everybody to their own way.

A 33-YEAR-OLD TRAVELING SALESMAN, BLACK, MARRIED, AN INACTIVE BAPTIST: Is everything too free today? Well, I guess each to his own, me, and the homosexuals and the group-sex people. If you dig this and I dig that, that's okay, we only got to have respect for each other. Now SM [sadomasochism] though, *that*'s not so good. I mean, give me a broad, I don't need no whip. That's sick, man!

So much for the overall movement toward permissiveness. As suggested earlier, however, the new attitudes are not uniformly distributed throughout the population, nor would one expect them to be. Many studies (by Kinsey, Harold Christensen, Winston Ehrmann, Ira Reiss, and other investigators) have shown that permissive sexual attitudes are more common among the young and among males, and are generally associated with higher education, higher occupational level, freedom from strong religious feeling, and political liberalism. Conservative sexual attitudes, *per contra*, are more common among older people and among females, the less educated, blue-collar workers, the devout and the politically conservative.[25]

The present survey, too, finds all these expected correlations. What is remarkable, however, is the magnitude of the age factor; with certain exceptions this appears to have emerged as the most powerful variable, now overshadowing the other major influences upon sexual attitudes—that is, accounting for larger differences than any of the classic institutional forces.

Only in the case of sexual issues that threaten no one and represent no danger to marriage or social stability do we find the young, the middle-aged and the aged in substantial accord. The statement "Sex is one of the most beautiful parts of life" won the agreement of nine-tenths or more of the men and women in every age group from under 25 to 55 and over. And some mildly threatening ideas—such as woman's right to initiate intercourse—are so obviously in harmony with the general cultural notion of equality within marriage that there is relatively little difference in the reactions of various age groups to it.

But such exceptions aside, permissiveness is very strongly associated with youth, and conservatism with age. Women under 25, for instance, are three and a half times as likely as women of 55 and over to believe that premarital intercourse makes for a better and more stable marriage (the percentages are 64 and 19 respectively). Again, nearly twice as large a proportion of people under 35 as of those 35 and over think homosexuality should be legal, and similarly large differences exist on the importance of virginity and the wrongness of masturbation. This does not mean, however, that permissive attitudes express only youthful irresponsibility and general rebelliousness. They may do so, in part, but they are also part of the contemporary culture and have been learned and adopted by every age group, though to a lesser and lesser degree all along the dimension of increasing age.

This raises the question: Do the differences associated with age represent a natural evolution from permissiveness to conservatism that is repeated in every generation, or is something new happening that does not replicate the past? One would expect that the status and habits that go with increasing age would naturally make people become more conservative about sex, as they do about politics, money and many other things. Ira Reiss and others have pointed out, too, that there is a strong tendency for the sexually permissive to become more conservative as their own children approach puberty, because as parents they feel responsible for what may happen.[26]

Nevertheless, the differences in attitudes between the very youngest group in our survey and the 35-to-44 group—old enough to have children close to puberty—are not usually large, nor does the difference between this latter group and those still older (45 to 54) show a sudden discontinuity. While there is undoubtedly some swing to conservatism due to the inherent nature of the life cycle, it is our feeling that the data suggest something more interesting than this: They indicate that during the past generation a major—and permanent—reevaluation of sexual attitudes has been occurring throughout our society, a process that has left its mark on each age group and recorded its history in the form of the growing attitudinal permissiveness and behavioral liberalism of the younger groups.

For although the changes all around us have affected nearly everyone at least in some degree, by far the greater part of one's attitudes toward sex are those acquired in the learning years of the late teens and young adulthood, and the attitudes of each age group therefore tend to indicate what the norms were for that group when it was at the formative stage. Here, for instance, is the striking record of the growing tolerance of men and women toward the use of cunnilingus (see Table 2).

Table 2

Cunnilingus Is Not Wrong: Total Sample, Percents Agreeing

	18–24	25–34	35–44	45–54	55 and over
Men	85	89	77	56	48
Women	86	89	81	67	47

(The paradoxical dip for those under 25 probably does not signify a revival of puritanism but rather the inexperience and inhibitions of the very youngest members of this group.) The acceptability of fellatio as part of male-female intercourse is virtually the same as that of cunnilingus in each age group, showing the same degree of change along the age dimension.

On so strongly forbidden a practice as anal intercourse, many people, as we noted earlier, express no opinion, which beclouds the picture. We can, however, clearly see the change that has come about by focusing upon those who find the practice wrong. Those reaching adulthood in the late 1920s and the 1930s are three to four times as likely to consider anal intercourse wrong as those who have just become adults or are still in the process —and this attitudinal change has been taking place for decades, as indicated by the figures for people of intermediate age groups (see Table 3).

But the real significance of what is happening begins to appear when we compare the importance of the age factor to the other major variables in determining attitudes. Formerly it was of less moment, in most cases, than such other factors as educational level or degree of religious feeling. Today it is generally as powerful as—and in many cases more powerful than—these or the other classic determinants of sexual attitudes. The pro-

Table 3

Anal Intercourse Is Wrong: Total Sample, Percents Agreeing

	18–24	25–34	35–44	45–54	55 and over
Men	12	17	36	48	51
Women	17	19	31	47	46

cess of change has been affecting all kinds of Americans, and significantly narrowing the gap—among the younger people—between the devout and the nondevout, blue-collar people and white-collar people, the college-educated and the noncollege-educated, the political liberals and the political conservatives.

As an example, in response to the statement "During sexual intercourse, the man should always take the lead," we got the predictable difference between men with at least some college education and men with only high-school education, but when we broke the sample into two halves by age—those under 35, and those 35 and older—we found the younger high-school men nearly as egalitarian as the older college men, and somewhat closer to college men of their own age than was true in the older half of this sample (see Table 4).

An even more striking example concerns fellatio, where the greater conservatism of noncollege women has virtually disappeared. Among women in the older half of our sample, the college-educated are considerably more permissive (three-quarters do not think fellatio wrong, as compared with a little over half of the noncollege women). Among women in the younger half of the sample, however, four-fifths of both the college-educated and the noncollege women no longer think it wrong.

Though the occupational factor continues to be important, younger persons are much more permissive than older persons at their own levels, and young blue-collar men are often as permissive as older white-collar men, as appears in Table 5.

As for the influence of religion, youth has again not only

Table 4
The Man Should Always Take Lead in Coitus:
Males, Percents Agreeing

	Under 35	35 and over
Some college or more	16	25
High school or less	28	40

Table 5
Homosexuality Should Be Legal: Males, Percents Agreeing

	Under 35	35 and over
White-collar	65	43
Blue-collar	41	27

greatly diminished the conservatism of devout and nondevout alike but on many questions narrowed the gap between them. Among men of 35 and over, twice as many of the nondevout as the devout feel that premarital intercourse makes for better marriages. Among the younger men, not only do substantially more of each group think well of premarital intercourse, but the magnitude of the difference between them is only half as great. Among women, permissiveness on this issue has increased among both the devout and the nondevout, but the gap has not narrowed among the young (the reason is not apparent). But on the subject of anal intercourse there is not only a remarkable shift away from conservatism among the younger devout women as well as the nondevout ones, but a distinct convergence of the attitudes of the two groups, as Table 6 makes clear.

The political factor tends to retain much of its power as a determinant of sexual views, but, even so, on a great variety of sexual questions the younger political conservatives have become more permissive, and their views tend to approach those of the political liberals. It may well be that, for the older group, more permissive sexual attitudes (and more liberated behavior) are considered a form of social protest, while younger people, even of a conservative political bent, regard them as a purely private and personal expression. As an example, see Table 7.

Table 6

Anal Intercourse Is Wrong: Females, Percents Agreeing

	Under 35	35 and over
Regular churchgoers	20	49
Nonattenders	12	24

Table 7

Premarital Intercourse Makes for Better Marriage:
Males, Percents Agreeing

	Under 35	35 and over
Political liberals	73	53
Political conservatives	60	39

╈ An Overview of Changes in Sexual Behavior in the Past Generation

Thus we have seen that during the past generation the sexual attitudes of Americans in general have shifted considerably in the direction of permissiveness, and among younger adults this shift has been so pronounced as to markedly diminish the attitudinal dissimilarities previously associated with differences in social class, educational attainments, religious feelings and political orientation.

But have there also been corresponding changes in overt behavior? Have most people merely become more tolerant of sexual liberation in others, or have they themselves become more liberated in their own actions? An uncritical reading of the more lurid accounts of contemporary sexual behavior would lead one to imagine that young Americans have no hesitancy about doing virtually anything to be found in the lexicon of sexual behavior, and that the casting off of all restraints, internal as well as external, is the true meaning of sexual liberation. Indeed, we found some advocates of sexual liberation who were embarrassed by their own inability to enjoy every activity suggested to them. As one young divorcée said, "I feel so silly—this fellow I'm seeing is keen on rimming me [*performing analingus on her*], but I always get embarrassed and turned off by it. I guess I'm not as loose as I'd like to be." And a young man said, "Some of my friends tell me I'm still hung-up because I can't bring myself to try sex with guys. Maybe they're right—I mean, what difference does it really make? But I'm chicken, or something; I just can't do it."

But most people read a different meaning into sexual liberation. They regard it not as an obligation to do anything and everything but as a freedom within which they have the right to remain highly selective, choosing only those sexual acts that meet their emotional needs. It is true that a number of practices that were proscribed and avoided by all but the sophisticates a generation or so ago have now been adopted, or at least tried out on occasion, by many people in various parts of American society; but a number of other practices have remained as generally unacceptable and as uncommon as they used to be. While many Americans now use forms of foreplay and coital variations that were shunned by the previous generation, and while they take a somewhat more unfettered enjoyment in their own sensations, by and large they have added to their repertoire only acts that are biologically and psychologically free from pathology, they have remained highly discriminating in the choice of their sexual partners and they have continued to regard their sexual acts as having deep emotional significance rather than as merely providing uncomplicated sensuous gratification.

Even masturbation continues to be linked to sexual acts of emotional significance; a large majority of men and women in every age group say that while masturbating they most commonly fantasize having intercourse with someone they love. But they do feel notably freer than formerly to administer such sexual relief to themselves in times of tension or deprivation. While we found only small increases in the percentages of all males and all females who have ever masturbated (over nine-tenths of our males and over six-tenths of our females have done so at some time in the course of their lives), we did find that girls are far more likely today to start masturbating early in adolescence, and that even boys begin somewhat earlier.[27] Moreover, as young adults, single males and single females masturbate considerably more frequently than formerly.[28] Both of these trends, we feel, indicate the lessening of guilt feelings. (They might also indicate increased sexual frustration, but since the very same single men and women are also having more intercourse, this possibility can be ruled out.)

What is even more indicative of lessened guilt feelings is the increase we found in masturbation among the married. It was surprising, in 1948 and 1953, to learn that any married people masturbated at all; today it may be equally surprising to learn that many more of them are doing so, and that the males are doing so far more often. Kinsey's data showed, for instance, that in the 1940s over four out of ten married men between the ages of 26 and 35 still masturbated,[29] while today, according to our own data, over seven out of ten married men in approximately the same age range do so. Moreover, the frequency with which married men masturbate has increased considerably: The median (the typical, or midpoint) individual, among married males who still masturbated in that age group in Kinsey's sample, did so about six times a year,[30] as compared with 24 times a year in our own. Among married women in the same age range, Kinsey found a third masturbating, the median frequency of those who did so being about ten times a year[31]; we found no increase in frequency among our own comparable married women, but more than twice as large a proportion of them was involved.*

Even allowing for any differences between Kinsey's survey methods and ours which might have slightly overstated—or, for that matter, understated—the change, the increases are remarkable. What can they signify? They might, of course, mean that the marital sex relations of young people today are inferior to those of a generation ago, but other data from our survey effectively eliminate this possibility. Alternatively, and more probably, the figures indicate that whenever sexual frustration does occur within marriage, due to sexual or emotional conflict, unavoidable separation, or abstinence due to illness, pregnancy and other extrinsic factors, young husbands and wives feel freer than their counterparts of a generation ago to turn to masturbation. That they do so without any residual feelings of guilt or self-contempt seems doubtful. We do feel, however, that such feelings must at least be far weaker in the young today than they were in the young a generation ago.

In the area of premarital intercourse, our figures confirm the popular impression: It will come as no surprise to anyone to learn that it is a good deal more acceptable and more common today than a generation ago. This applies to men as well as women. In Kinsey's study, well over one-quarter of unmarried American males (excluding those with only grade-school education) had not yet experienced intercourse by age 25[32]; in our own 1972 sample, the comparable figure is about 3 percent. The more significant increase in premarital intercourse has, however, taken place among females: One-third of the females (single and married combined) in Kinsey's sample had had premarital intercourse by the age of 25,[33] as compared with over two-thirds in our sample. Of his women who were married before or by 25, between 42 and 47 percent had had premarital

---

*We have used medians rather than means (arithmetical averages) in most comparisons because a mean often gives a distorted picture of typical activity, being pulled upwards by the high level of activity of one or a few individuals, while the great majority of individuals may have a far lower rate than the mean would indicate.

In all comparisons with Kinsey's data we use his raw figures, unless otherwise noted, and not his "U.S. Corrections"—a weighting he devised to correct his sampling errors, but which he abandoned after publishing the male volume.

intercourse,[34] as compared with 81 percent of ours. The double standard, it would appear, has been relegated to the scrap heap of history.

But if young women are much more likely than their mothers were to feel that they have a right to a complete sexual life before marriage, they do not exercise that right in a lighthearted and purely physical way; the inhibitions of the *demi-vierge* of the 1940s have been replaced not by free-and-easy swinging but by sexual freedom within the confines of emotional involvement, the new norm being, in sociologist Reiss's words, "permissiveness with affection."* In Kinsey's study, 46 percent of all married women who had had premarital intercourse had had it only with their fiancés[35]; in our sample, while twice as many had had premarital intercourse, an even larger proportion—slightly over half—had limited it to their fiancés, and among the youngest women in our sample the figure was still higher. It is very likely that in absolute terms there are more single young women today than formerly who are willing to have intercourse without any emotional ties, but in relative terms it remains true that most sexually liberated single girls feel liberated only within the context of affectionate or loving relationships.

The repertoire of sexual variations used by both unmarried and married people seems to have broadened considerably since Kinsey's time. Many younger Americans have now adopted, or at least occasionally experiment with, variations which only the sexually sophisticated used to employ. In the 1940s, for instance, only four out of ten of Kinsey's married males said they had ever kissed or tongued their own wives' genitals[36]; in contrast, 63 percent of all our males say they have done so in just the past year.** Only about four out of ten married males in Kinsey's sample said they had ever been fellated by their wives[37]; 58 percent in our sample say they have been in just the past year.** A remarkable aspect of this change

---

*Professor Reiss used this phrase to signify attitudinal tolerance, not actual behavior (which he did not measure in his 1963 survey). We use it here with both attitudes and behavior in mind; in our own terms, it might better be called "liberalism with affection."

**We omit from these comparisons the married males in Kinsey's sample who had eight or fewer years of education. His grade-school males had considerably lower levels of oral-genital experience than his high-school or college-educated males, and since our own sample had no grade-school males, the comparison would be distorted if we included those in Kinsey's sample. (See also Chapter 4, on techniques of marital foreplay.)

is that it has taken place in all age groups, though to the greatest extent among the young.[38]

As we expected, college-educated, nondevout, politically liberal, and white-collar people feel freer to use these and other advanced techniques of foreplay than do noncollege, devout, politically conservative, and blue-collar people. Yet here, too, as with sexual attitudes, the shift toward liberalism among the young is generally narrowing the gap and tending to bring about something close to a consensus or dominant sexual ethic among the young, despite the diversity of their life-styles. As an example, consider cunnilingus once more: In Kinsey's time about a sixth of all males with only high-school education ever performed this act on any female, while nearly half of all males with at least some college education did so.[39] In our own sample not only have more men in each category done so, but among younger men the gap has vanished—in fact, there now seems to be a gap in the opposite direction (see Table 8).

Table 8
*Ever Performed Cunnilingus: Males, Percents**

	Some college	No college
35 and over	68	50
Under 35	75	83

Our data include blacks, while Kinsey's sample was all white. On the question of cunnilingus, this understates the change since Kinsey's time.

But one need not suppose that cunnilingus has, in reality, become more popular with the lower-educated men than college men; the fact is that noncollege men start active heterosexual lives earlier and marry earlier than college men, and thus get around to cunnilingual activity sooner. In any event, it is apparent that lower-educated men no longer view the practice as unnatural, unmanly and disgusting but have adopted the college-educated men's view that it is natural, manly and aesthetically pleasing.

Still more remarkable is our evidence that the buttocks, and even the anus—regarded as erogenous and sexually attractive areas by many other cultures—are gaining some measure of acceptance among Americans. We do not see an increase in pathology in this trend, for there were few responses in our survey or our interviews indicative of obsessive anality, or of coprophilia and coprophagia (fecal fetishism). We do, however, find that rather large minorities of men and women have had at least some experience of nonpathological forms of anal stimulation. Kinsey, as mentioned earlier, offered no data on these matters and even noted, in his volume on the male, "Anal activity in the heterosexual is not frequent enough to make it possible to determine the incidence of individuals who are specifically responsive to such stimulation."[40] While we do not know how many people respond strongly to such stimulation or employ anal foreplay regularly, we did find that such techniques as fingering, kissing and even tonguing of the anus have been used, at least experimentally, by anywhere from a sizable minority to a majority of younger Americans and by a small but measurable minority of older ones, and that about a quarter of married couples under 35 use anal intercourse at least now and then.* Once again, not only do the young employ these practices more readily than older people, but among the young the factors of devoutness, occupational level, education and political orientation make relatively little difference. Liberation to regard the buttocks and anus as sexual objects is not yet general throughout our culture, but is becoming so.

The new freedom, in short, extends primarily to acts which are not pathological, which do not jeopardize the basic conception of marriage and which do not disjoin sexuality from affection or love. Major change has thus occurred within a framework of cultural continuity. A genuine overthrowing of the past and of all cultural values concerning sexual behavior would be evidenced by such things as (1) the displacement of vaginal coitus by nonvaginal sex acts *substituting* for it rather than *preliminary* to it, or by sex acts violating biological and/or psychological criteria of normality, such as sexual connection with animals, sadomasochistic acts and homosexuality; or (2) a major increase in sexual acts that fundamentally alter the connection between sex and marriage, such as mutually sanctioned extramarital affairs, mate-swapping and marital swinging; or (3) a growing

*Some readers may question whether anal intercourse can properly be classified as nonpathological. We do so because, as will appear in later chapters, nearly all of those who employ anal intercourse in heterosexual relations do so only as an occasional variation from vaginal intercourse, do so by mutual choice rather than by way of unilateral decision forced upon an unwilling partner, and do so, for the most part, without causing physical harm to either partner.

preference for sex acts devoid of emotional significance or performed with strangers.

As nearly as we can tell—many of these practices not having been surveyed a generation ago—there is no evidence that any such radical change or violent discontinuity with the past has occurred.

To generalize (details will follow in later chapters), we find, as to Point 1, that sex acts with animals are actually less common than when Kinsey was taking histories; homosexuality is not measurably more common than in his time (though there are, to be sure, difficulties in comparing our data to his on this issue); sadomasochistic acts, for all their popularity in humor and pornography, are very uncommon (less than 2 1/2 percent of our sample had had any sadistic sexual experience in the past year, a similar percentage had had any masochistic sexual experience in the past year, and for most of these people such experiences had been very few in number); and oral, anal and masturbatory methods of gratification have not been substituted, in any systematic or significant way, for vaginal intercourse.

As to Point 2, we find that those much publicized sexual practices that greatly alter the relationship between sex and marriage are far less common than they are generally alleged to be. Granted that our survey methods may have missed some fraction of the most unconventional persons in the country, we think it significant that in our total sample, which closely parallels the national population in most ways, only 2 percent of our married males and less than 2 percent of our married females have ever participated in mate-swapping with their spouses, and most of them on very few occasions. As for covert extramarital intercourse, despite the popular impression that it is virtually universal, its overall incidence has not changed for either sex; the only changes we do find are a moderate increase among men under 25, and a considerable one for women under 25—but even the latter increase only brings these young females close to, but not up to, the male level of activity. It is also worthy of note that the great majority of married people—including the youngest group—are not at all inclined to grant their mates permission for overt extramarital sex acts.

As to Point 3—sex devoid of emotional significance, or sex with strangers—a trend in this direction should go hand in hand with an increase in prostitution (there is no such increase), in group sex, especially with multiple partners (only 16 percent of all our males and 3 percent of all our females had ever had the latter kind of experience, and most of them rarely or only once) and in a considerable increase in premarital coitus of a purely physical or sensual sort (but this, as we saw a moment ago, is not what most young unmarried people are up to). Finally, in an attitude section of the questionnaire we offered the statement "Sex cannot be very satisfying without some emotional involvement between the partners"; there was very little difference in the reactions of the various age groups, large or very large majorities of all of them agreeing with the statement—most of them strongly.

To the majority of Americans, sexual liberation thus means the right to enjoy all the parts of the body, the right to employ caresses previously forbidden by civil or religious edict and social tradition and the right to be sensuous and exuberant rather than perfunctory and solemn—but all within the framework of meaningful relationships. Sex, for the great majority of Americans—including the liberated—continues to express loving feelings, or to engender them, or both. It has not been successfully disjoined from love and remade into a simple appetite, except by a tiny minority of swingers.

Which ought not surprise us, after all, for there is a wealth of evidence in the literature of psychology to show that the physical care and love given the child by the mother and the father promote digestion and other autonomic functions, create a sense of health and well-being and thus build into the nervous system a deep, abiding linkage between sensuous well-being and the state of loving. And being laid down in our nervous structure so early in life, this synthesis of sex and affection is not likely to be dissolved by the liberation of American sexuality from its heritage of guilt and shame.

A Typology of Contemporary Sexual Styles: Uptights, Swingers and Liberals

Studying attitudes and acts one by one, as we have been doing, is something like studying anatomy organ by organ; it tells us everything except what the whole living creature is like. We can, however, add to our comprehension of the state of American sexuality by looking at a few whole living creatures. In particular, we shall examine a chosen handful who exemplify the three major styles of present-day sexuality: the conservative (or, somewhat flippantly, the uptight), the revolutionary (or swinger) and the liberated (or liberal). This typology is based not so much on character structure as on social and subcultural identity. Most uptights, for instance, think and act as they do more because of their religious, ethnic, class and community affiliations than because of excessive Oedipal anxiety, feelings of unworthiness or other psychoneurotic factors. The three styles may, of course, parallel major psychological configurations, but more importantly they denote coexisting and competing cultural ideals: The uptight pattern is the sexual model of obsolescent traditionalism; the swinging pattern is that of antiestablishment anarchism; and the liberal pattern is the model of emergent progressivism that will soon, we think, dominate American society.

Of course, any such typology is only a convenient simplification—and thus falsification—of the diversity and individuality of real human beings. Yet in every society there are similarities in the behavior of different individuals, and men in all advanced civilizations have assembled these similarities into archetypes or patterns, given them labels and used them as symbols in abstract and generalized thinking. Without such conceptualizations we would be like those primitive peoples who had a word for, say, "duck," another for "pair of ducks" and yet another for "as many ducks as I have fingers on this hand," but no words for "one," "two" and "five," and hence no ability to perform generalized arithmetical calculations.

It would be impossible for us to think in any sophisticated and analytical fashion about the sexual behavior of men and women in past ages without such abstract labels as Apollonian and Dionysian, sacred and profane, celibate and licentious, or without such handy archetypes as the righteous but virile Old Testament patriarch; the dissolute ambisexual Roman voluptuary; the imploring frustrated troubadour and his chaste, unyielding lady; the frankly lustful Renaissance woman of Boccaccio (the impatient virgin, licentious nun or insatiable young wife of an old man); the compulsively conquering (but ever suave and poetic) Don Juan; the frail, pure, frigid Victorian goodwife (that "angel in the house," as one poet called her); and still others.

In America the several social classes have had somewhat differing ideals of sexual behavior. Nevertheless, there has long been a dominant pattern for men and another for women which middle-class people and upwardly mobile working-class people have generally taken as their models. The male model has been the stoical, taciturn frontiersman-scout-cowhand-seaman, ruggedly masculine but somewhat ascetic (he could spend weeks to months in the mountains, on the plains, at sea, without a woman), capable of intermittant bouts of drinking and wild debauchery but always respectful and deferential toward good women—including his wife, on whom he made only limited sexual demands and from whom he expected tender submissiveness but not exuberant passion. The female model has been the beautiful, flirtatious but innocent girl, resolute but feminine, marvelously desirable but sexually unawakened until, as a blushing bride and then as a blooming woman, she learns the meaning of a man's love and becomes a warm, accepting, sweetly yielding wife, lovingly but passively accepting his caresses and his flesh but never showing burning desire of her own and never actively *doing* anything.

These 19th-Century patterns have not yet disappeared; although they are being displaced by the ascendant liberals and even, to some extent, the maverick swingers, they still exist, somewhat modified but clearly recognizable, in the persons of the uptights.

Here, then, are some representatives (one male, one female) of each type. None perfectly or completely exemplifies the pattern, but we prefer to exhibit real people we interviewed rather than run the risk of distortion by fictionalizing or embellishing the cases.

MALE UPTIGHT

Not all uptights are middle-aged or old. Frank Mathers, for instance (all interviewees' names are, of course, fictitious) is only 25, and a good specimen of the sexual conservatism that still exists in a minority of the youthful population. Still single, Frank is currently in his sophomore year at a large university in eastern Texas after having spent five years in the navy. A tall, shambling, somewhat heavy young man, he has a cautious, neutral expression and a painfully deliberate manner of speech. He is the son of a chemical engineer and a housewife and was raised by them as a Presbyterian but switched in his teens, with his mother, to a minor Fundamentalist sect that offers more hellfire and brimstone. The Matherses, thoroughly conservative people in every way, told him nothing whatever about sex as he neared puberty, nor did he learn much from his playmates, most of whom came from similar homes. "Before I was twelve, I knew there were some differences between boys and girls, and by twelve I knew there was something called 'having sex,' but I didn't know what it was or how it was done. It wasn't until I was nearly fifteen that I finally heard the facts from some other fellows."

Even after puberty Frank's parents offered him no information, guidance or reading material about sex. When Frank was 15 his father finally asked him, "Do you know anything about girls?" and when Frank mumbled, "Yes," his father looked relieved and immediately changed the subject. Frank's ignorance had been so total that he had no idea what masturbation was, until, at 14, he played with his erect penis one night and to his utter astonishment and terror felt an electrifying sensation as strange white stuff jetted forth from him involuntarily. He was all but suffocated by guilt feelings—somehow he sensed that this must be one of the wicked things the preacher was always alluding to—but eventually it occurred to him that this was the very thing he'd heard other boys joking and boasting about, and this relieved his guilt somewhat. But he never told anyone of his discovery and always took great pains to leave no trace of his secret activity. He continues to masturbate today in "slack periods," but even when he has had no intercourse for months he permits himself such relief only once or twice a month. He says he could never admit doing so, not even to his closest friend, and is rather ashamed that he still finds it necessary to resort to it.

Until Frank was 19 his experience with girls was limited to necking; he never tried to touch any girl's breasts or pudendum. Frank says that this inhibition came from a fear of being rejected due to his being skinny and somewhat marked by facial acne; he does not see any connection between his inhibitions and his general upbringing. To this day he remains little interested in petting and foreplay, and explains that this kind of activity "just never occurs to me." His introduction to sex involved coitus without any preliminaries: He and two buddies were hitchhiking back to their naval base in a large southern city when they were picked up by a prostitute and her pimp. "Before I knew what was happening, the guy who sat in front worked out a deal with the pimp for all three of us at ten dollars a piece, and I was too drunk to be scared. Besides, it was something I wanted to do, to get over my hang-ups. She helped me along and got me started, and as soon as I figured out what to do, it went pretty fast. I felt kind of good about having done it, but actually it was just kind of nothing."

He had several further experiences of the same kind, and then met a cocktail waitress whose boy friend had just been killed in an auto accident and whom he tried to comfort. To his surprise, she invited him to come to her apartment and there suggested that he stay overnight with her. At first he had a problem in self-control—he was unable to delay his orgasm after intromission for more than a minute—but after a week or two of regular sex he was able to last two or three minutes. Taking advice from a friend, moreover, he began "trying to get her hot first, by using my hand on her. But whatever I did was for her sake, not mine, because I don't find it very exciting to play with a woman down there. I even tried eating it a few times, not because I liked it so much but because it seemed to excite her. But the reverse thing grosses me out. She was down there sucking me one time, and it felt good, but when I looked down and saw her doing it, it made me sick; it made me feel like I was going to vomit. I've never let anybody do that to me since then."

As the weeks wore on, he thought himself in love with her, and was briefly wretched when he was shipped out. They exchanged letters for a while, but after some months they simply stopped. In a number of ports around the world he sought girls, sometimes finding a prostitute, occasionally meeting a nonprofessional with whom he went to bed. With two of the latter he had affairs that lasted a few weeks, and with one of them the relationship was both passionate and close. Nevertheless, he has never had intercourse in any but the conventional male-above position, still prefers near-total darkness for sexual acts and has never suggested any variations to the women he has slept with. "I enjoy it the way I've been doing it. I've just never thought about any other way." One might wonder how, these days, it was possible never to think about any other way, but Frank never gets into discussions of sex with other men, does not read books or articles on sexual technique and avoids X-rated movies. "I'm not particularly interested in such things. They don't do anything for me, they don't get me excited or anything."

Recently, Frank met a high-school senior whom he is now dating. They sometimes neck a little, but he has not sought to do anything more. "She's a virgin, and she's only eighteen. I don't even get down to her breasts. I'll rub the back of her neck, like, or her knee, but I think that the proper place for anything else is in bed. I would like to have more of a sex life, but I don't feel I have to rape anyone or drive myself to it. I can wait."

The increasing sexual liberalism surrounding Frank has led him to pay lip service to certain modern ideas. He doesn't believe that hard-core pornography and X-rated movies ought to be illegal; he does feel, however, that people can and should combat them by avoiding them—and says, with evident pleasure, that he has heard that hard-core pornography is no longer selling well in Denmark, where it has been freely available for some years. He has no personal objection to homosexuals, as long as they keep their sexual activities private. And he would not want the law to punish mate-swappers, who, in his opinion, bring down suffering and punishment enough upon themselves.

Frank hopes to have a deep relationship with one woman someday. With her, he says, he would be willing to listen to suggestions for variations in intercourse, but he doubts that he himself would ever suggest any. Even with her, however, he would have some limits: He would not agree to fellatio or to anal intercourse. He considers himself idealistic about sex, and expresses his idealism with admirable, if slightly simple-minded, fervor: "I think the only way to enjoy sex is both parties really wanting to, not one person giving in to the other. But sex is a lot deeper than just what you do, it's not just one person and one person, but two people together, talking to each other and having trust in each other, and feeling comfortable. That's the way it's most fulfilling; that's the complete complement to life."

FEMALE UPTIGHT

Sally Gahaghan, 31 and married, is a good Catholic and married to one. Plump, blonde and neatly dressed, she has a schoolteacherish manner—and was, indeed, a teacher for several years, though now she is a full-time homemaker and mother, and the wife of a plumber. Sally, who now lives in California, grew up in an eastern industrial city with a large conservative Catholic population. When she neared puberty and began to ask questions about sex, her mother took some books out of the library and let her read them. They answered biological questions but left her ignorant of everything that dealt with sexual pleasure. Despite her mother's effort to be modern about the subject, Sally acquired a powerful sense of guilt about sex from the nuns who were her high-school teachers. "You'd get the impression that almost anything was a sin—even seeing any one boy too much, or wearing skirts that were too short or using any makeup whatever. Myself, I think it's a shame, all this over-modesty—it gives you the wrong slant on things. But still, when it comes right down to it, I feel I'd rather have my own two children in the Catholic school during some of these difficult years than exposed to all the ideas that are going around now."

Sally felt terribly guilty the first time she was kissed, at 16; she thought it might be a mortal sin. She never necked at all, and most of her socializing with boys took place in the halls at school. As a high-school senior she began going on actual dates with one boy, and it became a steady thing. After two and a half years, when they had begun talking about marriage, she permitted things to advance as far as heavy petting on a couple of occasions, and found it frightening but rather exciting. They had no actual intercourse, however, until they were married, and it was not at all satisfactory in the beginning or for some years. "I don't think sex, for me, is all that it seems to be for a lot of other people. I experienced a lot of pain in intercourse—that more than anything else—until I had a hysterectomy at twenty-nine. We already had three children and I didn't want to become pregnant again, so that operation really helped; I haven't experienced much pain since then, and I enjoy it more, even though I don't feel anything nearly as powerful as my husband does. The fact is, I don't climax often—maybe once every ten times or so—but I do like it at other times, because I enjoy the close feeling, and being held and all that."

She and her husband almost never deviate from the conventional male-above position, nor do they discuss such matters. "I would just as soon not discuss such things with him; I wouldn't raise the topic. Sometimes I have a strong physical thing, but mostly not. But even when I don't, I'm pleased that he is experiencing strong things, and I don't feel the need to analyze it or talk about it with him. And I don't want him to do any more of this or that for my sake, because actually I don't enjoy a lot of foreplay and different kinds of things. I don't know why I don't, but I wouldn't be surprised if it had to do with the things that were said to me when I was young. I don't like it being that way, but I am still me, whatever the influences have been."

She has read little sexual material, and even Elia Kazan's novel, *The Arrangement,* proved too strong for her taste. "I couldn't even keep reading it; I thought he was throwing in everything dirty just for erotic purposes, and this didn't appeal to me at all." She and her husband have never gone to a movie containing a nude sex scene. They think they probably should, in order to keep up with things, but they never seem to get around to it. On a recent plane ride, she was amazed at the language used in even a G-rated film, and rather disgusted by it.

She does not think that homosexuals or sodomists should be prosecuted; the only sexual acts she would like to see penalized are rape and sexual molestation of children. Married people, she feels, have a right to do anything together that they both want to do—but for herself this definitely does not include oral sex in either direction, while the very thought of anal intercourse, mate-swapping or group sex makes her almost nauseous. Even though she would not want people to be arrested and tried for these acts, she does believe that there is divine retribution for such sins, unless those who commit them confess, repent and do penance.

MALE SWINGER

If not all uptights are older people, neither are all swingers younger ones. Leo Zimmer, age 45, is a commercial artist (of no great success) who lives in New York. He is a short, ebullient, genial fellow whom one would take for a door-to-door salesman rather than an artist, and for a square rather than a swinger. Leo is Jewish, but not very; he was brought up with a minimum of religious training and ceased believing or attending services by the time he was 16. His parents, though they considered themselves enlightened, never told him anything about sex, but he read enough on the sly in their extensive collection of books and heard enough from boys in his own neighborhood in Brooklyn to know plenty, and early. Somehow—perhaps for purely physiological reasons, he says—he had a powerful sexual drive even in childhood. At five or six he was regularly trying to undress little girls in an empty garage; at nine he and a pal used to undress and take turns lying on each other and making coital movements (he had orgasms long before he could produce any emission); at eleven he began frequent, frenzied masturbation; and at fourteen he conned his younger sister into taking off her clothes and letting him lie on her and squirm around until he ejaculated all over her.

But in his teens he had no luck. Middle-class apartment-dwelling children have little privacy, and in any case all of Leo's dates were bourgeois Jewish girls who allowed no favors—or at least not to him. In retrospect he thinks he may have been so desperately needy, so driven and clumsy, that no ordinary girl could fail to be repelled. Not until he was 20 did he finally experience intercourse— "and then only by taking out a dreadfully homely girl who was said to be a sure thing. I got through an endless evening with her, and finally we did it. She was pimply and ugly and awful, and it was terribly degrading, but I did it because I had to."

At art school, one of his instructors was a beautiful woman in her thirties, who was (as he later realized) a genuine swinger. She sensed his pent-up passion and sought to seduce him, and although he felt at first that it was wrong because she was married, he gave in. Unfortunately, he was so inexperienced and so wildly desirous that he failed to please her, and she dropped him. He was crushed. "For years that was my life story—my need was so great and so obvious that I was always scaring everybody off. But it wasn't just sex—I was looking for affection, too, and I wasn't getting either." After a while, however, he did have some limited successes. He had an affair of some months' duration with a fellow student from whom he learned a great deal about foreplay, timing and free body movement, but he and she clashed emotionally, and she broke off with him. Once again, he was crushed. Other affairs followed, one after another, with increasing sexual expressivity and expertise on his part, but no improvement on the emotional plane.

In his late twenties, when Leo first heard about group sex, he was transfixed. That night he masturbated four times, while imagining scenes of orgiastic revelry. After a great deal of inquiring around, he finally got invited to a group-sex party, and took with him, as his required entrance fee (a willing female), a 17-year-old girl he was then dating who was as eager as he to experience the group scene. He loved it; she hated it. He outdid himself, having intercourse with nine different women and reaching seven climaxes, while his girl friend reluctantly had relations with four or five men, had not a single orgasm and felt exploited and shamed. Leo was obviously entranced by the experience, and his girl friend astutely went to other parties with him, while subtly making him feel guilty for exploiting her. In order not to lose her, he married her—at which point she abruptly refused to go anymore. The marriage was disastrous, both sexually and emotionally, and lasted only a year and a half, but Leo had found a way of life that satisfied him, and has practiced it ever since.

There is almost nothing sexual that he doesn't like to do—all the more so if there is a crowd around, so that he can move from one body to another, gorging himself with sensations and free of the need to observe the formalities of conversation, courting and personal interaction. He enjoys nothing better than being sandwiched between two or more girls whom he has only seen for the first time a moment ago, and for that matter he is perfectly happy being sandwiched between a girl and a man. "One time I was making it at a party with a girl, and some guy came into the room and started rimming me. My first impulse was to say, 'Lay off, you goddamned fairy!' but then I thought, 'Wait a minute—it feels *good*, why not enjoy it? What do I care?' A few weeks later I was with a married couple who had invited me home to make it with the wife, and when we got there the husband said, very apologetically, 'Don't take this wrong, but would you mind if I go up you while you're doing it?'—and oddly enough, it was just what I was thinking about at that moment. That was the first time I was penetrated anally, and it was a real *gas!* Just *marvelous!* But I would never dream of doing it without a woman there, and me in her. I love trios like that. In fact, I love all kinds of groups, with everybody pressing me on all sides, somebody's pussy in my face, somebody's finger in my behind, somebody's mouth on my penis—it's groovy!"

Unfortunately for Leo, virtually every girl he has ever taken to group-sex parties has eventually upbraided him for exploiting her. The problem, he says, is not his alone; very few of the swinging couples he knows have good relationships, and nearly always one person in each couple is highly sexed and likes the scene, while the other feels inadequate, degraded and used. Leo says he doesn't really like most of the swingers he meets; they're not people he would like to talk to or spend time with. "It's a real dilemma. How do you reconcile the fact that you want to have a physical ball with people you don't care for? You have to cut off a part of your own personality in order to use another part. But still, it's fantastic. You have five or six girls in one evening, and perform for hours on end, and have orgasm after orgasm, and it's a tremendous ego trip. You come home completely sated, and you can be puffed up by it for weeks. It's just a wild, wild thing."

The one thing Leo has never been able to find, though he has continued looking for it, is the right woman for him, one he could feel completely compatible with, emotionally and intellectually, and who would share his sexual enthusiasms and practices. His most intense relationship to date was one he had a few years ago with an 18-year-old girl. He and she would make love for five or six hours at a time, hardly stopping to rest, but there was nothing else between them. "We'd rip off our clothes the minute I walked in. It was insane, gorgeous! But she was always keeping me on the hook—if I was ten minutes late, she'd be off balling some other guy—and there wasn't any rapport whatever between us, except the chemistry."

For the past year he has been seeing a lot of a somewhat more mature girl with whom he does feel very genuine rapport— except that she refuses to swing. When the urge to do so comes over him, he arranges to take someone else to a party, tells his girl friend and endures her silent suffering with stoical calm. "We kiss and embrace before I go and after I come back, but it bothers her a great deal, and that bothers me. Still, it's like a hunger in me, and if I don't go, it would have severe consequences for our relationship. She tries to understand my need to go, and I try to sympathize with her reasons for not going."

He doesn't see this as an enduring solution to the problem, but cannot think of another. "I'd like to live with somebody who's really compatible and affectionate, but I can't have anyone around who'd cramp my style. I've been looking most of my life for the girl who could be both compatible and a swinger, and I haven't found one yet. I can find one thing or the other, but not both. I don't know what the answer is—I don't know if there's any answer at all. But I guess I've outgrown the desperate need for affection, so I might as well keep on having a ball.''

FEMALE SWINGER

If not all swingers are young, neither are they all irresponsible singles, cruising the bars and parties and waking up many a morning with a strange face on the next pillow. There are, of course, some of this kind, but the larger number of swingers are married people with children, homes, jobs and all the external apparatus of conventional middle-class life.

Toni Driscoll is one such person. She and her husband, Duncan, live in a large, untidy apartment in San Francisco, have a six-year-old son in grade school, go off to work every morning (he's a draftsman, she's a speech therapist), take their child to the beach on fine summer weekends and decorate a tree for him at Christmas. They also swing, and believe in it as a way of life.

Toni, dark-haired and blue-eyed, is a rather attractive woman in her mid-thirties, though somewhat sloppy (or perhaps consciously bohemian) in her dress and person. She is high-strung, energetic, talkative and strong-minded—the very opposite of her husband, a gaunt, languid, gray-haired man who rouses himself to speech with seeming effort. Toni grew up in the Midwest and was raised a Unitarian (she has been unaffiliated since her late teens). Her parents prided themselves on being liberal about sex as well as religion. Both of them walked around nude in front of her until she was 12 or 13 and made no effort to keep their sexual activities quiet or even private. This, plus the general feeling of permissiveness they conveyed to her, made Toni all but free from guilt, or so she says. She claims she felt none whatever when playing ''doctor'' with another girl at 12, petting with boys at 14 or beginning regular intercourse with a steady boy friend at 16. In all likelihood she would have felt no guilt at masturbating, either, but from 16 on, she says, she has always had all the sex she wanted, and has never felt any need to masturbate, though she has nothing against it.

She married the boy friend when she was 17 and had a very active sex life with him for a few years. It was not very satisfactory, however, since he tended to have his orgasm too swiftly, but she discovered that in the female-astride position she could have hers just as swiftly. Their sex life dwindled as the marriage faded in other ways. It did not occur to her to consider divorce, but it did occur to her to enrich her life with other men, and she took a part-time job, made a number of acquaintances and with very little timidity began a series of affairs, most of which she relished both sexually and emotionally. "Not that I was really in love with any of them, but I grew up with the idea that you have to be in love to have sex, so I managed to imagine that I was. But most of the time I knew inside myself that it was really just sexual." She felt no guilt about these affairs: "I wasn't hurting anybody—my husband didn't know, and our life together was functioning normally. And I wasn't thinking of leaving him for any other man. When I finally did leave him after several years of this, it was only because the marriage had become meaningless."

As a young divorcée she found life good. She had a decent job, met many men and slept around widely. Her husband had never conquered his early-ejaculation problem, but with men who had good control and who liked to teach her variations in the techniques of foreplay and in coital position, she played the diligent pupil, pleased to discover that there were almost no taboos she wasn't able to violate. A couple of the most important ones, however, could not be put to the test until she had remarried. "When Duncan and I started going together, we were both still seeing other people, and neither of us wanted to lose them. I did stop sleeping with mine, and he with his, but we both kept on seeing them socially, and this continued even after we were married, because we both refused to play the game of limiting each other in any way. I'd have lunch or dinner with one of my former lovers and come home and tell Duncan about it, and he'd ask if there'd been anything sexual about the meeting, and I'd say no, I hadn't let there be. And gradually it seemed to both of us that there was something artificial about my not having sex with someone I still liked, and the same was true for Duncan. Why should there be an arbitrary barrier to a relationship? Is it sinful to talk to someone else? To like someone else? And if not, is it sinful to have sex with him? We didn't think so, and both of us wanted to remain open to new experiences and not feel imprisoned by each other. So we agreed that each of us could go out with other people and have sex with them, and that this would only make us closer to each other."

Once Toni started, she was pretty active; for a while she was out three or four nights a week. (The advent of their child, later on, slowed her down somewhat.) Some of her companions were men she liked or even felt romantic about, and with whom she would spend long, pleasant evenings of talk, culminating in sex. Fairly often, however, at a party or on the job, she would meet someone new who was good for a purely sexual one-night stand. Duncan was doing much the same thing, and he and she would always tell each other how things had gone. The only problem with this way of life, she found, was that it was difficult to convince each new man that her husband knew all about it, approved and wasn't queer or impotent. Eventually she found it simpler to lie, and told each new partner that she was cheating on her husband.

One thing led to another. Telling each other about their experiences, they began to want to see each other in action, and started passing the word to some of their friends that they were open to the idea of swinging parties. Eventually they were invited to one and, after a period of initial stage fright, had a fine time, each of them performing with several partners in the course of a long evening. The party was one in which "closet swinging" was expressly disallowed; everything had to be out in the open. Toni took a particular delight in this aspect of it: "I like to see Duncan happy, and I enjoyed watching him having a wild time and looking so absolutely carried away by it all. He felt the same about watching me with other men—and it didn't seem the least bizarre or strange to either of us. I tried all sorts of things that night—I even got into a thing with another woman. She approached me, and I hesitated, but then I thought, 'I ought to try this, there really may be something in it.' I found it interesting—I liked the feel of her skin, I liked the *idea* of it, although it didn't really turn me on. But it turned Duncan on like crazy to see me with another woman. It was really worthwhile."

They got onto the regular circuit, only to discover that group sex had drawbacks. "Most of the women were nice, but many of the men were obnoxious—and I couldn't always refuse them. And there were too many rules about what you could and couldn't do—like you could have extra women at a party, but not extra men, and you couldn't date anybody's husband outside the party. So they really weren't sexually liberated at all; they were just as uptight as most other people. It really got to be rather boring."

After a while, Toni and Duncan dropped out of group sex and found things that suited them better. Each of them continued to have other partners outside the home, but they also began bringing partners into it for a night or even a weekend. They found the two-couple situation, with mate-exchanging and sex in each other's presence, a better arrangement than group sex, and sometimes they even settled happily for one guest of either sex, taking turns and having whoever was odd man remain in bed as observer and sometimes as simultaneous participant. Toni maintains that all of this is an adjunct to their marriage, and that they are simply sharing and communicating about sex as they do about all their other activities. She has never felt one moment's jealousy or insecurity, she says, and Duncan echoes the sentiment; one gets the impression, however, that she is more enamored of this way of life than is Duncan, who seems passive and accepting rather than overtly delighted by it all. But it is hard to be sure; the Driscolls convey very little actual emotion about their sex life other than a bland, somewhat smug pride in their own freedom from convention.

The one problem they acknowledge in their present way of life is the near impossibility of finding the right couple with whom to practice comarital sex. Such a couple would be one with considerable sexual appeal in each of the cross-matings but also personal and social appeal all around. "We've met dozens of couples who swing, and who would like to swing with us, but Duncan may be very turned on by the woman while I'm not attracted to the man, or vice versa. And even if both of us are turned on sexually, Duncan may find the man a pain, or maybe I can't stand the woman. It's difficult—it's really *terribly* difficult. But we keep on looking and trying, and meanwhile, even without the right couple, we live an infinitely better life than people who aren't liberated."

MALE LIBERAL

The liberal is more difficult to exemplify than the uptight or the swinger. Sexual liberalism covers a broad range of behavior, encompassing at one end persons who have selectively adopted certain liberal concepts and practices and made them part of traditional married life, and, at the other end, persons some of whose attitudes and behavior verge on sexual radicalism, and who find some difficulty harmonizing their polygamous or bizarre desires with their deep need for an intimate, monogamous love relationship.

An example of the former—the near-conservative liberal—is Kenneth Leach, the 40-year-old shop foreman we heard from earlier (see p. 25). Born in Danbury, a Connecticut factory town, he was the second of six children in a devoutly Catholic home. His father was a post-office employee, his mother a department-store saleslady (her mother took care of the children much of the time). Both Leaches were of Irish-American stock, conservative and lower-middle-class in outlook and quite incapable of discussing sex with their children. Not until Kenneth was 14 did his father so much as mention the subject, and then only to say, brusquely and apropos of nothing, "Do you have any questions you want to ask me about sex?" Kenneth, startled and embarrassed, said no, and his father never brought it up again until eight years later, when Kenneth was about to be married, at which point the elder Leach thrust a Catholic marriage manual at him and said, "Here. Read this."

Many of Kenneth's attitudes toward sex were instilled in him during childhood by his grandmother, a formidable opponent of temptation. "She was so strict that she wouldn't let me go to sleep with my hands under the covers for fear I might play with myself, and even when I went to the bathroom, I wasn't supposed to put my hands down there to aim it." In contrast, he gathered a good deal of sleazy sexual information (and misinformation) on the street from playmates and older boys, mostly of working-class background. Typically, this consisted of dirty jokes, boasting and endless speculations and assertions about the nature of female anatomy and responses. Kenneth found such talk exciting but disturbing; he felt greatly aroused but wicked, particularly when the talk caused him to have an erection. At 12 he bought some tattered girlie magazines from an older boy and hid them in a trunk in the cellar. "I felt terribly guilty about it, because the nuns in school were always warning us about 'impure thoughts and actions,' and when I would go down in the cellar and stare at the pictures in those magazines while masturbating, I felt sure that that was what they were talking about. It was terrifically exciting and felt wonderful, so it had to be sinful."

When Kenneth was a short, red-haired, freckled youth of 16 he began to go to parties and to date girls. Very timidly he tried to kiss his dates good-night, and sometimes succeeded, but not until he was 18 could he nerve himself up to touching a girl's breasts. He did this on a number of occasions with only one girl, and without attempting to undress her. It was intensely exciting, but afterward he would feel horribly sinful and could hardly wait for the chance to confess. "That always made me feel better—once I'd said I was sorry and was ordered to say a few prayers by way of punishment, it wasn't my problem anymore. But I never had a priest give me any real help with it—all they'd say was 'Take cold baths' or 'Play more sports' or something like that, and I did, but it didn't do any good."

He went into the service at 18 but made no effort to pick up girls during his months of basic training. After spending some time in combat in Korea, however, the feeling that he might die any day undercut his inhibitions, and during an R & R leave in Japan he went with a group of more experienced soldiers to a whorehouse and had his first sexual experience. It was, of course, a keen disappointment: "I was so embarrassed and awkward that I didn't play around, but went right at it and was all done in less time than it would have taken me to masturbate. Afterward I thought, 'You wait all your life for this, and then it's just nothing.'" Nonetheless, he thought the girl was nice, and hired her for the whole week. They went places together, she showed him the sights, and they had sex every night. But the sex, he says, "never did amount to anything—I never got over feeling awkward, and she never did anything but lay there and let me get on and off."

That was the sum total of his sexual experience until he returned home and started going with a girl, Bridgit O'Neal—also a good Catholic—with whom he fell in love. Over a period of seven or eight months they progressed slowly, and with much anxiety and soul-searching, from kissing to prolonged necking, and then to breast-touching, usually through her clothing but occasionally with his hand slipped inside. They never touched each other's genitals, although sometimes they lay pressed hard against each other, fully clothed, making timid coital movements. "It was really frustrating for both of us. We kept saying,

'It's not all right to do anything more now, but in three months it's going to be fine,' and that seemed ridiculous to us, but still we stuck with it."

The wedding night was a grim experience. Kenneth was jittery and unsure of what to do, while Bridgit, despite months of petting, was paralyzed, quaking and tearful. Kenneth made some clumsy efforts to consummate their union, but gave it up when she became semihysterical. The next night they tried again, and this time succeeded, though Kenneth was soaked with nervous sweat and Bridgit was in considerable pain. "It got easier in the next few days, but it didn't become satisfactory for a long while—and then not very. Bridgit didn't have an orgasm for over a year, and we were always afraid of pregnancy. It seemed that whenever we wanted to do it, it was the wrong time of the month, and when it was the *right* time, we felt we *had* to, even if we weren't in the mood. Or we'd do it in the not-quite-safe days and then feel tense and angry at ourselves afterward, and we'd sweat out the end of the month and hate the whole thing. When she did get pregnant, things were a little better for a while because at least there was nothing more to worry about. Even so, we were both still very hung-up and couldn't let go, or do anything except the straight routine thing. But we never talked about it or admitted to each other that we were both disappointed about our sex life.

"Finally, after we had our fifth kid and were at our wits' ends, we were living in New York and meeting some pretty progressive people and getting some new ideas, and began to wonder about things. We started to say, 'Let's think this out for ourselves—maybe it isn't right for the church to deny us contraceptives.' We were hoping the Pope would finally come out with something new on the matter, and when he didn't we became bitter and disillusioned. We stopped going to mass and joined a nonsectarian People's Church, and went to meetings of a discussion group on contraception and sexual problems. It opened our eyes to a lot of things. Bridgit started using the pill, and I bought books for us on sex techniques, and after a few months we began to feel changes taking place. In fact, we couldn't *believe* what was happening—it was so different that it was like beginning another life."

The change began with a general sense of relaxation and joyousness due to the absence of the fear of pregnancy. Instead of scheduling their lovemaking, they found themselves free to have sex whenever the mood was upon them, and without any foreboding feeling that there might be a price to pay. From their reading and the discussion-group meetings (both of which embarrassed Bridgit at first, but not for long) they learned to talk to each other about various sexual practices and became bold enough to try out some of them. The woman-astride position, they discovered, was not only exciting but easily produced powerful orgasms in Bridgit; rear-entry vaginal intercourse, which she found embarrassing but he found immensely exciting, they could manage on occasions when they'd had a drink or two; and the side and sitting positions, though not the most comfortable, seemed fun after their first clumsiness was overcome.

"Other things haven't come quite so easy. She's been saying for the last couple of years that she wants to loosen up about some of the preliminaries, and she has, but only in part. For instance, she has learned to like oral sex very much, when I do it to her—and I myself like it a lot, which surprised me—but the other way around is something else. She's making a big effort to like it, but it still isn't easy for her except when she's very turned on, and even then she can't make herself take it very far in or do it hard for fear I might let go in her mouth. Also, she still prefers the dark, but we're beginning to sneak in a little bit of light from the bathroom. But she's changed a lot, and I've changed so much I can't believe I'm the same guy, even though I know we can still improve a lot more."

These days, after 18 years of marriage, they make love three or four times a week—far more often than in their early years —and often luxuriate in it for half an hour to an hour. They look forward to it, talk to each other about it often and take a pride in the new selves they have found and in the new intimacy it has brought about between them. "It's just a different kind of marriage from the one we used to have—there's no other way to put it."

Kenneth and his wife are trying to pass along to their children the new attitudes they've acquired. In the last several years they have answered all the children's questions openly and honestly, bought them sex-education pamphlets and books and moved them from parochial to public schools. Kenneth was somewhat distressed at first to see hard-core pornography become openly available in the past few years; he feared it would harm his children. But he has come to think that it is probably better for such things to be out in the open than concealed, and that even if his children are exposed to such material, he'll know about it, be able to discuss it with them and thereby keep them from misinterpreting whatever they see. He does not think the law ought to control pornographic publishing or the showing of blue movies; pornography doesn't appeal to him, but he considers it psychologically more healthful not to have it bottled up.

As we heard Kenneth say earlier, he thinks that premarital sex between people who have a genuine emotional relationship is a good thing; it readies them for marriage and helps them avoid the pitfalls and problems he and Bridgit experienced. He expects his own children to have premarital sex experience, and is convinced that they'll be happier and better off for it. On the other hand, he disapproves of promiscuity, mate-swapping and group sex, all of which he thinks prevent or damage real relationships. Nevertheless, he does not think such things should be subject to legal interference; he feels that open discussion is the way to deal with them, and that those who, fully informed of the dangers, still want to behave in such ways, have a right to do so. "I have fantasies about such things once in a while, but not often, because I'm happy in my marriage. I always wonder about any person who has sex continually with different people— what's his problem, what's he trying to prove? I feel sorry for such people, because it's not a natural or happy way to act, but I don't look down on them or wish they could be stopped."

Kenneth does not expect that the process he and his wife have been undergoing will ever carry them beyond the borders of faithful monogamy. "We're still growing and changing, but I don't see any big radical change coming up. It'll just be more of the liberation inside ourselves and between us. Other people can screw around, switch off, do whatever they want—that's their business, but it isn't what I want. And I think that most youngsters today, including my own kids, are going to grow up feeling much the same way—free but loving, free but responsible."

FEMALE LIBERAL

Janet Whelan is at the far end of the liberal spectrum from Kenneth Leach. There are times when she acts and sounds al-

most like a swinger, though this is more a matter of passing
moods or conscious poses than of her inner needs. Janet is 26,
separated from her husband and lives in a tiny rented apartment
in Sausalito, where she leads the free-and-easy California single
life with no deep involvements and, for the time being, no long-
range plans. She's half flower child (though a trifle old for the
role) and half working woman; by day she is a trim, efficient
technician at a medical laboratory in San Francisco, but after
hours she puts on granny glasses, a Mother Hubbard and san-
dals, and mixes with assorted hippies, writers, drifters and radical graduate students, most of them single, nearly all of them
drug users, and every one of them dissenters from middle-class
mores and values. She herself is a gentle dissenter. Pleasant-
featured and almost pretty, though a little on the plump side,
her manner is sweet and a trifle vague. She thinks of herself as
loving, open and "cool."

Janet grew up in a suburb of Rochester, New York, the second
daughter of a mixed marriage. Her father was an Italian-Ameri-
can, her mother Jewish, but both were nonbelievers and educated, liberal people, though thoroughly suburban-bourgeois in
their tastes and habits. They freely discussed sex with her, but
always in an earnest, pedagogical fashion. The result was that
she had no great interest in the matter until well after puberty,
and was in fact somewhat prudish without having any religious
or moral reasons for being so.

In her early teens, nice-looking but somewhat chubby, she
dated a fair amount and had the usual middle-class-girl's experiences with local boys who tried to neck, or fumbled at her
breasts in the back seats of cars. For the most part she found
their kisses sloppy and their groping rude. But at 16 she fell in
love with a college junior who came from New York, an experienced and sophisticated youth who cared about her and was
both sensitive and skillful. "He knew I was naïve and unawakened, and he was very patient and smooth with me. He brought
me along so slowly, week by week, that I was never startled or
repelled by anything. First he introduced me to French kissing,
then to touching—we touched each other's fingertips for a long
while, then faces, then arms—and that's the way it went, over
half a year, all the way to intercourse. He was so gentle and slow
about the actual intercourse that I wasn't nervous or guilty, and
didn't even know for sure whether it had happened. I didn't

have an orgasm then, or ever, with him, but I didn't know the difference and never missed it."

The relationship slowly cooled after a while and became more friendly than passionate. Janet began going out with other young men, and during her college years dated a good deal. Sometimes she would feel infatuated, or "captured," as she puts it, by some new boy friend, and when this happened she would sleep with him, but since none of her boy friends was mature or particularly accomplished, sex remained for her simply a pleasant and friendly sort of thing. She suspected, from her reading, that she was fairly restricted in her responses, but had no idea what to do about it.

At 20, however, after half a dozen affairs, she began to secretly date a 30-year-old instructor at the university. He was sexually quite experienced and free, and undertook to educate her. He lavished foreplay upon her, held himself back in intercourse for half an hour at a time, taught her to move her body more freely and cajoled her into trying alternate positions. It helped, too, that at this time she was living off campus in rooms of her own, and could spend whole nights with him or even entire weekends without fear of intrusion or discovery. In the female-above position, one day, she suddenly felt a magical thing happening to her for the first time, and burst into convulsive, happy sobbing. She experienced orgasms from then on, though only about one out of every two or three times. Her lover also introduced her to certain other things she had heard about but never experienced and which, nervously but with a sense of adventure, she tried, one by one: daytime sex, cunnilingus, fellatio, 69, sex looking in a mirror, sex before a Polaroid camera with an automatic shutter release.

Actually, while she found all these things interesting and liked feeling free and daring, none of them seemed important to her. "What really suits me—what I really like—is the movement of my whole body against the man's whole body, because I want the feeling of union of two human beings, the wholeness of two persons becoming one. In all those other things, there's a limitation—you focus on this part or that part, you're not really relating to a person. I don't dislike any of those games, and I like feeling free to do them, but they don't really touch me."

After graduation she took a job in New York, and there met a graduate student in biology who had come on some errand to the laboratory where she was working. They liked each other, went out a few times, fell in love and shortly moved into the same apartment. For nearly two years their relationship—emotionally placid, sexually good—remained stable. Then they married, and at the same time he gave up his part-time job to enter an accelerated special program, she got a raise, and everything changed. She was now the only money-earner; he was the kept and junior partner. He grew surly, defensive and cold, claimed to be exhausted at night and rarely made love to her. "I have a great need for sex—not pure sex, you know, but a need to hold someone and be held, and he wasn't doing that. I felt rejected and miserable, and sometimes we fought a lot, and other times didn't talk to each other at all."

After half a year they separated, and she came to San Francisco, got a job and found a place to live in Sausalito. That was a year ago. Since then she has been enjoying her new freedom and expanding her sexual horizons. "Out here things are really cool—everyone's much less hung-up than in New York. I feel wide open to new people and new experiences, which I wasn't before. Not that I sleep all around—I have to really *feel* something about a man, I have to be totally *absorbed* by him, to go to bed with him. But it can happen fast. Just last week I looked into someone's eyes in a bookstore, and I knew at once that I wanted to know that person, to get involved with him. We went to a coffeehouse and talked all afternoon, and then went to my place and made love because our heads were really in the same place. But that doesn't happen often. Mostly it takes time, and when I do get involved with someone and see him regularly I don't sleep with other men at the same time, because it breaks up the feeling of being together, of being really into each other."

In this past year she has had several affairs that lasted a couple of months, and has gone to bed a few times with each of eight or nine other men. She has felt pleased with her own ability to try new things: She let one man use a vibrator on her (it amused her but did not really satisfy her), has tried half a dozen novel positions, let one lover give her a prolonged erotic massage, and with others has tried sex in the bathtub, on deserted beaches, while high on marijuana and while on an LSD trip. (Marijuana, she finds, usually makes her feel passionate and sometimes yields a particularly prolonged orgasm; LSD gives her an extraordinarily sensuous awareness of her body and her lover's but seems to prevent orgasm, although the total experience is so intimate and intense that she feels fulfilled and doesn't miss the climax.) One of her lovers urged her to let him try anal intercourse with her. She'd heard about it and was interested, though fearful, but it proved so painful when he attempted entry that she begged him to desist. She would like to try it again sometime, when she is more relaxed, particularly with a man who has a smaller penis. She also was urged by one man to have sex during her menstrual flow. The thought had always repelled her, but she decided this must be an old-fashioned prejudice, and tried it, feeling rather proud of herself for being able to enjoy it despite the messiness involved.

But some aspects of liberated sexuality do not attract her in the least. Hard-core pornography and blue movies strike her as rather disgusting—not for moral reasons but because they lack the human closeness and communication that she regards as the best thing about sex. "I can have an orgasm or not, and it doesn't matter, as long as I'm feeling very close to a man whom I'm all wrapped up in and the conversation and the touching and the holding are very intense. Or sometimes I can have an orgasm and be all released, and if we're really together I can go on to make love for hours without needing another." Group sex doesn't intrigue her at all; she has turned down a number of invitations to parties because sex, for her, is essentially a one-to-one experience. She is quite tolerant about homosexuality, but it has no attraction for her. Sadomasochistic and fetishistic practices she regards as sick; she wouldn't consider experimenting with them.

As pleased as Janet is with her present way of life, it involves one problem she has not solved: She still would like to find a man who would be absolutely right for her, and to whom she would want to be sexually faithful. But this would mean giving up the freedom to have new experiences and new loves. "I'd have to be faithful to any man I lived with, because it would tear me apart to be deeply involved with two men at the same time. Right now there's nobody important in my life, so I can sleep with more than one man and feel no problem. But if I find the really right man, I won't want anybody else—but I'll hate to be penned in again. Maybe it's marriage that is the trap—most of my married friends aren't happy, and I myself was happy enough with my husband until we got married. Marriage burdens love with a whole lot of rules and problems and complications. You get all bound up in *things,* and you get scared, and wonder if it's really right for you, and how you could ever get out if it isn't.

"Besides, we've messed up this earth so badly that it's going to come to an inglorious end in another generation or two, and I don't want to be responsible for creating someone who has to live with the mess we've made. I don't want children, so why marry? But of course I'm only twenty-six, and it's possible that after a while I won't enjoy living this way so much, or going from one man to another; I may want to settle down. But I won't worry about the future—I'm enjoying myself too much the way things are." Then, after a pause, she gives away the fact that, after all, the future *is* on her mind, and that her hopes are essentially old-fashioned: "I'm just not going to make any plans or count on anything until the ideal situation presents itself. I hope it will, before I get too old."

MALE, 24, CATHOLIC UPBRINGING: *I got to the point where I'd be half awake, and deriving great pleasure from moving my penis back and forth against the sheets until I'd have an orgasm without ever touching it with my hand. . . . I told myself I wasn't masturbating . . . but it gave me all kinds of awful feelings.*

FEMALE, 44, PRACTICING CATHOLIC: *I never did masturbate, never. I got into sex early and got married, so I didn't need it, but I don't even remember thinking about it . . . I don't have any desire for that, never did, not even when my husband was sick for a long while.*

MALE, 26, LIBERAL UPBRINGING: *I learned from the guys I played baseball with. I was in sixth grade, and one time they said, "Come on over—we have books and pictures, and we jack off together." . . . It seemed all right because eight or ten guys I'd known for a couple of years were all doing it. There didn't seem to be anything wrong about it.*

FEMALE, 28, NONRELIGIOUS LIBERAL UPBRINGING: *My parents always walked around naked, so it seemed perfectly all right to me to start investigating my own body. . . By the time I was twelve I became almost obsessed by masturbating. I sort of knew I ought not be doing it, but I must not have felt too strongly about that because I can remember even doing it secretly right at the dinner table.*

MALE, 35: *Whenever I travel, it takes about a week until I can't stand it anymore. . . . I tell myself, "It's either do it or go out on the town." But I'm not that kind of guy, so I do it, and I feel better—and also a little worse.*

FEMALE, 29: *I still do it when the man I live with is away and I feel the need. I enjoy sex with him a great deal more than I do masturbating, but . . . it gives me satisfaction and peace. . . .*

MALE, 25: *It's still true that in masturbating you have better control over your own penis and over your sensations, and you can prolong things without any trouble. So even though I'm sleeping with a great girl, I still masturbate sometimes, because the orgasm is better or because I just sometimes want to do something different.*

FEMALE, 27: *If I want to, for whatever reason, there's no reason on earth why I shouldn't, so I do. I like it, if I'm in the mood for it.*

CHAPTER

2

Masturbation

The Roots of Sexual Inhibition

It is our contention, based on our survey data, that the frequent assertions that a sexual revolution has conquered America are something less than accurate, for the changes that have taken place both in attitudes and in actual behavior have not, by and large, created any real break with the fundamental Western tradition linking sexual activity with love, nor have they brought about the existence of new social institutions competing with, or preempting sexuality from, marriage and family life. On the other hand, we find ample evidence that there has been a sweeping liberation of sexuality from a two-millenia-long tradition of Judeo-Christian asceticism. Nearly everyone can now think about, talk about and read about sex as freely as about food, politics or money. Most people have become grudgingly tolerant, even if not warmly approving, of many forms of sexual behavior they would formerly have regarded with loathing or even righteous indignation. And a considerable number of persons now practice and enjoy sexual acts they would previously have been afraid to perform, or would have performed at the cost of fear, guilt and self-contempt. What is as remarkable as the scope of this sexual liberation is the speed with which it has taken place. In the mere quarter-century since the present sexual era began with the publication of the first "Kinsey Report," the changes in sexual attitudes and in actual behavior in America have been of such proportions as have historically required one to several centuries to take place.

For all that, the liberation of sex is still far from complete. A substantial percentage of American men, and an even larger one of American women, retain many puritanical and antihedonistic feelings about sexual pleasure that color their judgment and attitudes, and limit the variety and frequency of their own sexual acts and the intensity of enjoyment they derive from those acts. Even in the relatively liberated part of the population, furthermore, nearly everyone still has at least some misgivings or guilt feelings about certain perfectly innocuous sexual acts he or she routinely performs or would like to perform.

This is most notably and most pointlessly true of masturbation. Kinsey reported that it was the second most important source of sexual gratification in the life of the average American male (heterosexual coitus being first), and the form of sexual activity which most reliably yielded orgasm for the average woman.[1] Today, as in his time, it is utilized regularly and frequently by nearly all single males and a majority of single females, and, though less frequently, by substantial percentages of married men and women. It is convenient, free, safe (it can cause neither venereal diseases nor pregnancies) and devoid of social or interpersonal difficulties. Thanks to the sexual-liberation movement, these facts about masturbation have been much publicized of late, and many modern sex educators have begun to speak approvingly of masturbation and to recommend it both for those with no available sexual partners and for those who are sexually inhibited. All this has had its effect upon the public: As our survey data will show, many people are less disapproving of masturbation, and many, even in adult life and even if married, use it more freely than their counterparts a generation ago.

Yet, aside from pubescent boys (who are often proud of their new accomplishment), most persons who masturbate remain more or less guilt-ridden about it, and nearly all of them are extremely secretive about their masturbating and would be horribly embarrassed to have anyone know the truth. In speaking of the act, practically everyone is jocular, condescending or scornful, thus tacitly implying that it is something he or she could never stoop to. Even though any reasonably well-informed single young man or woman knows that nearly every other single man or woman masturbates at least occasionally, almost no one will admit, even to an intimate friend, that he or she does so. It is far easier to admit that one does not believe in God, or was once a Communist, or was born illegitimately, than that one sometimes fondles a part of his own body to the point of orgastic release. Not even lovers, in their most intimate confessions, tell each other that this is still part of their repertoire of sexual behavior. Not even in the closest of marriages is one spouse apt to admit to the other that, during a long separation or illness that made intercourse impossible, he or she turned to self-relief. One 40-year-old man, a highly successful corporation lawyer, told us in his interview that he had been in psychoanalysis for a full year before he could bring himself to tell his doctor the thing he was most deeply ashamed of: the fact that he still masturbated.

It is not because the act is self-administered and pleasurable that it is so freighted with guilt, for we speak freely to friends of other self-administered pleasures—scratching an itch, sipping a good brandy, lingering in a hot bath, sailing a small boat alone, lying late in bed on a weekend—with no hint of shame on our part, or of disapproval on theirs. We see nothing wrong about giving ourselves pleasure, unless it be sexual in nature. But this casts a far larger net than it seems to, for through the onus placed upon autoerotic gratification, society instills in us a basic anxiety about or distrust of all sexual pleasure. It is through the elementary schooling we get about masturbation that we are made ready for more advanced education in the rest of society's edicts and limitations upon sexual enjoyment.

Elementary schooling is, in large part, composed of very early nonverbal learning. Perhaps precisely because it is nonverbal, it is the most influential sex education we receive. Many an infant discovers, while still in the crib, the pleasure of touching and playing with his or her sexual parts, or of stimulating them in some other way, such as rocking back and forth on a toy or tugging on a blanket pulled between the legs.[2] But most of these children soon learn that such simple pleasing acts have consequences wholly unlike any other. If their parents are the old-fashioned kind who smack the wicked hands and scold them, the message is plain enough. But even if their parents are the semi-enlightened type who freeze up in the effort not to show their revulsion and distress, the children sense disapproval far deeper and more sinister than any they have brought upon themselves by, say, throwing things or spitting out food.

As we will see in a subsequent chapter, the great majority of

American parents—even in this liberated era—provide very little explicit factual sex education for their children. But their communication of deep, shocked disapproval is education in a very real sense, for it transmits traditional social values to the child and tells him, in effect, what the world around him thinks of the thing he is doing, and what he himself should think of it. And because that part of our sex education lies deeper than words and antedates reasoning, it is particularly enduring and relatively resistant to the influence of the sexual-liberation movement.

Traditional Attitudes Toward Masturbation, and the Emergence of Permissiveness

Extreme social disapproval and condemnation by religious authorities have characterized the dominant Western attitude toward masturbation for a very long time. In many relatively primitive societies, masturbation by children of both sexes has been thought natural and even healthful, and no effort has been made to discourage it. In those societies, even adults who are known to masturbate have by and large been viewed with amusement or scorn rather than moral outrage.[3] But the ancient Jews, unlike most other peoples at their stage of social development, considered all masturbation a grave sin, with masturbation by an adult male being worst of all since it was a deliberate waste of seed provided by the Lord to increase the tribe. At times, in later Jewish history, the strict orthodox view even held that masturbation deserved the death penalty.[4]

The Catholic sex codes, first formulated by the Jewish founders of the church, have always severely condemned masturbation, classifying it as a mortal sin, which, if unexpiated, would cause one to be consigned to eternal hellfire.[5] Protestant theologians, when they appeared on the scene, took a somewhat less severe view of the act, but this did little to soften a tradition that was, by then, a millenium and a half old.[6] Indeed, the puritanical mind of Protestantism, taking a new tack, promised hell on earth, rather than eternal damnation, to masturbators. In 1760 a Swiss physician named Tissot published an immensely influential book entitled *L'onanisme: Dissertation sur les Maladies Produites par la Masturbation,* in which he asserted, on his own medical authority, that masturbation produced such dread disorders as epilepsy, feeblemindedness, impotence, bladder ailments, convulsions and paralysis. In France, England and America, generations of doctors read about and believed Tissot's doctrines, and a number of them wrote papers adding other diseases and malfunctions to his list. By the mid-19th Century it had been positively stated in a number of medical books and journals that masturbation could cause such minor disorders as pimples, falling hair, stooped shoulders and weak eyes, and such major ones as consumption, gonorrhea, uterine hemorrhage, dementia praecox (schizophrenia) and suicide.[7] For good measure, Richard von Krafft-Ebing claimed, in his monumental *Psychopathia Sexualis,* that masturbation was responsible for a wide variety of sexual deviations, severe degenerative neuroses and psychoses, and in some cases was the cause of lust murders.[8]

In one way or another, such ideas filtered down to the average person. Physicians and others wrote innumerable cautionary moral tracts for boys, warning them of the physical, mental and spiritual damage caused by "self-abuse," "self-pollution" or the "solitary vice," as it was variously called. Typically, a popular work called *What a Boy Should Know,* written by two doctors in 1909 and widely used for many years, informed its defenseless readers that

> . . . whenever unnatural emissions are produced . . . the body becomes "slack." A boy will not feel so vigorous and springy; he will be more easily tired; he will not have so good "an eye" for games. He will probably look pale and pasty, and he is lucky if he escapes indigestion and getting his bowels confined, both of which will probably give him spots and pimples on his face. . . .
>
> The results on the mind are the more severe and more easily recognized. . . . A boy who practices this habit can never be the best that Nature intended him to be. His wits are not so sharp. His memory is not so good. His power of fixing his attention on whatever he is doing is lessened. . . . A boy like this is a poor thing to look at. . . .
>
> [Finally,] the effect of self-abuse on a boy's character always tends to weaken it, and, in fact, to make him untrust-

worthy, unreliable, untruthful, and probably even dishonest.[9]

Such is the cultural tradition concerning masturbation, almost
unquestioned until recent years. But a feeble countercurrent
first set in toward the end of the 19th Century when a few
physicians, fighting off the preconceptions of Victorian morality,
dared to question the dread effects ascribed to masturbation.
Medical science was making great strides, and there simply was
no evidence to warrant the charges made by Tissot and his
followers. A few psychologists and psychiatrists, moreover, led
by Freud, were beginning to study sexual phenomena with a
certain amount of objectivity and to view masturbation without
the moral horror of their predecessors. But this was only a
partial liberation, for the emerging view of most liberal physicians and Freudian psychotherapists was that although masturbation produced no gross physical diseases or severe mental
disorders, it was an infantile form of sexual gratification and, if
continued beyond adolescence or indulged in to "excess" (a
term which was never defined), could fixate the masturbator on
the self as sexual object and render him or her incapable of adult
heterosexual adjustment; males would prove impotent, and
females frigid, in normal marital relations.[10] Even as up-to-date
and emancipated an author as the late great Dr. Abraham Stone,
coauthor with his wife, the late Dr. Hannah Stone, of *A Marriage
Manual*—published in 1935 and still selling briskly today—had
gentle but troubling comments to make about it: The dangers
of masturbation, he wrote in his 1952 revision, had been
"grossly exaggerated," and "as a rule," the practice would not
prevent good sexual adjustment in marriage—but "occasionally, young people who have practiced self-relief over a long
period of time may find it difficult to readjust their sex habits and
to derive complete satisfaction from the sex union in marriage."
In particular, women who have become used to clitoral orgasm
through masturbating "may later have some difficulty in attain-
ing adequate satisfaction from vaginal stimulation during intercourse."[11]

The qualified permissiveness of these physicians and psychotherapists, though a long way from the hellfire, the diseases and
the degeneracy threatened by the Victorian sex educators, was
still subtly damaging and worrisome to innumerable young men

and women: Anyone who knew that dangers lay in excess might wonder whether his own frequency was not excessive; anyone who had been told that masturbation was an immature form of sexual behavior could entertain grave self-doubts whenever he gave in to the desire, or even felt it; and anyone who thought that he might have been doing it too often or over too long a time was likely to fear that he might be sexually inadequate in marriage, and, fearing it, be so.

But at the leading edge of sexual liberation a handful of physicians and psychologists had begun to insist, as early as the 1920s, that according to their clinical experience masturbation in children or even in young adults was a useful preparation for heterosexuality, and that in persons deprived of sex partners it provided beneficial release from tension. Psychotherapist Wilhelm Reich and his followers reported that sexually blocked patients could be freed by a technique that involved teaching the patient, in the treatment office, to make coital pelvic movements and to build up sexual excitement in himself or herself to the point of orgasm, if possible.[12] Kinsey gave masturbation considerable cachet when he reported in 1948 that it was used more widely, and over a longer period of life, by better-educated and socially higher males than by those who were less educated and of the working class .[13] Moreover, though he had nothing to say about its effects upon marital sexual adjustment in the male, he found that premarital masturbation to orgasm by the female seemed to contribute to her capacity to respond with orgasm in coital relations.[14] Masters and Johnson, observing orgasms in both males and females in their Saint Louis clinic, also gave masturbation a good name when they reported, in *Human Sexual Response,* that, at least for the female, orgasm achieved by self-manipulation seemed to be stronger than that achieved in coitus.[15] By 1968 masturbation had become so respectable in some circles that Wardell Pomeroy, a longtime Kinsey associate, advised boys in his book *Boys and Sex* to masturbate as much as they wanted, desire being the reliable guide to proper frequency. While they were at it, he added, they might also try to see how slowly they could do it rather than how fast, since this would be good training for their later role as lovers.[16] In a companion book, *Girls and Sex,* he gave much the same encouragement to girls, but advised them, in the interests of successful future coitus, *not* to delay orgasm. In a seemingly unrelated development, some extremists of the women's liberation movement began to attack the claimed superiority of vaginal orgasm as male-chauvinist propaganda, and to view clitoral orgasm as the superior kind (or the only kind) and self-induced orgasm as better than an orgasm induced by the male oppressor.[17]

All this finally reached the great mass-cult middlebrow audience through the medium of paperback publishing and television. The anonymous authors of *The Sensuous Woman* and *The Sensuous Man*, for instance, enthusiastically urged everyone to masturbate freely and joyously as much as they wanted to, both for fun and for its good effects. The author of *The Sensuous Woman* called masturbation a splendid and essential way to train for lovemaking and, in itself, "one of the most gratifying human experiences," "wholesome, normal, and sound," and "good for you." She gave detailed and rather panting instructions on how to do it with fingers, vibrators, bidets or showers, dildoes and so on, urging her readers to practice diligently until they could not only reach an orgasm within a minute but regularly have three or four before stopping and sometimes go for the bundle —10 to 25 in a single session.[18] The author of *The Sensuous Man*, though making no claims about the training value of masturbation in men, was exultant about it as a form of fun. It was not as good as sex with a woman, but if no woman were handy it was good enough—a marvelous tension reliever, very satisfying, capable of yielding "an incredible feeling of pleasure and release" and totally harmless to self and society. "In short," he concluded on a rhapsodic note, "masturbation is terrific."[19]

Attitude Changes Toward Masturbation in the Past Generation

The tradition concerning masturbation is over two millenia old, while the countertradition barely existed two decades ago and has become a significant force only in the past ten years. That being the case, one could hardly expect the massive bulwark of tradition to have been completely torn down since Kinsey's time, nor has it been. Nonetheless, our data show that it has been badly battered and frequently breached; the classic attitudes toward masturbation, the frequency of masturbation (especially in adults) and the feelings of most masturbators about their own behavior have all undergone changes of striking magnitude and importance.

As one measure of attitude change, we offered questionnaire respondents the simplistic moral platitude "Masturbation is wrong," asking them to signify agreement or disagreement.* It might have been useful to have asked, in separate questions, whether they considered it wrong for children, and wrong for adults. Since, however, this item occurred in the context of a long series of other attitude questions relating to adult sexual practices, it is reasonable to assume that the replies refer essentially to postadolescent masturbation. Unfortunately, there is no comparable body of attitude data from the 1940s against which to contrast our own. Even Kinsey, though he had much to say about attitudes toward masturbation, presented little statistical information about them. But we are justified in assuming that any significant difference in attitudes between the older people in our sample and the younger ones would be at least a partial measure of the change occurring in the past generation: The 35-and-over respondents, even if they have been somewhat influenced by the new voices, will tend to reflect primarily the dominant social attitudes of their own formative period (roughly, 1915 to 1945) while the under-35 respondents will reflect the impact of the liberalizing influences existing during the past 30 years. And whatever change we do find, we can feel fairly sure that it will augur still greater change in the next generation, for as the attitudes of young parents grow more permissive, they will be less likely to impose guilt feelings upon their own children—who, in turn, will be even more receptive to scientific findings and nonmoralistic views concerning masturbation.

What, then, does our survey reveal? Somewhat to our own surprise we find that, even in the older half of our sample, men and women are not generally harsh in their views on masturbation: For each man who agrees that masturbation is wrong, a

---

*As with other attitude questions, respondents were offered five choices: Agree strongly, Agree somewhat, Disagree somewhat, Disagree strongly, Have no opinion. Since both "strong" and "somewhat" responses to this question proved to be of roughly equal dimensions, we present the results in collapsed (combined) form. Except where otherwise noted, the percentages are based on those who made some reply, the nonanswerers being omitted from our calculations.

little over two others disagree; and even among women, who
have traditionally been sexually more conservative than men,
for each one who agrees that it is wrong, two others disagree.
We cannot take these data to mean that a majority of older
people think well, or approvingly, of masturbation; in all likelihood they still regard it as immature behavior or as indicative
of personal inadequacy, and probably most of those older people who sometimes masturbate still experience guilt feelings or
self-contempt. Nevertheless, the majority of the older half of our
sample has at least begun to repudiate the categorical moral
condemnation of masturbation taught them during their own
childhood.

In the younger half of the sample, however, the vote is considerably clearer: For every male who says masturbation is wrong,
five others say it is not; and the same ratio holds true among
females. What is even more remarkable is the evidence of a
withering away of the moralistic tradition decade by decade. We
can see a continuing long-term shrinkage of disapproval when
we look at our entire sample arranged by age (see Table 9).

Table 9

Masturbation Is Wrong: Total Sample, Percents Agreeing

	18–24	25–34	35–44	45–54	55 and over
Males	15	16	27	28	29
Females	14	17	27	33	36

And Table 10 presents the corollary set of data, showing the
increasing percentages of people who, decade by decade, have
adopted the viewpoint of the countertradition.

We were concerned that there might be a bias in these figures,
since a sizable fraction of the younger age groups consisted of
single people and it is reasonable to suppose that single people
might be more inclined to justify masturbation than those who

Table 10

Masturbation Is Wrong: Total Sample, Percents Disagreeing

	18–24	25–34	35–44	45–54	55 and over
Males	80	81	67	67	63
Females	78	77	68	55	52

are not so often in need of it. But when we examined the responses of married people alone, we found that, age group for age group, the percentages of those who regard masturbation as wrong and those who do not were almost identical with those for the total sample. The countertradition is affecting not only those who currently benefit the most from it but nearly everyone in the younger segment of American society.

Kinsey and various other observers had noted that the taboos against masturbation were distinctly stronger at lower social levels of the population and among the less-educated than at higher levels and among the college-educated.[20] Our data indicate that this is still so. Both at the blue-collar and the white-collar occupational level, and among noncollege-educated people as well as college-educated, the traditional view is being eroded; the under-35 half of the sample is distinctly more permissive about masturbation than the 35-and-older half in every category. But the gap between the occupational categories and the gap between the educational categories does not narrow, among the young, as we reported it does elsewhere; in some cases it even seems to widen. This does not mean that blue-collar and noncollege-educated people have become more conservative about masturbation; in all likelihood, it simply indicates that among the more articulate parts of the society the permissive trend has developed faster. Perhaps this is truer of masturbation than of most other forms of sexual activity; people now freely discuss all kinds of sexual acts—and so strip away their traditional hostility toward them—but autoeroticism, by virtue of its historic position as the lowliest and most ignoble sexual act, is less freely discussed than other acts. This being so, it would follow that the more articulate part of the public would adopt the new outlook more rapidly than the less articulate part.

Changes in Masturbatory Behavior: Accumulative Incidence and Age at First Experience

It is, however, in measurements of actual behavior that we find more concrete and telling evidence of the extent to which masturbation has been stripped of much of its culturally imposed burden of sin, pathology and shame. One might suppose that the most obvious indication of that change would be in a marked increase in the total percentage of males and females who have ever masturbated. But while this is a revealing parameter for most kinds of formerly disapproved or deviant behavior, it is not so in the case of masturbation, an act so simple, so biologically natural and so likely to be spontaneously discovered on one's own that it has probably always been a part of the total life experience of nearly all men and a majority of women. This was known, at least intuitively, to most sex researchers prior to Kinsey, and confirmed and quantified by his finding that in his very large sample of Americans the accumulative incidence of masturbation, ever, or to orgasm, was 92 percent for males and for females was 62 percent ever, and 58 percent to orgasm.[21] ("Accumulative incidence" was Kinsey's projection of the ultimate lifetime experience of his total sample.) Our own results look virtually identical—94 percent of our males and 63 percent of our females have masturbated at some time—but this is not an accumulative incidence; it represents what has happened up to this time, in the lives of our respondents. Presumably, some of the younger people in the sample and at least a few of the more mature people who have not yet experienced masturbation will still do so during their lifetimes. Accordingly, our incidence data suggest at least a small overall increase since Kinsey's time.*

But where a sexual act had been experienced by nearly all males and by most females even before the advent of sexual liberation, we must look for change by means of more subtle tests, such as how early in life people first do it, how often they do it, when and why they do it and how they feel about it. The first of these tests is based on the common-sense assumption that the total weight of parental, religious and social disapproval, plus the warnings of folklore and the medical profession, will delay the beginning of masturbation until the growing power of the sexual drive and the increasing·strength of the teen-age or young-adult ego breaks through the psychosocial barriers. The corollary assumption would be that if those barriers have been weakened, the breakthrough will come sooner after puberty, or even concomitantly with it.

---

*Here, as in almost all of our comparisons with Kinsey's data, we have omitted our black respondents, in order to make the comparison with Kinsey's all-white sample as close as possible.

And we do, in fact, find that just such a shift has taken place. In Kinsey's sample, 45 percent of all males had masturbated by the time they were 13[22]; in our own sample, fully 63 percent have done so by that age. Among the females the shift is, as we might have anticipated, still more striking, since they have traditionally been subject to far greater psychosocial inhibiting forces than males. In Kinsey's sample only 15 percent had masturbated to orgasm by the time they were 13,[23] while in our own sample the figure is 33 percent, or more than twice as large. In every age grouping, our males and females seem to have begun somewhat earlier, on the average, than Kinsey's people in comparable age groupings a generation ago. Even within our own sample, our younger people started earlier than our older people. Evidently it has been far easier for people passing through adolescence and the teens in the past decade or so to perceive masturbation as acceptable, at least internally, than it was for people in their parents' generation.

Even those who are restrained by fear, guilt or ignorance tend today to acquire liberating information as they grow older, or, in the case of females, to experience masturbation in petting or marital sexual relations, and to try it themselves thereafter. As a result, more of the young married females in our sample have masturbated, at least at some time, than have our older females. The same change is revealed by a comparison of our figures with Kinsey's: 44 percent of his married females had experienced masturbation at some time or other while married,[24] as against 61 percent of ours.

Thus, even though our overall total incidences of masturbation are only slightly larger than Kinsey's accumulative incidences, there has been a major change in the age at which masturbation is first experienced: Both sexes are beginning it earlier than formerly, although females still begin masturbating, on the average, a good deal later than males, many females doing so for the first time in their dating or early marital years.

The tendency for both boys and girls to masturbate earlier does not, however, mean that it is now largely devoid of struggle and inner conflict. Americans exhibit a very wide range of feelings about their own desires to masturbate, some being thoroughly liberated from the tradition, a majority being partially liberated and ambivalent, and a minority still having the powerful negative feelings about it that their great-grandparents

did. Working-class men and women, and men and women without any college education, are still distinctly more apt to be
troubled by their own masturbatory desires or acts, or to believe
the folklore warnings about it, than are white-collar men and
women, and men and women who have had at least some college
education. Even more marked is the restraining effect of religion, though only on women. Those who attend services frequently, whether Protestant, Catholic or Jewish, are distinctly
less apt ever to have masturbated than those who never attend
services, as Table 11 illustrates:

Table 11

Ever Masturbated: All Faiths, by Regularity of Church Attendance, Percents

	Regular churchgoers	Irregular churchgoers	Nonchurch-goers
Males	92	92	93
Females	51	69	75

The survey data and the interviews suggest, moreover, that
among those who have ever masturbated, strong religious feelings tended to delay the beginning of such activity for both
males and females.

Such statements tell what is happening, but not how it feels
to the individuals involved. One can get a better sense both of
the torment that is still involved for many people and of the easy
hedonism of the liberated minority by listening to a few representative men and women talking about the approach to the first
masturbatory experiences. First, here are two men who might
well have grown up in an earlier and more repressive era:

A 38-YEAR-OLD SCHOOLTEACHER, PRESBYTERIAN, SMALL-
TOWN BACKGROUND: I can still vividly remember being three
or four, and naked in my crib, and having my mother come
in and fly completely off the handle. I was playing with
myself at the time, and it shocked the living daylights out
of her. When I was an adolescent and would get an erection, I'd want to grab it and do things to it—I'd be almost
sick with wanting to—but I felt too terrified. Finally one
time I did, and for days I lived with a sense that something
terrible was going to happen to me.

GRADUATE STUDENT, AGE 24, CATHOLIC, BLUE-COLLAR BIG-CITY BACKGROUND: The priests and my old man were always warning me about it, so I didn't dare try anything. But then I started having wet dreams, which I got excruciating pleasure from, and found very frightening. After a while I got to the point where I'd be half awake, and deriving great pleasure from moving my penis back and forth against the sheets until I'd have an orgasm without ever touching it with my hand, even though I wanted to and had to fight myself not to. It was stupid—I told myself I wasn't masturbating, the way I did it—but it gave me all kinds of awful feelings. I never did use my hand on it until I was eighteen or nineteen—and that made me feel even worse, at first.

A rather larger number of men, especially young ones, seem to experience less painful struggles, either because of weaker negative conditioning in childhood or the permissive attitudes and encouragement of their playmates:

THEOLOGY STUDENT, 25 YEARS OLD, RAISED A METHODIST IN SUBURB OF LARGE CITY: An older cousin of mine took two of us out to the garage and did it in front of us. I remember thinking that it seemed a very strange thing to do, and that people who were upright wouldn't do it, but it left a powerful impression on me. A couple of years later, when I began to get erections, I wanted to do it, and felt I shouldn't, but I remembered how he had looked when he was doing it, and the memory tempted me strongly. I worried, and held back, and fought it, but finally I gave in. The worry didn't stop me, and doing it didn't stop my worrying.

SALESMAN, 32, BLACK, RAISED AS A BAPTIST ON SOUTHERN FARM: I must have been eleven when I heard some older kids talking about it, and they went through the motions, and when I was alone, I tried it out. It worked—I had a rout! It was great! I didn't really feel guilty, either, because they were all doing it. I was scared I might get caught, but that didn't stop me. What did stop me was that I heard stories that if you jerk off, you go blind, so I gave it up for a while, but it wasn't easy.

And a few show no trace of the kind of conflict or inhibitions that ordinarily delay the beginning of masturbation or make it inwardly painful:

A 26-YEAR-OLD HIPPIE ARTISAN, RAISED BY DIVORCED CON-
GREGATIONALIST MOTHER IN PERMISSIVE RESORT TOWN: My
mother couldn't be open with me about it, so I learned
from the guys I played baseball with. I was in sixth grade,
and one time they said, "Come on over—we have books
and pictures, and we jack off together." So I went, and it
seemed all right because eight or ten guys I'd known for a
couple of years were all doing it. There didn't seem to be
anything wrong about it—it was all happy vibes. Afterwards, I got to doing it at home, too, but of course I made
every effort to keep it secret from my mother. I didn't really
feel guilty; but I knew she'd be against it.

Women, as the data show, are still considerably more likely to
be strongly inhibited about masturbating than are men, with the
result that some go through life without ever doing it, while a
good many others do so for the first time in early adulthood, and
with very ambivalent feelings. They talk about it in terms like
these:

CATHOLIC HOUSEWIFE, WORKING-CLASS, AGE 44, LARGE EAST-
ERN CITY: I never did masturbate, never. I got into sex early
and got married, so I didn't need it, but I don't even
remember thinking about it or knowing any other girls who
ever did it. A couple of years ago I read *The Sensuous Woman,*
and I couldn't *believe! This* is what happens? I says, *why?* I
mean, I don't have any desire for *that,* never did, not even
when my husband was sick for a long while.

A 40-YEAR-OLD MARRIED BUSINESSWOMAN, JEWISH, SEMIDE-
VOUT: I didn't even know about masturbation when I was
a girl. Or let's say I wasn't *onto* it. It just wasn't something
I could imagine myself doing. It wasn't until I'd been married many years that I read some material about masturbation in a feminist magazine, and I finally said to myself,
"I've got to try this," and I did. It was strictly experimental
—I felt rather excited and nervous, and sort of liked it, but
afterwards the secret weighed heavily on me for a while. I
only did it three times, in all, and then dropped it.

Other women, particularly young ones, began masturbating
relatively early and without much inner turmoil, although we
encountered no female who had the peer-group support or
group-masturbation experiences of some of our males:

HOUSEWIFE, 28, NONRELIGIOUS INTELLECTUAL JEWISH PAR-
ENTS, BIG-CITY BACKGROUND: My parents always walked
around naked, so it seemed perfectly all right to me to start
investigating my own body when I was seven. That passed,
but by the time I was twelve I became almost obsessed by
masturbating. I sort of knew I ought not be doing it, but I
must not have felt too strongly about that because I can
remember even doing it secretly right at the dinner table.

GRADUATE STUDENT, 27, NONRELIGIOUS (CHILD OF MIXED
MARRIAGE), BIG-CITY BACKGROUND: I played doctor with
other girls by the time I was five or six, although we got
caught and reprimanded once, but not harshly. When I was
twelve my best friend and I played sexual games and felt
each other, and that gave me the idea and started me masturbating, and I did it a lot. I kept it a secret from everyone
except two friends, who drew straws with me one time as
to whether we had to tell, and I lost. I was terribly embarrassed, but I told them.

Finally, one may get some inkling of the future from this brief
comment by one young well-educated mother about her own
daughters, who are 13 and 14, respectively:

They both have massage vibrators, and they use them to
masturbate with. Pretty often, too—Susie, for one, was doing it absolutely every night, at bedtime, last year. They
both told me about it without any hesitation, because
they'd heard Dr. Reuben on TV, and read about it in a
couple of books, and learned that it was perfectly all right,
and healthy, and relaxing. It bothers me, because I feel it's
wrong, somehow, but I know there's no evidence of that,
so I just listen to them, and say okay, and let it go at that.

Changes in Masturbatory Behavior: Frequency, Continuing Use, Use by the Married

The earlier beginning of masturbation in the adolescent years
thus does reveal, more sharply than the increase in total incidence, the impact of sexual liberation on contemporary behavior. But even more interesting and meaningful revelations
emerge from an analysis of the frequency of masturbation, the

number of years during which it is actively used and the continued use of masturbation beyond the adolescent years and
early teens by adults, and particularly by the married, for whom
heterosexual contact is easily and more or less continuously
available.

We begin with the hypothesis that the past generation of
sexual liberation should have resulted in measurable increases
both in the active incidence* and in the frequency of masturbation by late teen-agers and young single adults; but, more than
that, we hypothesize that there should also be increases in both
the active incidence and frequency of continued masturbation
by married adult males and females. These hypotheses may
seem strange to some readers. Surely (they may argue) an increase in masturbation by single people in their late teens or
early adulthood would be no evidence of liberation, since the
genuinely liberated should be enjoying more frequent and satisfying intercourse, and ought not need self-relief; by the same
token, and all the more so, an increase in masturbation by the
married would not be evidence of salutary sexual liberation but
an indication of a spreading inability of contemporary men and
women to achieve sexual satisfaction with each other in marriage.

We agree that a high frequency of masturbation in a single
person can be symptomatic of gross inadequacy in heterosexual
relationships or of neurotic compulsions, and that masturbation
by a married person may be the result of marital conflict, impotence or frigidity. But nothing else about our overall sample or
any component part of it indicates a rise in the overall incidence
of sexual, psychological or marital pathologies, as compared to
Kinsey's era, and it therefore seems unlikely that they account
for any significant increases we find in masturbation rates.

We also agree that sexual liberation should result in more
frequent, varied and satisfying intercourse for both single and
married persons, but this need not preclude a simultaneous rise
in masturbation; the two things could be compatible and coex-

---

*"Active incidence" signifies the percentage of an age group who have performed the
activity in question within a specified period of time; *e.g.*, if half of all females aged 18
to 24 masturbated at least once while they were in that age bracket, the active incidence
for the 18-to-24 cohort would be 50 percent; or if half of all females masturbated while
they were 18, the active incidence for age 18 would be 50 percent.

"Accumulative incidence," as indicated earlier, signifies the total percentage who have
ever performed the activity in question, even once, within a lifetime, or up to any
specified age.

isting results of the same cause. Indeed, as we will see in later chapters, our males and females, single and married alike, are generally having more frequent, more varied and more satisfying coital experiences than their counterparts of a generation ago. Any increase in masturbation is therefore not a case of *faute de mieux* but a natural and normal result of the lessening of psychosocial restraints against most forms of sexual expression.

This is not to argue that masturbation is a *should* for every liberated man or woman, or that those adults who never practice it are necessarily unliberated; the use of masturbation ought to be a matter of preference and need. There are many who find it so unrewarding compared to intercourse—for which they have ample opportunity—that they very rarely or never have any desire to masturbate; but there are others who, even though paired or happily married, do have occasion to need one or more of the various benefits offered by masturbation. The easing of inner restraints and of social disapproval does not force anyone to masturbate; it merely makes masturbation acceptable in situations where it can satisfy an unfilled want.

This is a very different thing from those special cases in which a man or woman masturbates compulsively, or relies on masturbation because other and more rewarding kinds of sexual satisfaction lie outside his or her capabilities. Certain militant feminists, denigrating the nature of heterosexual interaction, have urged women to use vibrators or their own fingers for sexual relief, and have waxed rhapsodic over the fact that a woman can give herself numerous orgasms in a single uninterrupted session. But while this kind of performance results in total sexual satiety, it yields none of the complex emotional satisfactions, and none of the replenishment of the ego, produced by loving heterosexual intercourse. Masters and Johnson, while judging the masturbatory orgasm to be physiologically more powerful in women than coital orgasm, noted drily that, nonetheless, it is "not necessarily as satisfying as that resulting from coition."[25] The few compulsive masturbators among our interview subjects all boastfully accounted for their masturbation as necessitated by their unusually powerful sexual desires and capacity—but in truth they seemed more driven than desirous, more sated than satisfied by their masturbating, and without exception they had only shallow and brittle relationships with their sexual partners. This statement by a 35-year-old man is illustrative:

I can have sex for two hours with a girl, and half an hour
later I'll wake up completely turned on, and have to masturbate to get back to sleep. I can come in a woman and stay
hard, which is very strange, and not feel I've had enough.
My whole life is oriented towards sex—everything I do is
aimed at getting it—but I get a *mental* satisfaction out of
balling, not a *sexual* satisfaction; I don't know if that makes
any sense. Anyway, I masturbate at least once a day, whether
or not I've been with a girl that day, because I need it.

But such cases are the exception; from other data yielded by
our survey and from the general tenor of the interviews we
conducted, it is clear that neither compulsive masturbation nor
frenzied hedonism accounts for any overall increase we may find
in general masturbatory activity, especially beyond the adolescent years; rather, it is explainable as one result of the unleash-
ing of natural sexual desires, concomitant with the increased use
of formerly rare techniques of coital foreplay and of variant
coital positions, and the increased frequency, duration and enjoyment of heterosexual intercourse.

These being our hypotheses, what do we find? First, let us
look at the experience of young single males. In Kinsey's survey
more than four out of five single young men had masturbated
at least once within a five-year period. In precise terms, the
active incidence for single males between the ages of 16 and 20
was 88 percent, and for single males between 21 and 25, 81
percent.[26] Our most nearly comparable group consists of a cohort ranging from 18 to 24 years in age; data for that group
should compare well with Kinsey's two cohorts combined and
recalculated. For our cohort the active incidence is 86 percent
—exactly the same as for his two cohorts recalculated as one.
But this does not mean that there has been no increase in active
incidence, for we defined it much more narrowly than Kinsey
did: We took it to mean any activity within a one-year period,
while he took it to mean any activity within a five-year period.
Obviously, if we had used the five-year measurement, our active-
incidence figures would have been higher than they are, though
by how large a percentage we cannot say. In any event, since our
figures are almost identical to Kinsey's, it is clear that there has
been an increase of some sort in the active incidence of masturbation by single males between the ages of 18 and 24.

We can make a somewhat more precise statement concerning the frequency with which these active individuals masturbate. In Kinsey's sample the median frequency for those single males in the 16-to-20 cohort who were masturbating was 57 times a year, and in the 21-to-25 cohort, 42 times a year.[27] Taking into account the size of these two samples and their age distribution, the Kinsey rate with which our own median frequency should be compared is 49 times a year; in our own sample the actual median proves to be just under 52 a year. There is thus evidence of at least a small increase in this age group.

A more striking change, however, is the far greater tendency of young single men in recent years to continue masturbating beyond their teens and into early adulthood. In Kinsey's sample, by age 30 over a fifth of his single men had ceased being "active" masturbators,[28] while in our own sample less than a tenth had stopped—this despite the fact that our males have more opportunity for, and experience of, coitus than their predecessors. Even more striking is the contrast in frequencies. By age 30 those of Kinsey's single males who were masturbating at all were doing so about 30 times a year (this, again, is the median, or most typical, rate),[29] while the median for our own comparable sample is a little over 60 times a year—even higher than for the younger cohort in our sample.

With women, some of the changes are far greater, and genuinely remarkable. A generation ago only a little over a quarter of all single girls in their upper teens, and only a little over a third of those in their early twenties, were masturbating[30]; today over 60 percent of girls 18 to 24 are doing so. (Once again, we must point out that even this remarkable increase understates the reality, since our definition of active incidence is so much more restrictive than was Kinsey's.) There is also a sharp increase in typical frequency as shown by medians: Kinsey's active single females in this age span were masturbating about 21 times a year[31]; our own do so about 37 times a year.

Beyond the age of 24 our sample is too small for statistically rigorous comparisons; it is at least suggestive, however, that by their late twenties and early thirties nearly half of Kinsey's single women were masturbating,[32] while over four-fifths of our comparable sample are doing so.

As interesting as the foregoing contrasts may be, what is far more interesting, and even astonishing, is the evidence of greatly increased use of masturbation by younger married men and women. Prior to Kinsey there had been almost no systematic collection of data in this area; it seems to have been taken for granted that masturbation all but ceased when marriage began. It was, therefore, startling—and at the same time immensely guilt-relieving to many persons—when Kinsey revealed in 1948 and 1953 that far larger numbers of young husbands and wives were masturbating, and far more often, than anyone had supposed. In their late twenties and in their early thirties, for instance, over four out of ten husbands still masturbated from time to time, their median frequency being about half a dozen times per year.[33] Today, half again as many husbands (72 percent) in our most nearly comparable cohort masturbate, and with a median frequency of about 24 times per year, a truly remarkable increase. In Kinsey's sample about a third of all wives in the same age range masturbated, and with a median frequency of some 10 times per year.[34] Today, although the median frequency is the same, over twice as many wives in this age group (68 percent) are actively involved.

In sum, far more women, both single and married, and far more married men masturbate today than formerly, and while typical frequencies have increased only slightly for young single men and not at all for married women, they have risen considerably for single women, single men of 30 and married men. These changes, though confusing at first sight, have a common thread of causality in the central ethos of sexual liberation. Formerly, men felt that masturbation was more or less acceptable for adolescents and even teen-agers, but not for young adults and certainly not married adults. They now see no evil in the practice at any time, if it does not preempt or replace heterosexual coitus. Formerly, girls were far more inhibited about masturbating than boys, and even in adulthood wives were, in general, somewhat less likely than husbands ever to permit themselves the solace of masturbation. Today, both young single females and adult married females have moved much closer to the male patterns of behavior as they are today, in consonance with the basic egalitarianism of sexual liberation.

The principal inhibitory demographic factors identified by Kinsey were lower occupational level, lower educational level and religious devoutness. These factors tended to reduce the likelihood that the individual would ever masturbate, or to delay the first such experience or restrict the incidence of active masturbation.[35] Today, the only one of these factors that still has significant influence is religious devoutness. In our sample, the nonreligious are more likely ever to masturbate, to start doing so early and to continue doing so in adult life and even (though at a reduced rate) in married life than are the devout. But here, as in most other areas, the inhibitory force is operating less effectively among the young than among older people.

Religious preference still has some noteworthy correlations with masturbatory activity, as it did a generation ago. To be sure, in our sample religious preference is somewhat allied with religious devoutness, the Jews being the least religious, the Protestants more so, and the Catholics most of all. But there are two correlations that deserve mention. First, while Catholics and Protestants have similar patterns of activity, Catholics who are active masturbators masturbate more frequently than Protestants. (One might speculate that the relieving effect of confession makes it easier for them to perform the act without prolonged guilt feelings.) Second, a much higher proportion of Jewish men than of Catholic or Protestant are currently active masturbators. Jewish women, too, are more likely to be active masturbators than non-Jewish women, though by a narrower margin.

At first glance, the large active incidence of masturbation for Jewish men is mystifying in view of the historical origins of the condemnation of masturbation and the severity with which it has been punishable in orthodox Judaism. We can suggest several explanations. One, already mentioned, is that our sample includes a smaller proportion of orthodox Jews than of devout Protestants and devout Catholics (orthodox Jews are ethnically somewhat insular and defensive, and thus hard to reach by sampling techniques). Another is that our Jewish sample is weighted toward higher occupational and educational levels, which introduces a liberal bias. Finally, Judaism, for all its moral strictness about sexual matters, has never been as generally ascetic and antisexual as was Christianity for most of the centuries since its beginnings. Kinsey, though his data on this point were admittedly inadequate, seemed to find Jewish husbands somewhat more active sexually with their wives than non-Jewish husbands.[36] Our data, though rather imperfect, seem to show that Jewish husbands are no less active, within marriage, than non-

Jewish husbands. If Jewish men, and especially Jewish husbands, masturbate more than non-Jews, it is not because they are all Portnoys, afflicted and compulsive, but perhaps because they are somewhat less blocked, by culture and upbringing, from perceiving masturbation as a normal and legitimate sexual activity.

Reasons for, and Rewards of, Masturbation; Fantasies Used in Masturbating

The trend is thus unmistakable: Throughout the population, males and females of all ages (but most notably the young), whether single or married, college-educated or not, religious or nonreligious, feel freer today than did their counterparts a generation ago to masturbate when they want to.

This raises two questions: Why do they want to, and just how free do they actually feel to do so? The questions are interconnected. The more "legitimate" the motive for masturbating ("legitimate" motives, for instance, include relieving intolerable sexual tension, training or sensitizing one's self for marital coitus and easing congestion in the prostate or in the vagina and uterus), the less guilty the act will make even the guilt-prone person feel; but conversely, the more liberated the individual is, the more likely he or she is to masturbate, at least occasionally, for sheer pleasure, self-indulgence, escape into fantasy or other hedonistic reasons.

We have no base line here against which to compare our findings. Kinsey did not publish data on the motives or mental processes leading to acts of masturbation; the implicit assumption in his discussions of the subject seems to be that masturbation is little more than a response to sexual hunger when other means of satisfying it are not easily available. Time and again he pointed out that masturbation bears an inverse relationship to other forms of outlet: The frequency of masturbation, for instance, is much lower for married men and women than for single men and women; single persons with high coital frequencies (working-class youths, for instance) masturbate much less than celibate singles; married women are particularly apt to masturbate when their husbands fail to satisfy them or are away;

and so on.[37] Similarly, Kinsey made much of the fact that the frequency of masturbation bore a direct relationship to the strength of the total sex drive: Since the orgastic potential of males declines slowly from the late teens on, typical masturbation frequencies diminish throughout life, while in females, whose orgastic potential peaks much later and remains on a high plateau, masturbation rates are nearly constant until after menopause.[38]

But while sexual hunger is undoubtedly a major cause of masturbatory acts, it is far from the only one. Kinsey, as many of his critics have pointed out, brought with him to the study of mankind a viewpoint—a bias, to put it bluntly—derived from his training in invertebrate zoology: He made little of, and often ignored, the mental and emotional components of sexual acts, preferring to observe and report solely on overt behavior. With the lower animals, and even with most mammals, this approach is sufficient; the frequency of their sexual acts shows a direct and invariable relationship to such factors as the time of year, the amount of daylight, the average outdoor temperature, the level of production of sex hormones in the body and the like. Most animals will copulate, at mating season or during the estrus of the female, with predictable frequencies (allowing, of course, for minor individual variations). They are, in short, chemically propelled, rather than "motivated" in a human sense.

Human beings, too, are chemically propelled toward sexual acts, but chemistry is only one of the propellants; our sex drive is greatly influenced by many nonbiological factors of a sort that play little or no part in animal behavior. A man or woman may experience an intense upsurge of sexual desire for days or even months during a period of boredom or emotional insecurity, or when confronting the onset of middle age. Conversely, during periods of worry, emotional conflict or career difficulties, a man or woman may feel almost none of his or her usual sexual desire. In an extramarital affair or in a period of single freedom after the breakup of a failing marriage, a man or woman may discover an intense sexual drive and unsuspected capacity in himself or herself. But rejoicing in it is often followed by disappointment when, after the novelty wears off, desire and capacity gradually return to their old level. And while it is true that a gross hormonal deficiency in a person of either sex will usually diminish sexual desire and capacity, it is also true that at perfectly normal and adequate levels of hormone production both men and women can exhibit anything from a high level of sexual drive and performance to little or none, depending on a variety of other factors.

This is as true of masturbation as it is of intercourse. We tend to think of masturbation chiefly as a response to biochemical pressure because most of us—most males, at any rate—experience it first, and most importantly, as the resort of desperate adolescents tormented by desire but lacking opportunities for intercourse. Much of the time it is no more than that, even beyond adolescence. However, for adults it is fairly often a way of satisfying any one of a number of other needs of emotional or intellectual origin.

For one thing, it can partially satisfy the psychological need for variety; it enables people to do, in fantasy, sexual things they do not ordinarily have the chance to do, or with partners they have no access to. Freud had maintained that fantasy is primarily a way of partially fulfilling unsatisfied needs; however, contemporary studies of fantasy indicate that it also serves to introduce variety and playlike stimulation into our mental lives.[39] Nearly half of the men in our total sample, and three out of ten women, said that seeing erotic pictures or movies increased their desire to masturbate—and almost as many married persons as single persons gave this response, even though the former have sexual partners readily available. (This is not to say that all these married people actually masturbate after seeing sexually exciting pictures or movies—far more often, indeed, they direct their sexual desires toward their marital partners—but they are, at least sometimes, aware of an increased desire to masturbate, whether or not they act upon that desire.) Reading erotic material is even more likely to engender such feelings than seeing pictures or movies, especially among females; half of our males and over half of our females acknowledged that it sometimes did so.

When people do turn to masturbation rather than to their regular coital partners after exposure to sexually stimulating material, it is generally to reenact, in fantasy, the acts they have just seen or read about, and often with partners drawn from those same sources or from their own imaginations, or with people they know but have no sexual relation with, rather than with their customary sexual partners. Nearly half of our males and over a fifth of our females said that among the fantasies they had at least sometimes employed during masturbation were thoughts of intercourse with a stranger, and considerably larger numbers had had thoughts of intercourse with acquaintances. The percentages of married males and married females utilizing such fantasies are somewhat lower than percentages for single persons, but still substantial, which is in accord with the finding, previously reported in another work by the author of the present volume, (*The Affair*, New York: World, 1969), that many men and women who are satisfactorily married, and who neither seek nor would be willing to be unfaithful in actuality, will at least occasionally indulge in fantasies of extramarital sex, such fantasies being a safe and acceptable substitute for the risky and unacceptable actuality.[40] From the data in our present survey it would seem that, at least some of the time, married men and women masturbate while having such fantasies. Such masturbating, it seems obvious, is not an expression of biological need but is an effort to vicariously add variety to their sex lives, and to experience the forbidden in imagination.

At the same time it remains true that among the various masturbation fantasies acknowledged by our respondents, the most commonly mentioned type involves thoughts of intercourse with a loved person; three-quarters of all men and four-fifths of all women said they had had such fantasies while masturbating, and the percentages were nearly the same for the married as for the single. Interestingly enough, while younger people feel somewhat freer to sometimes have daring or deviant masturbation fantasies, such as thoughts of intercourse with strangers, or of being forced (or forcing someone) to have sex, or of group sex, they are also the most likely to have fantasies of sex with a loved person. In statistical terms: Of nine fantasy themes investigated in our questionnaire, young men in the 25-to-34-year-old group mentioned, on the average, 3.3 themes as part of their masturbatory activity, while men of 55 and over mentioned only 1.7; for women, the widest range was an average of 2.6 for those of 18 to 24, with the range narrowing steadily to a minimum of 1.1 for women of 55 and over. The obvious conclusion is that young people are freer than older people to think of all kinds of things while masturbating, but that imagining sexual relations with someone they love is still, by far, the preferred kind of fantasy.

Kinsey, incidentally, made a sharp distinction between the role of fantasy in male masturbation and in female masturbation: For females, he reported, fantasy played a much smaller part in arousing desire, and was much less common as a part of the masturbatory act itself, than was true for males.[41] He seems to have thought that this was in considerable part due to neural differences between male and female,[42] but our own survey data, supported by our interview material, yield the strong impression that the differences Kinsey observed were culturally conditioned, for women today are far more likely to be aroused by erotic materials and fantasies, and to utilize fantasies while masturbating, than was true only a generation ago.

Although, as mentioned a moment ago, the young people in our sample feel freer than older people to use daring or deviant fantasies while masturbating, substantial percentages of men and women of all ages have at least sometimes indulged in such thoughts. In the sample as a whole (nearly three-quarters of which consists of people ranging from 25 to 77 years old), the more daring and/or deviant fantasies that had been used by at least some of our respondents were these:

Intercourse with strangers: As mentioned above, this fantasy was relatively common, having been used by 47 percent of all males and 21 percent of all females. The sex difference appears in younger as well as older groups; however, in the younger groups such fantasies have been had by more females, as well as more males, than in the older groups.

Sex with more than one person of the opposite sex at the same time: 33 percent of all males and 18 percent of all females have had this kind of fantasy while masturbating. Here, too, females and males in the younger groups feel considerably greater freedom to use such fantasies than do their older counterparts.

Doing sexual things you would never do in reality: This catchall category was acknowledged by only 19 percent of the males but by 28 percent of the females. Apparently males are not as willing as females to admit to themselves that various acts are outside the range of the possible for them.

Being forced to have sex: Not surprisingly, about twice as many females as males reported having had this fantasy (19 percent and 10 percent respectively). Interestingly, however, the fantasy was quite rare in older persons of either sex, and several times more common among the under-25s. Perhaps experience diminishes the attractiveness of the idea.

Forcing someone to have sex: Again not surprisingly, this is a strongly gender-associated fantasy, being acknowledged by 13 percent of our males but only 3 percent of our females. This may owe something to cultural conditioning, but undoubtedly owes far more to realistic mechanical factors.

Having sex with someone of the same sex: Only 7 percent of our males, as against 11 percent of our females, acknowledged having had such fantasies during masturbation. This would seem to suggest that homosexuality is much more threatening to the male ego than to the female ego; however, there was little difference in the use of homosexual fantasy between older and younger groups of females, but considerable difference between older and younger groups of males, the latter being several times as likely as the former to have used such fantasies. Apparently the threat to the male ego is diminishing.

From the above data it is more clear than ever that masturbation today cannot be accounted for solely in terms of biological drive but that it is often an outlet for forbidden or suppressed desires, and that these may arise even in persons having regular intercourse with nonmarital or marital partners, and in persons beyond the age when the biological drive is imperious and urgent.

Masturbation may even serve distinctly nonsexual goals. Even as lonely or unloved persons sometimes console themselves by eating, without regard to actual physiological need, so do many persons turn at times to masturbation to comfort themselves rather than because they feel actual sexual hunger. Over a quarter of our males and over a third of our females said that the urge to masturbate was aroused in them by feelings of loneliness; significantly, too, this response was far more often made by single people than by married people of like age. Autoerotic acts can also be triggered by nonsexual tensions such as those caused by career or personal problems; over a third of our males and nearly a third of our females said that the urge to masturbate could come about as a result of "general tension" that prevented sleep, rather than sexual tension *per se.* Similar percentages of men and women say that the urge to masturbate can be set off in them by a rejection of their sexual overtures; in such a case, masturbation is as likely to involve self-reassurance and revenge as relief from dammed-up desire.

It is true, nevertheless, that the most obvious reason for masturbating—the relief of sexual tension—is still the one named by the largest percentages of both men and women; over four-fifths of our males and over two-thirds of our females mention it, with young and unmarried persons doing so more often than older and married persons, and young single males mentioning it almost universally. But substantial majorities of older people, and of married people in nearly all age groups, also mention it, and we can therefore suppose that even people with regular sexual partners tend to regard masturbation as an alternative method of relief, or at least feel the desire to so use it (whether or not they do so) when the regular partner is not available because of illness, absence or emotional conflict.

But this is a less impressive measure of liberation than the fact that so many people are able to recognize as valid so many other reasons for masturbating. To use it for the relief of intolerable desire takes less daring and is less of a break with ascetic tradition than to use it for solace when lonely, or for fantasized variety or for vicarious experiences of unusual practices. This interpretation of the data is supported by the fact that the sexual conservatives in our sample (the devout, the working-class and the noncollege people) are less likely than the sexual liberals (the nondevout, the middle-class and the college-educated people) to give any of the unconventional or more sophisticated reasons for their own masturbation.

Some of the same contrasts appear in the data on sex dreams to orgasm. Here, too, younger respondents are more likely than older ones to have dreams involving deviant or daring sexual acts; apparently in many older persons these same ideas are somewhat more strongly repressed, and either seldom emerge or are immediately forgotten upon awakening. And once again, though the pattern is not consistent, there is some tendency for the sexual conservatives to dream less often of unconventional or "forbidden" sex acts.

The foregoing data and interpretations are an attempt to answer one of the two questions posed at the beginning of this section: Why do men and women masturbate today? The other question—how free do they feel to do so—has already been answered in large part by the data indicating that they start earlier in life than did their counterparts of a generation ago; that much larger percentages of them do so at times throughout much of adult life, even though paired or married; and that, with the exception of married women, those persons who do masturbate do so more frequently at every age than did comparable persons in Kinsey's time. But this is only the statistical measure of increased freedom; it tells us nothing of the painful ambivalence and conflicts still felt by many individuals, or of the striking differences in individual experiences, ranging from those of people who are still severely inhibited concerning masturbation to those of people who have almost no perceptible shred of inhibition remaining. To answer our question in human and individual terms, we need once again to hear some of them speak.

Here, for instance, are comments typical of those elicited from highly inhibited persons—uptights, as they were labeled in Chapter 1:

> FEMALE, 42: Oh, no, never, I couldn't *do* that. I think it's sick. I never have any such desire. It's disgusting to think of a grown married woman doing that to herself.

> FEMALE, 38: When I was in my teens, I tried not to, and wept and prayed, but I did it anyway. But that was only for a little while. As soon as I fell in love with a boy, at the age of sixteen, I got the strength to stop, and I felt clean and decent again—until the next time. And then I stopped again—and so it went.

> MALE, 43: I fought it until I was nineteen. But at twenty I said yes to Jesus, and I never did it again. I waited faithfully until I got married, although it wasn't easy, let me tell you.

These are extreme cases; the more common uptight experience involves resistance not strong enough to prevent or interrupt masturbation but strong enough to create considerable torment:

> MALE, 28: When I was fourteen I was like Portnoy—always rushing off to the bathroom when the urge came over me. I did it so much and so hard that my dick would get swollen and sore, but even that didn't stop me. By the time I was nineteen I was screwing, but there'd be times when I wouldn't be able to get anything, and I'd go back to jacking off—and then I felt really guilty and ashamed of myself, like I was a failure, like I had a secret weakness.

> MALE, 22: For a few years I didn't worry about it, but then I began to hear that it warps your mind, or that if you do

it when you're not a kid any longer you must be abnormal. So I felt lousy whenever I did it, and finally I quit.

FEMALE, 54: I was only ten when I felt I needed it, and had to have it, so I did it a lot—but always feeling oh-so-guilty. I thought everyone could see it written on my face. I've done it off and on, all my life, whenever the sex in my marriage has been poor—like right now—and I *still* feel hung-up about it, even living here [in California] where everybody is supposed to be so free.

FEMALE, 34: My parents caught me one time, and just *pounced* on me, and from then on I always felt as if terrible things would happen to me. But I couldn't stop until I started having regular sex, when I was about twenty.

Sexual liberals come in many grades, but for the most part they too feel considerable residual guilt and self-contempt about masturbating if they are well into adult life and if they masturbate for seemingly idle or unimportant reasons. But their feelings of guilt are minimal or nonexistent when they masturbate for reasons of health, sexual training or loyalty to an absent sexual partner (or if they can tell themselves that those are their reasons):

FEMALE, 29: I still do it when the man I live with is away and I feel the need. I enjoy sex with him a great deal more than I do masturbating, but it's a substitute, and it gives me satisfaction and peace, and keeps me from wanting to go looking for someone else.

MALE, 35: Whenever I travel, it takes about a week until I can't stand it anymore. I lie there at night trying to sleep, and the damn thing won't go away, and I tell myself, "It's either do it or go out on the town." But I'm not that kind of guy, so I do it, and I feel better—and also a little worse.

MALE, 57: Since my wife's change of life, she puts me off most of the time because she says it makes her sore. Well, okay; if that's the way it is, I'm going to take care of myself when I get horny, or I'd get bad-tempered.

FEMALE, 28: I thought I was frigid, even after three years of marriage, until I read this book and learned how to turn myself on. After I gave myself my first orgasm, I cried for half an hour, I was so relieved. Afterwards, I did it a lot, for many months, and I talked to my doctor and to my husband, and finally I began to make it in intercourse. But I still masturbate at times, to get myself worked up and ready, so I won't be too slow for him.

A minority of liberals are more thoroughly emancipated than this: They may masturbate, without guilt or self-dislike, for important reasons such as urgent desire, self-therapy or the preservation of marital vows, but they can also do so with equal psychic comfort for purely hedonistic ends. It is our impression that this kind of liberalism is quite rare in middle-aged and older persons and in most segments of the population, and is to be found chiefly among the young and in those social groups that are generally rather permissive. Here are some representative statements by such people:

MALE, 25: My best sexual experiences, taken all in all, have been with women—psychologically great stuff, with all the rolling around and the wild things you do and the feeling of being really knocked out. Yet, it's still true that in masturbating you have better control over your own penis and over your sensations, and you can prolong things without any trouble. So even though I'm sleeping with a great girl, I still masturbate sometimes, because the orgasm is better or because I just sometimes want to do something different.

FEMALE, 27: If I want to, for whatever reason, there's no reason on earth why I shouldn't, so I do. I *like* it, if I'm in the mood for it. But I don't get into that heavy bit with lotions and vibrators and all that. I really like sex with a man, and if you get used to a vibrator you're going to be disappointed in any man. The way I do it is good enough.

FEMALE, 34: I don't *need* it these days—my sex life is usually pretty busy—but I always take my vibrator with me when I travel, because you never know. Like I went to Acapulco a few months ago, and it was beautiful there, but at first I hadn't met any men. And everything just made me feel in the mood to enjoy myself, but I had forgotten to pack my vibrator at home—which was too bad, because it would have been groovy to have it there, right then.

MALE, 26: My wife and I have a great sex relationship, and always have had since before we were married. But we both still masturbate, because it seems a pleasant thing to do and because sometimes the urge comes over each one of us at times when we're alone—I'm away most of the day in the laboratory or the library, and she works at the [TV] studio until after midnight. I may suddenly have a momentary desire to ejaculate, and I run into the bathroom and do it. Or I may read something and it makes me fantasize having sex with some strange voluptuous woman—a belly dancer, maybe. Incidentally, I never have had intercourse with any woman other than my wife, so I enjoy these fantasies. There's nothing secret about it—I tell my wife if I've done it during the day, and she tells me if she has. It doesn't diminish our lovemaking at all, although sometimes one or the other of us isn't as eager as we might be—but then, sometimes it does just the opposite, because we try out with each other some of the exotic things we've been fantasizing.

As for swingers, we have too few cases to do more than offer a few impressions on their masturbatory habits. Some of them seem to masturbate in much the same fashion as the liberals just quoted, but rather more of them masturbate with the same emotionless physicality, the compulsiveness and the frequent deviant contexts (in fantasy) that they display in the rest of their swinging sexual behavior. For this reason they more properly belong in the next and final section of this chapter.

The Boundaries of Liberation

Throughout this discussion of the partial liberation of Americans from the fear and guilt traditionally associated with acts of masturbation, we have assumed that autoeroticism is not only essentially normal but good. Good, that is, in the sense meant by situation ethics rather than code ethics; the latter applies categorical rules and commandments, the former appraises each act in terms of the needs that motivate it and the consequences it entails. Since most acts of masturbation arise from normal needs and—assuming the elimination of severe guilt feelings—yield physical and mental pleasure at no cost to the individual or those around him, situation ethics finds such acts on the good side of the moral scale. We have seen, moreover, that pleasure is far from being the only good end of masturbation; it can be comforting, solacing, entertaining, vicariously adventurous and so on. It can even serve very practical goals: Masters and Johnson report that in some women masturbation can ease menstrual cramps and backache, and increase the rate of menstrual flow; some psychotherapists have been able to treat certain sexual disorders by first breaking down the patient's resistance to self-supplied pleasure; and marriage counselors and sex therapists sometimes recommend precoital self-stimulation for men who tend to have weak erections, and postcoital masturbation to orgasm for women who are left unsatisfied and tense by intercourse.[43]

But it is only fair to add that there is some danger involved in the total and uncritical acceptance of masturbation. It can be misused by—and prove hurtful to—certain persons with special psychosexual problems. Like eating, drinking, reading or televiewing, it can be used as an analgesic against psychic pain rather than as an activity desirable for its own sake; but an analgesic does nothing to cure the illness causing the pain and, by permitting the sufferer to ignore that illness, allows it to grow worse. The immature, the self-doubting and the socially inept; men who are afraid of or hostile to women, and vice versa; husbands and wives who are in conflict—all these and others can use masturbation as a neurotic and damaging solution to their problems. The likelihood of their doing so has surely been increased by the fact that some enthusiasts of sexual freedom have said, without qualification, that masturbation is categorically good, has no bad results whatever and can never be done to excess. Such is the implicit message of Kinsey's own writing on the subject, and the explicit message of a wide range of contemporary sexologists and popularizers, ranging from "J" and "M" to the superwholesome Dr. David Reuben, and from semipornographers writing in underground sex magazines to psychiatrist Mary Jane Sherfey, writing about multiple self-administered clitoral orgasms in the *Journal of the American Psychoanalytic Association*.[44] Such unqualified approval gives the unwary a distorted notion of the meaning of sexual liberation. Where masturbation is concerned, true liberation means the freedom to satisfy healthy needs but not neurotic ones; freedom to masturbate without thereby avoiding or blocking one's access to the far more rewarding interpersonal forms of sexual expression; freedom to masturbate voluntarily and by intelligent choice rather than compulsively and irrationally.

It is not truly liberated, for instance, to use masturbation as a continuing substitute for heterosexual relationships that are available but anxiety-producing. In the great majority of adolescents and teen-agers, masturbation is developmental—it is a normal part of the masturbation process and serves as a valuable precursor of heterosexual intercourse for which the immature are not psychologically or socially ready, but toward which they move, step by step. But, points out Dr. Hugo Beigel, a well-known New York psychologist and therapist, some young people who are particularly troubled by feelings of personal inadequacy and inferiority find it exceedingly difficult to take those steps to establish relationships with the opposite sex, and for them masturbation may be supportive as a crutch is, weakening rather than strengthening them.[45] The case is similar with adults who lose a mate through divorce or death. Most of them use masturbation as a helpful substitute until they establish new relationships, but a minority, lacking self-confidence or ego strength, may come to rely on it and use it as a way to avoid making the effort to seek another partner.[46]

In neither case is masturbation itself the problem. Rather, it is used as the solution to the real problem of weak ego, low self-esteem and lack of social skills. But it is a poor solution, for instead of correcting the basic difficulty, it aggravates it. Like any gratifying activity, it can be enjoyed by the healthy as a part of life—but can serve the unhealthy as a defense against life.

Another example: At any age, masturbation can be a way of carrying out a neurotic desire to avoid assuming an adult gender identity. As long ago as 1922, Alfred Adler observed that young women who resent their own femaleness, or who fear male domination, sometimes use masturbation to help them keep their distance from men.[47] Today, much the same use of it is earnestly advocated by some extremists in the women's-liberation movement, although, to be sure, they furiously reject the diagnosis of neurotic motivation and see female masturbation as a political and revolutionary act.

A final example: Among the married, masturbation is for the most part used substitutively and, to a limited extent, supplementally, but it is also sometimes misused to fend off one's mate when intercourse has become blighted by emotional conflict.[48] Here the analogy to the use of alcohol is particularly appropriate: It deadens discomfort, serves as an avoidance device and allows the underlying problem to go uncorrected and thus to worsen.

Our questionnaire did not include items designed to elicit information on the unhealthy use of masturbation, and we therefore have no survey data to offer. In our interview series, however, we came across some striking examples of it. The interview sample being as small as it is, we cannot assume that the proportion of persons in it who masturbate in a neurotic way can be projected to the general population; we can only say that we found such cases to be rare, but so serious that it would be unfair to overlook them or to report nothing but good in the contemporary liberation of masturbation. The following selected examples are no definitive overview of the subject, but they are, at least, cautionary tales.

The first concerns a 27-year-old divorcée from a well-to-do but restrictive background. Virginal at marriage, she remained nonorgasmic for several years and regarded herself, with loathing, as frigid. Although she had read a fair amount about masturbation, she could not bring herself to try it, either for training or relief. She briefly tried psychotherapy, however, and was urged by her maverick doctor to masturbate and to buy herself a vibrator to make the procedure easier and more effective. She did so, made the breakthrough and rather quickly became enamored of the activity and thoroughly habituated to it. But her marital relationship got no better; in fact, she began to detest her husband, considering it his fault that she had never had an orgasm in intercourse and she eventually divorced him. In the past five years she has had a series of affairs, trying everything from old men to teen-age boys and from a super-stud to a semipotent bisexual. Sometimes she has orgasm in intercourse, sometimes not; she never has any trouble however, having a whole series of them when masturbating. In her affairs she has found sex at its best in turbulent or shallow relationships with men who hardly care about her, while the only genuinely tender and warm relationship she has had was with a relatively old, feebly potent man whose lovemaking she always had to follow up with masturbation. More and deeper psychotherapy might have helped her find answers to her problems, but she seems to have settled for semipromiscuity and for the reliable consolations of her vibrator.

A 30-year-old bachelor, though intelligent and physically attractive, had been an ailing and overprotected child, and has been shy and socially inept since adolescence. In his college years he struggled to break out of his self-imprisonment, going on dates from time to time and making some efforts to establish intimacy with several girls. But having read widely in the literature of sexology, he was much gratified to learn that he need feel no guilt about masturbating. Thereafter, he did so not only regularly but at great length and with considerable frequency whenever he was turned down by any girl or found himself alone in the dormitory when everyone else was out on dates. After college, living alone in a big city, he retrogressed and became more encapsulated. In his loneliness and misery he added the consolations of marijuana to those of masturbation, and became a heavy user. At times he made efforts to meet and go out with girls, but when, on occasion, he did get into bed with one of them, anxiety usually made him impotent or prevented him from ejaculating. He finally managed to have one affair that lasted for six months, during which he was sexually adequate and thought he had outgrown his difficulties. When it broke up, however, he felt such a sense of personal failure that he became more reclusive than ever and addictively dependent upon both marijuana and masturbation. In the past three years he has dated rarely and has attempted intercourse only a few times and with only marginal success. Obviously, neither masturbation nor marijuana is the real reason for his disabilities, but both have exacerbated his basic disorder by robbing him of the impetus to cope with it in some realistic fashion.

Our final example is a case in which masturbation is playing a potentially ruinous part in the marriage of two attractive, intelligent people who, as they tell it, have had an extremely active, sensuous and uninhibited marital sex life in their eight years together. Both the husband and the wife, in separate interviews, described their lovemaking glowingly: They have done everything within the range of normality, they have done it often and they have done it at length—an hour to an hour and a half being common for them, with the wife having 10 to 15 orgasms before the session concludes with the husband's ejaculation. Recently, however, things have been somewhat different. The husband's responsibilities as temporary head of the drama department in a junior college have been greater than usual; he and his wife have been making plans for a year of study abroad, and worrying about the innumerable practical details of doing so; and the wife has been largely confined to home by their two preschool children. As they see it, it is the tension and fatigue resulting from all this that have brought about a sharp decline in the frequency of their lovemaking. However, because the husband is a high-strung individual and sometimes cannot get to sleep without an ejaculation, he deals with the situation by the simple expedient of masturbating—which he does openly and unashamedly, and which his wife accepts in a spirit of liberation. As he tells it:

> We've been under an awful lot of pressure recently—personal and business—so much so that lately, when I've really needed an orgasm to get to sleep and my wife has been simply too tired or not tuned in to me, I've begun masturbating myself in her presence, in bed, informing her what I'm doing and why. And she hasn't felt any embarrassment, nor have I, nor has either of us felt that she "ought" to do it for me when I can do it for myself just as well or better.

But before concluding that this is a good example of genuine liberation, listen to his hidden feelings about his wonderful sex life with his wife—feelings he admits to only after much prideful talk:

> When I first trained myself to perform for an hour or more without ejaculating, and was able to provide her with many, many climaxes, I felt a great deal of satisfaction, a great sense of power, a great inner contentment. But it didn't come from my own pleasure in the sex act; it came from the *giving* of pleasure. It's possible I never should have married —I don't seem to be capable of the kinds of feelings most

other people have, in marriage, or of being emotionally
open and giving to her, and it has been a big problem with
us. By putting on a tremendous sexual performance, I felt
I was paying off a debt, I was being a good boy, I was doing
my job. But when I realized the incredible disparitybetween
a woman's sexual capacity and a man's, I used to wonder
what to do, and to literally pray for help. And it was all my
own doing—I initially forced her to have multiple climaxes,
until it became a standard part of our lovemaking and an
expected thing.

Thus, for this man masturbation is not really a liberated act but
a neurotic adjustment to a serious marital and characterological
problem. There has long been a good deal of hostility in the
marriage—on the wife's part because of the husband's inability
to express emotional warmth, and on the husband's part because of the burden of making up, sexually, for his emotional
shortcomings. He is deceiving himself when he says that he and
she view his masturbating merely as a convenience in a difficult
period, and that it troubles neither of them. In reality, his masturbating is expressive of his resentment and anger, is worsen-
ing the very conflict that produced it and is having serious effects
upon her. For while she consciously knows nothing of his hidden feelings and has not even allowed herself to perceive the
present situation as a problem, she has symptoms enough that
reveal the state of her unconscious psyche: She has been tired
and depressed for months, is thinking about having an affair and
for the first time in her life feels the need to drink, every day,
to combat her tension and moodiness. Her husband could con-
ceivably learn through therapy to be emotionally open and giving; and, even without therapy, if he but told his wife honestly
of his feelings about their sex life, it is likely that she would
willingly change her expectations of the sex act. But neither
solution is possible as long as he continues to use masturbation
as a defense against lovemaking and as a barrier to communication. The prognosis is not good.

The liberation of sexuality is thus something like the production and distribution of consumer goods in American society:
Necessary and pleasure-giving things are readily available and

often at low prices, but it is still up to the consumer to know what he is getting and to spend wisely. The freeing of masturbation from the oppressive cultural tradition is undoubtedly a real boon, but the intelligent person's guiding principle remains, nevertheless, *caveat emptor.*

MALE, 26, LAWYER: *I got started late, and never knew what to do, but I learned a lot through petting. . . . But for years I never could seem to connect and actually get laid. I found out, though, that if I would lie up against a girl and rub up against her, I could come in my clothes . . . But it was messy and embarrassing.*

FEMALE, 27, ARTIST: *[At] college [I] fell in love with a guy, I saw him for three years and we would often spend hours in bed together and get very physical, and I would get a lot of satisfaction out of it and still, somehow, I never felt ready to do the real thing. . . . I'd get a peculiar panicky feeling, and feel ashamed and cowardly. . . .*

MALE, 25, GRADUATE STUDENT: *I'd been balling for several years and I thought I was pretty good, and then I met an older girl . . . and she said, "You don't just charge in like that; you try to create something in your partner." I felt stupid. I'd read about it, and I knew she was right.*

FEMALE, 28, GRADUATE STUDENT: *I felt very uptight about making love with the lights on, or about letting them [her premarital lovers] go down on me. . . . But it bothered me that I felt like that, and I talked it over a lot with two of them, hoping to work it out and become a better and more exciting woman.*

MALE, 27, SALESMAN: *What matters to me most is balling absolutely wildly with somebody new—real knockout stuff, really breaking through and getting to her, and getting the maximum possible turn-on for myself . . . The only thing I won't try is getting involved emotionally, because that would limit me. . . .*

FEMALE, 22, SECRETARY: *I haven't had all that many men, either, but I just love sex. I used to have a man friend who would meet me for lunch and a quickie, and that was practically the wildest of all, because it was like anything goes; it wasn't love, it was just passion!*

MALE, 24, CARPENTER: *I knew some of it was poor but I thought some was great —only I didn't know what great was. Because I've been going with a girl for a year, now, and with her everything we do is special, and very powerful but very sweet at the same time. I'm not just in there to have myself a time—I'm making love to her, and she to me, and we really get so close you wouldn't believe it.*

FEMALE, 23, GRADUATE STUDENT: *It was only after we started sleeping together that the relationship developed real depth—much more than my first affair—and the sex, as a result, has become much more satisfying than ever before. There isn't anything we don't feel free to do.*

CHAPTER

3

Sex and the Single Person

✗ The Changing American View of Premarital Sexual Behavior

For every species of animal other than man, sexual behavior under normal environmental conditions is virtually unvarying: Every pair of greylag geese goes through the same courting rituals; every pair of rats couples and disengages a dozen or more times before the male finally ejaculates; every pair of minks fights fiercely before copulation is effected. Only man is virtually without detailed genetic preprograming of his behavior and is thus free to invent most of the details of his own sex life.

And he has done so with infinite variety. The sexual signals of human beings, courting rituals, words and gestures, caresses, coital positions, and duration and pace of intercourse vary so widely among societies that there is no such thing as sexual behavior typical of the human male or human female; there is only sexual behavior typical of the human male or female in a given society at a given time—in American society, for instance, in 1972—and even then, as we have seen, there are major differences among age cohorts, religious and ethnic groups and other strata within the society.

But if there is no typical human-sexual-behavior pattern, does that mean that all of man's variations are equally natural and normal? Anthropologists of a generation or two ago, still reacting against the smug superiority of the Victorians, preached "cultural relativism," a value-free approach that held every culture to be as worthy of respect as any other, and every custom to be "valid" if it fit within its own culture and served valuable functions there.[1] But many anthropologists and sociologists today have gone beyond the status-quo passivity of relativism, insisting that although customs that involve exploitation, cruelty and pain for many or most of the people in a culture, or which create pathological conditions or shorten life, can be *understood* within the context of given cultures, they cannot be morally equated with those other customs that maximize gratification of basic needs, health and longevity.[2] Similarly, the sexual mores of various societies must be interpreted in their own context—but context notwithstanding, sexual mores are not necessarily of equal merit; some of them, even though they serve certain useful functions within a given society, do physical or emotional harm to many individuals or deprive them of gratifications that make for a better and happier life. The harem system of the Moorish sultans, though "valid" in its own setting, gratified a few at the expense of many. The suffering and self-denial of religious asceticism, understandable in given contexts, was nonetheless a needless deprivation, and dysfunctional in more ways than it was functional. The same thing is true of those painful and physiologically damaging mutilations of the penis, labia and clitoris that are part of puberty rites of many primitive peoples. It may be true that all these things serve certain purposes within their cultures, but they do so at an exorbitant cost.

Therefore, even though our genes prescribe no specific pattern of sexual behavior, we are justified in calling natural and normal any pattern which offers the majority of people in a society sexual and psychological satisfaction without interfering with their other major needs, and which simultaneously makes for the health and stability of society itself. To the extent that any pattern does the opposite, we are entitled to call it unnatural and abnormal. Here the biosocial meaning of "normal" tends to coincide with the statistical one, for that which is health-giving, rewarding and socially beneficial tends to be more common and widespread, while that which is unhealthy, punitive and socially disruptive tends to be rare. To take extreme examples, almost no society has attempted to impose celibacy on a majority of its members, and no society has permitted parent-child incest. Conversely, nearly every society has had some way of teaching the young what is expected of them sexually, and every society has had some form of marriage and family.[3]

All of which permits us to view in perspective the traditional sexual mores of the unmarried in our own society, and the distinctly different mores which have rather suddenly begun to replace them. The American sexual code long held that from puberty until marriage both male and female should be sexually continent; traditionally, under no conditions was sexual intercourse for the unmarried officially approved or considered right and good. This is in striking contrast to what has prevailed elsewhere throughout history. Other societies have dealt with premarital sexuality in widely varied ways, some of them being broadly permissive, others limiting and specifying the times, places and circumstances under which premarital intercourse was permissible, but very few banning it altogether. Anthropologist George P. Murdock and others have estimated that about 70 percent of the societies about whose sexual patterns there is reliable information have permitted premarital intercourse within varying limits; most of the others, moreover, have directed their prohibitions chiefly at females, with the aim of preventing out-of-wedlock births. Only about 5 percent of the societies in Murdock's roundup prohibited all intercourse for the unmarried.[4]

Western society has thus been most unusual in its proscription of premarital sexual activity. Statistically speaking, this is abnormal; and it is abnormal in the deeper sense, for the evidence amassed by psychotherapists, marriage counselors and sociologists has shown our society's ban on premarital sexual activity to be productive of much needless misery and innumerable emotional and sexual disorders and malfunctions. And if that ban has not caused social instability, neither has it been necessary for social stability; there are examples enough of sexually permissive societies which are far more stable than our own.

For all that, our tradition has an impressive and ancient provenance, starting with the early Old Testament Jews. Their extremely grave view of premarital sex is spelled out in *Deuteronomy*, in which it is ordered that if a man lies with a maiden betrothed to another, he and she shall both be stoned to death unless the episode took place outside the city, where her cries could not be heard, in which case only the man must die. If a man lies with a maiden who is not betrothed to another, he must pay her father 50 shekels—the same sum as the usual bride price—and must marry her, for he has taken away her value as a virgin. The virginity of a bride had to be proved by the display of a bloodied sheet the day after the wedding. If a bridegroom complained that he had been defrauded, and if his bride could not furnish the bloodied sheet, she was to be stoned to death "because she hath wrought folly in Israel, to play the whore in her father's house."[5] *Deuteronomy* said nothing, however, concerning premarital intercourse between those who were betrothed; it was not explicitly permitted, but neither was it named as a punishable wrong, since neither the father nor the groom was being robbed.

The Catholic church continued this tradition in modified form: Premarital intercourse did not merit stoning, but under any conditions—including intercourse between a betrothed man and woman—it was a deadly sin, which, if unconfessed and unforgiven by a priest, would cause the sinners to burn in eternal hellfire. But single males, with the convenient mechanism of confession and penance to save them from that fate, rarely held to strict premarital chastity and consorted at times with prostitutes and other available females. Single females, on the other hand, were under extreme social as well as religious pressure to remain chaste: A girl's betrothal could be broken if she lay with another man, and in many parts of Europe she had to furnish the bloody "tokens" of virginity to her in-laws after the wedding night or be forever disgraced and despised.[6] In Spain, Portugal and Latin American countries the cult of virginity led to the institution of the dueña (female chaperone): Virginity was rigorously protected by seeing to it that the nubile maiden was never alone with a young man, even momentarily, until the magical words making her his wife had been said.

The Protestants abandoned the device of confession and penance, but did nothing to ease the condemnation of premarital intercourse; ineradicable guilt and severe punishment (not just later on but in the present world) were the penalties of transgression. In Calvin's Geneva a fornicator could be exiled, and in the New England colonies he or she could be severely fined (in Plymouth Colony the figure was £10, a very substantial sum in those days) or expelled from the congregation (tantamount to social ostracism) if its members, after hearing a public confession read aloud, so voted.[7]

Even where Calvinism was not dominant, the rising middle class imposed a generally puritanical outlook upon both English and American society during the 18th Century. It was very commonly felt that even if a minister or congregation did not directly punish a sinner, God himself did so here on earth. Lust and lechery inevitably led the young man down the path of disease, disgrace and disaster—the Rake's Progress—the only alternative being to struggle against temptation, to pray for forgiveness for one's lapses and to seek the safety and satisfactions of marriage as early as possible. As for the young woman, she was supposed to remain wholly unawakened and untempted before marriage—in the words of the *Song of Songs,* "a spring shut up, a fountain sealed"—for let her but feel the heat of passion and once yield to a man's base desire, and she was ruined; the moment the unmentionable organ of generation and pollution entered her flesh, however briefly, she instantly became unmarriageable, dishonored and destined for the streets, the servant's quarters or the insane asylum. Unless, of course, she had the courage to do the right thing:

> When lovely woman stoops to folly,
>   And finds too late that men betray,
> What charm can soothe her melancholy,
>   What art can wash her guilt away?
>
> The only art her guilt to cover,
>   To hide her shame from every eye,
> To give repentance to her lover,
>   And wring his bosom, is—to die.

Perhaps Goldsmith's prescription was somewhat romanticized, but at the end of the 18th Century and for several generations thereafter, middle-class people could read his lines and agree, and weep with a delicious mixture of pain and pleasure.

In the 19th Century these middle-class values became dominant, particularly in America where there was no hedonistic leisured aristocracy. The puritanism of the bourgeoisie became official: In nearly every state, coitus was explicitly prohibited by law for unmarried juveniles, classified as "delinquent" behavior and made subject to corrective action. Coitus for the unmarried beyond juvenile status—in most states, those of 18 and over—was labeled "fornication," a crime punishable by fines or imprisonment or both. To this day, about half of the states still classify fornication as a crime subject to penalties ranging from a mere $10 fine in Rhode Island up to a possible $1000 fine and one year of imprisonment in Florida.[8] The laws are rarely enforced these days, but the fact that they remain upon the statute books shows how recently the values they reflect dominated American life.

We know, of course, that considerable numbers of young men violated the code with prostitutes, servant girls and the like. Nevertheless, most of them thought that what they were doing was wrong and made every effort to keep it concealed from the "decent" women in their lives. This attitude persisted, especially in the middle class, until recent times. Among men born before or around the turn of the 20th Century—men in their mid-forties and older at the time of Kinsey's fieldwork—Kinsey found that only a third of those with little education, but fully three-quarters of those with at least some college education, opposed premarital intercourse for males on moral grounds (and, to a lesser extent, on various other grounds as well).[9] Even among men a generation younger, who had been growing up during the Roaring Twenties, the era of "It" and "Makin' Whoopee," Kinsey found a fifth of the poorly educated but six-tenths of the college-educated expressing the same moral objections.[10] As for female premarital behavior, a number of minor surveys made between 1930 and 1950, chiefly of women college students and middle-class wives, showed that an overwhelming majority sternly disapproved of premarital female unchastity, and in 1953 Kinsey reported that 89 percent of all the women in his sample said that, for them, moral considerations above all had prevented them from having, or at least restricted their indulgence in, premarital coitus.[11]

The publication of the Kinsey studies marked the beginning of the present era of sexual liberation, but liberation was slow in picking up momentum; traditional attitudes toward premarital coitus continued to dominate the American mind until very recently. In both 1937 and 1959, as mentioned in Chapter 1, the Roper Agency asked a national sample of men and women how they felt about premarital intercourse and found that there had been virtually no change in all that time.[12] The figures appear in Table 12.

Table 12

"Do You Think It Is All Right for Either or Both Parties to a Marriage to Have Had Previous Sexual Intercourse?"—Roper (Percents)

	1937	1959
All right for both	22	22
All right for men only	8	8
All right for neither	56	54
Don't know or refused to answer	14	16

And a national adult sample taken by sociologist Ira L. Reiss in 1963, and subjected to sophisticated analysis, showed an even greater sexual conservatism among adults than the Roper polls.[13]

Even among college students, as late as the mid-1950s, sociologist Judson T. Landis found that 52 percent of male students and 65 percent of female students on 11 campuses believed sexual abstinence to be the proper premarital standard.[14] But signs of change began to appear—at least among the young— by the end of the 1950s. Reiss sampled high-school and college students in five institutions in Virginia and New York in 1959, and reported that 15 percent of the females and 24 percent of the males endorsed the standard of "permissiveness with affection"—a composite of various items in the questionnaire—and that considerably larger percentages endorsed premarital coitus for one sex or the other if engaged or in love.[15] Sociologist Harold T. Christensen, sampling students on a midwestern campus about the same time, and again (on the same campus) a decade later, found striking evidence of an increase in qualified permissiveness: Between 1958 and 1968 the percentage of males who approved of premarital coitus in a love relationship rose from 47 to 55, while that of females leaped from 17 to 38.[16]

Thus, despite the sharp break with Victorian prudery and antisexualism that took place during and right after World War I, the reigning attitude in America was, until very recently, one of general opposition to premarital sex, especially for girls; this, at least, was what people said publicly, and probably what they believed even when they increasingly departed from it in actuality. But among people of college age another attitude had begun to appear in the late 1950s, and gained ground with striking rapidity during the 1960s. This was the premarital sexual standard Professor Reiss termed "permissiveness with affection"—basically, a liberation of sexuality within the context of love relationships. And this limitation was what made it acceptable to a broad range of people, for it broke with tradition only in a limited sense, and harmonized sexual liberation with the larger needs of both the individual and of society. As Reiss himself put it in 1968, "Respectable, college-educated people have integrated this new philosophy with their generally liberal attitudes about the family, politics, and religion. And this represents a new and more lasting support for sexual permissiveness, since it is based on a positive philosophy rather than hedonism, despair, or desperation."[17]

Our own survey offers some interesting—and some startling—evidence of the further extensive change that has taken place in the mere handful of years since Reiss's 1959 and Christensen's 1968 samples. Viewing our sample as a whole (all age groups combined), we find a dramatically increased acceptance of the idea of premarital intercourse for women as well as for men in situations involving genuine emotional commitment.* Indeed, our entire sample—older people and noncollege people included—is more tolerant of premarital coitus under such conditions than were Christensen's college students in 1968 (see Table 13 for our figures).

Table 13

Premarital Coitus Is Acceptable: Total Sample, Percents Agreeing

	Males	Females
For a man:		
—where strong affection exists	75	55
—couple in love, but not engaged	82	68
—couple engaged	84	73
For a woman:		
—where strong affection exists	66	41
—couple in love, but not engaged	77	61
—couple engaged	81	68

*This is, of course, a change in an attitude, not in actual behavior; we will examine the latter further on.

Comparing figures in Table 13 vertically, we see that, at every level of commitment, premarital coitus is still deemed somewhat more acceptable for a man than for a woman. (This hardly makes sense when one is thinking of a couple in love or an engaged couple, but our respondents were answering the question about men and the one about women separately, and not thinking in terms of couples.) But if it is clear that the double standard has not yet wholly vanished, it is also clear that the differences in permissiveness associated with it are now relatively small. For instance, 82 percent of the men say it is all right for a man in a love relationship, 77 percent for a woman in a love relationship and so on. The greater sexual conservatism of women, in general, is also somewhat diminished: Comparing figures horizontally, we see that permissiveness among women is roughly three-quarters as common as among men. It is not overstating the case to say that, according to the above figures, the standard of "permissiveness with affection" now has become statistically dominant in the population as a whole.

But not in every segment of the population. The new attitude toward premarital intercourse is far more common in the younger half of the population—those people who are under 35 and went to high school in the mid-1950s or later—than in the older half. Our youngest age group (18 to 24) is, in general, the most permissive of all; the oldest (55 and over) is the least permissive. Table 14, for instance, shows one set of contrasting figures on the acceptability of premarital coitus where strong affection exists.

Table 14

Premarital Coitus Is Acceptable: Selected Age Cohorts, Percents Agreeing

	Males		Females	
	18–24	55 and over	18–24	55 and over
For a man:				
—where strong affection exists	86	57	73	32
For a woman:				
—where strong affection exists	80	48	59	11

Here "permissiveness with affection" is barely dominant among older men and definitely the minority attitude among older women, but just as definitely the majority attitude of both sexes among the young. At higher levels of emotional involvement (in love; engaged), coitus is even more widely acceptable to all age groups, but the gap between young and older persons remains. If the relationship is one of love, for instance, 90 percent of the young females say it is acceptable for a woman, while only 23 percent of older women agree.

Similarly, the standard of "permissiveness with affection" is very much more widespread among nonchurchgoers than among regular churchgoers—half again to several times as common, depending on age and sex. The contrast is greatest among women in the older half of our sample; here, strong affection seems justification enough for female premarital coitus to 46 percent of nonchurchgoers but to only 9 percent of regular churchgoers. Comparable, though smaller, contrasts exist between the college-educated and the noncollege-educated, with permissiveness in situations involving love or strong affection being more common among the former. The same is true of white-collar people as compared with blue-collar people.

The speed and magnitude with which the new attitude has been replacing the old one is remarkable. Just as remarkable is the fact that a rather more radical standard—the acceptability of premarital sex *in the absence of strong affection*—also seems to be gaining considerable ground. Here we must be cautious. Our questionnaire reads: "Is intercourse acceptable for an unmarried man (woman) when [there is] no strong affection?" This wording does not positively rule out lesser degrees of affection; had we asked if premarital coitus was acceptable "where there is no affection whatever," we would undoubtedly have gotten fewer yes votes, as certain other items in the questionnaire indicate. Be that as it may, we find it noteworthy that 60 percent of our males and 37 percent of our females consider premarital coitus acceptable for men, even where no strong affection exists, while 44 percent of our males and 20 percent of our females find it acceptable for women under the same circumstances. (In previous surveys by others, comparable questions elicited only very small percentages of permissive votes.) This more extreme permissiveness is, again, strongly associated with youth, as witness the figures in Table 15.

Startling as these figures are, they hardly justify the conclusion that a radically libertarian philosophy of sexuality is about to become dominant. First of all, as noted above, our question

Table 15

Premarital Coitus Is Acceptable: Selected Age Cohorts, Percents Agreeing

	Males		Females	
	18–24	55 and over	18–24	55 and over
For a man:				
—where no strong affection exists	71	46	47	15
For a woman:				
—where no strong affection exists	56	26	29	1

did not rule out lesser levels of affection. Second, far larger percentages of the very same people signified their approval of sex where there is strong affection, and still larger percentages where there is love. Finally, as we will see a little further on, in their actual behavior these same people follow primarily the standard of "permissiveness with affection." A more reasonable interpretation of the above figures might be that a growing number of young men and young women are no longer willing to condemn premarital intercourse even when the context is one of very mild affection, or none; they themselves may strongly prefer sex associated with love, and even limit themselves to it, but they do not criticize or find fault with casual sex in other unmarried males or females, nor do they rule it out altogether for themselves. This is, indeed, a remarkable and epochal change in attitude.

A final observation: One might cynically ascribe the overall permissiveness of the young to the fact that so many of them are unmarried and therefore adopt attitudes that justify what they are doing, or would like to be doing. But such cynicism is not borne out by the data. When we separate the replies of the married from those of the unmarried within the youngest group, the levels of permissiveness are nearly the same. The difference between the married and the unmarried is, however, larger in older age groups, particularly on the matter of premarital inter-course where there is no strong affection. But this is easy to understand; the older single persons have become practical, somewhat disillusioned and more inclined to take sexual satis-faction however they can get it, or at least have adopted attitudes harmonious with such behavior. Even so, they would still prefer

their sex allied with love, for they give this the highest acceptability rating.

Sex Education in America: Two Generations

What a curious thing is man, who has to be taught the most basic
behavior patterns: how to drink, how to eat, how to walk—and
even how to copulate! Spider and beetle, salmon and crab, spar-
row and chipmunk all know what to do sexually when the time
comes, without ever having been taught, or even, in the case of
the lower orders, without having seen it done. But not us: Lacking built-in instinctual guidance, we must be taught the words
and looks of courtship, the touches and caresses of sexual wooing, the signs and signals of readiness, the very positions and
movements of coitus. Without training, we are no better
equipped to copulate than we are to drive a car or sail a boat.
Indeed, even today doctors and marriage counselors still occasionally see young couples who, after months of marriage, have
not consummated their union because, having had excessively
prudish upbringing, they have no clear idea of what to do with
their sexual parts, and have taken ejaculation between the thighs
or at the unentered portals to constitute intercourse.[18]

Almost all human societies have therefore educated their
young in sexual matters, including the mechanics of copulation.
In some societies, parents, other elders or priestly persons have
explained the sex act in words. In others, songs, drawings and
sculpture have been used to explain what happens in intercourse. In still others, the young have had ample opportunity to
see or overhear adults doing it. And in some, the sexual act has
been publicly demonstrated during fertility rites or orgiastic
celebrations. American society, however, has long been without
any officially sanctioned system of teaching the young sexual
skills, and they have been forced to learn about them as best they
can, through gossip, rumor, accidental observation, trial and
error and the kind of tutelage provided by prostitutes and se-
ducers. No wonder so many men, even two generations ago,
were clumsy and brutish lovers; no wonder so many brides came
to the wedding bed without the least idea of what they were
about to experience or how they were supposed to act.

By the 1940s, to be sure, things had changed enough so that

few grooms or brides approached the nuptial bed in total ignorance. Yet such information as they had gathered had still, for the most part, come to them adventitiously or from underground sources. Although most people felt that sex education should be conducted by parents or other adults, Kinsey reported in the 1948 volume that, in actual fact, children learned most of what they knew about sex from other children.[19] In 1953 he estimated that no more than 5 percent of his female interviewees had received anything more than incidental information from their parents or religious mentors; all the rest had had to get most of their sexual information from their peers.[20]

One might imagine that the sexual liberation of the past generation would have made sexual education of the young a recognized and honorable activity, but by and large it has not done so. Even by the late 1960s, for instance, parents seemed to have remained largely aloof from sex education in general, let alone from instruction in the specifics of intercourse. Sociologists Roger Libby and Gilbert Nass interviewed a broad sample of parents in Manchester, Connecticut, in 1967 and 1968, and found that 87 percent of them handled sexual questions with their children by issuing orders rather than by means of discussions.[21] The most common parental attitudes encountered by Libby and Nass were epitomized by comments such as these:

"I try to keep them from knowing too much."

"My parents did not tell me about it. I don't discuss it, either."

"I think sex education corrupts the minds of fifteen-to-sixteen-year-olds."

"Kids know too much already."

"I just tell them to behave and keep their eyes open."

In 1969 the magazine *Psychology Today* invited its readers to fill out a sex questionnaire, and got some 20,000 responses. Within this sample (a self-selected one, to be sure), which was generally young, liberal and college-educated, less than a tenth of the men and about a sixth of the women said they had received most of their sex education from their parents, while two-thirds of the men and half of the women said that friends had been the major source. The only noteworthy change from Kinsey's time was the appearance of printed matter as the major source for nearly a quarter of both sexes; sexual liberation had made the publishing of all kinds of explicit sexual material, from scientific surveys to pornography, more feasible than formerly, and had made the reading of such materials socially more acceptable.[22]

Our own survey shows, in considerably more detail, that the situation has changed surprisingly little since Kinsey's time. It is undeniable that today's children, at any given age, know much more about procreation and about coitus than children of the same age did a generation ago, but not thanks to any broadly accepted, organized, institutionalized way of teaching them about sexual behavior. Friends are still the major source; reading, though second, is far less important; parents run a very poor third; and school programs are an even smaller factor.

Summarized in Table 16 are our respondents' answers to a question asking what their main source of knowledge about sexual matters had been while they were growing up. The figures indicate that despite the vastly increased availability of sexual information today, American parents still have a great reluctance to pass it along themselves, or to create any officially acknowledged mechanism for instruction in sexual behavior other than the printed word.

Table 16

Main Source of Sexual Information:
Total Sample, Percents*

	Males	Females
Friends	59	46
Reading	20	22
Mother	3	16
Father	6	1
School program	3	5
Adults outside home	6	4
Brothers, sisters	4	6
Other, and No Answer	7	7

*Add to more than 100 because some respondents checked more than one answer.

One might suppose that the situation had changed in very recent years, as we have already seen to be the case elsewhere in this study, but the figures for our youngest cohort—the people of under 25—are almost the same as those given above for the entire sample, the only notable exceptions being a small decrease in the importance of friends and a concomitant small increase in the importance of reading for under-25 males. It would appear that American sex education, at least as far as sexual behavior is concerned (as distinguished from biological information), has undergone no fundamental change since Kinsey's time; it is still up to the young to find out for themselves, as best they can, what to expect of the sex act and how to do it.

The data seem to contradict everyday experience. Do we not all know, have we not all heard, that parents are much more open about sexual matters with their children than was true a generation or so ago? But probably many parents think themselves candid and open just because, without actually giving their children any important information or guidance, they permit formerly unspeakable sexual matters to be mentioned aloud. The reality, however, is that two-thirds of our males and over four-fifths of our females said that their fathers had *never* talked to them about sexual matters before or during their high-school years, and three-quarters of the males and nearly half of the females said the same thing about their mothers. The minority of parents who did talk about sex generally did so too little or too late: Only 9 percent of our males, for instance, said they had learned anything new and important from talks with their fathers, and even fewer from their mothers. For females the figures are a little better: While only 8 percent learned anything new and important from their fathers, 28 percent did so from their mothers. Even so, half of all the talk between mothers and daughters was essentially useless, either coming too late or being too shallow. The data do show that somewhat larger percentages of the youngest people in the sample have had sex talks with their parents, but, again, these parent-child sex talks have only rarely contained new and important information for the males, and have done so only about half the time for the females. Surprisingly, too, white-collar people and college-educated people fare little better, as far as sex education at home is concerned, than blue-collar or noncollege people.

Our conclusion is that the traditional taboo on sexual communication between parent and child, and the native American reluctance to teach the young about sexual behavior, remain powerful bars to such education within the home, even at the upper social levels and even after a generation of sexual liberation. Despite everything, the prevailing tone of parent-child sex talks is one of discomfort, embarrassment and mutual resentment. From our interviews, here is a typical blue-collar Catholic man, of middle age, speaking about his sex education at home:

> When I was sixteen I started to go out with the daughter of friends of the family, and my dad said to me, "You lay a hand on that girl and I'll kill you." And later, when I was dating different girls, he handed me a rubber one day and again he said, not even looking at me, "If you ever get any girl in trouble, I'll kill you." And that was my sex education, as far as he was concerned.

And here, a generation younger, is a male graduate student from a wealthy and cultured New York home saying substantially the same thing:

> Neither of my parents ever really spoke to me about it. Mostly, I was warned about the potential of pregnancy; that was virtually all. Oh, there *was* a little hint of gentlemanly bragging by my father, to suggest that he enjoyed sex, but it was all terribly vague.

A young woman from a working-class family tells what is a very common story:

> My mother told me to "save myself for my husband," but that's the only thing I can remember her telling me. She did help me when I began menstruating, but even then she never really went into the matter, and I knew what it was about only because they had shown us a film in my Girl Scout troop.

And a well-educated woman in her thirties, despite the fact that her mother, a divorcée, had been a trained nurse and was the mistress of a wealthy man, has a similar tale to tell:

> She was so shy that she never told me a thing; she just gave me little hints now and then. When I was eleven or twelve, a friend's mother lent me a book about how babies are conceived and born, and told me not to read it but first to ask my mother if I could, and my mother studied it and heaved a great sigh of relief because now she didn't have to tell me anything. . . . One time I found her diaphragm

in a little box and asked her what it was, and she went into a real flap and told me it was none of my business and not ever to go near it again.

A minority did say that their parents had bought them helpful books, or had answered their questions, or initiated talks, or even drawn pictures for them and explained things with ease and naturalness. These men and women remembered with deep gratitude what their parents had done, but they were the exceptions.

School programs were named the main source of sex information by even fewer questionnaire respondents than were parents. This seems curious in view of the fact that there has been a considerable movement in the past decade to have the schools assume the burden that parents seem so unwilling to shoulder. Half of all persons under 35 in our sample did, in fact, get some sex education in public school or in college, but only very small percentages of males and females under 35 said that these programs had been their main source of information. In all likelihood, the explanation is that such programs deal primarily with biology, touching lightly or not at all upon the kind of thing young people most urgently want—explicit information as to how the various sex acts are performed.

Our major finding in this area, therefore, is that peers remain by far the most important source of sex information during the formative years of childhood and the teens, and that this is just about as true for people under 25 as it was for people of 55 and over; with occasional inconsistencies, moreover, it seems nearly as true for college-educated and white-collar people as for non-college-educated and blue-collar people. Throughout our sample the most important source of information about sexual behavior is still what it has long been—the oral tradition, composed of myths and facts, speculations and firsthand accounts, rumors and overheard adult conversations, that circulates among the young and continually filters down from the slightly older to the slightly younger. In interview after interview, men said they had learned nearly everything "on the street," or "from their pals," or "on the playground and in the locker room," while women said they had learned most of what they knew from playmates, closest friends, dormitory bull sessions and from boys who dated them and talked sex with them. In retrospect many of these people recall how enlightening—and also, sometimes, how misleading—this information was:

MALE, 48: I was ten when I first went to camp, and one kid in the bunk was a big-city wise guy and said he knew how a baby was made. None of the rest of us did, so he told us —he said the man stuck his thing in a hole in the woman's body and squirted some seeds in there. We were all disbelieving, and sort of shocked, but he said his older brother had told him. So then we asked him what hole, and he didn't know—not one of us knew—and after a lot of talk we decided it was probably the behind, because where else? I didn't get it straightened out until three years later.

FEMALE, 28: When I was twelve or thirteen, my three best friends and I used to talk about it all the time and try to figure it out, but we couldn't imagine why any girl would want a boy to urinate inside her. Then, later, another girl explained what the emission was—but she also said that a girl had an emission, too, just like a man's. I didn't learn better until I was seventeen.

The range of peer-group sex education is very broad. Boys and girls learn from other boys and girls the elements of anatomy, the various kinds of precoital activity, the changes that occur in the sexual organs during arousal, the basic coital positions and movements, and the like. Unfortunately, they also are likely to learn many nonfacts. Some say, for instance, that they were first told that coitus is ordinarily done either standing up or in the "doggy position," that sperm deposited in the vagina can be smelled on a woman's breath, that a woman cannot get pregnant unless she has an orgasm, and that a woman's resistance can be instantly and totally overcome if a man blows in her ear or rubs her belly slowly with a circular motion.

The caliber of peer-group education improves, of course, as the peer group gets older and accumulates better information and more actual experience. Attitudes, too, change as time passes; many of the views acquired early from immature companions are modified and liberalized later on as the peer group grows more knowing and sophisticated:

MALE, 22: Being brought up so strictly and all, I felt a whole lot of things were dirty and sinful. It wasn't until I was seventeen and went in the service that I started to feel differently. I was around other guys and they would talk about spending hours in bed with girls, doing "everything," and I'd ask what's everything, and they'd tell me. And they were good guys, they were my friends, and after a while I began to change my ideas about sex.

FEMALE, 26: I first heard about oral sex when I was only fourteen, and we all thought it was really sickening—especially a girl doing it to a man, taking it into her mouth; we all made terrible faces about it and felt like throwing up. But when I went to college the older girls were very cool about it and nobody seemed to think it was disgusting, and after a while I found myself thinking it might be interesting. As a matter of fact, because I was frightened to start balling, I got into oral sex first and stayed with it for a couple of years.

Part of the sexual education acquired from the peer group consists of actual experiences, but this is not a major source of learning for young children or even for most boys or girls in their early teens. A large percentage of boys and girls do, to be sure, play sex games—"doctor," "nurse" and the like—even before puberty, and small percentages of them engage briefly in a few homosexual experiments during and shortly after puberty, not so much because of homosexual desires *per se* but because same-sex partners are more open and trusting with each other at that age than opposite-sex partners. But most of this early experience is very limited and adds little to the total store of sexual information males or females possess prior to the beginning of regular heterosexual petting or intercourse in the late teens. So, at least, we may judge from the fact that less than 4 percent of our males and less than 3 percent of our females named "experience" as the major source of their sexual information while they were growing up. (These percentages are included in the category "Other, and No Answer" in Table 16.) After dating starts, experience does eventually become extremely important as a source of knowledge about refinements of erotic technique, as well as an influence in changing the individual's attitudes toward various practices. Indeed, for those who have various sexual partners during their adult life—and even, to a degree, for those who have only one partner—experience itself is a continuing source of sexual education over the years. But for very few people does it rank as the main source of their sexual education while they were growing up.

Reading, in contrast, is now the second most important source of sexual information during the period of growing up —and to judge by our interviews it may become even more important during the adult years, when most people are married and no longer discuss sexuality with their friends quite as intimately and freely as they used to. The term "reading" covers everything from pulp magazines and pornographic comic books to psychological, medical and anthropological studies of sexual behavior, which explains why our survey data show reading to be a main source of sexual information for noncollege people nearly as often as for the college-educated, and for blue-collar people nearly as often as for white-collar people. The interview material suggests that persons with less education and lower social status read chiefly the most popular kinds of erotic material—pulps and magazine articles when they are young, magazine articles and best-selling popular books when they are older—while persons from more literate and educated homes may read some of the same things but go on to ferret out all kinds of more serious and authoritative works. But it is our impression that, at every level, those who rated reading the main source of their information came from restrictive backgrounds, where sexual matters were not discussed in the home and where the peer group knew very little:

> FEMALE, 34, CONSERVATIVE JEWISH BACKGROUND: I hardly learned anything at home, and among my friends sex wasn't anything we talked about. When I was nineteen and getting serious with a boy, I finally went into a bookstore to buy a copy of Van de Velde; it took me an hour to get up the nerve to ask for it. But when I read it, it was a real education for me. I read and reread it as if I were studying for an exam, and most of the material was news to me.

> MALE, 25, POLISH-CATHOLIC BACKGROUND: I heard a little of this and that—mostly hints—and I got to be thirteen or fourteen and still didn't know how they do it. But some older guy showed me a bunch of eight-pagers [pornographic comic books], and I could finally see just what you do and all the kinds of ways you can do it. Later, when I got

brave enough, I started buying magazines and paperback books, and I guess I really educated myself, mostly, that way.

MALE, 55, PRESBYTERIAN BACKGROUND: My parents couldn't talk to me about it at all, and my friends didn't seem to know much either. But I was always a real bookworm, and on a high shelf in my father's library I found the works of Havelock Ellis and secretly went straight through the whole thing. And not only did I wind up knowing a lot more than most other teen-agers but I believe I got my very liberal feelings about sexual matters from those books.

But in recent years no one has had to secretly plow through the massive scholarly volumes of Havelock Ellis to get a liberal sex education; the freedom to publish popular, readable and very graphic sexual materials has increased so remarkably in the past generation that today a large proportion of Americans have, by the age of 18, read at least some sexually explicit materials covering various aspects of normal and abnormal sexual behavior. A number of our interviewees specifically credited certain mass magazines, and books by authors ranging from various pseudonymous pornographers to Masters and Johnson, with having eased their guilt feelings, introduced them to practices they had never known of and prepared them for a successful sex life:

MALE, 24: I used to haunt the pornographic bookstores and sneak as much reading as I could—and eventually I even bought some of those things—and I found out what things to do to arouse a woman, how important it was to pace myself, how to use sexy words and all that. And when I started actually making it with girls, I really did know what to do, although it took me a while to get around to trying some of the farther-out things I knew about.

But as important as reading has become, it is only fair to add that it, and such related sources as film, shows and television, are not an unmixed blessing, for some of these sources—especially those which are the work of enthusiasts and proselytizers—establish performance standards that make the naïve or gullible person feel inferior. Some young women, having read such materials, feel deficient because they fail to achieve orgasm every time, or because the orgasms they do achieve are not earth-shaking, or because they cannot manage a whole series of orgasms in rapid succession. Some young men consider themselves inadequate lovers or premature ejaculators because they cannot hold back more than five minutes; they believe—having read it, for instance, in Robert Chartham's *Sensuous Couple*—that every planned sex session ought to last an hour to an hour and a half.[23] And a number of our interviewees of both sexes seemed apologetic or defensive about the fact that, despite what they had read, they had no desire to lick whipped cream off someone else's sexual organs, have someone else explore their anuses with finger or tongue, or perform sexual acts with strangers at a swinging party.

For all that, it is still very likely that the increased freedom to publish is the single most important corrective to the lack of a formal and recognized system of sex education. Even though reading is still second to friends as the main source of information, the information passed along through the peer group is the end product of everything acquired by the members of that group; what is freely available in print thus filters down into popular knowledge, and is disseminated by oral means.

This, apparently, is the answer offered thus far by our sexually liberated society to the problem of education in sexual behavior. We can be grateful that this answer, at least, exists, but regretful that no more formal, regularized and institutionalized answer has been created. For despite the growth of freedom to talk, read and learn about sexual behavior, sexual learning remains largely a private, individually motivated and covert affair. Children hear and read far more and teach each other far more than formerly, but the social context of sexual learning is still basically unregulated and secretive, and still a matter of giggling, snickering, whispered conversations and furtive reading.

The result is that, despite the considerable degree of liberation we have achieved, it remains difficult for most people to obtain correct information in time to begin using their sexuality in a rational way. How short we are of the goal of real liberation may be suggested by the recent findings of demographers Melvin Zelnik and John Kantner of Johns Hopkins University, who recently studied the sexual behavior of 4611 teen-age girls and found that of those who had had coitus, more than three-quarters used contraceptive methods only sometimes, or never, their haphazardness being attributable in large part to ignorance and mistaken notions about the chances of becoming pregnant.[24] Further proof of the shortcomings of the laissez-faire system is the fact that gonorrhea is now the second most common infectious ailment among teen-agers, being surpassed only by the common cold. More generally, the defects in the sexual education of young Americans must be responsible for countless cases of psychosexual disability or limitation of function, for innumerable flawed marriages and for an unmeasurable amount of needless human unhappiness and frustration. Where education for adult sex life is concerned, we are still a long way from being liberated.

Petting: Incidence, Techniques, Importance

By 1920 or thereabouts, the changing conditions of American life brought about the spontaneous development of a new method of socializing among young unmarried people: In place of parental selection and chaperoned evenings in the family parlor, teen-agers and young adults chose their partners themselves, made their own arrangements to meet and went out of the home to spend their evenings at the movies, at parties or in the back seats of parked cars. In a word, dating had been invented.[25]

Dating posed a serious problem: It afforded the young the opportunity to experiment with physical love, but gave no sanction to premarital intercourse; it liberated the young from the watchful eye of the chaperone, but not from the traditional social values implanted in their consciences. The solution to the problem was another invention, namely, petting—that whole series of acts that lies beyond mere kissing but stops short of inserting the penis in the vagina. Petting was not formally sanctioned by parents—indeed, many were strongly opposed to it— but they opposed it far less strenuously than they did intercourse; it occupied a no-man's-land between old-fashioned virtue and the unthinkable freedom advocated by free-love radicals. In all probability, not too many parents were aware that petting could go far beyond occasional tentative fumbling and clutching—that it could, in fact, involve partial or total nudity, mutual masturbation, fellatio, cunnilingus and orgasm for one or both partners. But the young themselves knew, and while many of them, girls in particular, were temporarily troubled by each successive stage in intimacy, they generally felt that as long as the penis never entered the vagina—as long as they remained technically virginal—it was somehow all right. And more than all right; most young people considered petting to be far healthier and more natural than the restricted, touch-me-not courting of their elders. They saw nothing unnatural about their indulging in prolonged, intimate and intense foreplay while at the same time continuing to set great store by the avoidance of actual genital union.

Such was the new compromise between desire and purity. One can hardly find its like elsewhere. In a few sexually restrictive societies, petting without intercourse was practiced by engaged couples before marriage—we ourselves had something of the sort in the form of "bundling" in colonial New England—and medieval lords and ladies, though married, practiced something akin to petting in their courtly-love adulteries to keep their passions ennobled and pure. But in most societies petting without intercourse has been either unknown or practiced only during a very brief transitional stage of the life cycle.[26]

In 20th-Century America, however, petting came to occupy a most significant position in terms not only of the number of persons involved but of the number of years involved. Even in its "game" aspect, it was serious business: The boy tried to see how much he could get—and the girl how little she could give —by way of recompense for the time and money he had spent on her, and the better he "made out," the higher was his status among his fellows, while the less she gave in, the more desirable she was deemed.[27] But petting was also serious business in a deeper sense; it was the acceptable middle-class means of expressing erotic and emotional feelings before marriage. The more deeply a boy and girl cared about each other, the "further" they considered it all right to go. The standard enforced by the girls and grudgingly accepted by the boys held, in a general way, that kissing was all right if the two merely liked each other; "deep" or "French" kissing if they felt romantic about each other; breast touching through the clothing if they were halfway "serious" about each other, and with the bra off if they were somewhat more serious than that; and explorations "below the waist" or exposure of the naked penis to the girl's touch only if the couple considered themselves really in love.

Behavior of this kind was viewed as generally acceptable by middle-class youths in their upper teens, and at the time of Kinsey's first survey was most commonly and frequently practiced by single people in their early twenties. Kinsey found petting strongly associated with educational level. Although most young males did have some petting experience, those males who went only as far as grade school petted only very briefly before moving on to regular coitus, either prior to or within marriage. Virtually all of those males who went to high school, however, and especially those who went to college—and who, accordingly, married much later and held middle-class moral values— tended to adopt petting as a way of life over a period of some years.[28] Kinsey found much the same thing to be true of females, especially those born after 1920: The higher their level of education, the later they married, and the higher the percentage of them who ever petted and the longer they did so. In the younger generation of females, 94 percent of those who were still single at 20 had petted—about a quarter of them to the point of orgasm—and the percent who had petted to orgasm grew higher the longer they remained unmarried.[29]

Petting was thus a compromise, established by the 1920s, between premarital chastity and the new liberalism, and for a long while this compromise endured unchanged. Various surveys of students on one campus or another during the 1950s and 1960s, made by sociologists Winston Ehrmann and Ira Reiss, psychologist Keith Davis, author Vance Packard and many others, all agreed that although there was some general movement toward greater permissiveness and sexual liberalism, it remained true that, without emotional commitment, petting was considered more or less wrong, and that the degree of physical intimacy that seemed right, especially to girls, was directly proportional to the intensity and "seriousness" of the emotional relationship.[30]

Our own survey indicates that petting, as a compromise, has become more widely acceptable than ever—but at the same time has waned in importance. We find, first of all, that in very recent years there has been an abrupt increase in permissiveness concerning petting, both among parents and among the unmarried young. Reiss, for instance, who gathered data in 1959 and 1963 on attitudes toward petting, reported that a little over half of the adults in his national sample approved of petting for males who are in love, and a little under half for females who are in love[31]; in a roughly comparable group in our sample (all those of 25 and older), four-fifths of the males and nearly two-thirds of the females approve of it for persons who are in love. What is more striking is the comparison of Reiss's student sample (high school and college combined) with the students in our own sample: In Reiss's survey, somewhat over 80 percent approved of petting for engaged persons, and just under 80 percent for persons who are in love but not engaged,[32] while in our survey about 95 percent approve of it in either circumstance. But the contrasts, as indicated in Table 17, are still greater concerning petting where there is "strong affection" rather than love, and greater yet where there is "no strong affection."*

Similarly, when we compare the older half of our own survey sample with the younger half—the median ages of the two halves being roughly a generation apart—we find a major increase in permissiveness toward petting even when there is no major emotional commitment (see Table 18).

Emotional commitment thus remains very important to the

Table 17

Petting With and Without Strong Affection:
Student Samples, Percents Approving

	1959 (Reiss[33])		1972 Present survey	
	Approved for Males	Approved for Females	Approved by Males	Approved by Females
Where strong affection exists	67	57	88	78
Where no strong affection exists	34	18	68	30

*Reiss asked his respondents whether petting was acceptable for males and acceptable for females. We asked only if it was acceptable, without specifying for which sex, but the replies from our males and from our females clearly refer primarily to the respondents' own sex. Even if this were considered debatable, one could combine and reaverage Reiss's figures *for* each sex, and our replies *from* each sex, and still show a major increase in permissiveness concerning petting where there is strong affection but not love, and where there is no strong affection.

Table 18

Heavy Petting With and Without Strong Affection:
Total Sample by Age, Percents Approving

	Under 35		35 and over	
	Males	Females	Males	Females
Where strong affection exists	85	68	55	25
Where no strong affection exists	62	29	29	8

great majority as a justification or precondition for petting. This standard, however, is rapidly being joined by another, now held by a majority of younger males and a substantial minority of younger females, in which petting is also seen as acceptable even where there is little or no emotional involvement but only such motives as the desire for experience, or for sexual gratification, excitement, or simply for an ego boost. This is not to say that the majority of our respondents *prefer* petting without emotional involvement, or that they often indulge in it under such circumstances, but it is a reasonably safe assumption that they do, in fact, translate those attitudes into actual behavior at least now and then.

It is difficult, however, to measure the changes in actual behavior in the past generation, for neither Kinsey nor any other researcher provides a usable base line. While Kinsey compiled data on the episodes of petting that led to orgasm, these covered only a small part of all petting, as he himself pointed out.[34] As to the frequencies of all petting, he gave a number of reasons why it was hard to establish such figures reliably, offering no estimate whatever for males, and for females only the very loose statement that "the average frequencies of petting among unmarried females between the ages of fifteen and thirty-five . . . may range from about once in a week to once in a month."[35]

We can nonetheless make some rough comparisons of our incidence data with his to indicate the general magnitude of the changes that have occurred. There are minor increases in both active incidence and accumulative incidence—minor because the percentages were high even in Kinsey's day. Among unmarried girls, for instance, Kinsey reported that 88 percent of those between 16 and 20, and the same percentage of those between 21 and 25, were "actively" petting ("actively" signifying at least one episode within the five-year period)[36]; in our most nearly comparable cohort (18 to 24), 90 percent or better are doing so in the six-year period. Accumulative incidence shows similar small but definite increases: By age 25, 89 percent of Kinsey's single males had petted,[37] while in our own sample at least 95 percent—and probably more—have done so. (We cannot be more precise because we have data only for the cohort, and not year by year within it; accordingly, our total percentage of petting experience for under-25s includes some teen-age youths who have not yet petted but will very likely do so before age 25.)

It also seems very likely that both males and females are experiencing orgasm in their petting more often than was the case in Kinsey's time. Only a little over a quarter of Kinsey's males had ever petted to climax by age 25,[38] while at least two-thirds of our under-25 males had had at least one orgasm by various petting techniques in just the 12 months prior to completing their questionnaires. For women, the same thing appears to be true: About one out of four of the younger women in Kinsey's sample had experienced orgasm in petting by age 20, and about two-fifths had done so by 25[39]; in contrast, in our own sample of age 18-through-24 single girls, substantially more than half experienced orgasm through petting techniques in just the past year.

As was true of Kinsey's sample, in our survey a number of the males and females reporting orgasm through petting techniques had also had coital experience, and we considered the possibility that some of what we recorded as orgasms in petting may actually have been part of foreplay before or during long sessions of intercourse. However, after examining our own data on age at first intercourse, and making due allowance for this possibility, it is our conservative estimate that the percentages of unmarried males and females in their early twenties who are actively experiencing orgasm in petting sessions are close to twice what they were in Kinsey's time.

This is probably due in some degree to the diminution of

inner conflict, fear and inhibition on the part of males and, even more so, on the part of females. But probably it is also due in some degree to the increased freedom young single people now feel to employ highly stimulating and effective petting techniques. In Kinsey's sample, less than a third of the younger (under 26) males had ever been fellated, before marriage, by a female partner[40]; in our own most nearly comparable group, 72 percent have had the experience. In the youngest third of Kinsey's female sample, under a fifth of the virgins and only a little over half of the unmarried nonvirgins had ever used the petting technique of "apposition of genitalia"—simulated intercourse, body-to-body, without actual penile insertion[41]; we estimate that half of our virgin females and nine-tenths of our unmarried nonvirgin females have experienced this petting technique.

It comes as a distinct surprise, therefore, to find indications that petting is becoming *less* important in an overall sense than it was formerly. Kinsey asked married women who had petted before marriage how many petting partners they had had; the answers varied greatly, depending on how old they were when they married, but for the married female sample as a whole, the median number was just under eight.[42] For our own married white women, in contrast, the median number of premarital petting partners was down sharply to three. Kinsey published no figure on total number of petting partners for his males, but married white males in the older half of our sample had a median of 15 premarital petting partners, while married white males in the younger half had a median of 12.

A partial explanation of these decreases is that people are marrying a little younger today than in the period of Kinsey's fieldwork. The more cogent explanation, however, would seem to be that young men and more especially young women pet with fewer partners because they move on far sooner to fairly regular premarital intercourse. (The next section of this chapter will offer data on this point.) Thus, petting today is an acceptable compromise for a shorter period of years than formerly; its importance is changing from that of a long-term *modus vivendi* to that of a transitory apprenticeship stage, a period of training in physical actions and responses. Where Kinsey estimated that the median female with petting experience had such experiences over a 6.6-year period,[43] it is our impression that our own median female has closer to three or four years of petting, before marriage or regular premarital intercourse supplant it.

A generation ago, petting was immensely important to those who went to college and who, accordingly, married late; it was therefore very much a middle-class phenomenon, and it fit the middle-class need to preserve traditional morality while making it a bit more flexible. Lower-class and uneducated people—men in particular—found it an astonishing phenomenon; they considered the concentration upon foreplay techniques and the prolonged avoidance of genital union to be unnatural and almost perverted.[44] But during the past generation, as we noted in Chapter 1, the less-educated classes have learned a lot about the desirability of foreplay, while at the same time white-collar and better-educated young men and women have been growing increasingly impatient with petting as a *modus vivendi* and increasingly tolerant of premarital intercourse where there is emotional involvement. The distinctions between occupational classes and between educational levels are decreasing; petting is becoming more common and more freely used at the lower level—but less important and less stable at the upper level.

But even though petting is no longer as enduring a compromise as it used to be, it did or still does play a significant part in the lives of a majority of the people in our sample. Its continuing and widespread use signifies that restraints against premarital intercourse, though apparently much weakened, still exist. But are they the same restraints that were operative a generation ago? Do those who hold the line at petting have the same reasons for doing so, or have the reasons changed in some way? We asked all of our respondents who had never had premarital intercourse—that is, all singles who were still virginal, and all married persons who had been virginal until they married—what had restrained them. We then compared the responses of the older half of this total subsample with those of the younger half. There were, of course, considerably fewer such persons in the younger half of the married sample than in the older half, and more in the younger half of the single sample than in the older half. Our concern here, however, is not with the percentages of such persons within the age groups but with the relative importance of the various reasons for self-restraint within these subsamples.* Our findings appear in Table 20.

Table 20

Selected Reasons for No Premarital Sex: Persons Without
Premarital Coitus, Total National Sample, Percents

	Males		Females	
	Under 35	35-plus	Under 35	35-plus
Religious or moral reasons	69	80	92	91
Fear of what others would think	—	27	52	53
Fear of being caught	—	27	33	26
Fear of effect on future marriage	15	31	34	28
Fear of pregnancy	23	55	59	52
Fear of VD	15	44	24	28
Never met anyone desired it with	15	13	21	23
Desired partners weren't willing	39	29	3	4

The contrasts between the male and female reasons for avoiding premarital intercourse are interesting but hardly surprising. What is surprising is the stability of female reasons from one generation to the next, as contrasted with the changes in the male reasons from one generation to the next. As we will see in the next section, fewer males and far fewer females than for-

---

*For the record, however, here are the percentages of virginal single persons, and of married persons without premarital coital experience, within our survey sample. It is these persons whose reasons are given in Table 20.

Table 19

Single Persons Without Coital Experience:
Total National Sample, Percents

Males		Females	
18–34	35 and over	18–34	35 and over
13	0	23	*

Married Persons Without Premarital Coital Experience:
Total National Sample, Percents

Males		Females	
18–34	35 and over	18–34	35 and over
7	13	30	62

**Too small for computation.*

merly are wholly restrained from premarital coitus, but Table 20 indicates that among those females who are so restrained, all the traditional reasons for virginity still apply—guilt, the fear of God's wrath, the fear of parental anger, the fear of social ostracism, the expectation of dire practical consequences. For males, however, most of the traditional reasons have waned in importance, the only one that shows any noteworthy increase being the trivial one that girls weren't willing. The fairly obvious conclusion one can reach is one we have already come to from other findings—namely, that the double standard, though much eroded, still exists, even among some members of the younger generation of Americans.

How did these people—and the larger number who held the line for many years but finally yielded—view petting, after the initial excitement, novelty and fear wore off? From our interviews we have the impression that while it may have seemed an exciting and satisfying form of sexual behavior to many people a generation ago, more recently it has seemed so only to novices, and, even for them it soon comes to seem frustrating, disappointing and generally a poor substitute for what lies ahead. Our interviewees said things like this:

FEMALE, 36, HOUSEWIFE: When we became really serious about each other, we slowly got around to doing things I had never done before. I was eighteen then, but I had never let any boy touch me anywhere. But over the months we did more and more—and came as close as we could without actually having intercourse, which neither of us even dreamed of doing. It was terribly frustrating, and also I got tired of confessing it to the priest, because it didn't really seem sinful, and yet he insisted that it was. Finally I just stopped going to confession—but I still wouldn't have intercourse.

FEMALE, 34, TEACHER: I liked kissing games, holding hands and hugging, but I had this thing about remaining a virgin and I was afraid to let anybody start anything at all. [At seventeen] I started going out with a college sophomore, and I was terrified that he would know just what to do and I'd be helpless, but it turned out he was a Catholic and just as terrified as I was that we might go too far. So we would pet for hours and hours without ever doing more, and I loved it—but I'd get all strung up and have to masturbate as soon as I was alone, and that made me feel deeply ashamed.

MALE, 26, LAWYER: I got started late, and never knew what to do, but I learned a lot through petting. I found out, little by little, how to kiss properly—I used to press too hard—and how to do the little things to a girl's breast that would excite her. But for years I never could seem to connect and actually get laid. I found out, though, that if I would lie up against a girl and rub up against her, I could come in my clothes, and that relieved me. But it was messy, and embarrassing, and I always felt foolish about it.

MALE, 24, GRADUATE STUDENT: I did a lot of light petting in high school, and by the time I got to college and was going steady with a girl, we went further—we felt each other all over, and we'd dry-hump until we came. At first it seemed very exciting and daring, but it was never really satisfying and never really beautiful. I wanted to do the real thing so badly that I felt desperate, but the girl wouldn't, and I never thought of going elsewhere for it. I used to think sometimes, "What if I die in an accident, without ever knowing what it's like?" and that thought could make me frantic.

MALE, 30, SOCIAL WORKER: When I got to college, there was a lot of peer pressure on me—guys saying, "You're not a man if you haven't done it"—and I was much tormented by that. But I still had the moral values of my Methodist upbringing, and I kept myself chaste. Later, when I started going steady with Amy, we began to pet, and after a while it would get quite heavy, and then we'd both get frightened and guilty and make a pact to see each other but not touch each other. But that would collapse and we'd go further than ever. We'd even stay in bed all night, and masturbate each other to orgasm—and still we had some kind of conviction that it would be wrong to have real intercourse. At times we'd be ready to do it—and, at the very point of trying it, suddenly the vision of what we were doing would come down on us, and we'd stop and feel all torn up.

FEMALE, 27, ARTIST: By the time I was in high school, I thought I was very advanced and free because I'd let my boy friend see me completely nude. But I never felt ready for intercourse; I didn't feel old enough to deal with it. It was a real hang-up, because when I got to college and fell in love with a guy, I saw him for three years and we would often spend *hours* in bed together and get *very* physical, and I would get a lot of real satisfaction out of it and still, somehow, I never felt ready to do the real thing. I would try to think about it, and I'd get a peculiar panicky feeling, and feel ashamed and cowardly. It took me three years to finally get myself together and try it. Afterwards, I couldn't figure out what I'd been so afraid of.

Little wonder that the compromise has proven only a temporary one, and that petting seems destined to take its place as a historical curiosity, enduring chiefly as a brief learning stage in the lives of most Americans. In time the petting behavior of young people in Kinsey's time and in the recent past may seem as bizarre and unnatural to their grandchildren and great-grandchildren as the chaste and virtually kissless courtships of their grandparents and great-grandparents seemed to them.

Premarital Coitus: Incidence, Numbers and Types of Partners, Emotional Significance

Thus far in this chapter we have seen that during the past generation Americans in general—but especially the young—have grown increasingly tolerant of the general idea of premarital sexual activities, and that this greater tolerance has resulted in behavioral changes—specifically, earlier and more extensive petting, and some easing of the emotional prerequisites for petting behavior. Paradoxically, however, petting has become less important because, as we have said, there has been a major increase in premarital intercourse; it is this latter phenomenon that we are now about to document. In this section we will find out how early today's young adults began premarital intercourse, what percentage of them have done so by various ages, and under what emotional circumstances they do it. In the next section we will ask how frequent, free, and satisfying present-day premarital sex life is for most people.

The subject is of immense interest to the general public, but the intensity of this interest and the way in which the mass media cater to it distort and magnify the place actually occupied by premarital intercourse in the life cycle of the average American male and female. In those magazines that are addressed primarily to unmarried persons, and in much of contemporary fiction, television and cinema, attractive young women are commonly portrayed as remaining single, by choice, throughout their twenties, and handsome young men as doing so five or ten years longer, with members of both sexes enjoying an active sex life the whole time. The net impression is that premarital intercourse is the sexual *modus vivendi* of a major part of normal adult life—say, 10 to 20 years out of the 50 available. But this is a gross exaggeration of the reality. Only a very small minority of persons are actually involved in premarital sex for more than a very brief part of their adult lives. For one thing, a higher percentage of young people marry today than did two or three generations ago, and though the marriage rate declined somewhat during the 1950s, it turned upward again by 1963 and has been rising ever since.[45] For another, the young are marrying almost as early as did the people of a generation ago, the median age at first marriage today being a trifle under 21 for females and a little over 23 for males.[46] Premarital intercourse is thus not experienced over a ten-to-twenty-year span of life but more typically over a five- or six-year period by most males and a one- or two-year period by most females—and not regularly or actively, at that, until or unless the young male or female is living away from the parental home. This, rather than the gaudy lifestyle of the swinging singles, is the general reality.

Nonetheless, that reality has undergone great changes in recent generations, particularly in the two and a half decades since Kinsey published his first study. One of the less obvious but more revealing changes is in the role prostitution plays in the premarital lives of young men. A century ago, and even a generation ago, a considerable number of young males went to prostitutes for their sexual initiation, and some males—especially those in the lower social and educational levels—resorted to them often and regularly prior to marriage. The current wave of sexual liberation has made prostitution far more open and visible than ever before, as witness the burgeoning of "massage" and "body rub" establishments, commercially sponsored sex clubs, so-called dating bureaus, street-corner solicitation by addicted prostitutes, and hooker traffic in singles bars. Yet our data show that, despite all this, there have been distinct decreases in the past generation in the percentage of American males who are sexually initiated by prostitutes, in the percentage who ever have premarital intercourse with prostitutes and in the average frequency with which they have such experiences.

This is a continuation of a long-term trend that has coincided with—and in large part been the result of—the long-range emancipation of women and the decay of the double standard, for as dating partners have become sexual partners, prostitutes have become unnecessary and undesirable. Even in Kinsey's time, while as many younger men as older ones had had some experience with prostitutes, the younger men were averaging only half to two-thirds as many total contacts with them as the older men had had.[47] Kinsey also reported that the use of prostitutes was very strongly associated with lower educational and social status, where traditional views of women and of sexuality were most strongly entrenched. By age 20 nearly half of his noncollege single males, but only a fifth of his college-level single males, had experienced coitus with prostitutes; by age 25 the respective totals were nearly two-thirds for noncollege men but only a little over a quarter for college men; and even those upper-level males who did have such experiences had them only a quarter to a half as often as men at lower educational and social levels.[48] In a sense this foreshadowed the continuing decline of prostitution, for the direction of American evolution was toward mass higher education, with its associated middle-class attitudes concerning sex, women and love.

Because of certain technical limitations in Kinsey's accumulative-incidence data in this area, we can best see the change between his time and our own by comparing the experience of the older generation of married males in our own sample with the younger one: Table 21 reveals a sharp drop both at the college level and the noncollege level, in the total percentage who have had any premarital experience with prostitutes.

Table 21

Ever Had Premarital Coitus with a Prostitute:
All Married Males, Percents

	Under 35	35 and over
High school or less	30	61
Some college or more	19	52

Nor are prostitutes the initiators for as many males as formerly: Among our over-35 college men, 17 percent said their first coital experience had been in a house of prostitution, but only half as many of the under-35 college men said so. For noncollege men the figures were 20 percent and 5 percent, respectively. What is perhaps most significant, those younger men who have had premarital coitus with prostitutes have averaged far fewer contacts with them per year than their counterparts of a generation ago. Here, fortunately, we can make at least a crude comparison of our figures with Kinsey's. Only 3 percent of our single white males of the under-25 cohort had any experiences with prostitutes in the past year. Kinsey's active-incidence figures cover five-year periods and are roughly 31 percent for the 16-to-20 cohort and 29 percent for the 21-to-25 cohort.[49] A five-year active incidence is, of course, a wider net than a one-year active incidence, but even if we made the extreme (and unlikely) assumption that it yielded five times as large a sample as a one-year active incidence, Kinsey's figures cut by five would still be twice as large as our own. The comparison thus suggests that the use of prostitutes by single young males today is, at most, only about half as widespread as it was in the 1940s.* It is our impression, furthermore—based on the small number of prostitutes ever contacted by young men with such experience, as compared with their total number of other partners and with their overall quantity of coital experience with such other persons—that the part prostitution plays in their total outlet per year is only about a third to a half as large as in the total outlet of comparable young men a generation ago.

The overall decrease in the importance of prostitution is, as we have said, a by-product of the long-term change in women's status and position in society. Several generations ago, a young man in his teens or early twenties had relatively little hope of having frequent intercourse, if any, with a "decent" girl unless he was engaged to her, and often not even then. Prostitution was therefore a frequent choice of outlet for lower-class males, while for middle-class males the more common answers were masturbation or continence. But during and following World War I

---

*As usual, when making a direct comparison with Kinsey's data, which are based on an all-white sample, we use our own white subsample. The young blacks in our sample were more likely to visit prostitutes actively than the whites; the active-incidence figure for our total sample of under-25 males, whites and blacks together, is somewhat above 4 percent, rather than the 3 percent used above.

there was a marked liberation of attitudes toward sexuality in general and, in particular, toward premarital activities by the young of both sexes. What changed the premarital sexual pattern of the male was the growing freedom of the female; as "decent" girls became liberated enough to pet, or even in some cases to have intercourse, the lower-class male's resort to prostitution and the middle-class male's chastity both waned. According to an important study (primarily of middle-class people) published in 1938 by psychologist Lewis M. Terman, premarital virginity declined simultaneously for both males and females. Comparing people born prior to 1890 with people born in each of the next three decades, Terman found that male virginity at the time of marriage had shrunk from 51 percent to 14 percent, and female virginity from 87 percent to 32 percent. So dramatic was this shift that Terman expected it to continue unchecked, and predicted that virginity at marriage would be close to the vanishing point for males born after 1930 and for females born after 1940.[50]

Terman's sample was, however, small and far from representative. Kinsey, on the basis of his vastly larger and broader sample, agreed that a major change had occurred during the years 1916–1935 or thereabouts, but held that it had been of a more limited nature and, moreover, had leveled off. He found much less indication of change among males than Terman, for Kinsey's figures included lower-class males, and at that social level there had been very few virgin bridegrooms even in the generation born prior to the turn of the century. On the other hand, Kinsey did report changes among females that substantiated and refined Terman's data. The year 1900 had been something of a turning point, with women born before that year being far less likely to have any premarital intercourse than women born after it: By age 25, for instance, only 14 percent of the older women had had premarital intercourse, as compared with 36 percent of those born between 1900 and 1910.[51] But oddly enough the cohorts of those born later than 1910 showed only minor additional increases in premarital activity. Kinsey therefore disagreed with Terman's long-range prediction,[52] and implied that the classic inhibitory factors (religion, education and social class) had apparently come into a new balance with the forces of liberation.

Viewing his sample as a whole, Kinsey estimated that about

half of all females sooner or later had some premarital coital experience, while for males the figures ranged from 68 percent for the college-educated to 98 percent for those with only a grade-school education.[53] These are lifelong accumulative incidence data, however, and since our present focus of interest is on premarital intercourse of young persons, the more meaningful Kinsey figures are these, which pertain to the earlier part of life:

—By age 20, 53 percent of all males, but only 20 percent of all females, had had premarital intercourse. By age 25, 71 percent of all males and 33 percent of all females had done so.[54]*

—Religious devoutness was negatively correlated with premarital coital experience (the devout were far less likely to ever have such experience than the nondevout).[55]

—Educational level was strongly correlated with premarital coital experience, particularly for males. By age 20, 86 percent of grade-school men and 76 percent of high-school men—but only 44 percent of college men—had had premarital intercourse, and by age 25 the comparable figures were 90 and 84 respectively for the two less-educated categories, and 64 for the college men.[56]

—The same thing was true, though much less so, for females: At age 20, from 25 to 26 percent of the noncollege females had had premarital intercourse, as against 15 to 20 percent of the college and graduate-school females. By 25, however, the college-educated women were ahead of the noncollege women by a small margin, because the latter tended to marry earlier and thus to be removed from any further possibility of premarital experience.[57]

Not only were Kinsey's data far broader and more reliable than any others that existed, but for many years after the 1948 and 1953 volumes appeared it was Kinsey's predictions rather than Terman's that seemed to be correct. Despite the many outward signs of increasing sexual liberalism in the 1950s and early 1960s, almost all the post-Kinsey samplings and surveys—

---

*Kinsey's own figures for males run higher than those given here because he applied his "U.S. Corrections" to the raw data, though he did not do so in the case of the females. As explained earlier, we are using Kinsey's raw data rather than his corrections, since our own sample is more like his uncorrected one than like his corrections. On p. 550 of his male volume, he gives the figures 73 and 83 percent for males of 20 and 25 respectively as accumulative incidences of premarital intercourse. Using the raw data on the same page, we derived the above-given figures.

mostly small, to be sure, and chiefly limited to college students, usually on only one campus—showed little if any increase in nonvirginity between the mid-1940s and the mid-1960s.[58] As Ira Reiss summed up the situation in 1966: "There is a widespread belief that much has changed in terms of premarital sex behavior in the last 20 to 25 years. However, the evidence from all the available major studies is in strong agreement that although attitudes have changed considerably during this period . . . premarital coital rates have not."[59] If there had been any increase in the rates, he added, it had been only minor; the important change in the past quarter century lay in the greater acceptance of the new behavior, not in its widening adoption.*

But as has already been pointed out, attitudes are forerunners and shapers of behavior. Reiss and other sociologists may have been right that there was no major change in behavior in the quarter century prior to the mid-1960s, but the spread of permissive sexual attitudes and their gradual incorporation into the psychological mechanisms of the young were laying a groundwork for an abrupt, almost explosive change in behavior. By the end of the 1960s, the first signs of that change began to appear: Almost every new campus survey showed distinctly higher rates of premarital coitus than had been typical for the past two decades or so. Off the campus, the large-scale Zelnik and Kantner survey mentioned earlier in this chapter—a national sampling of 4611 girls between the ages of 15 and 19, made for the Commission on Population Growth and the American Future— reported that as of 1971, by age 19, 46 percent of the girls had had premarital intercourse. This figure suggests a very dramatic increase since Kinsey's time, although, since it includes the premarital experience of black girls (who were roughly twice as likely, in this age range, to have such experience as white girls), it overstates the change since Kinsey's time. When the data on white girls only in Zelnik and Kantner's survey are used, however, the comparison is fair—and still dramatic (see Table 22). At the same time, Zelnik and Kantner's data indicate that there is little promiscuity involved in this upsurge of premarital coitus; few of the white girls and even fewer of the black ones had had many partners, and about 60 percent of the nonvirgins of both

---

*But to do Professor Reiss no injustice, we must add that by 1972 he had reviewed the latest data from various sources and concluded that "indeed there had been an upsurge in the proportion of women nonvirginal at marriage during the 1960s."[60] As we will now see, he had good grounds for this revised opinion.

Table 22

Single White Females Having Ever Had
Premarital Intercourse, Percents

	1938–1949 (Kinsey*)	1971 (Zelnik & Kantner[61])
By age 15	3	11
By age 19	18 to 19*	40

*Kinsey (1953), pp. 286, 333; the span for age 19 is due to the imprecision of the graph and the lack of data for age 19 in the table.

races had had sex with only one male—whom about half of them hoped or intended to marry.

Our own survey likewise indicates that the growth of permissiveness in attitudes has been translated into an abrupt and major increase in actual premarital intercourse. For males, the big change is in that part of the population that goes to college. Even by age 17, half of those males who eventually went to college had had premarital coital experience—more than double the figure in Kinsey's comparable sample. Among the non-college men, too, there was an increase, but of much smaller proportions: By age 17 nearly three-quarters of our noncollege males had had premarital coitus, as compared with a little over two-thirds, for Kinsey's comparable sample.[62] At 20 and 25 Kinsey's figures are higher—and ours higher still.*

For females the changes are not only more dramatic but pertain to all educational levels, since educational status plays a much smaller part in the female pattern. By age 17 less than a tenth of all Kinsey's females—his accumulative-incidence data are for single and married combined—had had premarital coitus, and by age 25 only a third had done so.[63] Our own figures are strikingly higher: Among our white females, by age 17 nearly a fifth of our married sample and fully a third of our single sample had had premarital coitus, and by age 25 nearly half of our married sample and nearly three-quarters of our single sample had done so. In short, in their late teens and in their mid-twenties, the percentage of women who have had premarital coitus has roughly doubled since Kinsey's time.**

*See also p. 33.

**Again, we use white-only data in order to make fair comparisons with Kinsey's figures; like Zelnik and Kantner, we find a considerably higher incidence of premarital experiences among black females in their teens. At later ages, however, the rates converge.

Even this, however, understates the suddenness of the change, for much of this increase in the total sample is due to the altered behavior of the youngest cohort—those whose ages range from 18 to 24—in which 70 percent of the single white females and an astounding 80 percent of the married white females have had at least some premarital coital experience. In our 25-to-34 cohort, the figures are not so large, though they do show a pronounced increase over the older age groups; in other words, the change was beginning by 1965. We can see this even more clearly by looking at the proportions of married persons in each of our age cohorts (in our total sample) who had any premarital experience (see Table 23).

It is clear that to some extent the younger generation of American men, and to a very marked extent the younger generation of American women, are rapidly adopting a standard of behavior different from that of their elders. Terman, it now seems, was right after all, though he underestimated by some 15 to 20 years how long it would take for premarital virginity to disappear. It now appears likely that within another five to ten years only a tiny minority of females and an even smaller one of males, consisting of the deeply religious, the emotionally disturbed and the personally undesirable, will remain virginal through their teens or will be virginal at the time of marriage.

Why this has happened is a matter deserving of study in a separate research undertaking. There are some who think that the greater freedom of publishers to print and distribute sexual material has brought it about and others who think that sex education in the schools is largely responsible; these things, however, are outgrowths of the public's increased permissiveness and acceptance of sexuality as much as they are causes of it. Many people think that the rise in premarital intercourse has come about because parents let their children have cars as soon

Table 23

Ever Had Premarital Coitus: Total Married Sample, by Age, Percents

	18–24	25–34	35–44	45–54	55 and over
Males	95	92	86	89	84
Females	81	65	41	36	31

as they can drive, or permit their teen-agers to go off unchaper-oned on ski and beach weekends, while others think that the change owes much to the easing of rules, by college administra-tors, on intersex visiting in dormitories; but such things merely afford the young easier opportunities to do what they would do anyhow (albeit with more difficulty), provided they feel that it is right for them to do so. And as we have seen, the young have indeed increasingly come to view premarital intercourse as right, if the people involved have a deep emotional commitment to each other, or even if they merely feel strong affection that might someday become something deeper. It is the force of this conviction, translated into action, that has made parents and deans change their rules, rather than the reverse.

Yet the new freedom constitutes something less than a violent departure from the deeper cultural values of the past. The young are not, by and large, promiscuous; they want sex to be both exciting and emotionally meaningful. They regard premarital coitus, in general, as thoroughly justified when it grows out of and expresses a legitimate relationship, but much less so when it is a purely sensuous and casual indulgence. They are, in short, handling premarital intercourse much as the young of a generation ago handled petting.

Consider, first, the number of partners with whom the young have premarital sex. Though there are no data on this point in the Kinsey study of males, we can make the generational com-parison within our own survey sample. Typically, married males in the older half of our sample who had had any premarital coitus had six partners by the time they married (this is the median, a better measure here than the mean); the comparable figure for males in the younger half of the sample is exactly the same. For females, Kinsey did provide data: 53 percent of those with premarital coital experience had had only one partner,[64] while in our most nearly comparable sample 54 percent had had only one partner. Rechecking by means of the generational com-parison within our own sample, we find that of the married women in the older half of our sample, a little more than one-third had had some premarital coital experience, over half of them with only one partner; in the younger half of our sample, although over two-thirds had had premarital intercourse, it is still true that more than half (51 percent) of these women had had only one partner.

Casual or promiscuous sex does exist among today's single people, but in our sample it occurs chiefly among somewhat older single persons, and separated and divorced persons (whom we will look at later on); it is not typical of the great mass of single young people. The longer a male or female remains single, of course, the greater the number of sexual partners he or she is likely to have, and the likelier it is that he or she will sometimes or often relax the emotional prerequisites for intercourse. Our single males and females in the 25-to-34 cohort have not only had more coital partners than those in the younger group but have more partners per year. The median number of coital partners for single males under 25 in the past year was two, while single males of 25 to 34 had a median of four coital partners for the year. For single females the medians were two partners in the past year for under-25s, and three partners for those in the 25-to-34 cohort. This sounds a trifle more like the swinging single life that has lately been made so much of, but one must remember that only a small fraction of adult Americans are single at this time of life (nine-tenths of all males and over nine-tenths of all females have married by the halfway point in the 25-to-34 decade), and thus premarital-intercourse behavior for this age bracket is not typical of that of the great majority of Americans.

Not only the number of partners but the kinds of partners chosen reveal that some traditional values have been preserved within the new premarital morality. Our data on partner choice, set alongside Kinsey's,[65] show a remarkable constancy across the span of more than half a century (see Table 24). These figures suggest that the youngest group is, in a way, even less inclined to casual premarital coitus than its predecessor. However, the total number of women who are nonvirginal before marriage is so much larger today than formerly that there is undoubtedly a considerable absolute increase in the number of swinging young females around as compared with 10 years ago, let alone 25 or 50 years ago. Nonetheless, the overall significance of our data is that while today almost any "nice girl" will do, before marriage, what only the daring girl would do a generation ago, today's "nice" girl is still guiding herself according to romantic and historically rooted values.

Table 24

Types of Partners with Whom Married White Females
Had Premarital Coitus, Percents

	Kinsey		Present survey	
	Born before 1900	Born between 1910–1919	Born between 1938–1947	Born between 1948–1955
Fiancé only	40*	42*	49	53
Other males only	20	12	8	3
Fiancé and other males	40	46	43	43

On page 34 we cited the figure 46 as the percentage of married women with premarital coitus in Kinsey's sample who had had it only with their fiancés. The figures above do not contradict this; in the group not included in the above table (born between 1900 and 1909), the percentage was 48. More important, however, is the long-term trend we have sought to emphasize in the above table.

Males, on the other hand, typically have a handful of coital partners before marriage, and in many cases at least some of these relationships have been casual. But while the male pattern of premarital coitus today is far less restricted than the female one, it apparently includes no more casual sex than did that of a generation ago. Indeed, a growing body of research literature has established the fact that much of the current premarital coitus on campuses and in the big cities takes place between males and females who live together in what are essentially trial marriages or companionate marriages with firm emotional ties, conventional standards regarding fidelity and a definite social identity as a couple.[66]

Additional evidence that the sex ethic of contemporary youth is essentially liberal-romantic rather than radical-recreational comes from our data on the more daring—but impersonal and emotionless—forms of sexual behavior, such as partner-swapping and group sex. Few of our young single respondents had experimented with such sexual practices, and only on very few occasions; the regulars are more likely to be in their thirties or forties and married. Of our single people up to age 25, 15 percent of the males and 4 percent of the females had tried partner-swapping, but many of the males and all of the females had done so only once. Similarly, 17 percent of these young males and 5 percent of the females had experienced multiple-partner sex, but, a third of the males and the large majority of the females had had only one such experience.*

Where, then, are those wild teen-agers we have all heard about? Where are the "beautiful people," the "swinging singles," the sex-party habitués, the cheerful orgiasts? Where is the evidence that a "recreational philosophy" of sex, as opposed to a "romantic philosophy" of sex, is gaining adherents all over the land? Such people do exist; the evidence is in our averages and in our interviews, as we will see in the following section and in later chapters. But the main conclusion to be drawn from our data on premarital sex is that the explosive increase in premarital intercourse in the past half dozen or so years does not constitute a violent overthrowing of all cultural values concerning sexuality, but only of the unrealistic and unnatural prohibition of all premarital intercourse. The new sexual freedom operates largely within the framework of our long-held cherished cultural values of intimacy and love. Even while it asserts its freedom from marriage, it is an apprenticeship for marriage, and is considered successful by its participants when it grows, deepens and leads to ever-stronger commitment, and unsuccessful and a wasted effort when it does not.

Recreational sex is a reality, but we think that it does not clearly appear as a separate entity in our data or in most of our interviews because for most people it is not a viable alternative way of life. Instead, it is a vacation, a temporary escape, a kind of playlike behavior that meets the needs of many people during special and sharply delimited periods of their lives—at the conclusion of which they move on to, or return to, the romantic philosophy of sex. Recreational, casual or nonemotional intercourse briefly suits a large number of young males and a small number of young females when they are first exploring their own sexual potential and trying to garner basic experience. It meets the needs of many somewhat older single people on occa-

---

*Among the unmarried people in our sample, blacks were overrepresented, and since black males have higher incidences of the above activities than white males, the above figures are somewhat distorted. For the record, up to age 25, 12 percent of our single white males have experienced partner-swapping and 14 percent have experienced multiple-partner sex. The figures for single white females are the same as for the total single female sample.

For singles of all ages in the total national sample, the overall incidences for partner-swapping are 19 percent for males and 5 percent for females, and, for multiple-partner sex, 24 percent for males and 7 percent for females. Cf. pp. 271–273 for comparable figures for married persons.

sion, especially when recovering from the trauma of broken love affairs. It may also, from time to time, answer the needs of some married people during periods of boredom, depression or middle-age vapors. And it frequently helps newly separated or divorced people restore their self-confidence while temporarily avoiding premature new entanglements. It may even be the best lifelong choice for a small number of people who cannot tolerate intimacy and commitment. But for the great majority of Americans at the present time, the recreational philosophy of sex is viable only for brief periods; to meet their deeper needs for enduring love, security and intimacy, they turn to the romantic philosophy of sex.

Premarital Coitus: Techniques, Frequency, Satisfactions and Dissatisfactions

Many more young people are having premarital intercourse today than used to be the case, but this in itself does not tell us how genuinely liberated they are—how free from inner conflict about their own behavior, how unfettered and uninhibited in their sexual techniques, how capable of managing premarital coitus without doing physical or emotional harm to themselves or their partners. It would be unrealistic to expect that at this stage sexual liberation should have thoroughly transformed premarital coital experiences: The pressures of the total milieu —parental, religious and social—have abated but not disappeared, sex education remains woefully inadequate, the contemporary veneration of sexual wizardry and maximum coital performance makes many young people feel inadequate, and the suspicion or even contempt with which virginity in either sex is now regarded thrusts some young people into coital activity before they are emotionally or socially ready for it.

Not surprisingly, therefore, some males and many females in our sample—even in the youngest cohort—found their introductory premarital coital experiences frightening, disappointing or productive of emotional backlash. Their negative reactions have little to do with anything so trivial as tawdry or degrading surroundings; very few of our younger males and females had their first premarital coitus in parked cars, behind bushes or in sleazy roadside cabins, and only 3 percent of our under-25 males had their first coital experiences in whorehouses. Young people today generally have their first coital experiences in relatively aesthetic and comfortable circumstances: Close to two-thirds of our youngest singles had done so in their own homes or their partner's homes—a term that includes college dormitory rooms or off-campus quarters—while cars, rented rooms and the outdoors were all far less common than they had been among the older people in our sample.

Nonetheless, among our young single males who have had intercourse, only four out of ten found their first experience of it "very pleasurable," while another four out of ten found it only "mostly pleasurable," and two out of ten neutral to unpleasant. For our under-25 single females the initiation was even less likely to be easy and rewarding; only two out of ten with coital experience say that the first time was "very pleasurable," and a little over two more that it was "mostly pleasurable," while over half rate it as having been neutral or unpleasant. (Among our married respondents in the same age bracket, a considerably larger proportion of the males and a somewhat larger one of the females found their first coital experience very or mostly pleasurable. The difference is probably due to the fact that a substantial number of these early-marrying people had their first coital experience with the partners they eventually married.)

The lack of pleasure, to judge from our interview material, was due to many factors—nervousness, uncertainty, embarrassment, fear of failure, fear of discovery, lack of skill, physical discomfort and the like—while such pleasure as there was was more mental than physical. Among our interviewees only a few males and no females at all spoke of sensuous delight in the first act, but many young males voiced the gratification they had felt at "doing it at last," "making the big time," "actually experiencing it" and "finding out I was really a man." A few young females spoke in comparable terms, saying things like how pleased they felt to be "taking the big step," "getting rid of my virginity" or "becoming a woman," but this genre of pleasure is far less common among females than among males, whose sexual success is so curiously dependent on the involuntary but essential erection. In the national survey sample, four-fifths of our young males, but only a little over a third of our young females, reported feeling pride after the first coital experience.

Similarly, enough of the double standard still exists to make twice as many females as males regretful after their coital initiation. Conservatives who view the present sexual scene with alarm may suppose that the young feel no qualms or misgivings about sexual activity, but over a third of our young males and close to two-thirds of our young females with premarital coital experience report feeling regret after the first time, and some of them—particularly the females—characterized the feeling as having been extreme. Oddly enough, more females reported regret than did in Kinsey's survey, but his figure represents regret felt after as many as ten premarital coital experiences,[67] ours after the first one. When we compare the feelings, after first intercourse, of our own young single girls with those of our older women, we do find some decrease in the extent of regret, as we expected; it is rather surprising, nonetheless, that so many, even today, still do experience it.*

Why do they? The fear of pregnancy is the biggest single factor; two-thirds of the females and half of the males who felt regret named this as a cause. What may seem more surprising is that moral conflict still ranks fairly high; nearly half of the females and nearly a third of the males specified regret of a moral or religious nature. Half of the females and a quarter of the males felt bad afterward because first coitus "had not met [their] expectations"; this probably means that they were disappointed by their own performance or by their failure to have a peak experience. Smaller percentages named various other sources of regret, including the fear of public opinion, and worry about VD.

Although moral and religious feelings were a major cause of regret, this factor is not so much associated with religious preference as with degree of devoutness; among single people of all three major faiths, somewhat more of the regular churchgoers than the nonchurchgoers felt regret after first premarital coitus, a phenomenon which seemingly has not changed since Kinsey's time.[69] Yet there is a difference: Even though today's devout may feel regret afterward, their religious feelings do not keep them virginal; in overall incidence of premarital intercourse they are not like their devout counterparts of a generation ago but

---

*Similarly, Christensen found that "guilt or remorse" about the first premarital coitus dropped sharply, but by no means disappeared, between 1958 and 1968.[68]

like the nondevout of that time. This is apparent when one compares the data in the upper left quadrant of Table 25 with those in the lower right.

But although devoutness is no longer effectively keeping many young males or most young females from having premarital intercourse, it continues to act as a hobble upon them after they have begun such intercourse. Among our youngest single respondents, those regular churchgoers who are having premarital intercourse are doing so half or less than half as often as their nonchurchgoing peers, and far fewer of the former ever use oral foreplay or such variations as the on-the-side, female-above and rear-entry-vaginal positions for intercourse.

Religious devoutness does not, however, seem to inhibit orgasm; the percentage of churchgoing females who have orgasm fairly regularly in their premarital intercourse is roughly on a par with that of nonchurchgoing females, and the same is true for males. But reliability of orgasm is only one indicator of satisfaction; indeed, it is possible to get very little overall satisfaction from intercourse despite having orgasm every time. When we asked our younger single respondents how pleasurable intercourse had been for them, in general, during the past year, we found a clear-cut difference between the experiences of the devout and the nondevout, especially in the case of males (see Table 26).

Table 25

Married Persons Who Had Any Premarital Coitus: by Age and Regularity of Church Attendance, Percents

		Under 35	35 and over
Regular	Males	88	80
churchgoers	Females	55	27
Non-	Males	97	90
churchgoers	Females	90	62

Table 26

Intercourse in Past Year "Very Pleasurable": by Regularity of Church Attendance, Under-35 Single Persons, Percents

	Males	Females
Regular churchgoers	40	53
Nonchurchgoers	78	64

With repetition, familiarity and the acquisition of skill, persons of every degree of religious devoutness come to enjoy premarital coitus more than they did at the beginning. But for most of them, even today, it is far from easy and effortless, or free from worries, conflicts and emotional shortcomings. At the practical level the fear of pregnancy is a continuing concern for nearly all of the unmarried. (A small minority of the ultrahip, however, take no precautions and, allegedly, do not worry; their philosophy calls for "being natural" and "letting life happen to you.") The very young worry least and exercise the least care, probably because they lack maturity and knowledge enough to do so—and they pay the penalty: Zelnik and Kantner reported that 41 percent of their black teen-age girls and 10 percent of their whites had been, or were, pregnant.[70] But among our own 18-to-24-year-old singles there is a good deal of worry about pregnancy and a fairly determined effort to prevent it. While it is true that over half our males in this group use no birth-control methods at all, they are mostly relying, advisedly, on their partners to do so. Five-sixths of the females do use birth-control methods; unfortunately a sixth of these rely on rhythm or male withdrawal (the two least reliable methods), and a third are inconsistent in their use of birth control, employing it anywhere from "often" to "rarely." Even so, this is a good deal better than the performance of the younger girls surveyed by Zelnik and Kantner, three-quarters of whom never, or only sometimes, used birth-control methods. The typical young female in our sample is not basically irresponsible about the possibility of pregnancy but merely a bit slipshod. Nationally, the number of illegitimate births to teen-agers has more than doubled since 1940,[71] but this does not signify increased chance-taking and irresponsibility in the young; in fact, since premarital intercourse by females has much more than doubled in that time, it may signify the very opposite. In any event, in our own sample 61 percent of the under-25 single females who were having intercourse last year were on "the pill," the most reliable of existing methods, and among our over-25 single females the use of consistent and reliable contraceptive methods was still higher.

The aesthetic aspects of premarital intercourse are still often far from ideal, but in many ways the circumstances are generally rather more favorable than formerly. As with the first coital experience, the great preponderance of premarital coitus occurs in the bedroom in the home of one partner or the other. Kinsey, too, had said that half to three-quarters of all premarital intercourse, for his females, took place within the home,[72] but in his time most of this must have been clandestine and tense, performed in fear and desperation while the parents were asleep or out for the evening. Today, with four to five times as large a percentage of the young going to college, and with visiting and housing rules on campuses being relaxed year by year, much premarital coitus takes place away from the parental home and under relatively secure, unhurried and aesthetically adequate circumstances.

Like Kinsey, we find that the unmarried young do not, by and large, hurry their foreplay, though whether this is the result of sophistication, or of the need to court and be courted each time, or merely of fascination with the relatively novel processes is unclear. Whatever the case, we find that single people under 25 typically spend somewhere around 15 minutes in foreplay before beginning actual coitus. Most of these young single people, whatever else they may be doing by way of foreplay, spend at least half of the time manually playing with their partners' genitals, or having their partners do so to them, or both at the same time, and a quarter of them spend half or more of the time in oral-genital activity. The median for the 25-to-34 single cohort is about 20 minutes. The reason for the increase is not apparent, but it may be an effect of selectivity—that is, those who remained unmarried may tend to be persons who have particular requirements for, or are especially fascinated by, foreplay rather than coitus.

In itself, the amount of time spent on foreplay by single young people does not seem notably greater than a generation ago. (Kinsey's figures are not very precise on this point, but he did say that most females with extensive premarital intercourse reported upwards of 11 minutes of foreplay.[73]) There does, however, seem to be an astonishing increase in the amount of time spent in coitus itself. In contrast to the general impression that the coitus of unmarried young singles is very hurried—primarily due to the male's selfishness or lack of control—we find that the median duration of actual intercourse in the 18-to-24 cohort is 12 minutes, according to males, and 15 minutes, according to females, and, in the 25-to-34 cohort, 15 minutes, according to males and 17 minutes according to females.* Kinsey published no figures on the duration of intercourse for single persons, but he did make the celebrated observation that perhaps three-quarters of all married males reached orgasm within two minutes after intromission, and from other indications in his survey, single males were just about as speedy.[74] We can therefore reasonably suppose that most of Kinsey's unmarried males were reaching orgasm in a small fraction of the time spent in the act by single males today.

This is so astonishing a contrast that it behooves us to view the data with caution. Nearly all reports of time spent in intercourse are highly subjective, as anyone knows who has ever had reason to look at the clock before and after; and since nowadays nearly everyone, at every social and educational level, has become aware that it is considered meritorious to be able to prolong intercourse, there may have been a fair amount of unconscious exaggeration by our respondents. Yet, even making generous allowance for this, it seems quite likely that there has been a very considerable increase in the average duration of premarital intercourse, due in part to a conscious effort by both male and female to prolong the act as an achievement in itself, but also due in part to the generally more secure, relaxed and sensuous aura surrounding most premarital intercourse today. It is no mere coincidence that our under-25 married respondents are very much more inclined to rate their premarital sexual experiences as pleasurable than are our older married people.

Thus on the one hand there is ample evidence that numerous problems, fears and moral conflicts continue to surround the premarital intercourse of single young people—and on the other hand impressive evidence that the sexual liberation of the past generation, and especially the past decade, has enabled far more single young people to have full, adult sexual relationships, and to do so under conditions that make premarital intercourse considerably more enjoyable and more genuinely fulfilling than was true only a few years ago. And this is in accord with a general conclusion we have already come to in the preceding chapters of this survey—namely that the changes brought about by over two decades of sexual liberation are very real and of

---

*Differences in median figures for the two sexes are common in sex research; subjective factors create the minor distortions involved.

surprising magnitude, but that liberation still has far to go
before it has fully eradicated the ascetic, sin-pervaded view of
sex that has dominated Western civilization for two millenia.

At the present stage, moreover, a special (but probably transient) problem harasses many of the young. They believe that
premarital sex, under the proper conditions, is a good and
legitimate thing, and that they have a right to enjoy it; but
because one's own sexual liberation is now ranked so high in the
scale of cultural values, they feel compelled to seek and to reach
the very pinnacle of physical pleasure, since to do anything less
would imply that they were still inhibited and unliberated. What
one might call the "effort syndrome" thus frequently appears
after the fear, clumsiness and regret of the first experiences have
been dissipated. It is characterized by a conscious straining to
master the art, to achieve greater heights of ecstasy, to evoke
ever more intense responses in one's partner—in a word, to *do
better.* Rollo May sees this as a kind of neopuritanism in which
we pursue sexual pleasure with a dogged determination akin to
that with which our Puritan ancestors worked to achieve maximum business profits. Time and again our interviewees, while
telling us that premarital intercourse had become increasingly
pleasurable for them, revealed a nagging concern with performance and achievement. Here is how some of the younger men
sounded:

> MALE, 32, APPLIANCE REPAIRMAN: For a couple of years I was
> a real in-and-out type; I didn't know any better. I'd get all
> excited and just ride on through. But then I met this girl
> who taught me what it was all about. She would climb the
> walls when I touched her, and she let me know what it was
> that I did that got to her—and it was *her* enjoyment that got
> to *me.* Wow! Tremendous! It did more for me than my own
> pleasure ever did. I began to enjoy the playing with her
> even more than the intercourse, because I could see what
> I had the power to make happen, I could see that I was
> becoming a good lover.

> MALE, 25, GRADUATE STUDENT: I'd been balling for several
> years and I thought I was pretty good, and then I met an
> older girl and started in with her, and she said, "Hold it—
> I can see you have a lot to learn." I said, "Like what?" And
> she said, "You don't just charge in like that; you try to *create*

something in your partner." I felt stupid. I'd read about it, and I knew she was right, and I felt it was up to me to adapt and to improve. After a while I got much better at it and began to take some pride in what I could do.

MALE, 35, TRAVELING SALESMAN: I used to just get it done, and feel, well, that was another one! Then one time I said to this one girl that she was kind of dry, and she said that maybe I was in too much of a hurry, maybe I wasn't the great lover I thought I was. That started me wising up. I learned to put in my time first—and I also began to learn how to hold myself back for an hour or more of fucking and how to make a woman rise up higher and higher, and hit it again and again. I started perfecting myself, but it took years and years.

MALE, 28, AUTO MECHANIC: I've been reading up on it, lately, and trying things. Like I really work at getting the girl so hot before I stick it in that she's *ready!* And if I get in and she isn't ready, I make myself think about things like money problems, or I imagine I'm screwing some ugly old bag, and that takes the edge off my excitement. Since I've learned how to do that, I've had several girls tell me I'm quite a lover, I'm really good at it. I had one girl begging me to finish, after I'd made her come five times and she was exhausted and getting sore.

MALE, 33, ROCK MUSICIAN: Sometimes I'm really good; I can make a girl have orgasms until she's about half dead. But if I don't like the girl, or if I'm not feeling confident, it can be hard work—and sometimes I can't even cut the mustard, and that bothers me a lot when that happens.

MALE, 22, LAW STUDENT: I pride myself on being willing to do anything a girl wants me to do. Well, not *anything*—I wouldn't whip a girl, or let her whip me. But I'll do other things, even when I don't care for them. Like nobody's asked me to stick it up her behind yet, and the very thought makes me sort of sick, but I'd do it. But this one girl likes me to stick my finger in there, and I gladly do it for her, although I think it's a little disgusting.

Females, too, are frequently concerned about their own performance, even though they have none of the male's worry about potency and endurance. Typically, they wonder if they are "good" at it, compared to other girls, or seem free and passionate, or if their orgasms are as intense as they ought to be, or if they are doing all the things they should be doing. Here are a few comments which, though intended to portray joy in sexuality, reveal an underlying anxiety about performance:

FEMALE, 21, COLLEGE SENIOR: I can go on for hours. I might not even come, or maybe I'll come once and not again, but I could care less. I feel very giving and try hard to give my lover great happiness, and I think I succeed. The trouble is, men seem to be so hung-up about making the woman have an orgasm—so I often fake it, and go ape, and tell them they were fantastic.

FEMALE, 28, BANK TELLER: I wasn't much good at it, and didn't even know I wasn't. But a man I had an affair with for two years taught me how to move my body, how to feel my own rhythms and go with them and how to become aware of myself and him at the same time. It's a real art; it's something you have to study. I have always been open to suggestions, even when they frighten me—like my present lover wanted me to try anal, and I felt I really had to. It hurt and I didn't like it, and I asked him not to persist, afterwards. But at least I was willing to try it.

FEMALE, 24, LAW SECRETARY: When I was nineteen I overheard two men agreeing that some other girl was "a lousy lay." It made me wonder if I was a lousy lay and if my boy friend was just too polite to tell me, because sex wasn't a terrific thing for me, and that worried me. It was all sort of mechanical movement for me—no laughter, no craziness, no pure fun—because I felt I had to have an orgasm or he would think there was something wrong with me or with him. A fair amount of the time I did have one, but it was never easy.

FEMALE, 27, GRADUATE STUDENT: I had five lovers before I got married, and with all of them I felt very uptight about making love with the lights on, or about letting them go down on me or my doing it to them. But it bothered me that I felt like that, and I talked it over a lot with two of them, hoping to work it out and become a better and more exciting woman. Finally, I went beyond just talking and began to force myself to do the things I didn't like, and I gradually got used to them and they got easy for me.

FEMALE, 30, NURSE: A man I was going with got me to read several books on peak experiences and joy and that kind of thing. I had thought I was having a fine sex relationship with him, but this made me think differently—it made me feel inferior. I went through months of trying to be aware, and to let it all go—to blow my mind, to reach those peaks. Well, the sad truth is that I thought I was getting somewhere, but it was all a lot of bullshit. That affair was no good anyway. The man I'm seeing now likes the way I am, and so do I, and our sex life is just fine, without any effort to make it bigger than Bingo.

Closely related to this is another problem that the new freedom creates for a fair number of young people: They want sexual intimacy to be part of an emotional relationship, yet they have heard that it is old-fashioned and prudish of them not to be able to enjoy sex on a casual basis and for its own sake. This is related to the effort syndrome in that it understands sexual liberation to mean that one *ought* to be both able and willing to perform at any time and with anyone, regardless of the absence of feeling for that person. A number of our interviewees said things that suggest that this is a very real problem:

MALE, 26, ELECTRICIAN: While I was in the service I'd go into bars wanting to find a girl and get laid, but I'd want the girl to like me, so I'd talk to her and get really interested in her, and I'd find myself getting not just into a fucking relationship but something more. I'd begin to feel all screwed up about it; it wasn't what I wanted, which was just to ball someone without giving a damn.

FEMALE, 30, SCHOOLTEACHER: A lot of my friends, especially some commune people and some people in the drug scene, seem to be able to have sex without any involvement at all, just for the sheer physical thing, no delving into emotions or any of that. I wish I could do that—I've tried, but I can't get aroused, I can't feel a thing when I do. It's really ridiculous of me.

MALE, 24, GRADUATE STUDENT: I would say that for me, sex is definitely more satisfying with someone I care about—and still I feel a need to keep trying it out with other women I meet, women I don't even *like*. I can't understand it—I mean, have I got a Don Juan complex or something? If I like it best with the girl I'm seeing regularly, what makes me go to the trouble and expense of making it with other girls when I don't even enjoy it all that much with them?

FEMALE, 29, HOUSEWIFE: I had my first premarital affair when I was in college, and we really loved each other and the sex got very good over the course of a year. After we broke up I drifted into another thing with a man I didn't love at all, but I slept with him for weeks, and the sex was horrible for me. It wasn't his fault, it was mine; it was my hang-up.

From subjective evidence of this sort, we can draw only general conclusions about the increase in the enjoyment of premarital intercourse since Kinsey's time. But if we turn to objective and measurable acts, we get a different kind of evidence—devoid of internal response, but circumstantially convincing—that shows very definite increases in the overall incidence and frequency of premarital activity, and in the freedom that young males and females feel to use sensuous and exciting techniques that their counterparts of a generation ago avoided or used rarely and nervously. In the area of foreplay, for instance, Table 27 contrasts the extent to which four different acts were used

Table 27

Selected Techniques of Foreplay Used Premaritally:
White Males with More Than Grade-School
Education, Percents

	Kinsey[75] (adolescent to 25)	Present survey (18 to 24)
Male manual play with female genitals	91	90
Female manual play with male genitals	75	89
Fellatio	33	72
Cunnilingus	14	69

premaritally a generation ago and today.*The increase in the second technique is remarkable, and the increases in the third and fourth techniques are nothing short of astounding.

Similarly, there are very great increases in the percentages of single persons who use coital positions other than the conventional male-above posture. Kinsey published no data on premarital coital positions in his study of the male, but he did in his study of the female.[76] Comparing our own data with those in the latter, we find that our single people are at least twice as likely as Kinsey's were to make occasional to frequent use of such positional variations as female-above, on-the-side, sitting and standing. In some cases the increase is much greater: Rear-entry vaginal intercourse, for instance, is used with frequencies ranging from "sometimes" to "often" by 37 percent of our young single females, a six-fold increase over Kinsey's comparable sample. Anal intercourse was apparently so rare in Kinsey's time that, as noted earlier, he published no data on it; today, over one-sixth of the single males and the single females under 25 who have ever had coitus have tried anal intercourse, and 9 percent of the males and 6 percent of the females used it at least occasionally in just the past year.

As one would expect, there is also a clear-cut increase in the general frequency of premarital intercourse. For males the increase is significant, but not astonishing. In Kinsey's sample a little over half of the single males between 16 and 25 were having premarital intercourse, with a median frequency of about 23 times a year.[77]** Over three-quarters of our 18-to-24 single males were having intercourse, and their median frequency was 37 times a year. For females, however, the increase is not only significant but astonishing. A fifth of Kinsey's females were having premarital coitus between ages 16 and 20, with a median

---

*Here again we omit from Kinsey's sample those males with only grade-school education, since in our own 18-to-24 cohort we had no individuals with as little education. Elsewhere, it makes less difference; in the realm of oral-genital practices, however, Kinsey found very low incidences of experience in the grade-school males but considerably higher incidences at the high-school and college level. Had we included his grade-school males, the figures for fellatio and cunnilingus for his sample would have been even lower, exaggerating the change from his time to our own. It is impressive enough without such exaggeration.

**The above median of 23 for Kinsey's males does not include intercourse with prostitutes. There is no way to combine his data on intercourse with "companions" and with prostitutes; the combined median might have been either higher or lower by a few times per year. See Kinsey (1948), pp. 248, 250.

frequency of once every five to ten weeks, and a third of his women were having it between ages 21 and 25, with a typical frequency of once every three weeks.[78] In our own sample, two-thirds of the 18-to-24-year-olds had premarital coitus in just the past year, and dramatic as this contrast is, it understates the change, since our figure is a one-year activity record, while Kinsey's figures indicate any activity at all in five-year spans; even more impressive, the median frequency for our active females is a little over once a week, or anywhere from three to ten times the typical rates of young women a generation ago.

To sum up: Nearly twice as many unmarried males and two to three times as many unmarried females are having coitus in their late teens and early twenties as did a generation ago, with the males doing so about a third again as frequently and the females at least three times as frequently as their counterparts did.

Nonetheless, the social, practical and emotional obstacles are still real enough so that the median frequency for young single males is only about a fifth that of married males of the same age, while the median frequency for single young females is about half that of young married females. Marriage, as George Bernard Shaw so charmingly pointed out, combines a maximum of temptation with a maximum of opportunity.

Today's young single females are also a good deal more orgasmic than their counterparts of a generation ago. In Kinsey's sample only about half of the young females having premarital coitus had orgasms at all,[79] as compared with three-quarters in our sample; and a considerably larger proportion of our sample than of Kinsey's had orgasms in half or more of their coitus. In Kinsey's study the median frequency of orgasm for single women having coitus was about one every 20 weeks for females between 16 and 20, and one every six weeks for females from 21 to 25[80]; in our sample, single females of 18 to 24 who were having coitus were typically having more than one orgasm every two weeks.

But these are cold numerical abstractions; it is in the interview material that we hear young men and women speaking of premarital coitus in a way that suggests some of the freedom and joy it has begun to have. A small number are pure voluptuaries, delighted with their own ability to enjoy sex in a purely physical way:

MALE, 27, SALESMAN: What matters most to me is balling absolutely wildly with somebody new—real knockout stuff, really breaking through and getting *to* her, and getting the maximum possible turn-on for myself. I used to think, when I was eighteen or nineteen, that I enjoyed sex a whole bunch, but every year I've learned new things about women and about myself, and I can't get enough of it. The only thing I won't try is getting involved emotionally, because that would limit me, that would put an end to my way of life.

FEMALE, 22, SECRETARY: I started sort of slow, but I've learned a lot since I got going. I haven't had all that many men, either, but I just *love* sex. I used to have a man friend who would meet me for lunch and a quickie, and that was practically the wildest of all, because it was like anything goes; it wasn't love, it was just *passion!* I could go bananas, right out of my head, if he would just suck on my nipples a while, or use his tongue down below. I could come again and again from that alone. And me a nice Catholic girl! Or I was, once, and am I ever glad I'm not now!

But the predominant mood—at least of those young people beyond their first years of sexual experimenting—is a combination of pride and joy in the ability to have good sexual experiences, and a deep conviction that those experiences are at their best when they are part of a genuine, committed and essentially monogamous love relationship:

MALE, 24, PLANT SECURITY GUARD: I was so shy and naïve that I had made out only with prostitutes until I was twenty-one. I was a bum—spaced-out on grass, wasting my time, living like a hippie, all tied up in knots. But this girl, she was different, I could really talk to her. I got so interested in her that I shaved and cut my hair, and got my head straightened out and got a job. I started sleeping with her regularly, and she told me later that at first I was terrible, but that I had really come a long way. She taught me things, and I read up, and I got to feeling easier and freer, and it just got better and better. I do things now—and love doing them —that I used to think were for perverts only. Upside down, in the shower, doggie—you name it. Only thing I don't like is her going down on me; it makes me feel ashamed or something. But anything else is okay, and I guess that's because she and I are a thing, a real thing. We've been talking about marriage, but it wouldn't be much different from what we have now, living together and all.

FEMALE, 29, HOUSEWIFE: I slept around a bit before I was married, but with every fellow I tried I felt dirty. I hardly ever came, and even when I did, it didn't make me feel any better. I'd find myself hating each new man after the second or third time. But then I had some therapy, and I met this older man who was genuinely kind and loving—he was married, but that didn't matter, because it was so real and important—and with him sex was exciting and completely satisfying for the first time in my life. And even though I wasn't married to him, I never felt dirty. I felt beautiful.

MALE, 24, CARPENTER: I'd had all the usual growing-up things—back-of-the-car, making out on the living room couch, even sometimes staying over in a motel. And I knew some of it was poor but I thought some was great—only I didn't know what great was. Because I've been going with a girl for a year, now, and with her everything we do is special, and very powerful but very sweet at the same time. I'm not just in there to have myself a time—I'm making *love* to her, and she to me, and we really get so close you wouldn't believe it.

FEMALE, 23, GRADUATE STUDENT: He's only the second man I've ever slept with, although I began five years ago. The first one lasted four years, and the sex in it got quite good because he was terribly at ease about it and I picked up his attitude. But when it broke up, I went back to my high-school ways—nothing more than a little petting—because sex is very potent with me and I didn't want to risk letting anyone taint my feelings about it or hurt me. Actually, I did take somewhat of a chance the second time around, not waiting for it to be love but sleeping with him as soon as I felt he was genuinely interested in me and would deal with me honestly. And it was only *after* we started sleeping together that the relationship developed real depth—much more than my first affair—and the sex, as a result, has become much more satisfying than ever before. There isn't anything we don't feel free to do, and we stay with each other—he at my place, or I at his—four or five nights a week, and have sex nearly every night, and both look forward to Sundays, when we sometimes like to spend the whole afternoon smoking a little pot, and sipping wine, and making love, and listening to music, and making love again. Sometimes I have two or three orgasms in one session—that's something new, for me—because he's tremendously experienced, and I'm getting that way myself, and besides, it's a relationship with a future.

These several statements suggest the complexity of premarital sexual behavior today for the great majority of young people, and the mixture of concern and pride, of sensuality and emotional sincerity, of egocentrism and sharing that characterizes it. While some of the young and near-young singles stress the purely physical aspects of sexual liberation, far more of them speak of the special meaning sex has in a caring relationship, and the great majority of them have had their best sexual experiences with partners they love. The sex ethic of the great majority of single people today, including the youngest single people in our survey sample, is essentially liberal-romantic; the much touted philosophy of recreational sex remains definitely the choice of the minority.

MALE, 33, COLLEGE INSTRUCTOR: *Both my wife and I are terribly old-fashioned, but since being married our ideas about sex have changed a lot, partly from maturity but largely from the influence of the common culture—all the things one reads and hears about . . . Recently we saw a rerun of I Am Curious, Yellow, and came home and promptly tried out a position we had never thought of before.*

FEMALE, 45, BLUE-COLLAR HOMEMAKER: *After we'd been married a while, we felt there was a lot happening that we didn't understand, so I asked my husband if him and I should try to read up on it. So he went out and bought three books, and through them we found all different ways of caressing, and different positions, and it was very nice because we realized that these things weren't dirty.*

MALE, EARLY THIRTIES, LAWYER: *What with the children, and my responsibilities in my practice and my political activities, it's down to a couple of times a week. Also I would say that my wife isn't an ideal sexual partner—she's not as committed to oral sex as I would like, for one thing. . . . But I myself am not the world's greatest lover, because I just can't find the time or energy to work on it.*

FEMALE, 34, MIDDLE-CLASS BLACK: *Even now I still want it to be only at night, and with the lights out. . . . Sometimes I enjoy sex, sometimes not, but I always accommodate him. I like it fine, really, but I myself don't have an orgasm very often, and even when I do, there just isn't that strong physical whatever that my husband always seems to feel.*

MALE, MIDDLE-AGED, APPLIANCE DEALER: *I love my sex, and I've got a wife that loves it just as much as me. Our first five years of married life it was every day . . . Nowadays, even after twenty years of marriage, it's still about three times a week. . . . We'll lay on the couch watching TV and playing around with each other and half forgetting about the show. We'll carry on like that, laughing and horsing around, for half an hour or more, and then go to bed and get the bodies together, and it's tremendous.*

FEMALE, LATE TWENTIES, COLLEGE-EDUCATED HOMEMAKER: *We had varied our lovemaking before marriage, but in the first few years of marriage we varied it a lot more, and tried out many new things. We kept some, and dropped others . . . Sometimes there's a lot of foreplay, sometimes not, depending on the mood we're in. We both like oral acts very much. . . . We've tried just about everything possible, including my sitting up on him with my back towards him. We even use anal intercourse, although everything has to be just right. . . . We have sex less frequently now than we did seven years ago . . . [but] it's lots more exciting because of the familiarity and ease of it. . . .*

CHAPTER

4

Marital Sex

The Western Tradition Concerning Marital Sexual Pleasure

Every human society has forbidden sex between at least some kinds of partners, and sexual relations in all but one kind of partnership have been forbidden by at least some societies. The one universal exception, the one partnership within which sexual activity is everywhere deemed acceptable, is the husband-wife relationship.[1] But the universal acceptability of marital sex is not at all the same thing as universal freedom for husbands and wives to seek maximum enjoyment from their sexual activities; the social legitimacy of marital coitus does not necessarily signify the emotional legitimacy of pleasure. Accordingly, even though marital coitus has been approved everywhere, there are great variations, from society to society, in the precise sexual activities permitted to husbands and wives, in the inner feelings accompanying those activities and in the kinds of satisfaction they have obtained from their physical relationship.

Western civilization has long had the rare distinction of contaminating and restricting the sexual pleasure of married couples more severely than almost any other. From the beginnings of Christianity, marital sex was viewed not as a positive good, nor as a joy to be made the most of, but as an unavoidable lesser evil, preferable only to the far worse one of sex outside of marriage. Saint Paul formulated the doctrine in his *First Epistle to the Corinthians.* "I would that all men were even as I myself [*i.e.*, celibate]," he wrote. ". . . I say therefore to the unmarried and widows, it is good for them if they abide even as I. But if they cannot contain, let them marry: for it is better to marry than to burn." Later, various fathers of the church carried this antihedonistic and antisexual philosophy much further: Even marital sex, they said, was sinful if it was thoroughly enjoyable. In the 3rd Century A.D., for instance, Clement of Alexandria warned that married coitus remained sinless only if delight was restrained and confined, and in the 5th Century Saint Jerome asserted that "he who too ardently loves his own wife is an adulterer." By the 7th Century it was established church dogma that married intercourse was so incompatible with spiritual exercises that husbands and wives must abstain from sex for three days before taking communion. The same church that had made marriage a holy act thus characterized the essential sexual part of it as an unholy, even though permissible, lapse from purity.[2]

Such was the view that pervaded Western society and severely restricted the ability of men and women to take pleasure in married sexual relations. Although somewhat mitigated during periods of liberalism or learning, it remained generally dominant until modern times; indeed, in America in the late 18th and the 19th Century, its blighting effect was particularly strong, being intensified by the prudish middle-class view of the "good" woman as ethereal, passive and far above having any lustful or passionate feelings. Women's liberationists often assert that this view was part of the apparatus of male dominance, and that it was deliberately promulgated by men to keep women subordinate and enslaved, but although it may indeed have helped to do so, men did not consciously create it for that purpose. Its roots lay not in male dominance but in middle-class puritanism and the fundamentalist explanation of sin, which dichotomized womanhood into sinner and saint, Eve and Mary, whore and mother, minion of Satan and handmaiden of Christ. Besides, in many a non-Christian society, wives, although thoroughly subjugated, were quite capable of being highly sexual and passionate in marriage, these qualities being highly praised in them by men, as is apparent from even the most casual inspection of such classic Near Eastern marriage and sex manuals as the *Kama Sutra* and *The Perfumed Garden of the Shaykh Nefzawi.* In any case, even if the Christian-bourgeois view of woman helped keep her enslaved, it cost her oppressor dearly; he may have the right to enjoy her favors whenever he wished, but it was the right to relieve himself in a silent, inert, unresponding and unseen receptacle (inky darkness being the rule), who did her "conjugal duty" by allowing him to "take his pleasure."

Some wives, nonetheless, did enjoy sex, particularly (if we may trust playwrights and satirists) those wives of the very highest and the very lowest social levels. But in the 19th Century the majority of middle-class and working-class women found intercourse only tolerable at best, and a substantial minority regarded it as revolting, messy, vulgar, animalistic, shameful and degrading. Dr. William Hammond, an expert on sexual matters and onetime surgeon-general of the United States, asserted in a widely used medical textbook that, aside from prostitution, it was doubtful that women felt the slightest pleasurable sensation in one-tenth of their intercourse.[3] No reliable survey data on the matter exist, but at the end of the century many of the best-informed American and European doctors believed that female frigidity was widespread and perhaps even prevalent, their estimates of its incidence in American and European women running anywhere from 10 to 75 percent.[4]

But during the early part of the 20th Century the liberation and legitimation of human sexual enjoyment—even by the female—got under way. Freud opened up to view the hidden interior of human desire; women started struggling out of their bonds of helplessness, subservience and purity; and marital intercourse began to be viewed as a positive and healthful activity rather than a shameful and somewhat debilitating indulgence. Liberal doctors, scholars and feminists—Havelock Ellis, Ellen Key, Marie Stopes and Theodor Van de Velde, among others— argued for long and careful wooing of the wife by the husband, praised the aesthetic aspects of varied techniques of lovemaking and preached the emotional and physical importance of mutual orgasm.[5]

In the 1930s and 1940s, when Kinsey was doing his fieldwork, writers and social critics ranging from Sinclair Lewis to Philip Wylie were still scornfully portraying the typical American marital sex act as a crude, hasty, wordless Saturday-night grappling. But Kinsey's data partially gave them the lie; his figures proved that the early phase of sexual liberation had already had a considerable ameliorating effect. The younger married women in Kinsey's sample, for instance, were having somewhat less marital intercourse, at any given age, than older women had had at that same age, undoubtedly because wives' own wishes were beginning to count, but at the same time the percentage of such intercourse resulting in female orgasm was climbing, with something like a fifth more of the younger women than the older ones having orgasm most or all of the time, in any given year of married life.[6] At almost every age, in almost every stage of marriage and in nearly every detail—the degree of nudity during intercourse, the kinds of foreplay used, the use of positional variations—the differences between the older and the younger generation, though not large, were consistently in the direction of greater freedom, pleasure and mutuality. The beginnings of sexual egalitarianism and the legitimation of pleasure were changing marital sex as nothing else had in nearly two millenia.

Everything we have seen thus far in this survey points to the fact that since Kinsey's time those liberating forces have vastly increased in power. Accordingly, sex within marriage should now be far more sensuous, uninhibited and mutually satisfying; yet today there seems to be more and harsher criticism of married sex than ever. Many of the shriller voices in the women's-liberation movement portray married intercourse as male-chauvinist exploitation of the female body, with husbands being clumsy, hasty, brutal and selfish, and making no effort to delight or satisfy their wives, let alone consider, in the first place, whether their wives wish to be made love to. Many sexologists, moreover, have made sweeping statements about the prevalence of sexual incompetence or inadequacy in contemporary marriage. Masters and Johnson, for instance, have repeatedly said—while admitting it to be only a guess—that perhaps 50 percent of all American marriages suffer from sexual dysfunction of one sort or another.[7] Critics of monogamous marriage, and advocates of extramarital relations, have in increasing numbers scornfully portrayed married intercourse as stereotyped, dull and constricted, and nonmarital intercourse as varied, exciting and free.[8]

But our survey data appear to contradict this picture of contemporary married sex. They do not lead us to deny that there is still male chauvinism in many a marriage bed, or that many married people have sexual problems, or that for many people married sex eventually becomes overfamiliar and unexciting. They do, however, lead us to dispute the charge that these negative aspects of married sex are more prevalent or severe today than formerly (we believe, in fact, that the opposite is true), and to disagree with the assertion that they are the predominant and essential characteristics of contemporary marriage. How, then, is one to explain the widespread criticism of married sex? The answer, we think, is that the progress our society has made toward fuller and freer sexuality has revolutionized our expectations and made many of us so intolerant of our dissatisfactions that we forget the improvement that has taken place in our lives; like all partially liberated people, we are more discontented now than we were before our lot began to improve.

Yet improvement is widespread and real. The present survey, as we are about to see, indicates that since Kinsey's time marital sex in America has become a good deal more egalitarian (with husbands being more considerate of their wives' needs, and wives assuming more responsibility for the success of intercourse); that husbands and wives are much freer in terms of the kinds of foreplay and coital positions they use; that the conscious pursuit of sensuous pleasure in marriage has become much more acceptable to both sexes; and that there is a considerable increase in the percentage of marital sexual experiences that yield genuine satisfaction to both persons.

Contemporary Forces Tending to Liberate Married Sexual Behavior

Indeed, one could argue that the principal effect of sexual liberation upon American life has been to increase the freedom of husbands and, even more so, of wives to explore and enjoy a wide range of gratifying sexual practices within the marital relationship. Most discussions of sexual liberation concentrate upon its meaning for the unmarried, the unfaithful and the unconventional, but by far the largest number of people whose sexual behavior has been influenced by it are faithful (or relatively faithful) husbands and wives. All those social developments which have made male and female expectations of sex more nearly compatible, which have emancipated men and women from the guilt and inhibitions generated by fundamentalist religion, and which have broadened the average person's repertoire of sexual acts have affected sexual behavior within marriage as much as outside it, for marriage is not an enclave, impervious to outside influences, but a porous thing, penetrated through and through by the currents of the social milieu.

The most obvious of the openings through which external influences enter marriage is, of course, the sum total of attitudes and experiences that the partners bring with them at the outset. We have seen that the sexual attitudes of most young unmarried persons have become much more permissive in recent years, that this has brought about an increase in the amount—and an improvement in the caliber—of premarital sexual experience, and that while the overall change has been greater for females, it has been substantial even for males, especially those of the educated middle class. It would seem obvious that for a large proportion of younger married adults the difficulties of achieving sexual adjustment in marriage must have been reduced and that the range of sexual practices acceptable within most marriages must have been broadened.

Some experts have disputed the beneficent influence of premarital experience; in fact, a number of minor studies have shown small positive correlations between premarital sexual conservatism—specifically, virginity in females—and successful marriage, and a few sociologists and marriage researchers, among them Harvey Locke, Paul Popenoe, Ernest Burgess and Paul Wallin, have therefore held that premarital sexual experience does little or nothing to promote marital sexual adjustment or marital happiness.[9] But men and women with generally conservative attitudes are very likely to have different expectations of marriage from men and women with generally liberal attitudes, and marriages that the former rate "successful" or "happy" might not seem so to the latter. Similarly, most of the survey data on sexual adjustment come from self-appraisals, but the severely inhibited man or semifrigid woman is apt to term his or her married sex life satisfactory if it involves minimal demands and yields modest rewards, while the more liberated man or woman would probably view such a sex life as disappointing and perhaps even as a severe deprivation.

If we turn to objective and quantifiable activities rather than subjective self-appraisal, we find impressive evidence that successful premarital sexual experience does, indeed, bear a positive relationship to married sexual satisfaction for the wife and hence, inferentially, for the husband. Terman, Burgess and Wallin, and Kinsey all reported positive correlations between premarital orgastic experience for the woman and her orgastic regularity within marriage.[10] Kinsey, for instance, found that 57 percent of the females who had had 25 or more coital orgasms before marriage were having orgasms nearly all the time even in the first year of marriage, as compared with 29 to 44 percent of the females who had had no premarital coital experience.[11] Such data, alone, do not prove that the prior experience is the cause of the later success, for it could be that innately responsive females are more receptive to premarital experience and, by the same token, more responsive within marriage. But Kinsey, anticipating this argument, pointed out that for most females orgastic capacity develops only with years of experience, so that premarital experience tends to shorten the time necessary to achieve sexual success within marriage—a crucially important point, in view of the fact that more marital breakups occur in the first and second years of marriage than any subsequent ones.[12]

Whether or not women had had premarital coitus, however, Kinsey found their orgastic regularity increasing with the duration of the marriage, and continuing to improve even up to the twentieth year of marriage, a phenomenon most experts attributed to such internal processes in the marriage as the growth of intimacy and trust, growing familiarity of the partners with each other's physical needs, the slow wearing away of inhibitions, and the growing willingness of the wife to learn from the husband and to make little experiments at his suggestion. Today, however, the continuing improvement of the marital sexual relationship, though it still owes much to these internal factors, also owes a good deal to various external ones. For one thing, nowadays it grates on many a female to have her husband appropriate the role of teacher and innovator; she is willing to have him do so sometimes, provided he plays the role of pupil and follower at other times. In an egalitarian relationship, each partner is a source of suggestions and innovations, and with the society around them having become so permissive about the publishing, portraying and discussing of details of sexual technique, each partner has easy access to information and stimuli. A generation or more ago it was almost always the husband who suggested some novel activity—rear-entry coitus, say, or fellatio, or watching the action in a mirror—often to the alarm of the naïve wife, who feared her mate might be giving voice to some perversion or abnormality. Today the young wife is as likely as her husband to have heard and read about these and even far more fanciful novelties, thanks to the bumper crop of best-selling sex manuals, candid magazine articles and erotic novels, and to the new openness of talk about such things among her peers. Moreover, she is nearly as likely as her husband to regard such things as normal, intriguing and worth trying. What young males, and to a greater extent young females, may not have known at the outset of marriage, they no longer must discover for themselves or do without; indeed, they can scarcely avoid learning from the outside much of what was known to the ancient writers on the amorous arts, and a good deal that would have astonished even those venerables.*

All of this tends to liberalize the attitudes of both partners in marriage, to increase their repertoire of physical acts and to bring them closer to each other in their expectations and requirements. The sex manuals of the Van de Velde generation held that marital intercourse should always be "person-centered" (the term is Professor Reiss's)—that is, a primarily communicative and emotional act on the part of both partners, although in fact this was more typically the female attitude than the male one. Many of today's sex manuals pay only lip service to the communicative and emotional aspects of intercourse, stressing instead its earthy, sensuous, appetitive side—the "body-centered" attitude that used to be regarded as typically male. Male and female attitudes, as we measured them, still show some differences along this dimension, but our evidence suggests that American husbands and wives are moving toward a middle ground in which each can be both person-centered and body-centered, enjoying intercourse for both reasons at the same time, or, on occasion, for either one alone. This shift, we think, is due in considerable part to the continuing impact upon young married people of external influences and sources of information.

---

*We are unable, for instance, to find in the Hindu, Arabian or Chinese erotic guidebooks or in Japanese erotic art any reference to the use of edible substances applied to and licked off the genitals, the application of crushed ice to the genitals at the moment of orgasm, or analingus, although these are among the variations advocated in some contemporary sex manuals.

A number of items in our questionnaire survey indirectly indicate the impact of outside influences, but the most direct evidence comes from our interviews. Most of our middle-aged interviewees said that while they had recently become more permissive in their attitudes, their marital sex habits were too well established to be changed—and some of them candidly regretted that this was the case. But other middle-aged persons, and nearly all married persons under 35, said that books, magazines, films, erotic materials and discussions with friends had been important factors in expanding and liberating their married sex life. Here are a few typical comments:

FEMALE, 45, BLUE-COLLAR HOMEMAKER: After we'd been married a while, we felt there was a lot happening that we didn't understand, so I asked my husband if him and I should try to read up on it. So he went out and bought three books, and through them we found all different ways of caressing, and different positions, and it was very nice because we realized that these things weren't dirty. Like I could say to my husband, "Around the world in eighty days!" and he'd laugh and we'd really go at it, relaxed and having fun. Also, men talk about sex with each other, you know, and sometimes he'll come home and say, "Here's a thing I just heard about, and let's try it," and I'll say "Fine," and we do.

FEMALE, 28, BUSINESSWOMAN: By now, we have what I'd call a pretty wide range of specialties. We experimented even at the beginning, but we were pretty timid; it was reading and talking to friends that made the difference. We went through the *Kama Sutra,* and Henry Miller, and Frank Harris, and some of De Sade, and some of it was ridiculous, but a lot was eye-opening and stimulating. Even blue movies have sometimes given us an idea or two, although mostly they're just for laughs.

FEMALE, 37, WAITRESS: What changed our sex life was that a bunch of us girls on the same block started reading books and passing them around—everything from how-to-do-it sex books to real porno paperbacks. Some of the men said that that stuff was garbage, but I can tell you that my husband was always ready to try out anything I told him I'd read about. Some of it was great, some was awful—we just about wrecked my back, once, with this hassock bit—and some was just funny, like the honey business.

FEMALE, 34, TEACHER: All of a sudden, I kept hearing and reading about this multiple-orgasm thing, and I'd never realized before that it was normal. It sounded like the greatest, so my husband and I talked it over and decided to make a special try to see if I could. And I did, and wow! —I was really bowled over. He felt pretty proud of himself, too. We don't try for it as a regular thing, but whenever we do, it's really special.

MALE, 26, GRADUATE STUDENT: My wife was never willing to fool around as much as she now is. Not that we didn't have good, open sex, but in the last year she seems to have learned to *abandon* herself to it. I think this has come about from her exposure to other people's opinions—some of our friends talk quite openly about these things—and from reading things, like the Masters and Johnson studies, and even popular stuff like *The Sensuous Woman,* which is sometimes silly and overstated but makes a good case for itself.

MALE, 26, MECHANIC: My wife works, and at lunchtime she and all the girls talk about things, and she comes home one time and tells me she hears there's nothing like pornography for a turn-on. So I go along with it; I go out and buy an armful of stuff—mostly picture magazines—and bring it home. First, it embarrasses her, but then she gets to see it differently, and to like some of the things she sees. Same way with a stag film I borrowed and brought home to show her. Personally, I think it's good and wholesome; it stimulates and opens the mind.

MALE, 33, COLLEGE INSTRUCTOR: Both my wife and I are terribly old-fashioned, but since being married our ideas about sex have changed a lot, partly from maturity, but largely from the influence of the common culture—all the things one reads and hears about, the common coin, so to speak. Even a film can affect our life. Recently we saw a rerun of *I Am Curious, Yellow,* and came home and promptly tried out a position we had never thought of before—the one on the railing—and frankly, it seemed more trouble than it was worth, but we rather enjoyed making the experiment.

In addition to all the preceding milieu influences, which can be loosely termed didactic, there are three others worth mentioning that fall in somewhat different categories. The first is therapy; to be sure, most forms of therapy are partly informational, but primarily they involve conditioning and training. Clinics specializing in sex therapy, many of them patterned upon that of Masters and Johnson and using similar methods, have proliferated around the country; a survey by *The New York Times* in October 1972 located several dozen sex clinics in 20 cities, and many more must exist in other cities. The Masters-Johnson techniques have, however, had an even wider impact through the avenue of general-practice medicine and through the direct adoption, by readers, of the techniques of sex therapy described in their second book, *Human Sexual Inadequacy.*

The second special influence is that of contraception, which has achieved a new level of effectiveness and simplicity in recent years in three forms: pill, I.U.D. and vasectomy. Many millions of married couples have adopted one or another of these methods, and the simplicity and freedom from worry they provide has often brought new spontaneity and joyousness into married intercourse. Among the couples in our interview sample who were most enthusiastic about their sexual life were some who, desiring no more children, had sought the total security of vasectomy—and were dumbfounded at how much more excitement and delight they got from their sexual relationship as a result.

Finally, women's liberation has altered the sexual relationships of countless married couples—often for the better, sometimes for the worse. The topic is far too complex to be treated adequately here, but we must at least mention it because so many questionnaire responses reveal its influence. The beneficial effects have, in general, been an extension of those changes associated with the gradual emancipation of woman from her subservient, asexual, passive 19th-Century image. The harmful effects have come about in transferring to the sexual arena antagonisms and power struggles between husband and wife that have been exacerbated by the liberation movement. Even though a revision of the power balance between man and wife is often called for, the sexual relationship of the couple may suffer as a consequence. Many an angry woman gets even by deciding that her husband is a lousy lover and that she'll have no more of him except on her own terms; and many a man with traditional attitudes, alarmed or repelled by the new kind of woman, loses his drive or sexual self-assurance. Four out of five sexologists in a round-table discussion in the journal *Medical Aspects of Human Sexuality* held that impotence was definitely on the rise,[13] and a team of three psychiatrists writing in *Archives of General Psychiatry* recently identified a syndrome they called "the new impotence"—the failure of the male to function, as a result of the new assertiveness of women, which some men find so threatening that they cease being able to act as men.[14]

Even a liberated and reasonably secure male, furthermore, might well find at least one by-product of the women's-liberation movement too demanding for his taste. Psychiatrist Mary Jane Sherfey, borrowing loosely from Masters and Johnson and spinning her own version of prehistory, concocted a theory not long ago that all normal women are not only capable of multiple orgasms but that without some intervening force to stop them, they would all, by nature, be sexually insatiable. It was the male, says Dr. Sherfey, who forcibly suppressed female sexuality at the dawn of history to make civilized life possible (ungoverned, woman's sexual drive was too strong, impelling and aggressive to permit a settled family life) and who has kept telling woman ever since that she needs only one orgasm, if any, per coition.[15] As we have already noted, some militant feminists, finding this theory a powerful weapon against men, have written pridefully about the female orgasm potential and urged women to use fingers or vibrators to enjoy themselves without stint, rather than seek their primary gratification in marital coitus. But this can only seem an unhealthy and pathogenic view, except to those women who regard all marital intercourse, and marriage itself, as forms of enslavement by the male enemy.

Frequency of Marital Coitus a Generation Ago and Today

As we saw earlier, the Kinsey data show that the earlier stage of the liberation of women brought about a small but distinct decrease in the average frequency of marital intercourse. One might wonder, therefore, whether the later, and virtually explosive, stage of liberation of women that has taken place in the past decade has not greatly accentuated that trend and brought about something close to a sexual standoff within contemporary marriage. This is, indeed, the impression one gets from the writings of many critics and satirists of modern marriage. But critics and satirists, even if they are portraying something real, may be misled as to how widespread that reality is. To know whether what they see and portray is the general rule, we must turn to statistically representative survey data. Our own data tell a different story, contradicting both what the critics of marriage say and what the extrapolation of Kinsey's data seemed to forecast: We find that, by and large, contemporary marriages involve higher frequencies of marital intercourse than did those of a generation ago. With the smug assurance of hindsight, one can say that this was implicit in the Kinsey data. For although in his time the frequency of marital coitus was declining due to the wife's rising status and her growing right to have a voice in sexual matters, the regularity of her orgasm in marital coitus was rising due to a multitude of sexually liberating factors. This increase in orgastic reliability and overall sexual satisfaction eventually offset the forces that caused the initial drop in coital activity. Such, at least, is our interpretation of the data we are about to present in this and the next two sections of this chapter.

First, then, let us see exactly what has happened to the frequency of marital intercourse. In the past several generations a number of researchers have published estimates or survey data on this matter, but nearly all of the pre-Kinsey studies were based on small or special samples—patients in treatment, volunteer respondents and the like—or on groups covering too wide an age span to yield meaningful frequency data. The more recent studies are, in general, statistically more sophisticated, but because of the difficulty of gathering data in this area, they have often been based on what is most easily available, even when it is manifestly biased. A recent study published in the *Journal of Urology*, for instance, gives data on coital frequency based on information collected from 2801 male patients receiving urological treatment, over half of whom had prostatic hypertrophy or prostatitis.[16] But since it is highly likely that these disorders either made for unusual frequencies in them, or, conversely, were the result of unusual frequencies, these frequency data are a poor guide to normal behavior. Even the respected sociologist Robert Bell, seeking to gather data on the coital frequency of contemporary wives, sent out batches of questionnaires to colleagues in the field of family sociology, who handed them out at their own discretion. The returned sample—60 percent of the distributed questionnaires—is strongly biased in the direction of higher-educated employed women, and further distorted by the silence of the 40 percent who accepted questionnaires but decided not to tell about themselves.[17] Professor Bell's study is useful, within limits, but is hardly a reliable measurement of the changes in behavior of the general population since Kinsey.

For such reasons, the best comparisons we can make are those between our own data and those reported by Kinsey in his 1948 volume on the American male and his 1953 volume on the American female. Like Kinsey, however, we can repeat only what our respondents told us, which means that our data may involve subjective distortion—not outright lies, but underestimates or overestimates caused by the individual's feeling that he or she is having too little, or too much, coitus. Terman, Kinsey, Clark and Wallin, and Levinger have interviewed husband-wife pairs separately and compared their answers as to coital frequency: In some pairs, the spouses give different estimates, and when these estimates are correlated with desired frequency, it turns out that a partner who desires more coitus than he or she is having tends to understate the actual frequency, while one who desires less tends to overstate the actual frequency.[18] All who have researched this matter, prior to the present survey, agree that the bulk of such distortions lies in the direction of husbands wanting more intercourse than they were having, and hence giving lower estimates of actual intercourse than wives, and of wives wanting less than they were having, and hence giving higher estimates than husbands.

How much credence, then, can we put in data gathered in such fashion? Kinsey offered a careful analysis of male-female differences in estimates of frequency, based on interviews with over 700 husband-wife pairs. He found that most of them gave substantially the same estimates, and the differences in the remainder averaged out to be rather small.[19] It was, therefore, Kinsey's opinion that the averages derived from each sex were valid and reliable, even though slightly different. Clark and Wallin disagreed, but most other sex researchers have accepted

Kinsey's view and used his data. Recently sociologist J. Richard Udry and pediatrician Naomi M. Morris concocted an ingenious experiment that indicated that most females, at least, tell the truth about coital frequency. Udry and Morris, using a cover story to the effect that they were trying to correlate sexual behavior with hormone levels, obtained daily first-morning urine specimens from 58 female subjects plus reports as to whether or not the women had had coitus in the last 24 hours. They found, by microscopic examination of the urine specimens for spermatozoa, that the reports of coitus or no coitus were generally correct.[20]

All of which gives us good grounds for regarding the coital-frequency estimates of husbands and wives as reasonably trustworthy, even if slightly discrepant. Although the undersatisfied and the oversatisfied may distort their estimates somewhat, these people are in the minority; moreover, part of their distortions cancel each other out. The net result is that such distortions, though individually significant, have only a minor effect on the overall averages for all males and all females. If, therefore, we find that our data show consistent differences from Kinsey's, and of a magnitude considerably larger than the discrepancy between male and female averages, we can take this as evidence that significant change has taken place in the past generation.

And we do find such evidence. The data show that there has been an important, even historic, increase in the typical (median) frequency of marital coitus throughout the population. Convincingly, both husbands and wives report such increases. Moreover, the frequency is higher in every age group of each sex than for comparable groups in Kinsey's time.

It is hardly possible to overstate the importance of this finding and what it tells us about the net effect of the twin (and sometimes opposing) forces of sexual liberation and women's liberation. We present the data in detail in Tables 28 and 29 followed by our comments. The figures given in these tables are, of course, group averages and do not indicate the vast range of individual variation; among our 35-to-44-year-old males, for instance, the median rate of marital coitus is just under 100 per year, but some men in that group had intercourse with their wives only two or three times per year, and others several hundred times. Both of these are obvious extremes, but no one should take our group averages to represent norms to which all should seek to conform. We present both kinds of averages— means and medians—in Tables 28 and 29, since it is meaningful that both measures show increases since Kinsey's time. The means are the better measure of the total coital activity of each group, but tend to exaggerate the coital rate of the typical member of the group. The medians are better indicators of the typical frequency, since they represent the level of activity of the midpoint of a group, above which lie half the cases and below which lie the other half when ranked in the order of the frequency of marital coitus.

In the male table (Table 28) every 1972 mean and median is higher than the corresponding 1938–1946 mean and median, in many cases by anywhere from a quarter to a half—a very sub-

Table 28

Marital Coitus: Frequency Per Week As Estimated
*by Husbands, 1938–1946 and 1972**

| 1938–1946 (Kinsey)[21] | | | | 1972 (Present survey) | | |
Age	Mean	Median		Age	Mean	Median
16–25	3.3	2.3		18–24	3.7	3.5
26–35	2.5	1.9		25–34	2.8	3.0
36–45	1.8	1.4		35–44	2.2	2.0
46–55	1.3	.8		45–54	1.5	1.0
56–60	.8	.6		55 & over	1.0	1.0

Table 29

Marital Coitus: Frequency Per Week As Estimated
*by Wives, 1938–1949 and 1972**

| 1938–1949 (Kinsey)[22] | | | | 1972 (Present survey) | | |
Age	Mean	Median		Age	Mean	Median
16–25	3.2	2.6		18–24	3.3	3.0
26–35	2.5	2.0		25–34	2.6	2.1
36–45	1.9	1.4		35–44	2.0	2.0
46–55	1.3	.9		45–54	1.5	1.0
56–60	.8	.4		55 & over	1.0	1.0

*In both tables, Kinsey's data have been adapted by recalculating his five-year cohorts into ten-year cohorts to facilitate comparison with our own. The dates 1938–1946 and 1938–1949 refer to the years during which the interviews were conducted on which Kinsey's data are based; our own fieldwork was done, as indicated, in 1972. Our data are based on our white sample; as usual in making direct comparisons with Kinsey's data, we have omitted our blacks to make the samples more closely comparable.

stantial and remarkable change in a single generation. In the female table (Table 29) the increases are generally somewhat smaller but consistently in the same direction. The difference between the size of the increases shown in the male table and those shown in the female table is very likely due to an increase in perceptual accuracy by women. If, as we have suggested, the social emancipation of women in the past generation has made wives less apt to have marital coitus unwillingly than used to be the case, it would follow that they would be less likely to overestimate its frequency. If this is correct, then the increases shown in the female estimates must understate the change since Kinsey's time, since the 1938–1949 estimates were somewhat higher than reality, and the 1972 estimates closer to it. There is no corresponding reason to suppose that the 1972 estimates by males underestimate coital frequency any more or less than the 1938–1946 estimates. In any event, if we were to make the reasonable and conservative assumption that the actual truth lies about halfway between the averages derived from male estimates and those from female estimates, we would find increases in marital coital frequency of the order of magnitude shown in Table 30.

It thus appears that there has been a dramatic reversal of the decline in marital coital frequency that had taken place in the generation prior to the time of Kinsey's fieldwork. Since, as we have suggested, marital coitus today is very likely to represent the desires of both partners rather than of the husband alone, the rise in coital frequency must mean that, in general, today's wives find marital intercourse more rewarding than did their counterparts of a generation ago. As confirmation, we cite the fact that only about a tenth of our entire married female sample

Table 30

Marital Coitus: Frequency Per Week, Male and Female Estimates Combined, 1938–1946/9 and 1972

1938–1946/9 (Kinsey)		1972 (Present survey)	
Age	Median	Age	Median
16–25	2.45	18–24	3.25
26–35	1.95	25–34	2.55
36–45	1.40	35–44	2.00
46–55	.85	45–54	1.00
56–60	.50	55 & over	1.00

reported finding marital sex either neutral or unpleasant in the past year, and that even within this small minority, only a quarter said they would prefer less frequent intercourse with the spouse. In contrast, of the great majority of women who found their marital coitus mostly pleasurable or very pleasurable nearly three-quarters said the frequency was just about right, and a quarter would like it to be higher.

The general explanation of wives' increased appetite for marital coitus, it seems obvious, is that recent developments in sexual liberation have done much to rid women of those culturally created inhibitions, including the inability to convey their wishes to their husbands, that formerly stifled both desire and responsiveness. In addition, one other aspect of sexual liberation deserves special mention: This is the stimulative effect of printed and visual materials dealing with sex, which are now virtually omnipresent in daily life. Many of these materials not only convey new ideas but are meant to be erotically arousing. They succeed in the latter intent because sexual liberation has made most people more receptive to such stimuli than their counterparts of 20 or 25 years ago. Up to twice as many of the males and up to four times as many of the females in our sample as in Kinsey's say they can be sexually aroused by depictions of the nude body and by literature, pictures or film portraying sexual activities.[23] Interestingly enough, our data show that married females are much more arousable by erotic stimuli of various sorts, including out-and-out pornography, than are single females. This is probably because, despite the liberating developments of the past generation, erotic feelings still arise most freely, for most women, within the security of total interpersonal commitment. In any case, erotic stimuli of one sort or another are encountered anywhere from once a month to several times a week by more than four out of ten husbands and nearly three out of ten wives in the younger half of our sample—and according to studies made for the Commission on Obscenity and Pornography, each such exposure tends to increase the sexual activity between married partners for the ensuing couple of days.*[24]

---

*Even those females who deny being aroused by erotic stimuli may well respond with higher coital rates in the day or two after exposure. One study made for the Commission on Obscenity and Pornography found that many of the females who expressed disgust or annoyance when viewing pornographic films nevertheless had distinct clinical symptoms of arousal.[25] In Freudian terms, the ego disapproved but the id responded.

It is particularly noteworthy that the increases in coital frequency shown in Tables 28, 29 and 30 extend to older groups; sexual liberation, which in many ways seems associated with the young, is evidently having important effects throughout the population, making it possible for husbands and wives to remain somewhat more interested and active in marital coitus even after many years of marriage than used to be the case. The following are some of the factors probably associated with this shift:

—Increases in the variety of techniques used in foreplay and of positions used in intercourse (to be documented in the next section of this chapter) are keeping marital coitus more interesting.

—Sexual liberation has begun to counteract the puritan-bourgeois notion that sex is unsuitable and disgraceful for the middle-aged or elderly. Kinsey, Masters and Johnson, Isadore Rubin and others have shown that desire and physical capacity, though they wane with age (more in the male than in the female), do not disappear in physically healthy persons, except for psychological reasons, until late in the eighth decade of life.[26]

—Many older females used to lose interest in coitus because of the discomfort and irritation it caused after postmenopausal hormone deprivation had resulted in tissue inelasticity and in a lack of lubricating secretion. These postmenopausal changes are now easily controlled by estrogen-replacement therapy, and many women who once discouraged coitus are now continuing enjoyable coital activity with their husbands.[27]

Another interesting change revealed by the data is a shift in the nature of the discrepancies between the male and female estimates of frequency. In Kinsey's data, young females gave higher frequency estimates than did young males, while among older persons the opposite was true.[28] The explanation, valid at that time, was that young women wanted less than they were having, while older men were unable to provide as much as their wives wanted. Our own data show a very different picture: In the younger half of the sample it is the males, not the females, who give the higher estimates, though the reason can hardly be waning abilities (more likely, it is that liberated young females perceive their coital frequencies as lower than they would like). In the older half of the sample, desire and ability, on the part of both sexes, seem to be in accord, since there are no discrepancies whatever.

In Kinsey's time, education and occupational status, though they bore important relationships to the frequency of masturbation and premarital coitus, had little or no relationship to the frequency of marital coitus.[29] Nor do they today, according to our own data. Religion, on the other hand, did have an important relationship to marital coital frequency in Kinsey's time, and still does. Kinsey reported that less-devout husbands had 20 to 30 percent more marital intercourse than devout ones because the latter carried over into marriage their premarital moral views of sex.[30] For females, however, devoutness did not affect frequency because, according to Kinsey, the male had more control over the frequency of intercourse than the female.[31] Today, religion is still an inhibiting influence on marital coital frequency, but few husbands—especially among the young—are now wholly or principally in control of coital frequency; devoutness in the wife is now likely to cut down on coital frequency, but paradoxically, devoutness in the husband, is not. Perhaps sexual liberation has affected churchgoing males more than churchgoing females; or perhaps the balance of power has been reversed. In any event, the curious figures are given in Table 31.

In sum, we find a considerable increase in the frequency of marital intercourse at every age level, as compared to the same age levels a generation ago. Apparently, it is not just the young and single who are currently having more active sex lives than their counterparts in Kinsey's time, but married Americans of every age. Sexual liberation has had its greatest effect, at least in numerical terms, within the safe confines of the ancient and established institution of monogamous marriage.

Table 31

Marital Coitus: Median Frequency Per Week,
by Regularity of Church Attendance,
Under-35 Males and Females

	Regular churchgoers	Non-churchgoers
Females' estimates	2.0	3.0
Males' estimates	3.0	3.0

Techniques and Duration of Foreplay; Positions and Duration of Coitus

Not only are today's married Americans having intercourse more frequently, but they seem to be doing so more imaginatively, voluptuously and playfully than their counterparts of a generation ago. One indication is that most married couples are spending more time in foreplay than comparable couples did in the 1940s, the increase being greatest among people at the lower educational levels, where foreplay had been minimal.

This is a notable departure from the past. The Christian doctrine that sex was meant strictly for procreation, plus the traditional view of less-educated males that swift insertion and swift completion were their proper goals, had made erotic play preceding intromission seem, to most lower-level men, either unnecessary, unnatural or immoral. Kinsey asserted that many husbands, particularly at the lower educational levels, indulged in only the briefest sort of body contact, plus a perfunctory kiss or two, before proceeding to intromission and coital movement, and that these males were apt to view oral-genital play and even mouth-breast contact with suspicion, scorn or aversion.[32] College-level males, however, being part of a more sophisticated tradition, were likely to have heard or read about the importance of mutual satisfaction, the contribution of foreplay to female orgasm, and the high regard in which foreplay was held in many other societies. Accordingly, as Kinsey reported in the 1948 volume, the average college-level husband was more likely to engage in precoital activity for anywhere from five to fifteen minutes or more.[33] Most of these males manually and orally caressed the female breast and manually stimulated the female genitals, and many of them at least sometimes orally stimulated the female genitals.[34] Females interviewed by Kinsey and his staff confirmed these findings, although according to the female data each form of foreplay was used in a higher proportion of marriages than the male data indicated.[35] There are several possible explanations for the discrepancy (all of which may be right). For one thing, Kinsey's male sample included more very low-level individuals than did his female sample. For another, the difference between the degree of male interest and female interest in the more adventurous forms of foreplay may have caused underestimation by the males and overestimation by the females. And for a third, in Kinsey's time a good many college-educated men married noncollege women, with the result that the marital experience of the latter tended to become more sophisticated than that of noncollege married males.

In brief, Kinsey's findings were as follows[36]:

—Mouth-breast contact was rarely or never used in marriage, according to about four-tenths of the males with at least some high school but no college education and according to one-tenth of the females at the same educational level.* At the college level the percentages of those who said they rarely or never used it were only half as large, for each sex.

—Manual stimulation of the female genitals was rarely or never used in marriage, according to a fifth of the high-school-level husbands and a twentieth of the high-school-level wives. Among college-level people, again, the percentages reporting that this activity was rare or missing in their marriages were only about half as large for each sex. Manual stimulation of the penis by the wife was avoided by slightly to somewhat larger percentages, and here, too, the difference between educational levels was major.

—Cunnilingus and fellatio were totally avoided in marriage, according to the great majority of high-school-level husbands and according to half of high-school-level wives. At the college level, however, about four out of ten husbands and somewhat over half of the wives said they had used these techniques in their married sexual relations.

—Not only did Kinsey find that married men and women at higher educational levels were more likely than people at lower educational levels to have, at least occasionally, used each of the above and other techniques in their marital intercourse, but that at any educational level, younger married people were more likely than older married people to have done so.

The two parameters of education and age were predictive of future developments, since both were measurements of the leading edge of social change. Comparing our own data with

---

* The discrepancy between male and female estimates would be even greater if we included those males in Kinsey's sample who had had only some or little grade-school education. But since his female sample is deficient in persons at this level, as are both our male and female samples, we omit his grade-school males from this and the following comparisons.

Kinsey's, we find that every form of foreplay is now at least occasionally used in a larger percentage of marriages than in his time; that although the increases are largest among the young, they appear in all age groups; and that the noncollege and/or blue-collar segment of the population has come much closer to the college and/or white-collar segment of the population in its use of such practices.

In general, the more strongly an activity had been taboo, the greater the magnitude of the change. The increase in manual breast play, for instance, is small and limited to lower-level persons, since even in Kinsey's time this activity had been widely used by them, and had been all but universally used in upper-level marriages.[37] With mouth-breast contact, however, the changes are larger: Less than six-tenths of Kinsey's noncollege males said they frequently used this technique, as compared to over nine-tenths in our sample, while the percentages for college-level males rose from just over eight-tenths to just over nine-tenths.[38] Six-tenths to three-quarters of Kinsey's males, depending on educational level, said their wives touched or caressed their penises[39]; in our sample, over nine-tenths at each educational level said so. In every case the female data, though higher to begin with in Kinsey, showed changes in the same direction.[40]

But the most dramatic changes are those that have occurred in the formerly all-but-unmentionable oral-genital acts (which, incidentally, are still classified as punishable "crimes against nature" in the statutes of most of our states). We offer the comparisons in Table 32, but with two preliminary caveats. First, the discrepancies between the data derived from Kinsey's high-school males and those derived from his high-school females are quite large; in trying to gauge the change from his time to our own, we cannot rely solely on his male data, which probably exaggerate the change, nor on his female data, which probably understate it, but should look for the truth somewhere in the middle ground. Second, the comparisons of Kinsey's data with our own considerably understate the dimensions of change because his incidences of the use of oral-genital techniques are based on the number of persons who said they had *ever* or *on occasion* used them in marital sex relations,[41] while our own represent percentages of persons so using them *in just the last 12 months.* Had we accumulated data as Kinsey did on this point, our own figures would undoubtedly have been a good deal higher.*

With these qualifications, Table 32 presents our measurements of change since Kinsey's time in the incidence of oral-genital foreplay in marital sex relations.

Even if, for the sake of conservatism in interpreting the comparisons, we were arbitrarily to rely on Kinsey's female data, we would find a considerable increase in the incidence of oral-genital practices in married sexual behavior between his time and our own. If, more reasonably, we take the reality in his time to have lain roughly halfway between the data he derived from male interviews and those he derived from female interviews, we can only conclude that the increase has been of major and historic proportions—and even these figures, for reasons we have

Table 32

*Oral-Genital Foreplay Used in Marital Sex Relations:
by Educational Level, According to Married Males
and Married Females, 1938–1946,[42] 1938–1949,[43] and 1972*

	Percents of marriages in which fellatio is used		Percents of marriages in which cunnilingus is used	
	1938–1946 (Kinsey)	1972 (Present survey)	1938–1946 (Kinsey)	1972 (Present survey)
High-school males	15	54	15	56
College males	43	61	45	66
	1938–1949 (Kinsey)	1972 (Present survey)	1938–1949 (Kinsey)	1972 (Present survey)
High-school females	46	52	50	58
College females	52	72	58	72

---

*A third but minor caveat: Our breakdown by education does not permit us to extract blacks from the sample offered here, and since other survey data indicate that blacks are less accepting than whites of oral practices, the figures in Table 32 further understate the contrast between Kinsey's time and the present.

For the record, the comparisons between white and black active incidences of oral-genital activity in our sample are as follows:

Fellatio, last 12 months, percents		*Cunnilingus, last 12 months, percents*	
Married white females	60	Married white males	63
Married black females	50	Married black males	49
Single white females	67	Single white males	72
Single black females	48	Single black males	35

already given, understate the dimensions of the change. It seems undeniable that by 1972 both fellatio and cunnilingus had become part of the repertoire of sexual practices used within marriage by a majority of high-school-level Americans and by a large majority of those with at least some college education.

In the younger half of the college-level sample, the 1972 figures are even higher than those shown above. More than four-fifths of males and females under 35 used each of the oral practices in just the past year in their marital relations. Among the under-25 married males and females, even including those without college education, over nine-tenths of both the males and the females experienced both fellatio and cunnilingus with their mates during the past year. One can hardly doubt that within a generation there will be almost no American marriages, at any age level, where these two practices will not be used anywhere from occasionally to frequently.

The growing freedom to use formerly forbidden techniques of erotic arousal apparently extends, though in a small way, even to those most strongly condemned practices that involve the anus. Touching or probing the anus with the fingers or contacting it with lips or tongue was so rare and was viewed with such general revulsion and suspicion a generation ago that Kinsey failed to collect anything publishable on the incidence of such practices. In recent years, however, American males and even, to some extent, females have become relatively willing to admit that they find the buttocks sexually exciting—and finally the truth has begun to appear: that it is the most secret and sensitive part of that area that is the focal point of that sexual interest. Anal foreplay is now openly discussed—with qualified approval —in some contemporary sex manuals, and attitudes toward it, especially among younger persons, have undergone a rapid change from abhorrence and condemnation to neutrality, acceptance and even curiosity. Half of our younger married respondents indicated that they would find manual-anal foreplay, either as active or passive participants, acceptable with someone they loved, and over a third said they would find even oral-anal foreplay, in either role, acceptable under the same circumstances.

Although we failed to inquire whether such practices were used by our married respondents in the past year, we did find that well over half of the under-35 males and females in our sample have at least experienced manual-anal foreplay at some time or other, and over a quarter have experienced oral-anal foreplay. Since our single sample shows much lower incidences for the same age groups, it is clear that most of the accumulated anal-erotic experience of our married respondents occurred within marriage rather than before it. Only about half as many people in the 35-and-over half of our married sample have ever had either kind of experience, actively or passively. The percentages were smallest of all for those taking the active role in oral-anal foreplay: Only 11 percent of the 35-and-over females and 13 percent of the 35-and-over males have ever done so.

In our interviews we heard much that indicated the existence of qualitative differences, at least as important as the quantitative differences indicated above, between the way the younger and older people use oral-genital, manual-anal and oral-anal techniques. Among our older interviewees there were a number who, after a party at which they drank a good deal, or after some erotically stimulating event, might occasionally use fellatio, cunnilingus or even anal play, though ordinarily they felt squeamish about such acts or hesitant about suggesting them to their spouses. In contrast, most of the younger interviewees spoke as if they thoroughly enjoyed oral practices and took them as a matter of course, including them very frequently and naturally in their foreplay; a substantial minority, moreover, said that they also used manual-anal play anywhere from occasionally to fairly often. Oral-anal play, on the other hand, was rare and infrequent even among the younger interviewees, although the sample size was too small to permit more than an impressionistic judgment.

Another more precise measurement of the difference between age groups in the use of formerly forbidden practices was yielded by a questionnaire item asking what proportion of the time spent in foreplay was customarily given over to fellatio and cunnilingus. Among the under-25 men and women, six out of ten spent a quarter to half of their foreplay period in such activities, and two out of ten an even larger part of it. Among men and women of 45 and over, only two out of ten devoted a quarter to half of the foreplay period to oral-genital acts, and only about one out of twenty devoted more than that to them.

The increase in the use of such techniques of foreplay and in the amount of time typically devoted to them owes much to the general education of wives and (even more so) of husbands as to the usefulness of precoital activity in making coitus itself successful for the female. It is also attributable in part to the desire, now common to both men and women at almost all levels, to see themselves as sexually expert. But beyond this, liberation has undoubtedly given many people the internal freedom to relish such acts in themselves, practicing them not so much for utilitarian reasons as because they find them exciting and delightful.

In all likelihood it is for the same combination of reasons that the contemporary Americans we surveyed prolong foreplay more than comparable people did a generation ago. Precisely how much longer is hard to say, since Kinsey's figures on this matter are rudimentary. In the study of the female his figures suggest a median of about 12 minutes,[44] as compared to 15 in our own female sample; the increase is large enough to be significant. In the study of the male, however, Kinsey indicated that the foreplay of the less-educated husband was typically very brief, and that it was only the college-educated male who was likely to continue foreplay for as much as 5 to 15 minutes or more[45]; in our own sample the typical duration of foreplay, as estimated by noncollege men, is about 15 minutes—the same as for college-level men. Thus, there has apparently been a small increase in the typical duration of marital foreplay at the college level, but a substantial increase at the noncollege level, with husbands in the latter category now paying the same amount of attention to, or even taking as much pleasure in, foreplay as do upper-level men. In fact, while prolonged foreplay used to be most often a part of the courting and coital activities of unmarried persons, today it is equally a part of the sexual behavior of the married population: The median duration of foreplay for our single people under 25 is 15 minutes and of those age 25 to 34, is about 20 minutes, while that for married persons in both age groups is about 15 minutes.

While the difference between educational levels in the duration of marital foreplay has apparently vanished, and while differences along socioeconomic parameters such as religious devoutness and political orientation are inconsistent, we do find a consistent relationship between age and duration of foreplay, the youngest people prolonging it the most. The median duration of foreplay in the younger cohorts is as much as a third

longer than that in the oldest one, according to both male and
female estimates. This is probably due to several factors: the
lessened energy reserves and lessened enthusiasm of older people, but also, in all likelihood, some residual inhibitions that
prevent them from luxuriating in foreplay activities to the same
degree as younger people.*

In their actual coitus, as in their foreplay, contemporary husbands and wives testify to having a good deal more freedom, in
terms of the positional variations they use, than did married
couples a generation ago.[47] In the sample as a whole, the female-
above position is now used, at least occasionally, by nearly three-
quarters of all married couples, as compared with about a third
of all married couples in Kinsey's time. More than half of our
sample said they sometimes or often use the on-the-side position, whereas formerly only a little over a quarter did so. About
a twelfth of Kinsey's sample at least sometimes used the sitting
position, as compared with over a quarter of ours. Rear-entry
vaginal intercourse was used by something over a tenth of Kinsey's sample, but by four-tenths of ours. Kinsey had found variations in position to be more widely used by college-level people
than noncollege people, but, as in so many other areas, we find
that, in general, during the past generation lower-level people
have adopted the attitudes and practices once largely limited to
upper-level people.

Every coital position, without exception, is used sometimes to
often by more of the people in the younger half of our sample
than in the older half. This again can be taken as an indication
of the future of married sexual behavior. But to see the age-
related differences more sharply, let us omit from our consideration all who use such variations sometimes or rarely, and look
only at those who use them often: In this sharper focus, the
contrasts between our various age groups are truly noteworthy
and provide outstanding evidence as to how far the younger part
of our population has moved away from believing the male-
above position to be the only right and proper one. Combining
our male and female data and, for simplicity's sake, looking only

---

*Masters and Johnson, and others who have concerned themselves with sexual func-
tioning of older persons, have made much of the need for longer and more inventive
foreplay in older persons to offset the decreased responsiveness of both their tissues and
their psyches.[46] As their research-based suggestions become more widely known, we
may find the typical duration of foreplay among older persons increasing.

at the youngest, the central and the oldest of our five cohorts, we arrive at the data presented in Table 33. Some of the variations listed in Table 33 have been described by some psychoanalysts as degrading to the woman (rear-entry, for instance), or as expressive of an abnormal need for domination by the female (the female-above).[48] But each of these variations has been popular in various cultures where neither degradation of, nor domination by, the female was involved. It seems apparent that much of the psychological denigration of such positional variations is a quasi-scientific justification of deeply felt religious and antisensuous traditions. Today's young Americans, however, seem to feel that almost any feasible position is perfectly acceptable and potentially exciting to both partners. Nevertheless, by and large, none of these variations has supplanted the male-above position; they have merely been added to the repertoire —except in a limited number of cases where, for anatomical or neurotic reasons, some variant position is the only one in which one partner or the other can achieve orgasm.

Anal intercourse can also be considered a variant coital position, although from a biological, evolutionary and medical viewpoint it is more than merely variant; it involves tissues, nerve structures and microorganisms that are far from ideal for the purpose of coitus, to say nothing of its potential aesthetic hazards. But the larger part of the objections to it have been based on religious and cultural taboo—a taboo so strict that, until very recently, the practice was rarely mentioned even in professional literature, and was alluded to only in indirect terms even in so daring a book as *Lady Chatterley's Lover*.[49] In the past few years, however, the subject has emerged so far from the shadows as to be discussed freely in medical journals and in some of the racier sex manuals, and in 1973 portrayed by Marlon Brando (in simu-

Table 33

Percents of White Married Sample Often Using Specified
Variant Positions in Marital Coitus, by Selected Age Cohorts

Position	18–24	35 to 44	55 and over
Female-above	37	29	17
On-the-side	21	15	15
Rear-entry (vaginal)	20	8	1
Sitting	4	2	1

lated form) in the prestigious X-rated film *Last Tango in Paris*. (It has, of course, also been portrayed of late in actuality in many hard-core films.)

Even so, we were surprised to find how many people are now using it within marriage. While only a few scattered individuals in the 45-and-over cohorts have done so at all in the past year, in the 35-to-44 cohort about a seventh have, and in the 25-to-34 and under-25 cohorts nearly a quarter have. Most of these said they used it rarely, but over 6 percent of the under-35 people did so sometimes or often. Whether one personally finds this practice appealing, neutral or repellent, the increase in its use does not, as some may think, represent the brutalization and abuse of wives by sadistic husbands, but generally a more or less free choice by both partners of something they want to do together.

Finally, we find an increase in the median duration of coitus of such magnitude as to make most of our other indicators of change pale into insignificance. While it is true that prolongation of the act has lately become something of a cultural ideal, it is doubtful that any large number of husbands and wives would regularly and effortfully prolong coitus merely because of a wish to measure up to that ideal. It seems much more probable that the increase in typical duration reflects the more relaxed enjoyment, greater mutuality and increased variety that now characterize marital coitus.

As we pointed out earlier, Kinsey presented no detailed data on the duration of coitus from intromission to completion, but in the chapter on marital coitus in the male volume he did offer the often-quoted estimate that perhaps three-quarters of all males reached orgasm in two minutes or less after intromission.[50] Dr. Abraham Stone, one of the best-known and most respected clinicians and sex counselors of that period, agreed with Kinsey. In the 1952 revision of his well-known book, *A Marriage Manual*, he said that on the basis of his own extensive observations he would put the typical duration of coitus with active movements at one to two minutes.[51]* Kinsey viewed the speediness of the typical male with approval. He said that despite the emphasis in marriage manuals on the value of delay and control, speed in ejaculating was a sign of biological superi-

---

*Dickinson and Beam, and Popenoe, had earlier estimated the typical duration of coitus at five to ten minutes, but their samples were strongly biased and limited in size.[52]

ority in the male, even if unfortunate for that male's wife.[53]

But fashions change and sexual liberation has altered the goal of coitus in the minds of most men. Nowadays the goal is as much to maximize the enjoyment of the whole act as to reach its peak moment. Prolonging the act is no longer an act of altruism, done only for the female's sake, but something done for the sake of both partners. Despite all that we have heard in the past about how difficult it is for many a man to hold back his orgasm, the typical duration of coitus has increased so remarkably that we can only suppose the larger part of the problem to have been mental rather than physical. We suggest that formerly the man's chief desire was to reach orgasm, and that he found control difficult to achieve because it conflicted with his real wish; today, having a somewhat different balance of desires, he finds the prolonging of coitus not a hardship but a delight, and thus is better able to do it.

Unfortunately, we cannot be precise about the magnitude of the increase in duration, for in the male Kinsey study the figures are only rough approximations, and in his female study there are none at all. Our own figures, however, are clear enough: The median duration, as estimated by both the males and females in our married white sample, is on the order of ten minutes— something like five times as long as Kinsey's and Stone's estimates.*

Most astonishing of all is the fact that we find no major difference in median durations at different educational and occupational levels. Indeed, noncollege and blue-collar men appear to prolong coitus even more than their college-level and white-collar peers, though the differences are too small to be significant. Differences due to other demographic factors were either minor or inconsistent, and even the religiously devout and the politically conservative reported typical durations of coitus two to four times the durations reported by Kinsey and by Stone.

Another noteworthy finding is that it is the younger married people who spend longer on coitus, and the older people who finish sooner. It has often been said that young men are too highly charged to be able to control themselves and that maturity makes men better lovers because it slows them down

---

*It is also longer even than the duration estimated from the biased samples of Dickinson and Beam, and of Popenoe. Terman, in 1938, on the basis of a sample of largely middle-class wives, reported an average (arithmetic mean) of 12 minutes[54]; our own comparable average is over 14 minutes.

biologically. But our data give us further reason to think that desire and intention may play an even larger part in the prolongation of coitus than physical condition. For males and females combined, our younger cohorts report a median duration up to three minutes longer than our oldest, with the medians for intermediate age groups lying in between. Even if arousal is slower and control easier for the older male (sometimes, indeed, he may not be able to reach orgasm at all), it would appear that nowadays the sexually liberated, thoroughly motivated young man can hold himself back, and possesses both the physical and psychic energy to outlast the older man, despite the urgency with which his autonomic nervous system seeks release.

Our figures are so much higher than Kinsey's—even using medians, as we do, rather than means—that we have searched for hidden biases in our study. We have found none of any significance, but think it likely that some unconscious overestimation has entered into some of the estimates, or perhaps even most of them, due to the high regard with which extended coitus has recently come to be held. Yet, if the exaggeration were gross we would almost certainly find it confined to the male data; females, if they got short shrift, would perceive the time as too short because of their lack of orgastic satisfaction. Since this is not the case, we think that the exaggeration of the time spent in coitus is a minor factor. We stand convinced that a dramatic and historic change has taken place in the practice of marital coitus in America.

Satisfaction with Marital Coitus, Desired Frequency, Desired Amount of Variation

We have taken the increases in the frequency and duration of marital coitus, and in the variety of techniques employed, to signify increases in the general level of sexual pleasure within marriage and in the general level of satisfaction with marital sex life. We want to confirm this interpretation, however, since it is at least possible that the "effort syndrome" referred to earlier (page 162), though more apparent among the single, also affects the married, increasing their technical accomplishments without actually heightening the pleasure they obtain from marital sex.

Unfortunately, most measurements of sexual pleasure and satisfaction with marital sex life must rely on subjective and imprecise self-evaluations. What one individual means when he or she says that his or her married sex life is "very pleasurable" may be very different from what another individual means by the same term. The problem is compounded when one tries to compare the average levels of sexual pleasure or satisfaction at two or more different times in history, for it is most unlikely that men and women of even one generation ago would have used precisely the same internal standards as men and women of today in evaluating the satisfactoriness of their marital sex relationship. Researchers encounter comparable difficulties in all studies of pleasure, satisfaction and happiness that are based on self-evaluations. Repeatedly, for instance, they find that most people rate themselves as somewhat happier than most other people—a statistical impossibility that tells more about how people like to see themselves than about the actual state of their emotional lives. One has only to recall the deathbed utterance of the 19th-Century essayist, William Hazlitt, whose years were filled with domestic discord, unrequited love, money troubles and ill health, but who said in all earnestness, as he lay expiring, "Well, I have had a happy life!"

Orgasm, however, is an objective reality—and according to our survey data, there is no doubt that today more wives are having orgasm in nearly all of their marital intercourse, and fewer are having it rarely or never, than was true in Kinsey's time. If this is so—and we will produce the data shortly—we feel that it is a direct and precise measurement of the increase both in sexual pleasure and in the satisfactoriness of marital coitus for wives. Moreover, given the general nature of marital and sexual interaction today, it at least suggests comparably increased pleasure and satisfactoriness of marital coitus for husbands.

Some experts, to be sure, have questioned whether female orgasm is in fact related to female sexual pleasure and satisfaction. They base their doubts on certain studies of marital adjustment made by Terman and several others, which show only very small correlations between female orgasm regularity and satisfaction with marital sex.[55] But the lack of something one does not expect or feel entitled to is not experienced as a deprivation, and most of these studies were made a generation or two ago, before the great majority of women came to consider orgasm regularity not only exceedingly important but something of a right. More recent studies have shown a very different picture: There is, in the minds of contemporary women, a very strong relationship between orgasm regularity and overall pleasure of, or satisfaction with, marital coitus. In the early 1960s, for instance, sociologists Alexander L. Clark and Paul Wallin studied a group of women who had been married for some years, and reported that two-thirds of those who had orgasm all or most of the time said they enjoyed marital intercourse very much, as compared with one-sixth of those who rarely or never had orgasm.[56] Robert Bell's recent survey of married women shows similar strong correlations,[57] as does our own survey.

Kinsey and many other investigators have reported, furthermore, that while some women adjust well enough to occasional or frequent failure to reach orgasm in coitus, many others feel not only a sense of failure but considerable distress, both emotional and physical.[58] Marriage counselors and clinicians have often sought to reassure such women that they need not have orgasm every time, or even most of the time, in order to have a successful sex life and a good marriage, and that the distress they feel when they fail to have orgasm is largely self-imposed and unnecessary. Masters and Johnson, however, have observed that there is a very considerable vasocongestion of the pelvic organs and tissues during sexual arousal, and that after female orgasm this dissipates in ten to twenty minutes, whereas arousal without orgasm results in prolonged pelvic congestion and concomitant sensations of fullness, discomfort and even pain, accompanied by restlessness, irritability and general malaise.[59] Thus, it is not only cultural conditioning and personal expectations that make orgasm regularity a major factor in how contemporary women feel about their sex lives; physiology plays a significant part. Masters and Johnson have, in fact, shown in some detail that the female responses to excitation and release are biologically much more akin to those of the male than had been realized[60]—yet no one would expect any male to consider his marital coitus enjoyable or satisfactory if he frequently or usually failed to have orgasm.

As female orgasm has come to be deemed important or even essential, explanations of orgasm failure have multiplied. Many Freudians maintain that the nonorgasmic woman is resisting her own female nature and her need for male domination. Some marriage counselors and writers of sex manuals blame orgasm lack on insufficient foreplay, or on the husband's failure to set a romantic mood, or both. Certain sex researchers and physiologists, stressing the importance of clitoral contact during coitus, urge the use of positions other than the male-above, or even recommend surgical operations designed to free or move the clitoris. Many sex experts, linking the female's failure to have orgasm to the male's speed in reaching his own, advise males to pause, to move slowly, to think of other things and so to succeed in delaying their climax. Some others, however, claim that contrived and deliberate slowdowns dampen the female libido even more than that of the male. The most elaborate and weighty recent study of the subject, *The Female Orgasm* by psychologist Seymour Fisher, suggests that an unconscious fear that males may desert or abandon them is what keeps some women from "letting go" of conscious control sufficiently to have orgasm, while more self-sufficient women, having no such fear, can relinquish conscious control and let themselves be overwhelmed.

Probably there is some truth in each of these explanations. Each accounts for the orgasm failure of special samples of married females, or deals with special factors that can sometimes cause orgasm failure in almost any female. The larger truth, however, is that frequent female orgasm failure has diminished over a period of several generations, even as all those broad social changes were taking place that elevated women from their socially inferior status, made contemporary marriage a partnership and intimate friendship of equals, and liberated men and women sexually and gave them a far greater capacity for guilt-free pleasure. Virtually all the special explanations of orgasm failure or success thus deal with intervening causes, not fundamental ones. The fact is that orgasm regularity has increased almost in direct ratio to the progress of the twin liberations— the sexual and the female—over a period of three generations.

Toward the end of the 19th Century, for instance, as we noted earlier, women had only just begun to emerge from their sequestration, and the study of sexual behavior had only just begun to dispel some of the Victorian fog. At that time some of the best-informed doctors in Europe and America estimated frigidity to be the lot of anywhere from a tenth to two-thirds of all women.[61] An article published in the *Pacific Medical Journal* in 1907 even went so far as to claim that in New York State, where

the writer had made his observations, no less than 75 percent
of married women were frigid.[62]

Such estimates, based on clinical samples, were only educated
guesses; nonetheless, they undoubtedly indicate a common or
general tendency in female sexuality at that time. But things
were changing: Not only did the first wave of women's emancipation culminate in women gaining the vote in 1920, with all
that that implied, but the first wave of sexual liberation was
having its major effect on women born in the second and third
decades of the century. The results were still minimal in 1929,
when Hamilton published his classic study of 100 wives and
found 46 percent of them to have "a very inferior or wholly
lacking orgasm capacity," and a few years later a larger-scale
study by Dickinson yielded similar figures.[63] But the females
born shortly before and during the 1920s were growing up
under altered conditions, and by 1938 Terman, in his classic
study *Psychological Factors in Marital Happiness*, found that two-
thirds of the wives he queried had orgasm usually or all of the
time, while only one-third had it sometimes to never.[64]

Terman's sample was composed largely of middle-class and
educated women, among whom the changes were taking place
sooner than they were among lower-class and less-educated
women. But by the 1940s, when Kinsey was doing the fieldwork
for his study of the female, a majority of wives at all social and
educational levels were having orgasm most of the time. Trans-
lating Kinsey's data into verbal terms—taking, for instance, orgasm in 60 to 100 percent of marital coitus to be roughly equivalent to such terms, used by other researchers, as "regularly or
fairly regularly," and "always or usually"—we can summarize
some of his key findings as follows:

—For the sample as a whole, half of all wives were having
orgasm regularly even during the first year of marriage. But
orgasm regularity increased considerably during the first ten
years of marriage, and to a lesser extent even beyond that point.
By the tenth year, 59 percent of all wives were having orgasm
regularly or fairly regularly, and by the twentieth year of marriage 64 percent were doing so.[65]

—Orgasm regularity was clearly related to decade of birth
(and thus to the phase of social evolution during which the
individual was growing up). In their tenth year of marriage, 53
percent of wives born before 1900, but 63 percent of those born

between 1910 and 1919, were having orgasms regularly or fairly regularly. A third of the older wives were still having orgasms rarely or not at all (0 to 29 percent of the time) in their tenth year of marriage, but less than a quarter of the younger wives were similarly limited.[66]

—Educational level showed consistent but small correlations with orgasm regularity, the better-educated women having a slight advantage. By the tenth year of marriage, for instance, 62 percent of the college-level wives, but only 57 percent of the high-school wives, were having frequent or regular orgasm.[67]

—Differences in parental occupational level were weakly correlated with orgasm regularity, the upper-level females having slightly higher rates at every stage of marriage.[68]

—Somewhat surprisingly, the degree of religious devoutness had little or no relation to orgasm regularity.[69]

It is difficult to make direct comparisons between our own data and Kinsey's, for ours do not permit a breakdown of orgasm regularity by length of marriage. In addition, we preferred to ask our respondents not for the precise percentage of marital coitions resulting in orgasm but whether they had it "always or almost always," "about three-quarters [or half, or one-quarter] of the time," or "almost never or never." First, therefore, let us present our own data; then we will make such comparisons with Kinsey's data as we can. Table 34 summarizes orgasm regularity for all white married women in our sample, irrespective of age or duration of marriage.* The figures show considerably more orgasm regularity than was the case in Hamilton's sample or Dickinson's, and somewhat more than was the case in Terman's.

Table 34

Proportion of Marital Coitus Resulting in Orgasm:
Married White Females, 1972

Orgasm frequency	Percent of wives
All or almost all of the time	53
About 3/4 of the time	21
About 1/2 of the time	11
About 1/4 of the time	8
Almost none or none of the time	7

*Once again, our exclusion of the black females is by way of making our sample as nearly comparable as possible to the earlier surveys and to Kinsey's.

Where something like half to two-thirds of the women in those earlier studies had frequent or regular orgasms, three-quarters of ours do so, and where a third to nearly a half formerly had few or no orgasms, less than a sixth of ours are similarly limited.*

Comparisons of our data with Kinsey's however, must take into account the duration of marriage. Since the median duration of marriage among all presently married women in our sample is 15 years, we can guardedly compare the figures in Table 34 to those Kinsey gives for women in their fifteenth year of marriage. The two measures, though not precisely equivalent, are close enough to give some indication of the dimensions of change (see Table 35). While the figures on the second line are only roughly comparable, those on the top line, and those on the bottom two lines combined, are rather closely comparable. They indicate that since Kinsey's time there has been a distinct increase in the percentage of women who always or nearly always have orgasm in their marital coitus, and a very

Table 35

*Proportion of Marital Coitus Resulting in Orgasm:
Married White Females, 1938–1949 and 1972*

1938–1949 (Kinsey[70]): females in 15th year of marriage		1972 (Present survey): females with 15 years median duration of marriage	
Orgasm frequency	Percent of wives	Orgasm frequency	Percent of wives
90–100% of the time	45	All or almost all of the time	53
30–89% of the time	27	About 3/4 to about 1/2 of the time	32
1–29% of the time	16	About 1/4 of the time	8
None of the time	12	Almost none or none of the time	7

*The pre-Kinsey samplings, however, were largely middle-class in makeup, while our own is broader in scope. Since the lower-level wives slightly lower the averages, comparisons of our figures with Hamilton's, Dickinson's and Terman's understate the extent of change.

sharp decrease in the percentage who have orgasm in only a small part or none of their marital coitus.

Although in our opinion this general increase in orgasm regularity is due to the social evolution of the past generation, those broad changes still have not made women as orgastically free, early in marriage, as they eventually come to be through experience, continuing education and the growth of intimacy and trust. Our younger married women, though much more orgastic than were comparable women 30 or 40 years ago, are not quite as regularly orgastic as our women in their mid-thirties to mid-fifties. Among our women of 55 and over, however, orgasm regularity seems to be considerably lower than in the younger cohorts. This is probably due to a combination of reasons, including the residual inhibitions of the oldest women in our sample, diminished physical responsiveness, and still other factors. However, our information about the 55-and-over wives is unreliable, since 13 percent of them said they had had no marital coitus in the preceding year, while another 17 percent made no answer about coital frequency (perhaps because it was zero). Thus we have no way of knowing how orgastic these inactive older wives would have been if they had had coitus.

A minor note of some interest concerns orgasm regularity in married males. Kinsey, though he apparently gathered no detailed data on the point, flatly asserted that husbands achieved orgasm in virtually 100 percent of their marital coitus.[71] We did gather data on the matter, and found, somewhat to our surprise, that at every age small percentages of married men fail to have orgasm in their marital coitus as often as a quarter of the time, and a sprinkling of others fail to do so half or even more of the time. Eight percent of the men age 45 and up, in our sample, missed orgasm anywhere from occasionally to most of the time; 7 percent of the men between 25 and 44 failed to have orgasm at least a quarter of the time; and, surprisingly, 15 percent of the under-25 husbands failed to have orgasm about a quarter of the time or more often. We considered this last piece of information remarkable because although occasional failure to have orgasm is now considered by doctors to be entirely normal in mature and older men,[72] in younger men it is not. But from our interviews we get the impression that such failure in young men is quite different from that in older men: The failure of young men to reach orgasm is not due to normal fatigue, but more often because in the midst of coitus they sometimes have erectile failure due to anxiety, inexperience, awkwardness and other related reasons. It is also true that some young men, filled with youthful *hubris,* occasionally seek to have coitus repeatedly within a brief time period, and in such endeavors, though firmly erect, may be unable to reach a second or subsequent orgasm. (It would seem, though, that they must often pretend to, for the married females in our sample give higher estimates of their husbands' regularity of orgasm than do the married men themselves. The same thing, of course, is true, all the more so, the other way around.)

Throughout this book we have repeatedly noted that many of the differences in sexual behavior that Kinsey found to be associated with educational level seem to have diminished or even disappeared by 1972. This holds true of orgasm regularity in married females for our sample as a whole. Indeed, below the age of 35 slightly more of the high-school-level wives than college-level wives report very high orgasm regularity, and slightly fewer report no orgasm at all. But it is doubtful that this indicates any real orgasm superiority on the part of the less educated. College-level women tend to marry somewhat later than noncollege women and, having had less marital experience, have not yet increased their orgasm regularity, at any given age, as much as have the noncollege women.

Similarly, there is some tendency for blue-collar wives to report higher levels of orgasm regularity than do white-collar wives. The difference is small, however, and appears mostly in the younger half of the sample, the likely explanation again being that the young white-collar wives married somewhat later and have not yet caught up to the blue-collar wives. The net overall impression is that important differences between occupational groups, as with those between educational levels, have ceased to exist.

Our data on the relationship between religious devoutness and orgasm regularity are puzzling at first glance. In the older half of our sample the nondevout women are somewhat more orgastic than the devout, but in the younger half of the sample it is the devout who are more orgastic. If we assume, as seems reasonable, that there is some correlation between devoutness and lower educational attainment, the answer would again lie in the earlier marriages of the devout. For the sample as a whole, however, there is no relation between the degree of devoutness and orgasm regularity.

So much for the objective evidence, provided by orgasm regularity, as to the increased pleasure and satisfactoriness of marital coitus today. Let us now look at the subjective evidence, for whatever it is worth. Though we were well aware of the limitations inherent in self-estimates of pleasure and contentment, we asked our respondents how pleasurable, in general, they had found their marital sex relationship in the past 12 months. Their replies tell us, at the very least, something about their state of mind—how they feel about their marital coitus, if not what they feel during it. But comparisons of such self-evaluations with others made decades ago are of very dubious value, and in any case Kinsey's studies include no such data. We therefore present the following findings merely as an indication of the extent to which today's married Americans take a positive view of their married sex relationship:

—Two-thirds of our married males termed their marital coitus of the past year generally "very pleasurable"; there was little variation among the age groups. If we add to this all who termed their marital coitus "mostly pleasurable," the percentage of positive evaluations is 99 in the youngest cohort, and drops to no lower than 94 percent even in the 45-to-54 and 55-and-over cohorts.

—Roughly three-fifths of all married females under the age of 45 rated their marital coitus in the past year "very pleasurable," the proportion rising from 57 percent for the under-25 cohort to a high of 63 percent for the 35-to-44 cohort. Thereafter, however, there was a sharp drop, only 45 percent of the 45-to-54 group and 38 percent of the 55-and-over group viewing their marital coitus so favorably. (Again, the data for the oldest women are not altogether reliable, because of the failure of a fifth of this group to answer the question.) If, however, we add the "mostly pleasurable" to the "very pleasurable" responses, we get quite a different picture: Total positive appraisal starts at 88 percent for the under-25 women, reaches a high of 93 percent for those between 35 and 44, and then declines—but only moderately—to 91 and 83 percent respectively for women in the next two decades of life.

—Only 3 percent of all the males gave their recent marital

coitus either a neutral rating ("neither pleasurable nor non-pleasurable") or a frankly negative one ("mostly nonpleasurable" or "very nonpleasurable"), and nearly all of those who did so were 35 or older. Only 7 percent of all the females gave their recent marital coitus a neutral rating, and in sharp contrast to innumerable reports of the large numbers of wives who, two generations ago or less, found coitus anything from unpleasant to dreadful, only 2 percent of our married females found it "mostly" or "very nonpleasurable." (Even if we add those women who had no coitus in the past year by reason of "lack of desire" or "mutual agreement with spouse," the figure comes to only 3 percent.)

We also asked our respondents if they would like more marital coitus, or less, than they were currently having. This, too, is a subjective evaluation, and apt to be distorted by such factors as what respondents regard as the right or appropriate stance for themselves as contemporary males or females. Still, many investigators, including Kinsey, apparently considering this question less subject to such distortions than other kinds of self-evaluation, have gathered data on the matter. The changes in those data, from earlier decades to the present, are worth briefly noting. In the 1920s, according to an early survey cited by Robert Bell, two-thirds of wives desired coitus less often than their husbands.[73] Twenty-odd years later, Kinsey found the situation somewhat ameliorated; though he gave no precise data, he noted that many younger husbands wished coitus were somewhat more frequent, while many younger wives wished it were somewhat less so, but that in the later years of marriage the situation was often reversed.[74] The situation had altered still further by 1964, when Bell, in a small survey of young wives, found only 1 in 17 regarding her marital coitus as too frequent, but 1 in 4 as less frequent than she would like.[75]

Our own survey indicates that this trend has advanced still further. Less than 5 percent of the wives in our sample said they would like marital intercourse to be less frequent, and less than 1 percent of husbands felt the same way. At every age the majority of wives felt that the amount of marital coitus they were having was about right; the proportions ranged from six-tenths to seven-tenths, the higher levels being for those in the middle of life. Among husbands, satisfaction with frequency was nearly as high, the proportions ranging from just under half to six-tenths. Interestingly enough, it was among men of 45 and older that satisfaction with frequency was lowest, and not, as in Kinsey, because they wanted less, but because they wanted more. About four-tenths of the men at most ages, and about half the men of 45 and over, said they would like the frequency of marital coitus to be higher. This, however, was far from an exclusively male attitude, for more than one out of three young wives, and nearly one out of four among the 55-and-over women, said the same thing.

The desire for more coitus is in some cases an expression of a healthy appetite somewhat undersatisfied because of interference by other normal duties and concerns. In other cases, however, it signifies the limitation of sexual coitus by emotional problems within the marriage. Among both the men and the women in our sample, marital coitus was roughly 50 percent more frequent for those whose marriages were close than for those whose marriages were distant, and it was among the latter that the desire for more intercourse was most often voiced.

The most important conclusion to be drawn from all the above seems to be that the onetime conflict between the sexes as to the desired frequency of marital intercourse has greatly diminished. Majorities of both sexes are contented with the frequency they have, insignificant numbers of each would like less, and the desire for more is no longer exclusively or even primarily male. Some conflict of desire surely still exists; many of those who want more are undoubtedly married to spouses who, for any one of a number of reasons, do not—but who, to judge from the data, do not want less, either. It is probably also true that some men and women who want more are married to spouses who likewise want more—the pair being hampered by such obstacles as study, work, childcare, social life and illness. In any event, throughout our sample and most particularly among the younger people in it, males and females are now on something close to an equal footing as far as satisfaction with coital frequency is concerned. This, plus the fact that almost none of the younger husbands and wives would like coital frequency to be lower than it is, seems to us strong confirming evidence that marital coitus today is distinctly more rewarding for both husbands and wives than it was a generation ago.

Finally, as one last check on contemporary satisfaction with marital sex, we asked our respondents whether they would like more or less variation in their marital coitus than they presently have. We know from other questionnaire items that there is a good deal more variation in the coitus of the younger people than in that of the older ones, and that even in the older half of the sample many couples employ more variation than did their counterparts of a generation ago. But how much variation would they like? Here, traditional female conservatism still appeared, for at every age distinctly smaller percentages of females than males said they wanted more variation than they were having. A large majority of wives in every age group, and particularly in the older groups, said that they were content with the amount of variation in their marital coitus. Among the men, a smaller majority of the older ones felt so, as did less than half of the younger men. The impact of sexual liberation was clearly visible among the young of both sexes: While they are definitely having a good deal more variation than older persons, more than half of the under-25 husbands and over a third of the under-25 wives would like still more. Even among married people in their late thirties and early forties, over a third of the men and a quarter of the women expressed the desire for more variation.

All in all, however, the responses to this question, as to so many others in our survey, indicate a generally high level of interest in, enjoyment of and satisfaction with marital sex on the part of contemporary husbands and wives. This conclusion may annoy or disappoint those who are scornful or contemptuous of marital sex or critical of the effect of marriage upon sexual enjoyment, or who wish to compare it unfavorably with sex in the single life or the swinging life. We have felt obliged, however, to present the evidence we found, without regard to what we or anyone else would have preferred that we find.

Some Representative Voices: The Unliberated and the Liberated

Once again, to comprehend in human terms the meaning of these findings we must turn to a more impressionistic and immediate form of evidence. Our tables of frequencies and our computations of percentages and medians are an effort to explore sexual phenomena in a quantitative and intellectually rigorous fashion. But if we want to understand those phenomena as living realities, and to know how these experiences actually feel to the human beings who make up the statistics, we must meet those human beings in person and listen to them talking about their own lives.

Who, for instance, are the men and women whose sexual activities within marriage are deficient in pleasure, and how do they feel about it? Among our interviewees, a few of the people who found marital sex unrewarding, or who achieved sexual pleasure only with great difficulty, suffered from special problems of a manifestly pathological nature. One young woman said that in order to be aroused and to reach orgasm while having coitus with her husband, she had to secretly fantasy that she was being raped by some loathesome stranger, whipped with a studded belt or the like. A young man who had been a compulsive Peeping Tom before marriage proved to be only feebly potent with his wife, and for most of the eight years of his marriage could achieve full erection and orgasm only when his wife was fellating him. A woman of 25 who had been having intercourse since she was 14 had never been able to have orgasm except when astride her partner and in full control of movement. This, she claimed, was because she needed unusually strong clitoral contact, but she also admitted that when her husband sought to bring her to orgasm by manual or oral stimulation of the clitoris, she could not relax enough to let his ministrations succeed. One overweight and low-sexed young man, though still in his early twenties, said that he had coitus only about once a week, and that from intromission to orgasm it usually lasted about 45 seconds. This seemed just right to him, and when his wife questioned whether their lovemaking wasn't less frequent and a lot quicker than was the case for most people their age, he brusquely told her that whatever other people might do, he and she were doing what was right for themselves.

But these and similar cases did not seem to us to be typical. Rather, it was our impression that most of those whose marital coitus was infrequent, routine and unexciting in comparison to that of others of their age group were people with inhibitions and built-in limitations stemming not from individual pathology but from conditioning to a familial or subcultural norm. In these people a limited capacity for pleasure was not so much a symptom of sickness as a by-product of education in an antihedonistic value system.

Listen, for instance, to a bright, attractive lawyer in his early thirties, whose generally conservative Episcopalian background and upbringing are reflected in a measured, unemotional manner of speech, and whose marital sex life, after only eight years, is as bland and colorless as his words:

> I would say that when we have sex, it's better than it was when I was single, but it's not as frequent. My wife would probably like it more often, but what with the children, and my responsibilities in my practice and my political activities, it's down to a couple of times a week. Also I would say that my wife isn't an ideal sexual partner—she's not as committed to oral sex as I would like, for one thing; she'll kiss it, but she won't do more than that. But I myself am not the world's greatest lover, because I just can't find the time or energy to work on it. I wouldn't say that I've ever reached a zenith of sexual experience with a woman, and being realistic I have to say that I'm not inclined to spend the time and effort it would require.

The next, a 45-year-old man raised in a stiffly moral middle-class Jewish home, had poured his youthful energies into business rather than sex. Though he remained single until he was 30, even in the busiest of his bachelor years he had averaged only about one act of intercourse every month or so, without feeling particularly deprived. He was much the same in marriage: In talking about marital coitus he uses language so flat and drab as to suggest that here, too, his drive and enjoyment of sex are thoroughly constricted:

> We do it maybe once a week now, or less. The underlying reason for the slowdown is that we're both pretty busy. It's not that we don't enjoy sex. We do, but I have a lot of meetings and I get home late and she's asleep, and anyway I'm tired. I would perhaps enjoy a bit more activity, but I'm not discontented about it in any way. . . . Mostly she does have orgasm—not that we ever discuss it, but I feel pretty sure she does. . . . Our typical sex act is about like this: I'll be reading in bed and maybe doze off, and then I roll over and decide I'd like a little action. Sometimes it's very rapid —a minute or so—but sometimes it goes on longer, ten minutes, say, half before I put it in, half inside.

Similarly neutral and affectless accounts were given by most of the married women who remain sexually unliberated. A department-store buyer in her late thirties, though she claims she has orgasm a fair amount of the time, talks about her married sex life in a way that conveys a sense of aridity and joylessness:

> I was a very restrained person, not all that free, before marriage, and I guess I still am inhibited in some directions. About varying our position, for instance. I'm uncomfortable in some positions, I really am—I mean uncomfortable mentally, not just physically. Yes, that's the right word for it: uncomfortable. [How about other things, such as oral-genital contacts?] Well, we do that occasionally. [How do you feel about it?] It doesn't bother me. [In either direction?] No, it doesn't bother me. [Do you and your husband discuss what you or he might like to do?] No, no, we don't. I don't know why not. Maybe we're in agreement and don't need to. I just haven't ever thought about it.

A 34-year-old black woman, quite middle-class in status and tastes and raised by strict Southern Baptist parents, said that as a result of her upbringing it had taken her six years of married life to begin to find sex pleasurable, and that even now, a decade later, she is still rather restricted in her enjoyment of it:

> I knew that after you got married you were supposed to have intercourse, but there was something in me that said it was wrong. I never could relax, I felt that what we were doing was dirty, wicked. The feeling gradually eased up over the years, especially after we had the second baby and I got sterilized and wasn't afraid of getting pregnant anymore. But even now I still want it to be only at night, and with the lights out. *He* wants to leave the lights on, and I say, "You leave the lights on and I'm not doing it!" And sometimes we have an argument because he wants me to take my nightgown off and I like to keep it on. Sometimes he picks up new ideas from the men and wants to try a new position, and we'll do that, but I just like best to be on my back. I don't like to do lewd things or illegal things—you know what I mean. . . . Sometimes I enjoy sex, sometimes not, but I always accommodate him. I like it fine, really, but I myself don't have an orgasm very often, and even when I do, there just isn't that strong physical whatever that my husband always seems to feel.

Some sexually inhibited persons seem thoroughly puzzled and annoyed by their own limitations; although capable of experiencing sexual pleasure when using traditionally approved methods, they meet with little success when they try to increase their enjoyment through variant techniques that they have read or heard about. A bright, smartly dressed waitress who says she really likes sex, and who has had several affairs and is now in her second marriage, replied somewhat regretfully, when asked about oral sex, "Well, I feel that if both of you want it and enjoy it, it's not wrong, but *I* can't do it. I wish I could, but I just can't make myself do it." Others do manage to make such experiments, but their misgivings and negative reactions keep them from adopting the new experiences as part of their regular repertoire. A young auto mechanic hesitantly revealed that once, when he and his wife were taking a shower together, they decided to have intercourse then and there. When asked why he sounded so hesitant, he apologetically said, "Well, it seemed right at the time, but I guess it was sort of peculiar of us. I mean, most people just don't *do* things like that, do they?" Another young blue-collar husband who seemed very pleased with his marital sex life was deeply perplexed by two of his own blocks:

> Me on my back, I don't like that. I don't know why. Just bothers me, that's all. And the other thing is her going down on me—I don't like that, either, which is funny, because my going down on her, I like *that*; it really turns me on. But the other way, I don't know, I just don't enjoy it, I don't like her to do it. Guys I know all say it's so great, but I can't see what's great about it. I wish I could figure that one out.

Even those who have adopted enough of the values of sexual liberation to employ a wide range of techniques of foreplay and coitus may fail to enjoy many of those practices, although they continue to use them with grim determination, as if trying by force to make themselves experience pleasure. This is part of the "effort syndrome" we referred to earlier, which recognizes sexual liberation as a worthy goal but mistakenly identifies it with the liberated acts themselves rather than with liberated feelings about those acts. The effort syndrome is probably more common among the unmarried, many of whom seek to project an image of proficiency, versatility and sexual freedom to their partners, but because it involves one's self-image, it also affects married persons. Some of our married interviewees, for instance, had learned to make regular use of practices they originally found embarrassing or unpleasant and which, though now tolerable, still gave them no particular pleasure. This was true of both men and women, though more often of the latter. Generally, the acts in question were variant coital positions or oral practices, but included such seemingly unthreatening practices as sex play in the bathtub, watching one's own sexual activity in a mirror, or playfully enacting roles (Sleeping Beauty or innocent youth, brazen hussy or bold seducer). Such people, though determined to do things they do not enjoy, are critical of themselves for failing to enjoy them. The following statement, by a formerly very proper and inhibited young woman who has been married for three years and now enjoys coitus thoroughly, is typical:

> He certainly has been a good teacher—he'll try and try something new, with my okay, but if he sees it isn't going to work, he knows enough to stop or switch. I've come a long way—but not nearly long enough. For instance, he likes a lot of light and I don't; it embarrasses me. But that's something I'm working on; I'm making myself get used to letting a little light come in from the bathroom. I still don't much like it, but I mustn't be like that! And oral—that's another one of my little things. I'm still working that out. I do it, but I gag. I was just beginning to get beyond that and not mind it when I got pregnant and suddenly got turned off again. Originally, the whole area of the male parts looked ugly to me—just awful—and I still don't think it's very pretty, but I'm coming along.

Far freer in behavior than this woman, yet even less able than she to feel actual pleasure, is the youthful drama professor whose case was related, in part, in the chapter on masturbation (see pages 102–104). He had fallen into the habit of putting on a "tremendous sexual performance," partly to compensate for his inability to be warm and communicative in other ways, and partly because, having been an avid reader of erudite sexual material, he sought to cast himself in the image of the ideal lover. He had become expert at varying coitus in many ways, and had trained himself to prolong it for an hour to an hour and a half, until his wife had had many orgasms. But he himself got very little actual sexual pleasure from all this, his pleasure being far more mental—a matter of pride in his own generosity and in his power to overwhelm her with sensation. As he put it:

> When my mind was in good shape I would be able to mount her and concentrate on the flower patterns in the wallpaper or something else, and bring her to climax ten times or more without ejaculating. I perceive my own value in terms of my capacity to make another person happy, especially in the sexual area, and so it gave me enjoyment to provide her with extreme pleasure. But I myself got little physical reward out of it—indeed, her attempts to reciprocate with inventive forms of love play, at which she is quite uninhibited, were not particularly meaningful to me. I sensed no erotic increment as a result of her efforts, and generally I allowed her to pursue them simply to give her some feeling of reciprocity.

Not surprisingly, he eventually came to find this entire situation burdensome and oppressive, and at the time of the interview was avoiding marital intercourse as much as possible. Liberated sexuality, in his case, had proven only another entrapment.

Those who are genuinely liberated sound very different from this. Even when the range of their acts is narrower or their performance less heroic, their words convey a sense of spontaneity and comfortable self-acceptance; they not only enjoy their sexual activities but are at ease with their own pleasure. They perform well, though many of them are not the greatest of performers, and they have a wide range of variations in their sexual interaction, though not necessarily the very widest. What is of the essence is that their enjoyment of the sexual relationship in marriage is untainted by embarrassment, shame or any sense of wrongness about the things they do or feel.

Some of our interviewees identified their own sexual liberation with breakthroughs in specific areas of their behavior and feeling. For one man it consisted of finding himself able to make love to his wife during her menses; for another, discovering that during intercourse he could describe his sensations to his wife in graphic words, which immensely excited her and thus intensified his own pleasure. For one woman it lay in finding herself able at last to sprawl out, legs unabashedly apart, and luxuriate in having her husband mouth her genitals; for another it was in learning to yield so fully to her own sensations as to succeed in having several end-to-end orgasms lasting nearly a minute.

But the interviewees we identify as being most truly liberated have a broader, more holistic view of the matter. They see their own enjoyment of marital sexuality as an entirety, rather than as consisting of one or several meritorious achievements. Not that such people are necessarily intellectual about the matter; here, for instance, is as good an exposition of sexual liberation within marriage as any we heard, although the speaker is a genial, beefy, unsophisticated appliance dealer in a small midwestern city—and, incidentally, an exemplar of sexual liberation among the middle-aged:

I love my sex, and I've got a wife that loves it just as much as me. Our first five years of married life it was every day with us, and sometimes twice a day because my job would allow me to stop off at home at lunchtime for a quickie. Nowadays, even after twenty years of marriage, it's still about three times a week—and with the kids finally all in school, we've even started up again on that lunchtime business once in a while. Most of the time, naturally, it's in the evening, after the kids are in bed. My wife puts some of that damned perfume on and I know right away that she wants it tonight, and that really gets me going. We'll lay on the couch watching TV and playing around with each other and half forgetting about the show. We'll carry on like that, laughing and horsing around, for half an hour or more, and then go to bed and get the bodies together, and it's tremendous. She can wiggle that ass of hers around like you wouldn't believe, and any position I want to use, she couldn't care less. I like doing all kinds of things to her— the only thing I don't do is go down on her, because I had a very bad experience with that when I was in high school with a girl who really stunk, and it's had no appeal for me ever since. But all sorts of other things are fine with me. And she does all kinds of things to me, including taking it in her mouth and really working on it. And sometimes I kid her about stuff I've seen in some stag movie the boys have been showing down at the garage, and would you believe she often wants me to *show* her how it went? After all these years?

A young man of 25—the product of a sophisticated New York home, an Ivy League education, and four years of graduate study—used much more elegant and up-to-date language than the appliance dealer, yet the inner message of his account was much the same:

> We began sleeping together when we were both under-graduates, and we more or less lived together for a while after graduating. The sex was good even then, but in the three years since we got married it has changed and im-proved a great deal. We're more flexible about speed, for one thing. Sometimes, when our conversation or reading has made us both very excited, it may take only a minute or two, and we get a real kick out of that. But other times we lie around in each other's arms making a lot of interest-ing kinds of physical contact for half an hour or more, and then even after we put it together we may spend fifteen or twenty minutes before we come, and we get really wrung out by it—and we love that, too. In the beginning I found it difficult to control myself, but now I find it no trouble to maintain control until she's thoroughly excited and coming herself—and then I can't help myself, it carries me away. Before we were married I'd often stay in afterwards, and after a rest we'd continue and I'd come again. Nowadays we don't do that very often, and when we do, I don't always bother to come, but just ball for a while for the sheer fun of it. We're down to about three times a week, what with hard work and a lot of career worries, but we've become a lot more experimental, particularly because her exposure to other opinions and her reading has made her willing to try things and to let herself go. From ordinary experiment-ing with various kinds of touches and positions, we've gone on to fooling around with more exotic things like, say, an exaggerated form of cunnilingus with her draped over the back of a chair. The other night I said to her, "Let's go out to dinner, and come home and have a real romantic fuck on the sofa, with candles and wine," and she joined right in and loved the idea. It isn't that we *program* our sex—it's

that we sometimes take time to consciously enhance our pleasure with finesse and the heightening of sensuality.

Similar feelings were expressed by women we interviewed, some of them young and educated, but others middle-aged and of the working-class. An example of the latter is a 45-year-old woman, formerly Catholic but now Lutheran, and married to a Jewish longshoreman:

It hasn't been so good lately since he got sick and went in for his operation, but for twenty-some years it's been mostly very, very good. At first, we'd do it every night, maybe twice, maybe three times, and I liked it fine even though I wasn't getting climaxes very often. But as time went by, it got better—more petting, more kinds of different things—and I began climaxing regularly, right along with him. By the time I was thirty we were talking about every kind of technique and really going at everything. Not just two or three positions but every kind of position, and every kind of technique. Truthfully, I like oral technique— done to me, I mean; I really like that very much. Not as a steady diet, though—and I always want the final part to be real intercourse. Sometimes I find wild books and magazines hidden in my son's room and I read them, and I'm practically panting, I can't wait for my husband to come home so we can do something I've read about. But I don't like everything—I don't get stimulated by the idea of beatings and freaky things like that. And I can't swallow the sperm; I draw the line at that. I know it's done and there's nothing wrong with it, but I just don't like it, okay?

Far removed from this woman in background and general life-style but with very similar feelings about marital sexuality is a young college-educated wife, now temporarily retired from teaching to care for her own preschool daughter. Reared in an educated and enlightened home in a large eastern city, she acquired a core of liberal attitudes about sex long before marriage, and in her late teens yearned to experience intercourse, but not without being in love. When it finally happened during her senior year in college, it proved physically more difficult than she and her lover had anticipated; but loving each other, and being half liberated, they found the mechanical problems more

absurd than grim, and laughed (somewhat hysterically) and
went on with it. After a few times it grew easier, then exciting,
then fulfilling. Meanwhile, the emotional attachment grew along
with it, and a year and a half later they were married. Let her tell
the rest:

> I thought it was quite good before we got married, and no
> doubt it was, but being married and having our own place
> made a big difference in my whole mental state about sex.
> Of course, there had been a certain excitement before mar-
> riage—we were always trying to get together, and find some
> privacy and keep it hidden—but that was an artificial excite-
> ment. Once we could take our minds off those extraneous
> concerns and pay more attention to each other, it rapidly
> got very much better, and we took a lot more time and
> seemed to penetrate much deeper into total feeling. We
> had varied our lovemaking before marriage, but in the first
> few years of marriage we varied it a lot more, and tried out
> many new things. We kept some and dropped others as we
> came to understand what we both enjoyed most. Some-
> times there's a lot of foreplay, sometimes not, depending
> on the mood we're in. We both like oral acts very much,
> with the one limitation that he doesn't like me to bring him
> too close to climax that way because it makes it difficult for
> him to last long inside me. Now I, as it happens, can climax
> more than once, and I just *love* to do so, so we try to arrange
> it so that he sends me off into one and then another, and
> then joins me for the grand finale—and I do mean grand!
> The best position for me is the standard one, but I also get
> great pleasure out of being on hands and knees and being
> entered from the rear, which he likes best. We've tried just
> about everything possible, including my sitting up on him
> with my back towards him. We even use anal intercourse,
> although everything has to be just right, in terms of my
> stomach and bowels, for me to want to do that. At first we
> did that very rarely because there was pain, but he found
> it very exciting, so I persisted and learned to relax so that
> there is no pain, and now—though I don't know how it's
> physiologically possible—I actually climax in that position.
> . . . We have sex less frequently now than we did seven years
> ago, at the beginning of marriage, because it's not so novel

a thing anymore, but at the same time it's lots more exciting because of the familiarity and ease of it, and a much richer and freer experience than ever before. The only thing that limits it is when we're unhappy with each other about something, because it isn't possible for either of us to enjoy the physical thing unless we're emotionally in tune.

Relationship between Marital Success and the Liberation of Marital Sex

Finally, we must try to offer an answer to the question that has been implicit throughout this chapter: Does the liberation of sexuality within marriage have any bearing upon the quality of the husband-wife relationship? Or stated another way: Is there a direct relationship between the degree of sexual pleasure within marriage and the overall success of the marital relationship?

The answer may seem obvious to the layman, but it has not been obvious to behavioral scientists; indeed, some earlier studies failed to show any strong correlation between sexual adjustment and marital happiness or success.[76] But since contemporary husbands and wives expect and want the sexual side of marriage to be intensely pleasurable and deeply gratifying to both partners, it may be far more closely associated with the success or failure of their overall relationship than was the case for their grandparents or even for their parents.

Two of the items in our questionnaire should provide us with evidence as to whether such an association exists. One is a question as to how pleasurable the respondent's sexual relationship with his or her spouse has been in the past year. The other is a question asking the respondent how "close" the marriage is. The latter item is our effort to appraise marital success without using the terms "happy" or "happiness," which, as we have said, yield results of low validity. We think that self-appraisals of closeness, though still subjective, are more likely to be based on factual content than are self-appraisals of happiness, and in our society today closeness is a valid measure of marital success, if not all but synonymous with it.

The analysis of the data offered in earlier parts of this survey has already shown that, contrary to what some sexual-freedom advocates have said, sexual pleasure and emotional intimacy are still strongly linked for most people. We expected, therefore, to find a positive relationship between the pleasure obtained from marital coitus and the closeness of the marital relationship. And we did find such a relationship—an even stronger one than we had anticipated. The results in brief:

—A large majority of married men and married women for whom marital sex had been very pleasurable in the past year rated their marriages as very close.

—Of those men and women for whom marital sex in the past year had been either lacking in pleasure or actually displeasing, virtually none rated their marriages as being very close, and only a few as being fairly close.

—Among the people who rated their marriages as not close or as very distant, six-tenths of the women and four-tenths of the men found the sexual side of things unrewarding or even unpleasant.

For the figures in detail, see Table 36.

Comparing the figures in the upper part of Table 36 with those in the lower part, we see that one traditional difference between males and females still exists to a limited extent: The data in the third column indicate that more men than women can find some pleasure in sexual relations even when the relationship is emotionally cool or distant. But the differences between the male figures and the female figures are not nearly so impressive as the high degree of congruence between them. Note especially the data of the top lines and the bottom lines of both parts: These represent the extremes of the sexual-pleasure scale and are the best indicators of the association between sexual pleasure and marital closeness; on these lines the connections between the two factors are unmistakable, and very similar in degree.

There is little doubt in our minds that a cause-and-effect relationship exists today between sexual pleasure in marriage and the overall success of the marital relationship. But which is cause, and which is effect? One might argue very plausibly that sexual success, since it involves communication and shared experience, creates emotional closeness. But one might also argue, with equal plausibility, that it is the intimacy and trust of a genuinely close relationship that permits the partners

Table 36
Sexual Pleasure by Marital Closeness:
Total Sample, Percents

MARRIED MALES

Marital relationship:

	Very close	Fairly close	Not too close, or very distant
Marital sex life in past year was:			
Very pleasurable	79	45	12
Mostly pleasurable	20	50	47
Neither pleasurable nor nonpleasurable	1	2	17
Mostly or very nonpleasurable	—	3	24
	100%	100%	100%

MARRIED FEMALES

Marital relationship:

	Very close	Fairly close	Not too close, or very distant
Marital sex life in past year was:			
Very pleasurable	70	30	10
Mostly pleasurable	26	58	28
Neither pleasurable nor nonpleasurable	1	8	45
Mostly or very nonpleasurable	3	4	17
	100%	100%	100%

to become sexually free with each other.

We cannot decide the issue on the basis of our data but must content ourselves with offering the suggestion, derived from insights gained through our interviews, that under some conditions one thing causes the other, under other conditions the opposite is true, and in most cases the two phenomena are reciprocal, each being both cause and effect of the other. In any event, we find no support for the sexually radical-chic notion that sexual pleasure is no longer allied to, dependent upon or productive of love. The connection is not total and categorical; many people, at times, can experience sexual pleasure with a partner they have little positive feeling for, and some people can deeply love a partner with whom sexual relations are faulty. But the evidence of our own survey is quite clear: The husband and wife who have a free and intensely pleasurable sexual relationship are much more likely to be emotionally close than the husband and wife who do not, and the close marriage is much more likely to involve genuinely liberated marital sex than the distant one. History has come full cycle, *mirabile dictu*, and restored to married men and women what Paul and the fathers of the church took away from them so long ago.

MALE, 48, PRINT-SHOP FOREMAN: *I was shaken up pretty badly by the break-up of my marriage. I didn't even date for half a year. Then I started in, and gradually got into the sex thing, and realized that I'd been pretty stuffy and blocked as a sex partner up to then. I opened up and learned a hell of a lot from different women; I had a real ball. But I didn't want to get too close to anybody. . . . I always laid it right on the line, and those who didn't like it got out, and those who did had a ball right along with me.*

FEMALE, 32, REAL-ESTATE SALESWOMAN: *[After my divorce] I used to fight off every guy I didn't feel keen on sleeping with, because I had my principles. But so many times it wound up getting nasty that finally I decided it wasn't worth the trouble. . . . If some guy makes a big thing about it, I simply stay cool and let him have it. Big deal! . . . Sometimes I even have an orgasm with a man I don't like, or find repulsive, but that worries me; it's kind of perverse.*

MALE, 40, ELECTRICIAN: *It's wrong to play around [extramaritally], once you've made your commitment; it's dishonest. It's not like I haven't been tempted—I sure have—but I haven't given in because I figure if I did, I would be so miserable and disgusted with myself that I wouldn't know what to do.*

FEMALE, 35, ASSEMBLY-LINE WORKER: *I had the chance [for extramarital sex] just a month ago, and turned it off before it got started. I'm not at all sure it would make me any happier if I did it, but I do feel sure it would definitely make my husband very unhappy. Even if he didn't know about it, I'd be thinking within myself that if he knew, he would be unhappy, and that's something I don't want to live with.*

MALE, 45, PHYSICIAN: *At first, I was all torn up about it [an extramarital affair], but I couldn't give it up. It made me feel totally different—younger and more attractive than I had in twenty years, completely reawakened inside. . . . [Yet] she was no good at all, sexually. Despite all her sexiness, she was frigid. . . . Still, for months I couldn't break it off; I felt as if I were hooked on some drug.*

FEMALE, 33, WRITER: *My husband had been all right as a lover, at least as far as being always ready for it, and able to control his orgasm. But his whole style was basically uptight. . . . I didn't know any better myself, until I had my first affair. Then I was bowled over—my lover was so sensitive, so expressive. . . . After we had been together a few times, I would almost seem to lose consciousness for a little while during my orgasm. It was unbelievable.*

CHAPTER

5

Postmarital and

Extramarital Sex

Sexual Fidelity: Functions, Dysfunctions, Alternatives

None of the many restrictions that Christianity has placed upon sexual expression has been more highly valued—and more burdensome—than the doctrine that husband and wife must limit themselves sexually to each other from marriage until death. While our pious great-grandfathers may have regarded this as the natural and only moral way of life, it is so rare a pattern in anthropological and historical perspective that one is forced to consider it, if not unnatural, at least idiosyncratic and no more moral than any one of a hundred other alternatives. Reviewing the data available for 185 primitive societies that had been studied by anthropologists, Professors Clellan S. Ford and Frank A. Beach reported in *Patterns of Sexual Behavior* that fewer than one-sixth of those societies had formal restrictions to a single mate, all the rest permitting various forms of polygamous union.[1] In 39 percent of the societies on which information had been gathered concerning the mores of extramarital sex, there was formal approval of extramarital liaisons of specified types, and in a number of others there was tacit toleration of discreet extramarital liaisons for men, and, in some, for women as well.[2] Moreover, in many of these societies and in such major civilized cultures as those of ancient Greece and Rome, there was another avenue of escape from lifelong single mateship—divorce, a route which at certain times and in some social circles was heavily traveled.

The rarity of lifelong sexually-exclusive monogamy in human societies indicates that it is far from being the most natural choice for the human species, and that neither male nor female is instinctively driven to seek it. On the other hand, neither does the human animal instinctively gravitate toward any other specific pattern of mating; hence the great variety of our sexual mores and marital arrangements. Among subhuman animals it is quite otherwise: Mating behavior varies very widely from species to species, but each has a highly specific and virtually invariable pattern that is determined by genetic mechanisms which are activated by external stimuli. In most animal species, mateship consists only of a brief period of active copulation; in some others, it includes companionship and cooperation beyond the copulatory period, throughout gestation and the rearing of the young; and in a few birds and mammals it is a lifetime bonding.[3] But in every case the mating behavior of a species varies as little as that species' distinctive physical characteristics.

The behavior of the human being, in contrast, is governed in only the most general way by genetic mechanisms. We eat, speak and live in social groups because of biological drives—but exactly what we eat, what language we speak and what kinds of social groups we live in are determined by our childhood experiences and by the culture around us. So, too, with our sexual behavior and family life; familial and cultural influences, rather than biology, dictate how many sex partners we are likely to have during our lifetime, what we will regard as the natural terms and conditions of marriage, and how these two things will be related.

Only rarely in human history have those familial and cultural factors conspired to make lifelong sexually-exclusive monogamy the preferred choice of most or all of the people in a society. The panorama of humanity's other choices—polygyny, polyandry, concubinage, prostitution, divorce, extramarital love affairs, courtly love, the cult of the *cavaliere servente,* wife-exchange, ceremonial orgiastic festivals and so on and on—is proof positive that no one pattern of sexual behavior and mating is instinctive and natural for us, and that lifelong sexually-exclusive monogamy is perhaps the unlikeliest choice of all. Unlikely

not only for the male but for the female as well, for while it is
true that the female has generally been the more monogamously
inclined of the two sexes, the male has usually had power over
her, and has educated and coerced her into being so. As Ford
and Beach point out, in societies having no sexual double standard and in which a variety of liaisons are permitted, "women
avail themselves as eagerly of their opportunity as do the men."[4]

None of this means that lifelong sexually-exclusive monogamy is unworkable or pathogenic. It does mean that it is
difficult, and works best when it is a necessary prerequisite to the
obtaining of certain major rewards. The pioneer husband and
wife on the American frontier needed each other's help for
sheer survival as well as for companionship; sexual fidelity, accordingly, was the price each paid in order to be uninterruptedly
assured of those benefits. In the close-knit, devoutly religious
towns of colonial New England, husband and wife were bound
together not only by practical needs but by the fact that to stray
from rectitude was to risk public ostracism and even expulsion
from the community; under such conditions fidelity became not
only worthwhile but almost easy. "Hail wedded love!" sang
Milton, the great poet of Puritanism, "by thee adulterous lust
was driv'n from men/Among the bestial herds to range"—but
more often the truth, at least in Puritan New England, was that
adulterous lust was driven underground by implacable preach-
ers and pitiless neighbors.

Not that fidelity has always had to be forced upon unwilling
men and women. The human being is the most educable and
malleable of all living creatures and, if taught from infancy on
that sexual fidelity is the key to both sexual rapture and abiding
love, will tend to believe and live by that doctrine. But since it
is a wholly learned behavior pattern and has no genetic rein-
forcement, it can also be unlearned under the pressure of such
forces as disenchantment, marital conflict, boredom, sexual
deprivation due to the spouse's illness or absence, unsought
intimacy arising from a close working relationship with an other-
sex partner and the like. Thus, even when lifelong single mateship is the dominant pattern in a society, many a husband and
wife will have individual reasons for finding it unrewarding or
even insupportable, and will try to circumvent the rule in ways
ranging from romantic, long-lasting secret love affairs to tawdry
quickies with prostitutes or strangers. A substantial part of

Western literature is devoted to accounts of the innumerable efforts of men (and to a lesser extent, of women) to outwit their mates, neighbors, churches and consciences, and to venture beyond the confines of sexually-exclusive mateship without getting caught or paying any penalty.

Nothing has ever wholly restrained the extramarital impulse —not the idealizing of romantic and lifelong love, nor the strictures of the Catholic church (which defines adultery as a mortal sin), nor the severely punitive rules of the Puritan churches (which fined adulterers or even drove them from church and community), nor the laws passed in many a Protestant country making adultery a crime against the state. (Even today, four-fifths of the states in our own country have laws—rarely enforced, but still on the books—making extramarital coitus a crime punishable by anything from a ten-dollar fine in Maryland to as much as five years' imprisonment in Maine, Oklahoma, South Dakota and Vermont.[5]) But if these several impediments never wholly restrained the impulse, they did block it or drive it underground most of the time, particularly among men and women of the middle class and especially in the Protestant nations.

It was no mere coincidence, therefore, that with the rise to power of that Protestant middle class in northern Europe, a different and more acceptable escape from single mateship eventually became available in the form of divorce. Though it long remained costly, difficult and socially damaging, and though no one took this drastic step merely for the sake of sexual variety, divorce did at least provide a solution of desperation for men and women who found their marriages intolerable for various reasons, including gross sexual maladjustment.

Divorce did not and could not become widespread until both liberalization of the laws and the growth of employment opportunities for women made it feasible for marriage to be broken at will. This began to happen during the latter part of the 19th Century. Between 1867 and 1971 the divorce rate per 1000 population in the United States increased nearly twelvefold until, in the latter year, there were more than one-third as many divorces as marriages throughout the nation, and in some localities—California's Marin County, for instance—one divorce for every marriage.[6]

None of this, however, means that marriage has been dying

out, for the great majority of divorced people eventually re-marry. It means, rather, that divorce and subsequent remarriage has come to be a major modification of the traditional Western expectation that marriage would be a lifelong exclusive bond. It is not in idle jest that sociologists call the emerging American pattern of divorce and remarriage "sequential polygamy"; it is something very different from lifetime single mateship, but by preserving the appearance of monogamy—by not *looking* like polygamy—it has been able to win sanction in our monogamous society. But that sanction is very recent; only a generation or two ago the divorced person was—except in the "smart" set—something of a pariah, set apart and whispered about, as much for the presumed immorality of his or her return to single life as for violating the vow of lifelong faithfulness to one mate.

Just how sexually free divorced people were, between mar-riages, a generation ago, or are today, is a question we will shortly look into. In any case, it is clear that divorce and remar-riage is a major alternative to extramarital relationships. As sociologist Jessie Bernard has put it, traditonal marriage re-quires both exclusivity and permanence, but in modern life these two things have tended to become incompatible. The modern alternatives have become exclusivity-and-divorce or permanence-and-infidelity.[7]*

Any number of sexual innovators, over the past 60 or 70 years, have argued for a third alternative—a combination of permanence with permissiveness: that is, permanent adherence to the marriage, for the sake of child-rearing and social stability, combined with freedom for each partner to have additional emotional and physical relationships outside of the marriage. But thus far, all variations upon this theme have proven disrup-tive to the marriages of most of those who have practiced them, and too threatening to the majority of those who have not to be seriously tried out. Relatively few people, even today, manage to make permissive marriage work at all, let alone work better than exclusive marriage. For although marriage no longer has the structural support of religion, community, law or practical necessity, today there is something else that makes exclusivity,

---

*The two are not, however, mutually exclusive. Fairly often, extramarital sex precedes the breakup of marriage, either as a preliminary step to gain self-confidence or as an adventure that backfires and produces an unwanted divorce.

or the appearance of it, immensely important—namely, the loneliness and disconnectedness of modern life, which creates a deep need in modern man and woman to belong, and to have a binding emotional connection with someone else. And since for most people sex is so closely bound up with deep emotions, extramarital sexual acts are severely threatening to the emotional identity and security that marriage seems to offer.[8]

It thus remains true, even after a generation of rapid change in sexual attitudes and behavior, that there are still only two major alternatives to lifelong single mateship in the United States: one, secret extramarital relationships; the other, the breakup of the existing marriage, temporary return to single life and eventual remarriage. In this part of our survey we will seek to ascertain how the sexual liberation of the past generation has affected the use of each alternative: specifically, whether there has been any measurable increase in the incidence of extramarital and postmarital sexual activity; whether the spectrum of practices involved in either has been broadened; and whether the people having such experiences today feel less inhibition and guilt, and derive greater pleasure, than did their predecessors.

First, then, we will look at the more conventional and acceptable of the two alternatives—the sexual behavior of those who have left the world of marriage and rejoined the world of single people.

Postmarital Coitus: Incidence, Frequency, Number of Partners, Techniques, Overall Pleasure

Before presenting our findings on postmarital sexual behavior, we must explain why comparisons of Kinsey's data in this area with our own have only limited value. Readers who find such explanations of no interest may prefer to skip the next three paragraphs, although they run the risk of taking our ensuing discussion to be more definitive than we consider it to be.

Kinsey used the terms "postmarital" and "previously married" to refer not only to the separated and divorced but to the widowed; all his relevant data lump these categories together. But widowed persons, though living in a postmarital phase of life, have arrived at it in very different fashion and have very different psychosexual needs from the separated and divorced (whom we shall refer to, from now on, simply as "divorced"). Indeed, a later study by Dr. Paul Gebhard (Kinsey's successor as director of the Institute of Sex Research), using Institute data, shows that widowed women of any given age are less likely to be having coitus in any given year than divorced women of the same age, and that even those widows who have coitus do so less often than comparable divorced women.[9] A study published in 1966 by the author of the present volume yielded similar findings concerning widowers and divorced men of the same age.[10] The general explanation is that most divorced persons need sexual and emotional experiences that are more gratifying than those they had in marriage, and hence ego-restoring, while most widowed persons cherish the memories of their marriages, and fear or resent anything that might devalue them. Kinsey's combining of the divorced and the widowed thus yields a blurred picture of postmarital behavior, particularly insofar as such behavior is the alternative to sexual infidelity.

We therefore set out to study the postmarital sexual behavior of the divorced apart from that of the widowed. (Because of limitations of time and manpower, we eliminated the widowed from our survey altogether, since some three-quarters of all widowers and two-thirds of all widows are 65 or older and, as a group, are sexually relatively inactive.[11]) But how were we to measure the change in the sexual behavior of the divorced if there existed no comparable data on the preceding generation? We found the following solution: (a) if we limit our comparisons to data for persons under 55, we eliminate more than three-quarters of the widowers from Kinsey's "postmarital" males and nearly three-quarters of the widows from his "previously married" females[12]; (b) based on census data, and allowing for the fact that Kinsey counted long-separated persons as equivalent to divorced persons, his under-55 "postmarital" males probably consisted of about one-third widowed and two-thirds divorced persons, and his under-55 "previously married" females probably consisted of about one-quarter widowed and three-quarters divorced persons[13]; (c) these fractions of widowed persons in the under-55 Kinsey sample, as we know from Gebhard's analysis, make the group averages of coital incidence and frequency lower for females (and probably for males) than they would have been for divorced persons alone, but based on Gebhard's figures we can judge that the distortion this causes is an understatement of female coital incidence ranging from 1 or 2 percent to somewhere on the order of 10 to 20 percent, depending on the age group. Frequencies likewise would be understated, generally by about one-eighth.[14] We have no similar basis for estimating the underreporting of postmarital activity for males, but if we assume that much the same difference existed between divorced and widowed males as between divorced and widowed females, the Kinsey postmarital data would understate divorced coital incidence and frequency by slightly larger margins than the above.

It may be asked why, since Gebhard did give figures for the divorced alone, we did not use his data as the base line. We had two reasons for not doing so. First, his figures deal only with females. Second, they represent an accumulation of female interview material gathered from 1939 to 1956—a span considerably wider than that represented by the data in the Kinsey volume on the female, and too wide to yield a focused picture of behavior at a particular stage of social evolution. The same, of course, is somewhat true of Kinsey's own data (which Gebhard's include, and add to), but the material included in that volume was all gathered prior to 1950, and thus is more suitable for our purposes.

So much by way of explanation. Let us proceed to our findings.

Public discussion of the effects of sexual liberation has been very little concerned with changes in the behavior of the divorced. It was more or less assumed, a generation or so ago, that the "gay divorcée" and her male equivalent led a rather loose and free life that hardly needed further sexual liberation. Indeed, Kinsey explicitly stated that the postmarital male, "in spite of customs and laws . . . continues to have almost as active a sexual life as when he was married,"[15] and that "the postmarital patterns for the females are rather close to those of the married females."[16] But his own data gave a somewhat more conservative picture of the situation: While it was true that, in general, neither males nor females reverted to the sexual behavior characteristic of the unmarried young, it was also true that at nearly every age the proportion of postmarital persons having any coitus at all was distinctly smaller than that of married persons, with the disparity becoming considerable among middle-aged and older persons. An example: At age 50, only 2 percent of married males were having no coitus at all with their wives, while 18 percent of postmarital men were having no coitus at all.[17] Equally revealing are the figures on frequency: Even those post-marital males in Kinsey's sample who were having coitus were doing so only about half to two-thirds as often as married men.[18]

The popular notion that the divorced man led a life of unbridled profligacy was thus hardly accurate, as Kinsey's statement quoted above indicates. This is hardly surprising. Unlike the married man, the divorced man had to locate partners who were both appealing to him and potentially willing, and then had to invest considerable time, effort and money on nearly every occasion that might lead to a sexual encounter. Even more important than these impediments was the general stumbling block of the social disapproval of sex between unmarried persons. Fearful of gossip, trouble with the neighbors, damage to his social position or career, and run-ins with police, he had to exercise great discretion, limiting his sexual encounters to times and places that held no danger of discovery. As a result, even though his internal inhibitions were far fewer than those of the single young man, externally he was little freer, unless he lived in the anonymity of a big-city apartment house.

All these social impediments operated even more strongly in the case of postmarital females. Many of them, moreover, were also severely restricted in their activities by the presence of dependent children. Even in relatively young age groups, a third or more of the postmarital women were having no coitus at all, while in the older groups a majority of postmarital women were inactive. An example: At age 50, when only 7 percent of married women were no longer having coitus with their husbands, 53 percent of postmarital women were having no coitus at all. By age 55 the contrast was even more striking: 12 percent of wives had ceased marital coitus, while 64 percent of postmarital females were coitally inactive.[19] As to frequency, in most age groups, even those postmarital females who were having coitus were doing so only about one-third as often as married females.[20] Typically, the previously married female in her early thirties—an age at which nearly all such persons in Kinsey's sample were divorcées, rather than widows—was having inter-course about once every two weeks, while her married peer was having intercourse four times in the same period, and more than a quarter of the previously married females in this age bracket were having none at all.

Our own sample of divorced males and females, though pro-portionate within our survey sample to the divorced segment of the national population, is too small to warrant statistical analy-sis by ten-year age cohorts or by such other parameters as edu-cational or occupational level. Taking the group as a whole, however, and comparing it to Kinsey's under-55 postmarital sample taken as a whole, we find ample evidence that sexual liberation has affected postmarital behavior as significantly as it has premarital and marital behavior, even though those changes have received relatively little public attention.

For one thing, while anywhere from 4 percent to 18 percent of postmarital males in the cohorts up to age 55 were coitally inactive in Kinsey's time (the figures being higher among the older men),[21] none of ours was; 100 percent of our divorced men had had intercourse during the past year. Because of the smallness of the sample (40 cases), we cannot take ours to be a completely reliable figure, although it is probably not far from the truth. As for Kinsey's figures, even if one allows for the possible underreporting of postmarital activity due to the inclu-sion of widowers, there would still be significant percentages of coitally inactive males in every age group—a definite contrast with our own.

The contrast in female incidence figures is more striking, and is equally likely to be a genuine, though not wholly accurate, indication of change. Roughly a third of Kinsey's younger post-marital females, and a majority of those beyond the mid-forties, were coitally inactive,[22] as compared with only a tenth of all our divorced women. Here, too, the comparison is imprecise: A larger 1972 sample might have yielded a result slightly to one side or the other, while allowing for the understatement of coital activity in Kinsey's figures, due to the inclusion of widows, would somewhat reduce the above percentages of celibate post-marital women. Yet even taking both things into account, it seems safe to say that celibacy in divorced women is a rarity today, and only about one-quarter as common as it was a gener-ation ago.

Frequencies, again, tell us even more about the nature of the change that has taken place. The median coital frequency for our divorced males is more than twice a week—more than double the median coital frequency for coitally active postmarital males in Kinsey's sample.[23] And while the coitally active postmarital males in Kinsey's sample had less coitus than his married men, in our own sample the median coital rate of divorced men is apparently a trifle higher than that of married men. For our divorced females the median frequency of coitally active respondents was almost twice a week—roughly four times greater than the median for comparable females in Kinsey's sample,[24] and approximately the same as the rate for married women in our sample across the same age range. Against increases of such magnitude, the understatement of coital frequency for divorced males and females in Kinsey's sample, due to his inclusion of widowers and widows, is inconsequential.

Increases of such magnitude make it indisputable that in a single generation sexual liberation has drastically altered the entire *mise en scène* of postmarital sexual behavior. Divorced males have been largely freed from many of the social and internal constraints upon normal heterosexual behavior that existed as recently as a generation ago. And divorced females, who were even more constrained by tradition and circumstance than males a generation ago, have, in relative terms, experienced an even greater degree of liberation and now enjoy nearly as much freedom as divorced males. Which is not to say that divorced men and women are, by and large, promiscuous, or flagrantly open about their sexual activities. Some do become promiscuous—usually for a limited time only—and a few are flagrantly open, but most, while no longer elaborately concealing the reality of their lives, have much the same standards of taste and privacy as do married persons or mature single persons. In short, sexual liberation has affected postmarital sex much as it has premarital sex, bringing greater honesty, enjoyment and flexibility into the sexual behavior of the divorced but without displacing their major values.

On the other hand, it is true that their relative maturity and their traumatic marital experiences make them somewhat more experimental, and often more casual, about sex than the unmarried young of high-school and college age, or even than single persons in their mid-twenties. For one thing, the divorced are likely to have a number of different sexual partners each year, until or unless they enter into a deep relationship in which marriage is the implicit possible goal. Among our divorced males, the number of intercourse partners in the past year ranged from one to several dozen, with the median figure being eight, as compared with only two for our under-25 single males and four for single males of 25 to 34. (Interestingly, anywhere from 37 to 61 percent of Kinsey's postmarital males, depending on age, included prostitutes among their coital partners.[25] In our own sample, only 20 percent had done so within the year prior to the survey.) For our divorced women who were actively having coitus, the median number of partners in the past year was four, as compared with two for single females under 25, and three for single females of 25 to 34. Both divorced men and divorced women also had had a number of petting partners in the course of the past year—more, on the whole, than they did coital partners. But to judge by their coital rates, petting was not used as a substitute for intercourse as it still is to some extent among younger singles, but rather as a testing process and, in some cases, a delaying tactic.

Since Kinsey published no data on the number of coital partners per year for previously married persons, we cannot say how great an increase these figures represent. It would be reasonable to suppose, however, that the increase is of the same general magnitude as that in coital frequency—anywhere from, say, twofold to fourfold. Nor does Kinsey say anything about the techniques of foreplay or the coital positions used by postmarital males and females, so we cannot assert unequivocally that liberation has made changes in these respects. Nevertheless, we think that it has, for in the interviews for the present study, as well as in those conducted by the author for his own recent study of the divorced,[26] there was a good deal of evidence that most divorced persons experience their postmarital coitus as being more sensuous, free and varied than their marital coitus. And since marital coitus itself has been much liberated in recent years, it stands to reason that postmarital sex must also have been.

This is only speculative. More concretely, our survey data show that the sexual intercourse of divorced persons today is at least as innovative, sensuous and varied as that of the younger married people in our sample (the most liberated subsample within our survey aside from a very small contingent of far-out experimentalists and sexual radicals). Nine-tenths of our divorced men, for instance, and over eight-tenths of our divorced women had at least some oral-genital experience within the past year—a proportion considerably larger than that we find among younger singles, somewhat higher than that among married people in general, and about the same as that among the youngest married people. As for coital positions, divorced men and women were more likely to use most of the variations we asked about than even the under-25 married people in our sample. A fifth of our divorced people, for instance (combining male and female responses), said they often use the sitting position, as compared with only about a twentieth of our youngest married group; and over a quarter of our divorced people said they often use rear-entry vaginal intercourse, as compared with a fifth of the young married group. Half of our divorced people reported having had anal intercourse at least once in the past year—twice as many as among our youngest married cohort.

It is sometimes said that such sexual experimentation and variation by divorced persons indicate not healthy hedonism but a cold-blooded concentration upon genital sensation without interpersonal meaning, often involving the exploitation of one partner by another—particularly of the female by the male. In our interviews we got the impression that this was sometimes, but not generally, the case. Only a minority of divorced persons seem either chronically detached or coldly exploitative, though many pass through a phase of one or both kinds of behavior. As for the majority, most of them do encounter some emotionally impenetrable or exploitative sexual partners as they make their rounds, but are not firmly tied to those with whom they have bad experiences, and need not, and generally do not, repeat them. Nor apparently do they permit sexual variations that they dislike, in order to stay on good terms with their partners. In our survey sample, not one divorced person said that he or she would prefer less variety in sexual practices than he or she was now having.

Moreover, there appears to be a high overall level of satisfaction among the divorced with their own sexual activities. As we observed in the previous chapter, the most objective measurement of satisfaction available is orgasm regularity in the female. Since Kinsey gives no such figures for postmarital females, we will have to use Gebhard's data, even though they provide a less

sharply focused picture of behavior of a generation ago. Gebhard reported that it was usual for both divorced women and
widowed women to have higher orgasm rates postmaritally than
they had had in their marriages (although this was much truer
of divorced women than of widows).[27] This was due partly to
psychological reasons ("rebound") and partly to the fact that
marital sex had been failing as the marriage failed. However, the
satisfaction of divorced women was high not just relative to their
own marital experience but in absolute terms: Except for very
young women (under 26), about half to two-thirds of the divorced women in Gebhard's study had orgasm in 90 to 100
percent of their postmarital coitus, while considerably fewer
than half of Kinsey's married women did as well.[28] But in 1972
divorced women were even more regularly orgasmic than this:
Over four-fifths of those divorced women in our sample who
answered our question on orgasmic regularity said that they had
been reaching orgasm in three-quarters to all of their postmarital coitus.

Kinsey includes no data on self-evaluation of the overall pleasure of postmarital sex. While we thus have nothing with which
to compare our own findings as to perceived or self-evaluated
overall pleasure, those findings do contrast sharply with the
general picture of postmarital sex to be found in fiction and
reportage of the 1940s, and which we found in our interviews
with people who had been in the postmarital phase of life a
generation ago. Two-thirds of our currently divorced females
and nine-tenths of our currently divorced males rated their postmarital coitus as very pleasurable in general. If we add those
who rated it as mostly pleasurable, the total affirmative vote
comes to nine-tenths for the females and more than nine-tenths
for the males. Only a few males and females rated their postmarital sex as neither pleasurable nor nonpleasurable, and none
at all gave it either a mildly or strongly negative rating. Although
precise comparisons are not warranted because of the small size
of our sample, the divorced apparently perceive their postmarital coitus as being as pleasurable as the married do theirs. But
we must add a reservation: Our survey inquired specifically
about pleasure, rather than total satisfaction. From our interviews it is apparent that for a number of divorced men and
women, postmarital sex often involves powerful physical pleasures but lacks comparable emotional fulfillment. For many

men, and even more women, coitus with a loved partner is more totally rewarding than coitus with a sexually more exciting but unloved partner.

Our conclusions are thus generally positive. Postmarital sex has apparently been much liberated in the past 20-odd years, and by and large this liberation has made life for the divorced more healthful, satisfying and exciting. But our report would be incomplete if we did not add that the sex life of the divorced is far from problem-free and far from wholly liberated. The divorce experience in general is one of crisis, alienation, transition and recuperation, and this pertains to the sexual behavior involved in it as well as to its nonsexual aspects. In our interviews with both currently divorced and with remarried persons, we heard much about the varied pains and pleasures involved in postmarital sex at different stages of the process. Our material does not warrant any attempt to present the whole spectrum of such experience, nor would this be the place to do so even if it did, but we can at least briefly exemplify some of the wide-ranging reactions of the divorced to their postmarital sexual encounters.

The introduction to the liberated world of postmarital sex is anxiety-producing and even somewhat shocking to many of those who had been faithfully married for some time. They are not only unsure of themselves because of the divorce trauma, but unfamiliar with the mores of a sexual marketplace that is faster paced, more callow and more cynical than the one they knew as young singles. This is especially true for females, as exemplified by a fairly typical comment:

FEMALE, 34, INSURANCE ANALYST: I was nervous enough on my first date after ten years of marriage, just wondering whether I'd have any problem later on, or how I'd handle it, when this clod asked me straight out—even before dinner was over—"How about it?" I was so dumb, and so unsure of what was happening, that I actually said, "How about what?" Oh, God, I was so embarrassed! And then there were all the gropers, the grabbers, the smoochers, the dirty-talkers, the guys who swore they were in love with me after an hour or two. I was no prude, and I was plenty frustrated, but I was damned if I'd trade my bod' for dinner. I didn't come that cheap.

Men, too, are often troubled, especially at first, by the sexual expectations of their partners and by the lack of self-assurance that is the frequent result of marital failure. A typical statement:

MALE, 41, BUILDING CONTRACTOR: My marriage had been so rotten in its last two years that I almost never felt any sexual desire—I sometimes thought my organs looked half atrophied—and even when we did go at it once in a while, I was as likely to fail as not. I lost all belief in myself as a man. After I left her I couldn't bring myself to try it with anyone else for nearly a year, and then, when I did, I was in a cold sweat and only half-hard, and just barely made it—if you can call an orgasm coaxed out of a semilimp dick "making it." But things slowly got a little better and a little better, with one girl, until after a while I was functioning marvelously. With *her,* that is—because for several years my first time or two with any new woman was always a time of nervousness and worry, wondering whether I would or wouldn't. About half the time, the first time with each new woman was poor.

Despite such alarms and anxieties, five out of six divorced people begin having coitus within the first year after separation from their spouses, and very few of them retreat to temporary or permanent celibacy. Indeed, as we have seen, most of them begin to get considerable pleasure from their postmarital coitus and go on to lead fairly active sexual lives. Nonetheless, unless the divorced man or woman is emotionally involved with his or her sexual partner, much of postmarital coitus is a price the woman feels obliged to pay for the time and money spent upon her, and the proof of manliness the man feels obliged to exhibit even when he feels no real desire. Two examples:

FEMALE, 32, REAL-ESTATE SALESWOMAN: I used to fight off every guy I didn't feel keen on sleeping with, because I had my principles. But so many times it wound up getting nasty that finally I decided it wasn't worth the trouble; it was just part of the cost of taking a chance on a new person. If some guy makes a big thing about it, I simply stay cool and let him have it. Big deal! What's the difference?—it's not like I haven't been laid plenty of times before. Sometimes I even have an orgasm with a man I don't like, or find repulsive, but that worries me; it's kind of perverse. Afterwards I feel disgusted with myself, and try to wash it all away in the shower—I practically boil myself for half an hour.

MALE, 35, STATIONERY SALESMAN: It took me three years to get it through my head that I didn't have to screw every woman I took out. I used to make an all-out try with every one of them—and let me tell you, if I didn't find the gal appealing, it could be a rough trip, and afterwards I'd be furious with myself. But somehow I *had* to. I felt that if I didn't come on like the superstud of all time, they'd think I was a fag, or hung-up or something.

Still, as we have seen, in general most divorced people find postmarital coitus more pleasurable than they did marital coitus or at least coitus in that deteriorating phase of marriage which is most recent and clear in their memories. In addition to—or perhaps because of—the pleasure involved, their postmarital coital experiences renew and restore their egos, broaden their sexual horizons and often reveal them to themselves as being more sensuous and responsive than they had realized.

Even so, their sexual relationships often continue to be anxiety-producing for another reason. Because of the trauma of marital failure, the divorced tend to be more apprehensive about emotional involvement than young single people, and to feel torn between their own desire for, and fear of, intimacy and commitment.

MALE, 29, SHIPPING CLERK: It was a fortunate thing for me that I had to go into the army after we broke up, because it kept me on the move, with no time to get wrapped up with anybody. I would just hunt for pickups in bars, and ball around all I could, and get into all kinds of wild scenes. I all but screwed myself sick a number of times. I saw myself as the greatest cock walking. But if any girl made noises like she was getting fond of me, or if I myself felt any such feelings starting up, I got really nervous, I got the mean reds, I turned into a sonofabitch and busted out of it. It took me two years to wash all that out of my system and get my act back together so I could have a real thing going again with a girl.

FEMALE, 31, COMPUTER PROGRAMMER: I had always thought that sex with my husband was very good, but after we broke

up and I was dating some older and really hip guys, I began
to find out what it was all about. One man I went out with
for a while taught me how to be really aware of my own
body and my reactions; it was fascinating, watching myself.
Another man was so sensuous about every little detail, even
without grass, that I became that way myself. One of the
fellows I'm seeing now is getting me to see the fun-and-
games side of sex. My only problem is that I have this fear
of getting trapped again. I hate being alone, but I get into
a panic whenever I feel someone closing in on me or think
I'm letting myself get too involved with someone.

Most divorced people pass through these several stages of
personal reconstruction over a period of time. Then, slowly
reintegrating their restored or newly acquired sexuality with
their deeper emotional needs, they enter into intimate relationships, which, if they endure and deepen, are eventually formal-
ized as marriage. But by the time they are deeply committed to
such relationships, they cease sounding like people leading the
postmarital life; their sexual experiences, and their feelings
about them, are very much of a piece with those of the happily
married. The following man speaks not only for himself but for
many other men and women who have passed through postmarital life and on into a new monogamous love relationship:

MALE, 48, PRINT-SHOP FOREMAN: I was shaken up pretty
badly by the breakup of my marriage. I didn't even date for
half a year. Then I started in, and gradually got into the sex
thing, and realized that I'd been pretty stuffy and blocked
as a sex partner up to then. I opened up and learned a hell
of a lot from different women; I had a real ball. But I didn't
want to get too close to anybody. I was honest about it—
I always laid it right on the line, and those who didn't like
it got out, and those who did had a ball right along with me.
There was one gal who'd been married to a homosexual
and was really ripe, just like me. We went at it hot and heavy
for a couple of years. Sometimes we'd screw for two or
three hours, off and on, until we were so exhausted and
hungry and thirsty that we had to stop and feed ourselves
before we could get back to it. With her, I learned how to
work up to it slowly and carefully, and excite her in all sorts

of little ways, and then, when I was finally in the saddle, pace myself so I could last for an hour, maybe, while she had one, two, three—or half a dozen—climaxes. It was great; it was a good life.

I wasn't planning ever to marry again, but then I met a girl I liked, and *more* than liked. After a while I realized she was someone I hadn't thought existed anywhere. I didn't feel the least fear of getting totally wrapped up in her, and she felt the same about me. Our sex was just fine—about as good as any I'd been having—but it was only part of the whole magoo, and we both knew after a few months that we just had to be married to each other. We've been married for ten years and we still feel the same. The sex is still fine, too. Naturally, we don't do it nearly as often as we used to, and we don't try to make it last as long either, but it's great anyway. It's still a big thing in our lives, and yet *not* a big thing, in a way—I mean, it's not what we're thinking about or planning or working on all the time; it's just there, part of us, like breathing and sleeping.

Extramarital Coitus: Attitudes, Incidence

In those aspects of sexual behavior we have thus far examined, we have found that sexual liberation has not produced sexual anomie. Despite the extensive changes it has made in the feelings most Americans have about their own sexual parts and sexual sensations, about the legitimacy of maximizing pleasure and about the acceptability and normality of a wide variety of techniques of foreplay and coitus, sexual liberation has not dismantled the romantic-passionate concept of sex and replaced it with the recreational one. The latter attitude toward sex now coexists with the former in our society, and in many a person's feelings, but the former remains the dominant ideal. While most Americans—especially the young—now feel far freer than formerly to be sensation-oriented at times, for the great majority of them sex remains intimately allied to their deepest emotions and inextricably interwoven with their conceptions of loyalty, love and marriage. The web of meaning and social structure surrounding sex has been stretched and reshaped, but not torn asunder.

The traditional sexual exclusivity of marriage is a case in point. In sharp contrast to most of our findings thus far, our data in this area suggest that in the past generation there has been almost no measurable increase in the number of American husbands who ever have extramarital experience, and only a limited increase in the number of American wives who do so. The overall incidence for our sample of married men of all ages appears to be basically unchanged from that of a generation ago. Only among men under 25 do we find any significant increase, but even that increase is of moderate proportions. As for our sample of married women, there is no evidence of any overall increase in incidence compared to a generation ago. Among wives under 25, however, there is a very large increase, but even this has only brought the incidence of extramarital behavior for these young women close to—but not yet on a par with—the incidence of extramarital behavior among under-25 husbands.

These findings will seem surprising if not unbelievable to many persons. In the last decade, and especially in the last four or five years, we have all been subjected to a barrage of propaganda to the effect that sexual exclusivity in marriage is obsolescent. An endless stream of books and articles and an endless parade of guests on TV talk shows have informed us that such exclusivity is archaic, or male-chauvinist, or unsuited to modern life, or unnecessary, or absurd, and that a number of alternatives are more workable, more sensible and more fun. Books advocating permissive marriage have outsold almost everything but diet books (the O'Neills' *Open Marriage* was on the best-seller lists during almost all of 1972); articles on group marriage have become a staple of women's magazines and have even appeared in the respectable *New York Times*; discussions of marital swinging and what used to be called "orgies"—a word that already sounds quaint and old-fashioned—have become almost commonplace in periodicals and on late-night TV; and novels about group marital experimentation (by Robert Rimmer and others) are among the cult books of the college crowd. A number of sociologists and psychotherapists have begun to maintain that extramarital behavior can be good for the individual and for the marriage: O. Spurgeon English, an eminent psychiatrist associated with Temple University, has written that extramarital affairs are often "a self-chosen means to a greater sense of living"; Gerhard Neubeck, former president of the American

Association of Marriage Counselors, has argued that such affairs can benefit marriage by reducing the burden each mate places on the other; and psychotherapist-sexologist Albert Ellis maintains that "sexual adventuring" outside of marriage can do a lot to stimulate personality growth.[29] In early 1973, when New York Yankee pitchers Mike Kekich and Fritz Peterson told the world about their mate-swapping experiment, it appeared that the new doctrine had penetrated the square, wholesome heartland of American culture.

Not only has all this talk convinced most people that extramarital behavior is now far more widespread than formerly, but some authorities have provided factitious proof by quoting other authorities who have said that it is "logical" or "reasonable" to assume that there have been significant increases since Kinsey's survey. Thus, what begins as speculation and assumption is transformed, by citation, into ostensible evidence. In reality, however, there has been no survey of respectable dimensions since Kinsey's work to provide any factual support for these speculations or to validate the popular impression.

Indeed, a few thoughtful investigators have found some reason to suspect that the increases in extramarital activity were either small or nonexistent. Various recent attitude surveys, for one thing, have shown little weakening of the traditional disapproval of extramarital behavior. Sociologist Harold Christensen, for one, sampled midwestern American attitudes on the matter in 1958 and again in 1968—a decade in which, as we have seen, sexual liberation was making major strides—and found that the great majority of people, in both years, were strongly against extramarital behavior under all conditions.[30] A national poll conducted by *McCall's* magazine in 1966 found a large majority of persons condemning extramarital sex even under circumstances often thought of as extenuating.[31] In 1968, the author of the present volume conducted a national questionnaire survey of his own, chiefly limited to middle-class and lower-middle-class persons, and found a large majority of respondents saying they always, or usually, disapprove of extramarital behavior; even those in the sample who themselves had had such affairs were more often than not generally disapproving.[32] The seeming permissiveness of Americans today concerning extramarital sex is apparently more a matter of public attitude than real conviction.

In the present survey we did not explore attitudes toward extramarital sex in general, but several of our specific questions touched on the matter, and the answers to them suggest that things had not changed much by 1972. Three-quarters of our females, for instance, and over three-fifths of our males, agreed with the statement "Mate-swapping is wrong." Even in the youngest segment of our sample it was only the single who were considerably less critical. We also asked for reactions to certain hypothetical extramarital situations: Would the respondent object if his or her mate were to pet with another person? Or have occasional extramarital sex experiences? Or have an extramarital love affair? And would the respondent's mate object if the respondent himself or herself did any one of these things? The responses were remarkably traditional: Anywhere from 80 to 98 percent said they, or their mates, would object to each of these activities. Wives were no more accepting of husbands' extramarital actions than the other way around, and, most revealingly, the young in our sample were no readier to accept extramarital activity in their mates, even hypothetically, than were older persons.

All of which is very strange indeed. How is one to reconcile the public's current interest in the subject of extramarital sex with its continuing disapproval of it? The glib answer is to say that Americans are hypocritical about sex, but we have seen that in many other cases of sexual behavior this is ceasing to be the case. A more thoughtful answer might be that the majority of people have always experienced extramarital desires, at least from time to time, and kept them hidden; in today's climate of open discussion those desires are being manifested in the form of discussion and of an unconcealed appetite for vicarious experience. At the same time most people continue to disapprove of such behavior because they believe that when it becomes a reality rather than a fantasy, it undermines and endangers the most important human relationship in their lives.

We regard this as the likely explanation of our survey findings. We cannot, however, make as fine-grained an analysis of change in this area as we have in some other areas of sexual behavior because of certain limitations of both Kinsey's extramarital data and our own. Kinsey's information on extramarital behavior, at least that of males, is curiously skimpy. He himself says, without explanation, that "because of the inadequacy of the record it has been impossible to construct accumulative-incidence curves by the usual techniques, and we can only estimate from these active-incidence figures."[33] And while he did provide accumulative-incidence data for females, the figures are seriously exaggerated by an overweighting of his female sample with divorced women, a problem we will return to in a moment. For our part, while we do have data on the percentages of males and females who have ever experienced extramarital sex (these being loosely equivalent to accumulative incidences), we failed to collect sufficiently detailed data to establish the active incidence for any but the youngest cohort, or the frequency for any cohort. Despite these limitations, we think we can furnish reasonably illuminating answers to at least some key questions about the scope and nature of extramarital behavior today as compared with Kinsey's time.

The first question: How many men a generation ago had, and how many today have had, any extramarital coitus at all? Though Kinsey did not construct an accumulative-incidence curve to show what percentage of men, by any given age, had ever had extramarital experience, he did make the rough estimate, based on the percentages of those who had activity in each five-year cohort, that "about half of all the married males have intercourse with women other than their wives, at some time while they are married."[34] In our most closely comparable group—a merging of our married and divorced white men—we find that only 41 percent have ever had extramarital coitus. Our sample, however, includes men of all ages, and unquestionably some of the younger men who have not yet had any extramarital experience will eventually have some. Accordingly, the lifetime accumulative incidence of our whole sample will be somewhat higher, though not by a substantial amount since two-thirds of all those men who have extramarital intercourse do so for the first time within the first five years of marriage. A reasonable estimate would be that the ultimate accumulative incidence will probably be close to, but not above, 50 percent. Confirming this projection is another characteristic of extramarital behavior shown by the figures: Our "ever had extramarital intercourse" percentages show no increase after age 44, which is grounds to suppose that our sample will ultimately have, at most, an accumulative incidence about the same as that of the 35-to-44 cohort, or just under 50 percent. The percentages, by age, are shown in Table 37.

Table 37

Ever Had Extramarital Intercourse: Married and Currently Divorced White Males, Percents

Under 25	32
25–34	41
35–44	47
45–54	38
55 and over	43

The somewhat low figure for the 45-to-54 cohort is in all likelihood a mere statistical error due to the smallness of the sample. In any case, the overall impression is one of a relatively flat curve of accumulative incidence, and this suggests an eventual lifetime figure, for today's white males, of about the same magnitude as that in Kinsey's sample. It is worth noting in passing that the figures in Table 37 are slightly lower than they would have been had we used our total sample, which includes blacks. We did not do so, of course, since in measuring the change with Kinsey's time we were obliged to choose that part of our sample which most nearly matches his.

But while the incidence for the entire married white male sample shows no increase over Kinsey's figure, closer examination does show some increase in the youngest cohort. We can draw this conclusion, despite the absence of any accumulative-incidence curve in Kinsey's study, by using Kinsey's active-incidence data for males of the same age. Since our under-25 married males are the youngest cohort in our series and have had no earlier period of married experience, the "ever had extramarital intercourse" figure for this cohort in Table 37 is also an active incidence. It can therefore be compared with Kinsey's active-incidence data. The figure for Kinsey's married males of 16 to 20 is 35.4 percent, and for married males of 21 to 25, 24.4 percent.[35] Our own cohort partly overlaps these two, however, and we therefore need to weight Kinsey's figures to match our own sample before making the comparison. Since one-fifth of our 18-to-24 group is under 21, and four-fifths are from 21 to 24, a rebalanced active incidence for the Kinsey sample, comparable to our own, comes to 26.6 percent. Our own 18-to-24 cohort, as shown in Table 37, has an incidence of 32 percent.

The indicated increase, although significant, is modest in comparison with the increases we have found in premarital coitus and the use of oral techniques and positional variations. The 18-to-24 cohort may, as it grows older, somewhat outstrip today's 25-to-34 and older cohorts, but probably by no greater a margin than they now outstrip the young married males of Kinsey's time. It is even possible that there will be no overall increase whatever, for as we will see in the next section, those who have extramarital coitus today do not wait as long before beginning to do so as was true in Kinsey's era. It may be that the increase in the youngest group reflects only this, rather than that the percentage who will ever do so is on the rise.

The picture is thus one of rather little change since Kinsey's time in the incidence of extramarital behavior by males. Nor is there any evidence of large-scale changes along any of our special demographic parameters. Kinsey, for instance, found a tendency for married males at the lower educational levels to be more active, extramaritally, in youth, and less so by their forties, while at higher educational levels the active incidence was lowest in the early twenties, and highest in the upper thirties.[36] While our own figures are not active incidences (except for the youngest cohort), we find that, under 35, considerably more noncollege men than college men have had extramarital experience, but that the gap narrows among the males of 35 and over. This suggests little change since Kinsey's time. Again, Kinsey reported that extramarital intercourse was a good deal more common among religiously inactive males than among devout males[37]; this still seems to be the case, although the spread is distinctly greater in the older half of the sample than in the younger half.

The data for female extramarital behavior, as we indicated at the outset, paint a somewhat different picture. In the female volume, Kinsey did furnish accumulative-incidence calculations for each age rather than a guesswork lifetime figure. As in the male volume, these incidences are based on the experiences not only of individuals who were married at the time of the interviews but also of those who had been separated, divorced or widowed. In the male volume this worked out well enough, since the proportion of separated, divorced and widowed men to presently married men in his sample was close to that in the national population at that time.[38] In the female volume, however, the situation was quite different. In Kinsey's female sample, the ratio of previously married (separated, divorced and widowed) women to presently married women is 1 to 2.2, although the ratio in the U.S. population at that time was about 1 to 4[39]; and in the portion of the female sample with which we are most concerned—women of 45 or less (since Kinsey's accumulative-incidence data break off at this age)—the situation is far worse, the ratio in Kinsey's sample being 1 to 3.7, although at the time it was only about 1 to 31 in the U.S. population.[40] This causes a serious exaggeration of extramarital incidence rates: The great majority of previously married women below age 45 were separated or divorced rather than widowed, and there is good reason to believe that both the active and the accumulative incidences of extramarital experience of the separated and divorced were much higher than those of presently married women. Gebhard reported, for instance, that 31 percent of divorced women had extramarital coitus in the last year of marriage—twice as high a rate as for any five-year period for Kinsey's combined married-plus-previously-married female sample.[41] Kinsey himself did not give separate accumulative incidences for the several categories of ever-married women. Gebhard, however, found that 34 percent of divorced women had had extramarital coitus,[42] which is anywhere from a third larger to four times larger than the accumulative incidences, at various ages, of Kinsey's entire ever-married sample,[43] and, obviously, must be still higher than the incidences for the presently married women within that sample.[44] Our own survey data show a difference of the same order of magnitude: Only 17 percent of our presently married white females, but 52 percent of our divorced white females, have had extramarital coitus.

To make a reasonable comparison of our data with Kinsey's, and a fair appraisal of the changes that have taken place in a generation, we therefore have to provide ourselves with corrected accumulative incidences for Kinsey's time, removing the exaggeration caused by the disproportion of the separated and divorced in his sample. We assume, on the basis of our own survey data plus the clues provided by Gebhard, that separated and divorced females have an accumulative incidence of extramarital coitus something like two to three times as large as that of presently married females—say, 2.5 times. Using this ratio, plus the actual proportions of married persons and separated-divorced persons in the U.S. population at the time rather than those in Kinsey's sample, we were able to come up with figures which we believe more nearly represent the actual accumulative incidences for presently married plus previously married white women in Kinsey's era. His own published accumulative-incidence figures[45] and our adaptations of them[46] are shown in Table 38.

Now we are in a position to compare our own "ever had" figures (which are crude approximations of accumulative incidences), for married and divorced women combined, with what we consider to be relatively correct accumulative incidences for Kinsey's time. Kinsey gives no overall figures for his total sample, but our own figure is 18 percent, which by inspection is clearly of the same order as the rebalanced Kinsey figures in Table 38 and suggests no overall change. When we break this down by age, we see that indeed there has been no change of any consequence except below age 25—where, however, the change is of historic dimensions (see Table 39).

Table 38

Accumulative Incidence of Extramarital Intercourse,
White Females: As Given by Kinsey,
and Rebalanced, Percents

	As given by Kinsey	Rebalanced
By 25	9	8
By 35	23	19
By 45	26	20

Table 39

Ever Had Extramarital Intercourse: Married and Currently
Divorced White Females, Two Generations, Percents

1938–1949 (Adapted from Kinsey)		1972 (Present survey)	
Age	%	Age	%
By 25	8	18 to 24	24
By 35	19	25 to 34	21
By 45	20	35 to 44	18
[By 55	18–20*]	45 to 54	12
[55 and up	18–20*]	55 and up	15

*Kinsey did not extend his accumulative-incidence curve beyond 45 on the grounds that there was no further accumulation beyond that point. This might mean that that curve was flat from there on, or, more likely, that it dropped; certain other curves of this type show declines among the oldest individuals, due to their greater sexual conservatism. It is reasonable to suppose, therefore, that the missing data would be somewhat under 20 percent. (See, for comparison, Table 37.)

The comparisons in Table 39 are admittedly imprecise, but they do entitle us to draw certain major conclusions. First, it seems clear that there has been no increase of any consequence for women in the entire age range above 24. The increase in the 25-to-34 age cohort is too small to have any statistical significance, and the same is true of the apparent decrease for the next cohort. As for the two cohorts beyond 44, our figures are considerably smaller than the by-age-45 figure provided by Kinsey, which we think is applicable to the next two age brackets, but we doubt that the apparent decrease among women of 45 and over is real. When Kinsey was doing most of his fieldwork, resistance to talking about sex at all was even stronger in most females than in most males; accordingly, like many others who have studied Kinsey's work closely we feel that his sample was overweighted with the unconventional and the daring, and that his incidences for socially disapproved sexual behavior are therefore often somewhat high. Our previous rebalancing of his data did not affect this kind of distortion; even the adjusted accumulative-incidence data in Table 38 are probably too high, at least in the older age cohorts.

All of which leads us to suspect that our oldest two cohorts were probably about as active, extramaritally, as comparable females in Kinsey's time. But clearly not more so, even though they were teen-agers or young adults at the time of Kinsey's fieldwork, and according to his own analysis should eventually have shown distinctly higher incidences of extramarital behavior than his sample as a whole.[47] They do not; we conclude that there has been no such increase among them, or among women of any age group from 25 up.

It is quite another story when we turn our attention to the under-25 cohort. Here the increase in extramarital experience between Kinsey's time and today is of such magnitude as to completely outweigh any and all uncertainties and errors inherent in the data, or in our method of making comparisons, and to leave no doubt that for all the uncertainties and imperfections of the data, something major has happened.

The comparison, in this age group, is less conjectural and less error-prone than that for any other age group. For while the comparison of Kinsey's accumulative incidences, rebalanced by us, with our own "ever had" accumulations, is filled with statistical hazards, in the case of our youngest cohort the "ever had" figure is also, by definition, a six-year active-incidence figure. Thus, it provides a very fair and reliable comparison with the active incidence for Kinsey's 16-to-20 and 21-to-25 cohorts. Here again, as in the case of males, we need to rebalance the Kinsey data to make a cohort comparable to our own, one-fifth of which is under 21 and four-fifths of which is 21 to 24. Starting with Kinsey's raw data, an active-incidence figure for a cohort comparable to our own would be 8.4; correcting this for his overrepresentation of divorced women makes the figure somewhat less than 8, as against a 24-percent active incidence for our 18-to-24 cohort.[48] In simplest terms, the experience of extramarital intercourse is three times as widespread among married white women of 18 to 24 today as it was a generation ago. The change is dramatic, to say the least.

But what does it signify? Since we found no evidence of an overall increase among males and only a relatively small one among the under-25 males, and since the very large increase among females under 25 only brings them close to, but still below, the incidence for males in the same age bracket, it would seem that where extramarital coitus is concerned, sexual liberation has brought about something close to equality rather than a revolutionary change in values. A generation ago, only a third as many young wives as young husbands ventured outside of marriage; today, three-quarters as many young wives as young husbands do so. The change is not a radical break with the ideal of sexual fidelity, but a radical break with the double standard. Kinsey was of the opinion that the difference he observed between the male and female incidences of extramarital behavior was due to biological differences in the nervous system.[49] Undoubtedly, some of the differences between human male and female sexual behavior are biologically based, but our data strongly suggest that extramarital behavior is not one of them: Woman will go outside marriage for sex as often as will man, if she and her society think that she has as much right to do so as he.

This, as far as we can tell from our data, is the major change in extramarital behavior since Kinsey's time. Some people are, of course, involved in widely touted innovations in extramarital behavior, which we will look at a little later—"swinging," in particular—but there is nothing in our data to show that the innovations have made any important change as yet, in the overall percentages of males and females who have ever experienced extramarital coitus. The behavior of the under-25 females does suggest that, in the next 20 years or so, overall female experience will double or triple, bringing it more or less to the same level as overall male experience. Meanwhile, however, the deluge of contemporary talk about infidelity, affairs, open marriage, swapping and swinging means not that more is happening but that people discuss such things more openly than they used to, and that those who do such things do them more frequently and regularly than formerly.

Finally, we find some relatively limited change in the relationships formerly shown by Kinsey between various demographic factors and the incidence of extramarital coitus. Religious devoutness, for instance, had a strong negative correlation with the incidence of extramarital behavior in wives in Kinsey's time. To give an extreme example, only 7 percent of devout Protestant women in their early thirties reported any extramarital experience, as against 28 percent of nondevout Protestant women in the same age group.[50] In our own sample, religion is still a potent restraining influence, though less so than formerly. Among our 35-and-over women, for instance, a quarter of the nonchurchgoers, but only half as many who attend church regularly, have ever had extramarital experience.

We conclude that in the area of extramarital behavior sexual liberation has not made widespread changes, as it has in premarital and marital sexual behavior. All sorts of predictions abound as to the future of marriage, and particularly as to the growth of nonexclusive, permissive or polygamous adaptations of it, but such evidence as we possess does not show these alternatives to be dominant or even common as yet. Sexual liberation, we repeat, has thus far brought freedom, but not anomie.

Extramarital Coitus: When Begun, Number of Partners, Secrecy versus Permissiveness, Coital Variations, Orgasm Regularity, Overall Pleasure

Quantitatively, therefore, sexual liberation has made only limited changes in American extramarital behavior. But what about qualitatively? Has extramarital coitus become emotionally more rewarding and less conflicted? Is it more freely sensuous, uninhibited and satisfying than formerly?

Some of these questions are very difficult to investigate, for much of what passes for the sexual gratification of extramarital coitus turns out, upon close inspection, to be nonsexual in nature. The intense pleasure some people experience during their extramarital acts may, for instance, owe less to the sexual acts being performed than to the revenge being taken against their mates, or to the excitement of doing something forbidden and dangerous, or to feelings of personal desirability and success engendered by those acts, or even to the rediscovery of a lost capacity for romantic love. Furthermore, two respondents may each rate their extramarital experiences as having been generally "very pleasurable," but what one of them means by the term may be so different from what the other means that the answers should not be made part of the same statistic. The point may be illustrated by two brief excerpts from our interview transcripts. First, a 39-year-old working woman talks about an extramarital relationship she had for five years:

> My husband is a very unhappy man—he's never achieved anything he meant to achieve, and as a consequence he's always angry at everything, including me. As for our sex life, it's adequate—well, actually, it's always been a borderline thing, because his ejaculation comes almost immediately upon penetration. For years, he was always bothered by fantasies of my sleeping with various men I worked with, and he made my life miserable about it, but it wasn't true and I had no intention of ever making it true. Then, finally, I did meet a man through business, one of the nicest human beings I'd ever met in my life, and I did have an affair with him that lasted for years. It was absolutely delightful. He was completely different from my husband, sexually—very gentle, interested in me, patient, not at all selfish. The sex became very good after I got over my guilt feelings. But that wasn't why I went into the whole thing—I went into it because it was a *personal* relationship, a quite beautiful thing, and I treasure the memory of it. We never considered divorce and remarriage—I'm a Catholic—but the relationship brought real happiness into my life for years.

And now, in contrast, a brief reminiscence by the interviewee we called Leo Zimmer, the group-sex swinger we heard from in Chapter 1 (pages 45–49). In the following excerpt he recalls his feelings about swinging as a species of extramarital sex:

> I married my wife after we'd gone swinging together a number of times, but as soon as I did, she wanted to cut out on the group scene. I couldn't do without it. Married sex was okay, but it didn't give me everything I needed. I insisted on swinging, because I really dug meeting a bunch of brand-new women and, inside half an hour, having one of them in front of me, and another in back, and a couple more on the side, all of us busily doing every kind of thing to each other. What I needed was to ball myself to exhaustion every once in a while, with as many new and different bodies as possible, and go home completely sated. It was a terrific ego trip; it would puff me up for days or even weeks—and for that length of time, at least, I'd be satisfied with marriage.

One can hardly make a valid generalization about the pleasures of extramarital sex that will encompass both of these cases. They are, however, extremes; the great majority of extramarital experiences involve neither as deep and tender an intimacy as the former, nor as coldly impersonal an egocentrism as the latter. We can therefore cautiously make certain generalizations about the quality of contemporary extramarital behavior as shown by our data, recognizing that these conclusions apply primarily to the middle range of activities and may completely fail to fit those at one extreme or the other of the spectrum.

The first generalization is that sexual liberation seems to have made very little change in the emotional context of extramarital behavior. Even though the words "adultery" and "infidelity" have become somewhat unfashionable among sexual liberals because of their moralistic overtones and their inapplicability to mutually sanctioned extramarital acts, the evidence of our survey indicates that nearly all extramarital activity is still adulterous and unfaithful in the emotional sense; that is, by far the largest part of extramarital activity is secret and furtive, violative of the emotional entente existing between the spouses, productive of internal conflict and guilt feelings on the part of the one engaging in such acts, and anywhere from infuriating to shattering to the other if he or she discovers the truth.

Nevertheless, it appears that nowadays the classic restraints of fear and guilt do not hold back extramarital behavior as long as they used to. Kinsey published no data as to how long persons who had had extramarital experiences had been married before they began them, but we can get some idea of the change that has taken place in the past generation by comparing the older half of our sample with the younger half. Men of 35 and older who have ever had extramarital coitus did so for the first time after an average of six or seven years of marriage; in contrast, men under 35 began after only one to three years. Similarly, women of 35 and older with extramarital experience began, on the average, after about ten years of marriage, while women under 35 did so after only two to six years.

Although Kinsey provided no tabulated figures on this subject, he did say that less-educated and lower-class males were far more apt than better-educated and upper-class males not only to begin extramarital coitus early in married life but to taper off earlier.[51] There was a similar but less clear-cut relationship in the case of females. While our own sample is too small for detailed analysis by age within the demographic breakdowns, we can report that we see no evidence of gross differences of this sort. As nearly as we can tell, blue-collar and white-collar men, high-school-level and college-level men, now wait about the same length of time before having their first extramarital experiences. The same thing is true of women. This is in accord with our other findings about the narrowing of cultural differences in the area of sexual behavior.

We did, however, find one interesting correlation of quite another sort: Those divorced people in our sample who had had extramarital coitus had begun doing so much earlier in marriage than those people who have had such experiences but are still married. The median figure for both divorced males and divorced females was about one year, or only a fraction as long as the comparable figures for the still-married. The question to be answered is what the relation is between early onset of extramarital activity and subsequent divorce. From interview material, we get the impression that early extramarital activity by those who later get divorced is, in some cases, the result of the early recognition that the marriage is a hopeless mistake, and in other cases is the result of neurotic traits that would have irreparably injured the marriage even without the added insult of infidelity. In either case it is not extramarital activity, in itself, that is the ultimate cause of divorce; both that activity, and divorce, are results of other and deeper-lying causes. But this is not to exculpate extramarital behavior altogether; it is a proximate cause of divorce, if not the ultimate one, at least in the minds of many who ought to know best: In our survey, over half of the divorced males and females with extramarital histories say that their extramarital acts did play a part in their separations or divorces. Apparently, for many contemporary people—and certainly, for most of those who have had extramarital relationships and whose marriages have subsequently broken up—sexual activity outside of marriage has lost none of its traditional significance as a serious breach of trust and intimacy and a major offense against the marital partner.

But these are the people whose marriages failed. Those whose marriages remain intact tell another story. Kinsey claimed that in most cases the extramarital relationships of his interviewees (especially if kept secret) had caused no serious marital difficulties, and in some cases had improved marital sexual adjustment.[52] Many of our own presently married males and females with extramarital experience likewise feel that their marriages have not been adversely affected, and a small number think that it has actually benefited their marital sex relationships. From our interviews and from the evidence of other studies, we think that this is sometimes an accurate assessment but that more often the individual who feels that his or her extramarital behavior has harmed nothing, and perhaps done some good, is seeking to rationalize his or her behavior, or failing to perceive what is actually happening to the marriage. Many supposedly unharmed or even benefited marriages suffer unseen emotional decay as a result of the external intimacy, and later collapse with a suddenness that takes the partners by surprise.

Although those people who have extramarital sexual experience tend to begin it earlier in married life than used to be the case, their behavior seems no more inclined toward promiscuity than that of their precursors. We infer this from a comparison of the numbers of extramarital partners had by females in our own sample with data published by Kinsey on the same point (there are no comparable data in his male volume). His figures and ours are given in Table 40. The similarity between the two sets of figures is remarkable, particularly since, as we saw earlier, there has been a threefold increase in the incidence of extramarital behavior among under-25 women. Apparently, that abrupt expansion of extramarital activity has taken place within the traditional context that such behavior has long had; it is still no lighthearted frolic, no idle amusement even for the liberated young, but is, as it has always been for most people, serious business.

Table 40

Number of Extramarital Partners: Married and Formerly Married White Females with Extramarital Experience, Percents

	1938–1949 (Kinsey[53])	1972 (Present survey)
1 only	41	40
2 to 5	40	44
6 to 10	11	10
11 to 20	5	4
21 to 30	1	2
31 plus	2	0

Another important indication that extramarital coitus has not become notably more acceptable or less threatening to marriage is the fact that it is still largely a secret activity, diligently concealed from the spouse. In Kinsey's sample, half of the married women with extramarital experience said their husbands had presumably never known, nor even suspected, the truth, and another tenth said their husbands had suspected but not known.[54] Today, sexual liberation notwithstanding, the proportion of wives with extramarital experience who say their husbands were wholly in the dark is slightly larger than in Kinsey's sample, as is the proportion whose husbands suspected but did not actually know. Kinsey gives no comparable data for males. For the record, however, we note that half of our married men with extramarital experience say their wives have had no idea, and another three-tenths say their wives have only suspected. Only one-fifth of the women and one-fifth of the men say that their mates have actually known about their extramarital activities. Nor does the situation seem to be changing among the younger people. Somewhat more of our under-35 than our

35-and-older respondents say that their spouses have known, but the increase is offset by a decline in the number whose spouses have merely suspected; perhaps the young have less tolerance of an ambiguous situation in marriage than do older people. All in all, there is no decrease among the young in the percentage of spouses who know nothing of the extramarital activities of their mates.

Apparently, the general feeling that extramarital behavior must be kept secret—unless one means to wound the spouse or to provoke a break—has not weakened. This is an enlightening finding in view of the fact that various researchers have recently maintained that, for a fair number of sophisticated persons, extramarital experience may represent a relatively normal, relatively guilt-free quest for variety and renewal. As sociologist Robert N. Whitehurst sees it, secret extramarital activity can be "an extension of fairly normal (meaning nonpathological) behavior . . . without strong guilt feelings, without underlying intrapsychic complications or other commonly described neurotic symptoms."[55] Maybe so; but our data indicate that there is still a very great emphasis on secrecy, based on the clear recognition that such extramarital acts will be perceived by the spouse as disloyalty, partial abandonment and a repudiation of marital love. And this means that for the person engaged in extramarital acts there must be internal conflict, even if no perceived guilt.

Indeed, it is said by advocates of sexually permissive marriage that secrecy is the main problem in extramarital relations, since it involves the loss of intimacy and trust between spouses, the threat of unseen and unknown emotional involvements, and the resentment felt by the deceiver about his or her need to deceive. Accordingly, they argue, spouses have only to grant each other the right to have outside sexual relationships freely, without any need for secrecy, and all such difficulties will disappear; in fact, the open and mutual acceptance of extramarital behavior will increase the closeness and trust of the partners and the security of their marriage.

This is said to be the great advantage of the two swinging alternatives to sexually exclusive monogamy—mate-swapping and group sex—both of which require total openness and mutual permissiveness. Some advocates of alternative marital life-styles say that these practices are already fairly common among the young and are destined to become more so in the immediate future. British biologist and sexologist Alex Comfort, for one, asserts that group sex for the married will soon be widespread because today's young people, in his opinion, "shy away from the idea of total self-surrender."[56] Other enthusiasts think the future is already here, and has even been around for a while. Almost a decade ago, William and Jerrey Breedlove, in a book entitled *Swap Clubs,* estimated that eight million American couples were involved in marital swinging.[57] The Breedloves, however, based their estimate on a projection of the number of ads in swingers' magazines, taking these to represent only a tiny percentage of the total phenomenon. The method has little to recommend it; most swingers know that the great majority of such ads are fake, or at least not serious in intent. As one knowledgeable group-sex participant told us, "Most of the people who put those ads in get their kicks from the letters and pictures they receive; they don't really swing. I've answered plenty of them, and nine times out of ten they're phonies." A careful and impartial observer, anthropologist Gilbert Bartell, recently reviewed the fragmentary evidence available (including his own) and ventured the educated guess that, as of late 1970, half a million to a million married people—at most, 1 percent of the married population—were involved in swinging.[58]

Bartell's estimate, we think, comes close to being right. Our own total married sample, consisting of 691 males and 740 females, is not large enough to enable us to speak definitively about the incidence of mate-swapping and group sex today, but is large enough to provide at least some idea of its probable order of magnitude. Despite all the jokes, cartoons, articles, exposés, movies and pornographic and semipornographic fiction about marital swinging, we think it is still very rare.

For one thing, only 2 percent of our married males and less than 2 percent of our married females have ever participated in mate-swapping with their spouses, and many of these males and most of these females have had only one such experience. (In addition, a few of our married people had had mate-swapping experiences before marriage or outside of marriage.) To be sure, among our younger married people the figures seem to run slightly higher, although the absolute numbers are so small that our percentages are not reliable. Apparently, some 5 percent of husbands and about 2 percent of wives under 25 have engaged in mate-swapping (some of this, however, may have been premarital), and in the 25-to-34 cohort the figures are 5 percent for husbands and a little over 1 percent for wives. But most of these have done so only occasionally; those who practice mate-swapping with frequency or regularity are too few in number to justify precise percentaging, and amount to tiny fractions of 1 percent of our married males and females.*

As for group sex, it is apparently just as rare, if not rarer, although our data on this point leave much to be desired. We asked our married respondents whether they had ever had sexual relations while other people were doing likewise in the same room, and were surprised to find that 18 percent of the married males and 6 percent of the married females had done so; this seemed out of keeping with our incidences for mate-swapping. Upon closer examination, however, it appeared that our question had been ambiguous, having failed to specify whether the sexual activity under discussion had been had as a married person or prior to marriage. Judging, however, from the identities of the partners involved in such reported experiences, it is clear that over half of the male responses and at least a third of the female responses refer to premarital experiences. In any case, three-quarters of the married males and three-quarters of the married females who have ever had this kind of sexual experience, whether before or during marriage, have done so only once. In the under-25 married cohort, while the figures were much higher—38 percent for males and 22 percent for females —some of this was premarital, and, in any case, most of the individuals involved have had only one such experience.**

Much the same proved true of our data on group sexual experiences involving simultaneous physical contact among three or more persons (the phenomenon inelegantly but succinctly

---

*Swapping, whether on a two-couple or group-sex basis, seems considerably more widespread among those who remain single for some time. The incidence of partner-swapping among our single males and females in the under-25 and 25-to-34 cohorts are several times as great as among married males and females of the same ages. (See pp. 153–154.)

**Among our single people, there are slightly larger incidences of sex in the presence of others, some 40 percent of our single males and 23 percent of our single females having had such experiences. Once again, however, nearly half the males and over two-thirds of the females have done so only once.

known to swingers as "cluster-fucking"). This species of activity, although a current commonplace in humor and erotica, is so out of keeping with traditional Western attitudes toward sex, even among enlightened and liberal persons, that we were surprised to find that 13 percent of our married males have had such experiences. But less than 2 percent of married females have had any, and when we sought to explain this discrepancy, examining our data as to the identity of the partners involved and the participation of the spouse, it became evident that over four-fifths of the males and two-thirds of the females with multiple-partner experiences had had them prior to marriage or, in a few cases, extramaritally. We estimate that under 3 percent of our married males and under 1 percent of our married females have experienced multiple-partner sex with the spouse present. In any case, whether maritally or otherwise, over two-thirds of the males and nearly all of the females with experience of this kind have had it only once.*

There are undoubtedly several reasons, aside from the obvious ones of inhibition and morality, why marital swinging is so rare even though it seems to fascinate a large number of Americans. For one, while it is supposed to eliminate the problems stemming from secrecy, a number of observers—including some who are more enthusiastic about the swinging scene than Gilbert Bartell—report that jealousy and competitiveness often exist among swingers. Many males, furthermore, experience a great deal of anxiety about their performance in a situation where size, style and endurance are so easily compared. More mundane problems include the complexities of getting compatible and desirable people together, the danger of public exposure, the fear of disease and various unaesthetic aspects of group encounters, both physical and social. All this has been adequately reported elsewhere, and some of our interviewees with mate-swapping and group-sex experience confirmed these reports.

But some also confirmed what the advocates and enthusiasts

---

*Among our single people, there has been a somewhat larger accumulative experience of multiple-partner sex. As noted earlier, in the single sample as a whole (all ages combined), 24 percent of the males and 7 percent of the females acknowledge having had such experiences, a third of the males and half of the females having done so only once. (See footnote, p. 154.)

have claimed—namely, that marital swinging can provide physically intense experiences, that it can be immensely ego-gratifying and that it is a temporary release from confinement and
responsibility and a brief chance to live out one's wildest fantasies. In the end, however, for nearly all contemporary husbands
and wives, its advantages are heavily outweighed by the mani-
fold conflicts, emotional problems and practical dangers involved. This, at any rate, is the apparent meaning of the rarity
and self-limiting nature of such behavior among married Americans in the early 1970s.

Even if extramarital sexual behavior still takes place largely
within the old familiar context of secrecy and infidelity, one
would expect it to be characterized by the same sensuous and
voluptuous freedom that is now becoming a part of marital sex.
Indeed, for many reasons one might suppose that extramarital
sex would generally be even more physically uninhibited and
sensuously abandoned than marital sex. But this does not appear to be the case; our data indicate that people with extramarital experience are somewhat less free and uninhibited in those
relations than are most married people in their marital relations.

This may seem strange, since we have all been told time and
again, in novels and drama, that extramarital passions are tem-
pestuous and unfettered while those of marriage are pale, routine and restricted. Nor is this wholly fictitious; many of those
who have extramarital experiences do claim that they find themselves far more passionate and sensuous and far more deeply
gratified by sex outside of marriage than by sex within it. But
these people have special reasons for perceiving things this way.
Some of them have ventured outside of marriage precisely because of special sexual difficulties within it. Others have uncon-
sciously contrived to make their marital sex poor in order to
justify seeking sex elsewhere. Still others, as suggested earlier,
mistake the delights of revenge, excitement or ego gratification
for deep sexual pleasure. Thus, extramarital sex may well seem
superior to marital sex to many of those who have had particular
reason to experience both, but when one compares the quality
of extramarital sex in general to that of marital sex in general,
the opposite appears to be true. Some specifics:

—Even as in Kinsey's time, a fair number of married males and females confine their extramarital activities to various forms of petting, despite the limitation of satisfaction this imposes on them. They seem to feel that the avoidance of full genital union and full satisfaction minimizes the wrongdoing. The figures: About a tenth of our married males and of our married females have had extramarital experience limited to petting. Needless to say, there is no comparable limitation in married sexual relations.

—Most nontraditional coital positions are used less frequently in extramarital intercourse than in marital intercourse. In some cases the difference is small, in other cases considerable. Surprisingly, the differences between coital variety within marriage and outside it are greater in the younger half of the sample than in the older half, perhaps because of the greater insecurity of the young in untested or unproven situations. Of our under-35 married males, for instance, nine out of ten said they sometimes or often used the female-above position in marital coitus, but among under-35 males having extramarital coitus, only seven out of ten did so in the extramarital relationships, possibly because that position suggests female domination to insecure men. Similarly, of our under-35 married females, 47 percent said they sometimes or often used rear-entry vaginal intercourse in marriage, but only 28 percent of the females with extramarital experiences did so in the extramarital context, possibly because of its seeming impersonality or coldness.

—Two other variations were, however, more common in extramarital relations than in marriage, and for good reason. The first is coitus while standing, a position more likely to be chosen on the basis of necessity than of sensuous considerations. The second is anal intercourse, reported by our males to be used more often extramaritally than maritally, but by our females less often. The likely explanation is twofold. First, since many women find anal intercourse painful and without sexual reward, males are more likely to engage in it outside of marriage, where they have a better chance of having coitus with women about whose discomforts or wishes they are not greatly concerned. Second, even those women who are liberated enough to be willing to try anal intercourse are likelier to do so within marriage, where they feel more secure and more nearly certain that they are not being exploited.

These indicators suggest that even if many individuals find their extramarital coitus freer and more satisfying than their marital coitus, the comparison does not hold true for extramarital intercourse as a whole when compared to marital intercourse as a whole. Even stronger evidence of this is provided by our information as to the regularity with which marital and extramarital coitus results in orgasm for the female. We acknowledge that this is a limited measure of the total satisfaction derived from intercourse by the female, and only an indirect measure of the satisfaction derived from intercourse by the male, but it is the best we have. Our data indicate that in extramarital coitus, while females reach orgasm in a majority of their copulations, they do so distinctly less often than do women in marital intercourse. Table 41 tells the story, but we must point out again that the comparison made here is not between the marital and extramarital coitus of the same individuals. The comparison is between the marital coitus of all married women in our sample and the extramarital coitus of that small segment of our married women who have had any.

It appears from the data in Table 41 that extramarital intercourse is reasonably successful for women in terms of orgasm regularity, but distinctly less so than marital coitus in general. The tension, guilt and lack of emotional security that often characterize extramarital coitus may prevent many women from letting go and responding totally. (The same thing is probably

Table 41

Frequency of Orgasm in Marital Coitus
and in Extramarital Coitus:
Married White Females, Percents

Orgasm frequency	In marital coitus	In extramarital coitus
All or almost all of the time	53	39
About 3/4 of the time	21	12
About 1/2 of the time	11	7
About 1/4 of the time	8	7
Almost none or none of the time	7	35

true, though to a lesser extent, of men.) Moreover, marital coitus has become considerably more pleasurable since Kinsey's time; perhaps extramarital sex was formerly better by comparison but has simply stood still while marital sex has advanced beyond it. This last point is conjectural; we do not know precisely what the orgasm rate in extramarital coitus was a generation ago. Kinsey says only that about 85 percent of all women having extramarital coitus had responded "at least on occasion" to the point of orgasm (a total incidence about the same as that for married women in his sample in the tenth year of marriage) and that "orgasm in the extramarital relationships had occurred in a high proportion of the contacts."[59] These statements do not lend themselves to quantitative comparisons with our own findings, but we do get the general impression that the females in our own sample are doing no better than, and possibly not even as well as, the women in Kinsey's sample in their extramarital coitus. It may be, of course, that the comparison is distorted by the fact that so many more very young women are now having extramarital relationships. Since very young women do not have the high orgasm regularity of more mature women, they may be biasing the comparison.

But as we have noted, the satisfactions of extramarital coitus are inadequately measured by orgasm regularity. For many men and women the physical delights of the act are much outweighed by its various psychic rewards, in particular the renewed sense of personal desirability, the illusion of recaptured youth, the intensity of awareness and the rediscovery of poetry and passion. At the same time, along with these positive satisfactions many men and women continue to feel severe tensions, the nagging fear of discovery and the torment of inner conflict and guilt. For a few people extramarital coitus has provided untarnished peak experience; for a few others it has been a sordid exercise in meaningless sensuality; and for most people it has yielded a mixture of satisfactions and frustrations, rewards and penalties that add up to less overall pleasure, on balance, than marital coitus provides the average male and female. We base this conclusion on the ratings our respondents gave their marital and extramarital coitus, as shown in Table 42.* The con-

---

*As we said earlier, such subjective evaluations may not accurately represent reality; the two sets of evaluations in the table are, however, comparable to each other.

Table 42

*Overall Pleasure of Marital and Extramarital
Sexual Relations: All Married Respondents
and All Respondents with Extramarital Experience,
Percents*

| | Males | | Females | |
	Marital sex	Extra-marital sex	Marital sex	Extra-marital sex
Very pleasurable	67	47	55	37
Mostly pleasurable	30	43	35	37
Neither pleasurable nor nonpleasurable	2	6	7	14
Mostly nonpleasurable	1	1	2	8
Very nonpleasurable	1	2	1	5

trasts, though not great, definitely contradict the popular and
fictional clichés. We wondered, however, whether the lower
pleasure ratings given to extramarital intercourse were the result of inhibitions and guilt feelings existing chiefly among older
people but partly or largely erased in the younger people. This
proved not to be the case: Except for the 55-and-over group,
which rated extramarital intercourse as less pleasurable than did
any other cohort, the ratings given it by all other age groups
were much the same. Young married people nowadays talk more
about extramarital sex—and more openly—than young married
people did a generation ago, and they are seemingly less cen-
sorious about it in others, more aware of their own extramarital
desires and more conscious of the alternatives now being
recommended and tried. But for a whole series of social and
emotional reasons, they are not freely and easily making it part
of their lives, and those of them who do have such experiences
still find them by and large less pleasurable than married people
in general find their marital sexual relations.

Extramarital Coitus: Some Representative Voices

To come closer to the human reality behind our statistical generalizations, we turn once again to the individual histories in our
interview sample. The excerpts that follow are not an attempt

to illustrate the whole range of emotions and experiences involved in extramarital sexual relations, but only the major ways in which sexual liberation has altered them—or, against all expectation, failed do so.

We stress "failed to do so," for the majority of husbands and the great majority of wives in present-day America have never had extramarital coitus, even though neither religion, community pressure, the forces of the law nor practical necessity any longer pose as serious obstacles to extramarital behavior as formerly. One would think, to read Kinsey, that the weakening of these social controls would have automatically resulted in a major upsurge of extramarital activity, but evidently there are factors other than social penalties at work. Such factors are personal and internal and have to do with the individual's own sense of right and wrong (as contrasted with divine or clerical injunctions and punishments), and with his or her feelings about the nature of marital intimacy, trust and love.

At first glance this statement seems to contradict one of our own questionnaire-survey findings. When we asked our subjects to check off, from a given list, the reasons why they had avoided extramarital coitus, the one checked most often by female respondents, and second most often by male respondents, was "Felt it was wrong for religious or moral reasons." But we erred in lumping religious and moral reasons together, for when we interviewed people in depth it became abundantly clear that fear of God's wrath, or strict and unquestioning adherence to the Seventh Commandment, was the controlling factor in only a very few cases, while choice, based on a personal ethical judgment, was far more general. Only rarely did we hear statements like these:

> FEMALE, 54, HOUSEWIFE, BLUE-COLLAR: I'm a good Catholic, and I mean a *good* one. It's a sin to commit adultery, and there's no exceptions. I couldn't do it if I wanted to—and I've never wanted to, not for an instant.

> MALE, 30, MINISTER: Of course I've felt temptation, but I believe in the [Baptist] values I was taught as a boy—and I believe that those who sin are going to have to pay for it. That's not a very fashionable view today, but it wasn't in Sodom and Gomorrah, either.

More often when our interviewees spoke of extramarital sex as being "wrong" or "immoral" they were judging it in terms of a personal system of ethics which, in some cases, had its roots in religious teachings, but operated from within them as a moral force rather than as an external punitive power. They expressed it in varying ways, according to their social and educational background:

> MALE, 40, ELECTRICIAN: I ran around until I found the girl of my choice, but I always intended that once I made my decision and got married, there'd never be anybody else. It's wrong to play around, once you've made your commitment; it's dishonest. It's not like I haven't been tempted— I sure *have*—but I haven't given in, because I figure if I did, I would be so miserable and so disgusted with myself that I wouldn't know what to do.

> MALE, 36, TEACHER: I've thought about it a lot—who hasn't? —but nothing in my life has ever brought me even close to it. Not that I never feel any hankering to know how it would be. As a matter of fact, my wife has a lovely figure, but she's very slim, and if there's one thing I would really love to do, it would be to make love to a woman with great big voluptuous breasts. But I have a sense of values that keeps me from even looking around for it. It sounds old-fashioned, but it's a matter of principle.

> FEMALE, 43, HOUSEWIFE, WHITE-COLLAR: It's just a matter of right and wrong, I guess. I would feel dirty or cheap, or something. I mean, there are better ways to do it. If my marriage went sour, I wouldn't have to sneak around and cheat; I could get a divorce, and keep my self-respect and hope to remarry.

But most often those interviewees who spoke of avoiding extramarital sex for moral reasons had in mind something more specific and situational than did the last three speakers —namely, a concern about the possibility of damaging their marriages or hurting their marital partners. In large part our respondents' choice of "religious or moral reasons" was an alternate way of expressing another sentiment offered in the same multiple-choice question—namely "Concern about causing trouble in your marriage," the reason most often cited by men, and third most often by women.*

In the course of our interviewing, it became obvious that moral reasons and concern about one's marriage were one and the same—and that this one is quite clearly the major restraining force among people today, including the sexually liberated young. Older people and younger ones, blue-collar people and white-collar people, males and females expressed similar feelings—though in a variety of styles—to the effect that extramarital sex was disloyal and a betrayal of trust, that it gravely endangered the emotional integrity of the marriage, and that it could be damaging or devastating to the spouse. All this, it was felt, made extramarital sex ethically wrong. Here are some representative statements:

FEMALE, 28, JEWELRY DESIGNER: I fantasize about it sometimes, but knowing myself I know I'd get really involved with the other person, and that would be unfair to Sam, because I'd probably love him less or end up leaving him. So even though I'd very much like to have some other sexual experiences while I'm still young and attractive, I avoid them on principle.

FEMALE, 38, FORMER TEACHER: One time I did come very close to it. It was more an intellectual thing than a big physical attraction, and I discussed it with my husband openly, thinking that he'd understand and that it wouldn't bother him. He said that it was my choice to make, and that he wouldn't tell me what to do or not to do, but I could see that he was crushed and that it made him feel inadequate and insufficient. I just couldn't do it to him. I broke away from the other man before anything happened. Since then, I know I'll never take a chance on harming him again, or damaging our relationship. Actually, I think we're closer today than ever because of my facing up to reality.

FEMALE, 35, ASSEMBLY-LINE WORKER: I'm determined not to get into that kind of a situation at all. I had the chance just

---

*The second most often cited by women was "Never had the desire/interest/opportunity," which, in large part, is the expression of moral sentiment so strong as to repress desire altogether. Other reasons cited, but only by minorities of men and women, included fear of VD, fear of what people would think, doubts about own sexual adequacy and failure ever to meet anyone desirable enough.

a month ago, and turned it off before it got started. I'm not at all sure it would make me any happier if I did it, but I do feel sure it would definitely make my husband very unhappy. Even if he didn't know about it, I'd be thinking within myself that *if* he knew, he *would* be unhappy, and that's something I don't want to live with. It would really harm my feelings about him, it would show in my behavior —and that would be bad for him and for me.

MALE, 26, STORE CLERK: Even if I was tempted by some great opportunity, I would be very hesitant. I would try to fight it off, because that's part of what I believe in. My wife and I, we made a deal: Nobody touches you, I won't touch nobody. That you can believe in—and everybody needs something to believe in.

MALE, 47, TELEVISION EXECUTIVE: I certainly don't think of it as "wrong" in any absolute sense—what's right or wrong all depends on the situation—and many a time I've had the desire, sometimes very strongly. But my wife and I have a very good and rare kind of marriage, and I know it would hurt her badly, despite all her liberal thinking, if I slept with some other woman, and it would make her feel terribly insecure. Frankly, from what I've seen among my friends, she'd be right to feel insecure, because even if these things start out as fun and games, all too often they wind up with serious feelings. So I simply don't let myself do it; I don't even let myself get into any situation where I'd have to struggle against it.

A few men and women, particularly at the working-class level, were very earthy and mundane about the dangers. They spoke of practical risks—"She'd kill me, if she ever found out," "If he ever found me stepping out, he'd walk out the door and never come back." But even these people made such statements with a jocular air and, when queried further, admitted with some embarrassment that what really concerned them was the danger of the erosion of trust and love.

Even when secrecy was hypothetically ruled out in favor of openness and permissiveness, most of our interviewees still saw extramarital relationships as seriously endangering the trust and intimacy of marriage. A number of them, especially in the younger age groups, said that they and their spouses had discussed the possibilities of open marriage, mate-swapping and swinging, but that one partner or the other, or both, felt that despite the granting of mutual permission and the open, honest context of such extramarital experience, it would entail such grave risks to the marital relationship as to outweigh the possible rewards:

MALE, 26, PH.D. CANDIDATE: We've talked a lot about whether it wouldn't be possible to openly have sexual experiences with other people and still remain emotionally faithful to each other. We've heard and read a great deal about it, and we know people who claim that they're doing it and making it work. But whenever we get right down to it and try to think how to go about it—with whom, or when, or where—we both feel very threatened. We've more or less come to the conclusion that, for us, sexual fidelity and emotional fidelity are tied together. My wife, even more than I, is frightened by the thought of taking any chance of either one of us getting drawn into something that might damage our marriage. And yet, to tell you the truth, each one of us would very much like to have other experiences, because we had practically none with other people before getting married.

The last statement is particularly interesting because it articulates a special contemporary problem—the conflict felt by liberal but nonswinging people who happen to live in a swinging community. Such people lack peer-group support for their private values, and if most of the people around them are engaging in overt extramarital activity, they may come to wonder if their own sexual fidelity is not a defect or the product of neurosis:

FEMALE, 48, LOWER-MIDDLE-CLASS HOUSEWIFE: I've been asked, often enough—I've had my chances, even lately—but I've always found it easy to say no. I just don't seem to have any real desire for it, I never get those kind of thoughts, I never have the feeling that that's something I really want to do. Which worries me—I think I must have something wrong with me, sexually.

MALE, 29, LEATHERCRAFT ARTISAN: I figure I have some real heavy hang-ups left over from my upbringing. I was raised to think that if you're sleeping with one person, or married to them, you shouldn't be out doing it with someone else. Intellectually, I know better. There's no reason why two people should have to not sleep with anybody else as long as they live, just because they're living together. But that seems to be the way I and most other people my age feel. Like if my wife was sleeping around with other men, I don't know how we could continue our relationship. I couldn't hack it. Either you live together just like buddies, and ball everybody else, or you're a thing together and don't ball anybody else. That's the way it is with me—but I think it's crazy of me, it's just plain madness.

So much for those interviewees whose behavior had not been affected by sexual liberation, although their feelings about extramarital sex had been made more complicated. As for those who had actually had such experiences, the majority had many of these same fears and moral misgivings before any one of several circumstances or motives propelled them on, sometimes after minor struggles and sometimes after major ones, past all obstacles. None of our female interviewees and very few of our male interviewees began their extramarital experiences without any internal conflicts or struggles whatever. Those few who did so were men whose social or familial background had given them a mental set toward extramarital behavior more like that of persons from some other culture altogether. A lower-class black, age 35, put it this way:

[Before you married, did you have any intention of limiting yourself sexually to your wife?] Well, I just never thought about that. You could say I never *meant* to, but I just never gave it no thought. I'd been having other girls every time I could manage it, up till I was married, so why should I stop? When I first was married, I was fucking everything I seen, but later on I got a little choosy, because sometimes I'd come home all fucked out and I could barely make it with my wife. So I figured, okay, unless they got something special to offer, I don't screw them. [At first, after you were married, did you ever think there was any reason why you shouldn't do it?] The only reason would be if I thought there was something wrong with a girl, a disease that I didn't want to take home.

And a commercial artist, nearing 40, explained his own effort-less entry into extramarital activity as follows:

> I'd always needed a lot of variety, so I knew before I got married that I'd be cheating sooner or later. So what differ-ence whether I started right away or not? I cheated on my honeymoon—I wasn't married twenty-four hours before I did it. We went to this classy hotel in the Springs, and in the morning she went to the beauty shop and I was out by the pool, and some good-looking woman starts rapping with me and tells me she's off by herself, away from her husband for the weekend, and why didn't we spend some time together? So I said, "I have a prior commitment—but what are you doing right now?" So while my wife was get-ting her hair done, I was up in this gal's room, boffing her. I thought it was a riot! I mean, how many people would have the guts to do something like that? That's the way my mind works—I like the challenge.

But such cases were rare. Nearly all other interviewees with extramarital experience told of initial struggles with fear, anx-iety and guilt, sometimes relatively short-lived and minor, some-times protracted and agonizing. Generally, such feelings abated somewhat after the beginning of extramarital coitus; most of these people, like raw troops in combat, rookie policemen or novice criminals, found that successful and unpenalized experi-ence counteracted fear, anxiety and guilt feelings. The principal influence of sexual liberation was to provide them with a set of handy, up-to-date rationalizations that made it easier for them to justify to themselves what they were doing. A few others, however, felt no such amelioration; fear and guilt continued unabated, and sometimes even became worse as the individuals in question experienced near-discovery or saw their marital rela-tionships decaying. Such people tended to wrench themselves out of their extramarital involvements and to avoid them there-after.

Despite the influence of sexual liberation on sexual behavior in general, extramarital relations generally take place in a con-text of so many emotional and practical problems that many of the men and women involved sometimes or even usually fail to function at the top of their sexual form. But they may function rather poorly and still find the experience intensely rewarding for quite a few other reasons. The following excerpts are quite typical of the experiences of a number of our interviewees:

MALE, 45, PHYSICIAN: She was twenty years younger than I and very seductive, and she had this fantastic, long-legged, high-breasted body. She took the initiative one afternoon when she was the last one in my office, and I couldn't stop myself; it just happened, right then and there, on the waiting-room couch—the first time for me, after fifteen years of marriage. At first I was all torn up about it, but I couldn't give it up. It made me feel totally different—younger and more attractive than I had in twenty years, completely reawakened inside. A young girl, so sexy and so marvelous to look at and touch, wanting me! It went on for months. I'd meet her and have relations with her at least once or twice a week, usually at her place, sometimes at my office after hours. And now listen to the funny part—she was *no* good at all, sexually. Despite all her sexiness, she was frigid, and she'd lie there obviously getting nothing out of it. So even though I'd enjoy the whole situation and the buildup, when it came to the actual act I'd do it in a minute or two and get it over with. And still, for months I couldn't break it off; I felt as if I were hooked on some drug.

FEMALE, 37, HOUSEWIFE, WHITE-COLLAR: It was I who sought the thing out and got it started, and I didn't feel at all inhibited or embarrassed about what we were doing, so it was really very odd that I couldn't seem to have an orgasm with him. It wasn't his fault—he was good in bed—and there wasn't anything basically wrong with me, because I have no such inability at home. I had to laugh at myself. I had figured this thing would be the great fling of my life. As a matter of fact, despite the orgasm problem I did get a great kick out of it, because it was something I had really wanted to do at least once in my lifetime, and I just loved the excitement of it and was very surprised that sexually I couldn't achieve anything for myself. But it didn't matter, because there was real satisfaction in it.

FEMALE, 27, DENTAL TECHNICIAN: Since things started going badly in my marriage, I've had five of these relationships, and I have to admit that the sex in them isn't as good as sex with my husband used to be, because there just isn't the knowledge of the little movements and special things that get me excited. That takes a lot of time for anyone to get to know. But when I'm with a man I enjoy, and I spend an evening with him making love with him, it builds up my ego no end. I've learned a number of new things, sexually, and some of them are fun, but it's being *wanted* by another man, and feeling close to him, that gives me the boost.

MALE, 37, MAGAZINE EDITOR: Finally, after months of this buildup of feeling between us, we were able to be with each other for a whole weekend during a medical convention we were both covering. We spent most of the time together, a lot of it in my room. I felt light and heady, I felt a sense of self-abandonment, I had no embarrassment or guilt even though I had never done anything like this before. And I felt a sort of strength and masculinity that I had never felt before. But not in bed, strangely enough. In fact, I performed miserably. First, I couldn't get a firm erection for the longest while. Then I got one, more or less, and ejaculated prematurely. Then back to the first problem; then back to the second one. But she didn't seem to mind; she just clung to me, and I to her, and we rejoiced in each other, and I had this great sense of manliness and pride. Which is just the opposite of what I have in my marriage, where sexually I'm quite competent and reliable and don't feel manly at all.

Some interviewees did find their extramarital experiences, or at least part of them, far more physically successful, free and gratifying than their marital sexual experiences. The role that sexual liberation played in this was often secondhand; many of these people had learned to be sexually liberated within marriage, and merely replicated those experiences outside it after the marital relationship had deteriorated for one reason or another:

FEMALE, 30, HOUSEWIFE, WHITE-COLLAR: I'm married to the most sexy guy, technically, that I've ever known. He can always get it up, and he can keep screwing for hours if you want him to, and he'll try *anything* at all. But I can never

come with him, because I hate him—because I want a divorce and he won't give it to me. But with the men I've been
having affairs with, it's something else—I mean, I have
orgasms right and left, I can let go and feel really lustful,
I get carried away, I go right out of my head. But I only do
so with men I have a real feeling for, a warm affectionate
thing or a romantic crush, even if I know it's going to last
only a very short time.

MALE, 46, BUSINESSMAN: It was as if I discovered all over
again what sex can be—what it used to be for me. This girl
and I would laugh and tease each other, and play around
and try all sorts of kinky positions and crazy gimmicks just
for fun. Then finally we'd get serious and bang away, moan-
ing and yelling, and it would knock us out. When I came,
I'd feel as if I was practically turning inside out. But when
I was first married, it was almost that way with my wife for
a couple of years. Then came the children, and other problems, and we drifted apart in many ways, and the sex got
less frequent and less interesting. After a while we were
doing it only once in a while and in a very halfhearted way.
I'd forgotten what it could be like when it was great.

And, there was a small minority of persons for whom sexual
liberation, operating directly within an extramarital relationship, had brought a heightened, intensified and widened kind of
sexual experience unlike anything they had previously known:

FEMALE, 33, WRITER: My husband had been all right as a
lover, at least as far as being always ready for it, and able
to control his orgasm. But his whole style was basically
uptight—he was more *athletic* about it than expressive. He
never could relax and be imaginative or poetic with words
or with his body. What he did, really, was to pump away
vigorously, and keep it up without ever a word, with his
eyes closed. I didn't know any better myself, until I had my
first affair. Then I was bowled over—my lover was so sensitive, so expressive (I never even knew anyone could talk
about it while it was happening), he made me so aware of
my own body and of his, and of our feelings, he did such
marvelous things with his hands and his mouth and his face
and his whole body. After we had been together a few

times, I would almost seem to lose consciousness for a little while during my orgasm. It was unbelievable.

MALE, 44, LAWYER: I never went over the hill until seven years ago, and then only because I fell into something without planning it or seeking it. And even when I could see what was about to happen, I thought it would be a one-time thing. But that first night was a revelation to me. My wife is a big, affectionate, warm woman, and she was always willing enough, but very placid in her sexual responses. I just didn't know what the difference was, or what I myself was capable of. I'd started going with her when we were in college, and had never laid another woman, except for a couple of whores. And there I was, that first time, with a woman responding in all kinds of ways I had only heard and read about, and I was hitting a peak I had never hit before—and coming back, in a little while, for more, and letting her do things I would never have asked my wife to do, and doing things to her that I would have been afraid to even suggest at home. Between midafternoon and midnight we did it five times, and I knew my whole life had changed. I couldn't quit and go back to the way I'd been living, and I never have. I've moved on from one to another, and not all of them have been great, but at least I know what it's all about now, and I know what to look for.

Finally, although we interviewed only a baker's dozen of marital swingers, we noted even within that small sample the same extremes of experiences in swinging that have been reported by Denfeld and Gordon, the Smiths, Bartell, Symonds and others.[60] At the one pole, some participants spoke of the extraordinary and unparalleled physical sensations experienced in the wholly uninhibited group-sex situation. At the other pole, we found a few men who, despite their emotional excitement at being in a group-sex situation, had difficulty getting or maintaining erections, and a few women who, similarly, while tremendously stimulated by the situation, rarely or never reached climax.

In between were what we take to be the majority—people who experience various levels of sensuous pleasure and orgastic release, but whose primary reward in the group experience is that of doing forbidden, daring, ego-gratifying, voyeuristic and exhibitionistic things, all with the approval of the group. Significantly, one man admitted that as much as he enjoyed swinging parties (at which he functioned heroically, performing with one woman after another), he almost never had an orgasm at them and could not make himself have one. After such an event, however, he and his wife would go home and have coitus, at which time he would reach orgasm easily and swiftly. One woman, who rarely has orgasm at a swinging party even though immensely titillated by the *mise en scène*, told us that she played the part of scientific researcher one night when the party was winding up after six hours of constant activity: She asked each guest to jot down, anonymously, how many orgasms he or she had had in the course of that whole evening. To her amazement, she found that the average—excluding one female who had had 15—was only a little over one per person, which was not at all the impression the participants had managed to give. Another man, who usually does have several orgasms at such events, claims that the best thing about group-sex parties is that they provide new stimulus for his fantasy life, and that he has "the big one" afterward with his own wife, particularly when visualizing her as he saw her at the party in the act of coitus or, better yet, fellating some other man.

Our impression is that, by and large, swinging does not so much offer freedom to experience the maximum sensuous and emotional possibilities of sex as it does freedom from the social and interpersonal requirements of intercourse—the customary proprieties, the privacy, the need for communication, the expectation of emotional significance. What gives swinging its particular worth, for those who enjoy it, is the chance to violate rules and obligations they have been taught since childhood. As for maximum sensuous gratification and sexual satisfaction, only a few persons seem to achieve it in the swinging situation. For most persons sexual liberation, at least at this point in our history, has brought not freedom to swing but freedom to be more responsive and more deeply gratified within meaningful interpersonal relationships.

"God, sometimes I wish we'd never published that statistic!"—Dr. Paul Gebhard, Kinsey colleague, referring to Kinsey's estimate that 37 percent of American males had one or more homosexual experiences.

MALE, 49, MARRIED, DESCRIBING HOMOSEXUAL EXPERIENCE AT AGE 12: *We were crazy to know how it [coitus] felt, and we talked it over and decided we could get at least some idea by trying it with each other. First, we tried to do it between the thighs, but that was awkward and embarrassing. . . . So then he suggested that we could stick it in the anus. We tried that, but neither one of us could relax the sphincter sufficiently. . . . Finally, we had the brilliant idea of trying sixty-nine, and that worked, it really worked! . . . But one minute after I ejaculated, I felt sick and disgusted, and horribly guilty. . . .*

FEMALE, 23, RECENT CONVERT TO HOMOSEXUALITY: *It's right for me. I have my preferences, though—I can't stand a real butch who only wants to play the aggressive role and who won't let her partner do anything to her. . . . Touching and stroking and kissing and all that sort of thing—a woman will do that much better, and longer and more lovingly, than a man. For the past year I've been trying out as many women as possible, but right now I'm seeing one woman who excites me emotionally. When she calls, I feel just the way I used to when a man I was excited about would call.*

MALE, EARLY 40S, MARRIED: *I was about eleven. My grandfather had had a heart attack, and my mother was sleeping downstairs to be near him, so I asked could I please sleep in the big double bed with my father? Well, we're in bed [coughing] . . . and he was sleeping with his back to me, and I cuddled up to him and slept that way. And the second night, I awakened and my penis was erect, and he [sighing, long pause] . . . he was attempting to put my penis in his anus. . . .*

FEMALE, EARLY 20S, SINGLE, RECALLING EXPERIENCE AT AGE 13: *My father, God love him—I'm sure he must have thought it was right—he tried to show me. And I guess he did it the wrong way [nervous laughter]. . . . My mother was very Catholic and I couldn't talk to her about it [sex], and so he decided—he was a very shy man—and he decided, instead of telling me or saying a man is built this way and a woman this way, and you do this step and the next step, instead he showed me. Not that he actually had intercourse with me—no!—but everything leading up to that [wild giggling].*

CHAPTER

6

Deviant Sexual Behavior

The Meanings of Deviance: A Typology

One of the less admirable effects of sexual liberation is that it has made fashionable the avoidance or repudiation of two concepts essential to the scientific understanding of sexual behavior: the concepts embodied in the dichotomies "normal-abnormal" and "conforming-deviant." Most sexual radicals and many sexual liberals, hypersensitive to any suspicion that they might harbor the least trace of obsolete moralistic attitudes, think of the terms "abnormal" and "deviant" as being pejorative and as having roughly the same connotations as "sinful," "degenerate" and "perverted." Yet the terms in question, and the dichotomies of which each is half, rest on biological, psychological and sociological premises rather than moral ones. The misunderstanding and denigration of these terms is unfortunate, for it produces intellectual obscurantism and prevents analytic thinking. If we make no distinctions between the normal and the abnormal, or between the conforming and the deviant, we limit our ability to make meaningful generalizations about what we observe, rational decisions about our own sexual behavior and intelligent appraisals of the social benefit or harm of laws and customs governing sexual behavior. It is as if we were to decide that numbers were pejorative and moralistic, and thereupon sought to shop, drive our cars, fly our planes and operate our businesses and governments without using the simplest arithmetic and even without counting.

Kinsey himself was partly to blame. In his zealous effort to replace moralistic thinking with dispassionate scientific inquiry, he stretched the meaning of the term "normal" to include much behavior that had been considered beyond the pale. This was generally salutary, but he introduced two serious confusions into the discussion. Time and again he suggested that whatever was common and normal among other mammals was, by that token, normal in human beings; and equally often he said that whatever was relatively common among human beings in various societies was, by that token, biologically and psychologically normal in human beings everywhere.[1]

The first argument—that what is common among mammals is part of mankind's "fundamental mammalian heritage" and therefore is normal in human beings—is valid only in a limited sense. The biological and psychological determinants of sexual behavior in most subhuman species differ in many respects from those in the human being. Nearly all the subhuman mammals, for instance, mate only during estrus; in contrast, the hormonal and neural characteristics of the male and female human being give them year-round sexual responsiveness, with the result that seasonal mating, in the human species, would be distinctly unnatural.[2] Moreover, sexual acts that serve a useful biological purpose for many other species may serve no such purpose in the human being, and may even be dysfunctional. In many mammals, for instance, a certain amount of pain, inflicted by the male upon the female, is needed to produce sexual arousal and to bring about the release of the egg from the ovary, while neither thing is true of human beings[3]; indeed, for many human females, pain abruptly shuts off erotic impulses and leads to efforts to avoid coitus. Finally, even when a given genre of sexual behavior is observed in all mammals, including mankind, the precise way in which it is done by one species may be suitable for that animal but grossly unsuitable for others, including the human animal. Most male apes, for example, ejaculate very soon after intromission (the chimpanzee's average time is about seven to ten seconds),[4] but such dispatch is wholly unsuited to the needs of many other primates or of many men and most women. All that one can legitimately say is that any genre of sexual activity that is frequently exhibited by most mammals under normal environmental conditions is biologically and psychologically normal for the human being—but only in a general sense;

the specific details of normal behavior are determined by the specialized needs of human males and human females, and not by those of any closely related species.

The second argument—that any form of behavior more or less common among other human societies is therefore biologically and psychologically normal for persons in our own society —is likewise of limited validity. Merely because a practice has been observed in a number of societies does not mean that it has been *functional* for all those involved in it. Slave prostitution, the castration of captured enemies and the rape of the enemies' women have all been fairly common in the annals of human history, but distinctly dysfunctional, biologically and psychologically, for the victims. Moreover, since such behavior is far from universal, it cannot be instinctive (as is the relationship between predator and prey in the lower orders) but must be the product of specific social conditions; in any society where it is not sanctioned, its normality depends on the degree to which it is in conflict with the cultural norms of that society. What one can legitimately say, therefore, is that any sexual act that has been observed in many societies, and that has few or no adverse effects upon most of the persons involved in it or upon the societies themselves, may be considered natural or normal even when practiced in a milieu in which it is mildly to moderately deviant. We have seen this to be true of masturbation, premarital intercourse, many forms of foreplay and most variant coital positions in our own society. But any piece of behavior which destroys life or diminishes the chances of survival or satisfaction of most individuals in a society, or jeopardizes the society itself, may be viewed as abnormal, even when sanctioned by that society. Finally, any piece of behavior that is in extreme conflict with the values and norms of a given society must be considered abnormal within the context of that society: Puberty-rite mutilations, concubinage and pedophilia, for instance, all of which are acceptable in many other societies, are so totally in conflict with our own concepts of mental health and individual rights that these acts, when performed in the context of American life, must be regarded as pathological.[5]

In seeking to slay the dragon of moralistic prejudice, Kinsey achieved overkill. Following his lead, many sex researchers and sexual liberals became increasingly loath to make any value judgments about many forms of sexual behavior. Lately some of them have gone as far as to argue that virtually all sexual acts are normal in themselves, and that any abnormality appearing in the deviant individual is not an inherent part of his sexual syndrome but the result of society's hostility toward him, or its labeling of his behavior as abnormal.[6] As the *reductio ad absurdum*, a few have even refused to acknowledge that deviant behavior is deviant, misconstruing that term to mean biologically or psychologically abnormal, when in fact it only means not in conformity with the social norms of the society in question. Here, for instance, is a specimen of the kind of semantic and logical nonsense that results from the effort to be totally uncritical and nonjudgmental:

> If a human being, from time to time, enjoys unusual sex participations, such as being beaten while he is having sex relations, or copulation with animals . . . we may justifiably call him odd, or peculiar, or statistically unusual. But we may not, from a psychological (or biological) standpoint, justifiably call him abnormal, perverted, or deviant. If, however, this same man *mainly* or *only* enjoys sex relations of some special sort, then we may, psychologically speaking, call him fixated, neurotic, or abnormal.*

Redefining the meaning of abnormality in this fashion is like saying that it is all right to eat feces, provided one makes it a part of a balanced diet, or to steal, provided one also works for a living. It is, in fact, not a redefinition but a repudiation of the concept of abnormality. But in addition to so misusing (and thereby rejecting) the concept of abnormality, the quoted author misuses (and thereby rejects) the concept of deviance by equating it with psychological or biological abnormality and thus finds it inapplicable to the examples he offers. In actual fact, being beaten during sex and having intercourse with animals are both very strongly in conflict with our existing norms; quite apart from the issue of normality or abnormality, they are socially deviant, and redefining the term to make it meaningless cannot alter that reality.

But we would argue that being beaten while having sex, and copulating with animals, even when not the main or only forms of sexual gratification used by an individual, are not only deviant

---

*Albert Ellis, *The American Sexual Tragedy* (New York: Lyle Stuart, 1962), p. 94.

but abnormal in both the statistical and functional senses: the statistical because they are, by every measurement, rare; the functional because the weight of the evidence indicates that they are part of behavior syndromes in which loving, fulfilling, emotionally supportive psychosocial relationships are almost never present.[7] Many sexual radicals argue that if a person wants to be whipped during sex or to copulate with an animal, there is nothing wrong with his doing so as long as no other person is hurt thereby. But his desires may be part of a self-limiting or self-damaging syndrome, and to grant him the absolute right to indulge such desires, without asking whether he is competent to judge the larger meaning of the acts involved, is akin to justifying a child's wish not to go to school, or a depressed person's preference for suicide rather than therapy.

It is imperative, therefore, for the individual in a liberated society, and for the society itself, to continue to make the distinctions between the normal and the abnormal, the conforming and the deviant, and to clearly recognize the difference between these two dichotomies. Only by identifying a given pattern as conforming or deviant and as functionally normal or abnormal can we evaluate its probable consequences for individual and society, come to rational conclusions about it and deal with it intelligently and constructively.

Borrowing from sociologists John Gagnon and William Simon[8]—both longtime associates of the Institute for Sex Research—we divide sexually deviant acts into three general categories. The first consists of those acts which are moderately deviant in our own society but which, though socially disapproved, are very common, rarely in open conflict with the social order and distinctly useful as adjuncts to the accepted mores. Such acts are very likely to be biologically and psychologically normal even though deviant; indeed, Gagnon and Simon label this category "normal deviance," giving, as examples, masturbation, premarital intercourse and heterosexual mouth-genital contacts. (As we have already seen, these three types of activity are rapidly becoming increasingly acceptable. It may be that in another 10 or 20 years they will no longer be classifiable as normal deviance but will be part of the accepted mores, and within the law.) One might add to this list of practices certain others that are more strongly disapproved of but have recently become part of the experience of many normal persons and rarely come into overt conflict with our social institutions. These include anal foreplay, sex in the presence of others, promiscuity and perhaps secret individual extramarital relations (we say "perhaps" because the latter still appears to be frequently dysfunctional).

Mate-swapping and group sex, on the other hand, particularly when practiced by married persons, seem to fit more readily into a second category of deviance: behavior which, though fairly common, is not only more strongly disapproved of by society than normal deviance but which by its very nature is more visible and more often in overt conflict with other components of the social structure. To minimize the effects of that conflict, such behavior tends to generate social structures of its own within which to recruit and train its participants and to conduct its functions apart from the dominant social institutions. Gagnon and Simon's two principal examples are female prostitution and male and female homosexuality. Apart from the issue of biological normality, these two behavior patterns are so strongly disapproved of in our society and so alien to the rest of social life that they are generally chosen only by persons with special needs. Such needs range from the purely situational (the prostitution of the female junkie, the homosexuality of prisoners) to the unmistakably neurotic (the prostitution of the middle-class runaway, the homosexuality of the "mama's boy").

It is important to note, however, that as the social pressure against a given behavior pattern in this category of deviance decreases, the pattern becomes an easier choice, and thus more possible for persons whose needs are only marginally or not at all abnormal. As we have already seen, many of those who have had mate-swapping and group-sex experiences are essentially normal persons who were merely curious and experimentally inclined. Similarly, overt homosexuality has recently become an acceptable choice for many former "closet" gays who, except in their sexual actions, are virtually indistinguishable from heterosexuals in appearance, behavior or psychological-test responses. In December 1973, the board of trustees of the American Psychiatric Association voted to reclassify homosexuality as a "sexual orientation disturbance" rather than a "mental disorder," and Dr. Judd Marmor, former vice-president of the A.P.A., has even categorized homosexuality as "merely a variant sexual preference."[9] This last position may be a case of throwing out the baby with the bathwater. It is surely a liberal move to recognize that homosexuality is not always a symptom of mental disorder—but to classify it as merely variant, and on a par with heterosexual behavior, is to ignore the weight of biological, psychological and anthropological evidence. Homosexual behavior has never been the main choice, or even a customary minor part of the sexual pattern, of any mammal living in the free state. The occasional mounting of male animals by other males—apes in particular—is not true homosexuality but is in part playful and learning behavior in the immature, and in part a way of avoiding violent fighting between two males. The weaker one signifies submissiveness by "presenting" his rear, the stronger signifies dominance by mounting and making a few routine penile thrusts without intromission or ejaculation.[10] In human societies male homosexuality has never been accorded equal status with heterosexuality, probably because of its socially dysfunctional nature. It has either been strictly forbidden, or half-tolerantly viewed as a peculiarity, or recognized and sanctioned within sharply defined limits (being acceptable, most often, in children, young unmarried males, and, in some societies, in adult male transvestites and shamans).[11] Female homosexuality has been still rarer, and still more narrowly restricted to certain age groups and certain categories of persons.[12] Even in its least restricted and least deviant adult manifestations, homosexuality has generally been a diversion for males who were married and did most of their copulating with females. Such was the case in ancient Athens, where, despite the propaganda of our contemporary homophiles, many eminent intellectuals (including Plato himself in his later days) felt that homosexuality was contrary to nature, and either scorned it or condemned it.[13]

Biologically, moreover, homosexuality is abnormal in the sense that no children can be born of it. It is true, of course, that even contraception is abnormal in this sense, but the heterosexual couple using contraception has it within their power to be fertile or not, as they choose; and even when they choose not to, they are still employing the neural, hormonal and muscular responses of sexuality in the fashion which evolution, with the goal of reproduction, cunningly designed to provide maximum reward. There is also recent evidence that homosexuality may be related to certain biological pathologies: Research on animals and human beings by the late distinguished endocrinologist William C. Young, by Dr. John Money (medical psychologist of Johns Hopkins University), and by others has shown that virilizing hormonal imbalances in the mother during gestation lay down important male patterns of reactivity in the developing neural structure of a female fetus, who later on, in childhood and beyond, exhibits classically male patterns of play and aggressiveness.[14] Comparable congenital "errors," it is thought, may underlie some or much of the classically female behavior of some male homosexuals. Moreover, a recent study conducted by Dr. Robert Kolodny at the Reproductive Biology Research Foundation in Saint Louis (the Masters and Johnson laboratories) found both significantly lower levels of plasma testosterone and lower sperm counts in a group of homosexual males than in a matching group of heterosexual males.[15] (Dr. Kolodny has said, however, that the cause-and-effect relationship remains unproven, and that it is at least possible that the hormone deficit is somehow a result, not a cause, of the homosexual behavior.)

Although homosexuality in our own society thus often falls into the category of socially structured and subcultural deviance, Gagnon and Simon say that in some of its manifestations it falls into yet another category, which they call "pathological deviance." This includes forms of behavior that are the product of pathogenic family and personality factors and are biologically and psychologically so aberrant, and socially so disruptive, that they generate no supportive structures or subcultures of their own and remain almost wholly in conflict with law, custom and existing institutions. Among the forms of homosexuality that clearly fall into this category are the "tearoom trade" (public-toilet fellatio or masturbation between strangers), the use of male prostitutes, and pederasty (sexual connection with very young boys). Other examples of pathological deviance named by Gagnon and Simon are incest, sexual contact with children of either sex, exhibitionism, voyeurism and aggressive or assaultive offenses. We would add to the list sadomasochistic practices (Gagnon and Simon's "aggressive and assaultive offenses" apparently refers primarily to rape), bestiality (sexual contact with animals), urolagnia (sexual arousal by the partner's urination), coprophilia and coprophagia (sexual arousal by the partner's defecation), transvestism, transsexualism and necrophilia.

In previous chapters we have already presented our findings

concerning the major forms of normal deviance and, aside from homosexuality, of socially structured deviance. In this chapter we will offer our data on homosexuality and on the three forms of pathological deviance—sadomasochism, incest and bestiality —about which we were able to collect data in sufficient quantity to warrant the drawing of conclusions. The other forms of pathological deviance are so rare that we could not obtain statistically meaningful data within the limits of our sample size. This may seem odd when on every side we hear about sexual deviations until it sometimes seems that they must now be very common. Pornographic films, fiction, freak-rock performers, magazine articles, books of erotic technique, and magazines catering to all sorts of pathological sexual specialties make it seem as if pathological deviants form a substantial minority of our population. The classified pages of any one of scores of underground sex periodicals contain innumerable appeals from deviants or those who serve them for profit. A recent issue of the *Berkeley Barb,* for instance, offered scores of ads like the following:*

STEVE 23 yr stud musclebuilder
46" chest 17" arms blond hair
5'9" Domination, water sports,
s/m, some equipment.

HANDSOME YOUNG MASCULINE
Ex-Marine dominant! S&M WATER
sports toys, will do your thing
whatever's right. Bi-sexual stud.

ARRIVING S[an] F[rancisco] TO FORM ELITE
slave club. Europe's premiere dominatrix
seeking connections, generous
male submissives and aggressive
gals for gainful exchange.

I love to massage women's feet
so let's get your feet and my hands
together.

---

*Some of the terms used may not be familiar to every reader. A few of the more recondite: "water sports" (urolagnia); "s/m" (sadomasochism); "equipment" (dildoes, whips, shackles, etc.); "toys" (same as equipment); "D&S" (dominance and submission); "French modeling" (fellatio).

ORALIST & SWEDISH VIBRATOR
EXPERT seeks attractive female
21 or over. Will do it
your way and add in fringe benefits.

GAY MALE 36, will satisfy any
unusual male fetish.

DOMINANT COUPLE
INTO D&S AND S&M
want to meet submissive
young couples for mutual
pleasure.

BUXOM BLOND TRANSSEXUAL
WILL DO FRENCH MODELING

But one cannot judge the incidence of any form of pathologically deviant behavior from the number of such advertisements or from the quantity of reading matter about such behavior. The advertisements, as we have already noted, are often meant to produce titillating correspondence, not actual contact, and fictional representations of deviant acts generally provide a fantasy life that the readers have no intention of seeking to put into practice. Fairly sizable numbers of our men and women have sometimes or often fantasied pathologically deviant acts while masturbating or having normal coitus, yet the incidence of behavior carrying out those fantasies is very small. We do not take this to mean that there is a large reservoir of pathological deviancy held in check solely by fear of the law or of other practical consequences. Our interpretation, stemming from psychodynamic psychology, is that nearly every child experiences a wide variety of infantile sexual desires, most of which he or she gives up during the process of socialization and maturation; in adulthood, however, the old infantile wishes still live on in the childlike unconscious, from which they sometimes emerge in the form of dreams or the free associations of psychotherapy—or, in today's freer milieu, in the form of conscious fantasies. But generally even those persons who now feel relatively free to think about such acts recognize that it would be most unwise to perform them in reality. It is akin to the way in which most of us have occasional fantasies of avenging ourselves on someone with whom we are extremely angry—but while the child within us prompts such fantasies, the adult knows that to act them out would be self-defeating and self-destructive.

Homosexuality: Incidence, Frequency, Techniques

Thus, while sexual liberation has brought about a great increase in the freedom to think about sexual acts that are more than moderately deviant, it has resulted in little measurable increase in their actual use. This is nowhere more apparent than in the case of homosexuality. On every side there is abundant evidence of a major shift toward liberalism in the public attitude concerning homosexuality, yet our survey data provide no evidence of an increase in the incidence of actual homosexual behavior.

The liberalization has been evidenced in many ways: the growth of freedom to portray and discuss homosexuality openly, dispassionately and even sympathetically, in fiction, nonfiction and drama; the greatly increased public consumption of such materials; the tempering of medical opinion and legal penalties concerning homosexuality; the abandonment of cover stories and pretense by large numbers of homosexuals; and the efforts of Gay Liberation action groups to win legal and social equality with heterosexuals—a movement which is as much a product of the liberalized climate as a cause of it. But while these new freedoms create the impression that the incidence of homosexual behavior has greatly increased, our survey, as just stated, does not confirm this impression in any way. Astonishing or even incredible as this may seem to the average person, it will come as no surprise to most professional sex researchers. As Arno Karlen pointed out in 1971 in his comprehensive and learned review of the subject, *Sexuality and Homosexuality: A New View,* no recent study has even hinted at an increase in homosexuality since Kinsey's time.[16]

To measure the new liberalism toward homosexuality, we asked a number of attitude questions on the subject. Kinsey himself published no comparable data in the male volume, but he did make frequent allusions to the intense public hostility toward male homosexuality, the severity of the laws dealing with it and the Judeo-Christian tradition that held homosexual acts between males to be "abominable," "detestable," "unnatural" and, of course, immoral. Our results can be viewed against this general perspective, and specifically compared with data Kinsey did provide, on two attitude questions, in the female volume. The salient points are these:

—A little over one-third of Kinsey's females expressed disapproval of homosexual behavior in general[17]; so do the same number in our female sample. But well over half his females were noncommittal on the matter, and fewer than a tenth were definitely tolerant, whereas in our own sample only a tenth are noncommittal, and half are tolerant.

—Under 60 percent of Kinsey's females said they would remain friendly with someone they learned was homosexual[18]; 68 percent of our own females say they would, and in the under-35 half of the sample the figure is above 75 percent.

—A little over half of the males and close to half of the females in our total sample agree with the statement "There is some homosexuality in all of us." In the younger cohorts of the sample the proportions of those who agree are distinctly larger.

—Nearly half of our males and our females think homosexuality should be legal; about four-tenths think it should not, the remainder having no opinion. In the younger half of the sample, six-tenths think it should be legal, three-tenths do not, and one-tenth has no opinion.

—Even the highly debatable statement "Being homosexual is just as natural as being heterosexual" wins agreement from nearly a quarter of our males and slightly more than a quarter of our females. As expected, the proportions of those agreeing with the statement are somewhat higher among single people and those under 35 than among the married and those of 35 and over.

One would expect that this degree of tolerance would result in a high incidence of at least occasional fantasizing of homosexual acts, since with increased tolerance such fantasies should be less threatening and less productive of guilt feelings. At first glance, this does not seem to be the case, for as we noted in Chapter 2, only 7 percent of the males and 11 percent of the females who have ever masturbated say they have ever employed a homosexual fantasy while doing so, and even in the younger half of the sample the percentages are only 9 and 12 respectively. But this apparent lack of suppressed desire conflicts with the evidence of the greatly enlarged market for written and dramatic material about homosexual life and acts. The explanation of the paradox is, we think, that in most people homosexual desires, though part of the original and residual childish potential, are so remote from and so unsuited to the adult's real needs and self-image that fantasies of one's self performing such acts are deliberately avoided. But reading about such acts or seeing them portrayed in dramatic form is another matter; *other* people are the vehicles of the fantasy experience, and it therefore becomes far more acceptable to the adult ego. The public appetite for vicarious experience of homosexual behavior has increased without being matched by an increase in actual homosexual activity because the desires satisfied by the vicarious experience belong to the child within, rather than to the adult self and the reality of adult life.

But what hard evidence is there that homosexuality has not actually increased in incidence, despite the increases in the incidence of so many other forms of previously disapproved sexual behavior? Before we offer our evidence, we feel obliged to say that, in some respects, Kinsey's data on male homosexuality are the least satisfactory of any he presented—and that our own data on homosexuality, as we will shortly explain, are the least satisfactory in our own survey. Thus, such comparisons as we will be able to make with Kinsey's figures will be of a gross order. Rather than enabling us to make any precise quantitative statements about the level of homosexuality today as compared with a generation ago, they will enable us only to conclude that there is no indication of any increase since Kinsey's time.

Prior to Kinsey's work, the only quantitative estimates of homosexual behavior dealt only with males and were based on wholly inadequate samples. In addition, they failed to discriminate between the fleeting experimental homosexuality of youth and the more serious homosexuality of adulthood. Kinsey's survey of homosexuality, on the other hand, was monumental in scope, depth and analytic detail—and deeply shocking to the public. For while it had always been supposed that only a small percent of the population was homosexually inclined, Kinsey reported that at least 37 percent of all American males and 20 percent of all American females had some actual homosexual experience in the course of their lives, and that substantial additional percentages had responded erotically to persons of the same sex even though overt physical acts had not taken place.[19] These figures, particularly the one concerning males, were at first a national scandal. After a while, however, they became an accepted part of the national mythology of sexual behavior. Unfortunately, they are misleading and distorted.

Kinsey had quite properly objected to the earlier characterizations of heterosexuality and homosexuality as two distinct and wholly separate patterns of behavior. What really existed, he said, was a continuum, ranging from total heterosexuality to total homosexuality, with a number of gradations in between.[20] He found it convenient to set up seven categories, ranging from 0 to 6, to represent the spectrum from total heterosexuality to total homosexuality. This concept is taxonomically sound and useful, but it can be—and has very generally been—misconstrued to mean that many people have a *continuing* mixture of homosexual and heterosexual in their natures, when in fact many people have brief experimental homosexual experiences that do not carry over into their adult behavior. Kinsey himself was aware of this, yet time and again he ignored his own careful analyses to make sweeping statements in which he added up all who rated anywhere from 1 to 6 on his scale, and thus produced those various totals that so shocked the nation.

If we turn to Kinsey's own detailed data rather than his more general statements, we find that, beyond the age of 15, not 37 percent but only 25 percent of the male population had anything more than incidental homosexual experiences of any sort.[21] Nor does this mean that the 25 percent were homosexually active during any substantial part of their adult lives, for Kinsey's criteria included those who had only "definite responses" to homosexual stimuli but no overt activity, and for as little as three years of their lives beyond age 15.[22] Only 10 percent of American males, even according to Kinsey's very generous criteria, were "more or less exclusively homosexual" for three years or more beyond the age of 15.[23] The figures, in short, though startling enough, were not nearly so shocking as many popularizers, homosexual spokesmen and Kinsey himself made them out to be.

Even more troublesome is the fact that in this area of sexual behavior Kinsey's survey methods had grave methodological flaws that produced a serious exaggeration of incidence data. Over a period of some years Kinsey made strenuous efforts to secure histories from homosexuals, frequenting gay bars in large cities, soliciting interviews with people he met there and, with their cooperation, being passed along from one interviewee to another within the homosexual world.[24] This yielded invaluable descriptive material, but hardly provided a sound basis for estimating the incidence of homosexuality throughout the nation—a task that would have required representative, rather than selective, case-collecting. Kinsey himself and his coworkers were aware of this and, as a control and verification of their individual case-collecting, sought to obtain a number of "hundred-percent samples"—groups such as men's clubs, college classes and the like whose entire membership, constituting a more nearly random sampling than his individually collected cases, had agreed to participate in Kinsey's survey.[25] In most other areas of sexual behavior the data Kinsey got from such hundred-percent samples tallied closely with those derived from all his other case-collecting; in the case of male homosexuality, however, there was a very wide divergence, the hundred-percent samples yielding incidences anywhere from a quarter to a half lower than those of his individual volunteer samples.[26] One must presume that this was a result of his having so energetically sought and collected a surplus of homosexual histories. For all that, in publishing his data and drawing his conclusions he combined the cases from both types of sample, even though the hundred-percent samples accounted for only a quarter of the total input.[27] Inevitably his findings seriously exaggerated the reality.

The result is that this part of Kinsey's heroic undertaking has been both a service and a disservice to behavioral science and to the public understanding of the subject. Many of its details are valuable additions to knowledge, but the built-in exaggerations and distortions have misled countless people and become self-perpetuating myths. A single example of the nonsense that has been endlessly reiterated, supposedly *ex cathedra,* will serve —particularly since it appears in a book edited by two respected sociologists in the field of sexuality and family life:

> Dr. Kinsey and his associates . . . delivered a body blow to homosexual mythology . . . for the stereotyped homosexual —the effeminate, mincing dandy—clearly was not one of every three males, and this meant that the great majority of persons who had expressed homosexual inclinations looked just like those who despised them. . . . Kinsey forced society to see that, instead of having just heterosexuals and homosexuals, it had many active bisexuals, and many more who were potentially so.*

---

*Donald J. Cantor, "The Homosexual Revolution," in *The New Sexual Revolution,* edited by Lester A. Kirkendall and Robert N. Whitehurst (New York: Donald W. Brown, Inc., 1971), pp. 86–87.

To deal with the errors in these few lines would take three times the space of the quotation. Suffice it to say that Kinsey did not show that one out of three American males had expressed homosexual inclinations, but that one out of three had performed at least one overt homosexual act at some time in their lives—most of them during adolescence and the teens—and that only a very limited number of American males are bisexual or "potentially so" in adult life.

Those who know the subject best have long been unhappy with the Kinsey statistics on male homosexuality. Dr. Wardell Pomeroy, a key figure at the Kinsey Institute for 13 years and coauthor of the male and female Kinsey volumes, says in his recent history, *Dr. Kinsey and the Institute for Sex Research,* "The magic 37 percent of males who had one or more homosexual experiences was, no doubt, overestimated. Probably 33 percent would have been closer to the mark."[28] Other close associates and Institute members are even more outspoken. In an interview with Arno Karlen, Dr. Paul Gebhard, coauthor of three Institute volumes and director of the Institute ever since Kinsey's death, bluntly said, "God, sometimes I wish we'd never published that statistic!" going on to explain that many of those included in the famous 37-percent figure had only limited homosexual experiences, early in life, and were thoroughly heterosexual thereafter.[29] Sociologist William Simon, who was for a number of years a research associate in the Kinsey Institute and has since done special work on homosexuality, told Karlen that, on the basis of his knowledge of the original Kinsey data and information from other sources, he would estimate that only "2 to 3 per cent of the male population has a serious, long-term homosexual pattern. Another 7 or 8 per cent have casual or episodic homosexual experience. That makes about 10 per cent of the male population who've had more than fleeting or experimental homosexual events in their lives."[30] Psychiatrist Irving Bieber, coauthor with several others in 1962 of *Homosexuality: A Psychoanalytic Study*—the most ambitious and best-known work of its type—recently said in a medical journal that he diagnoses as homosexual only those adults who engage repetitively in homosexual behavior; according to that standard, "a more realistic evaluation [than Kinsey's] is that 1 to 2 per cent of American adult males are exclusively homosexual and another 3 to 4 per cent are bisexual."[31]*

Because female homosexuality has been less intensively studied, and less alarming to society, Kinsey's data in this area have not been subjected to the same kinds of critical attacks. The female data apparently have somewhat similar shortcomings, but to a much lesser degree; unfortunately, they present still other hazards of their own. Fewer than three-tenths of Kinsey's females were married when interviewed,[32] and since his own analysis shows homosexuality to be very much more common among single and divorced women than among the married, any active-incidence data for his whole female sample must be seriously exaggerated. By using his figures for unmarried and married females considered separately, we can avoid this distortion —but when it comes to accumulative incidences, even this is no help, for in the female volume Kinsey based the accumulative incidence of homosexual behavior not on data collected from persons who were single or married when interviewed, but on the basis of acts occurring *while* the individuals were single or *while* they were married.[33] This was a procedure quite different from that used in the male volume and tended to exaggerate the homosexual experience of the single sample and to understate that of the married one.

It is clear that these data offer no firm basis on which to make comparisons of the extent of homosexual behavior a generation ago and today. Were we to use Kinsey's data as they stand uncritically, our own survey would seem to show a sharp decline in homosexuality. If, however, we adjust his figures downward in accordance with his hundred-percent sample guidelines, and if, furthermore, we exclude fleeting or early experimental experiences from the totals, as do some of Kinsey's colleagues and critics, we come closer to a valid basis of comparison, and one which shows far smaller apparent declines.

But now we admit to a shortcoming in our own sample that probably accounts for those apparent minor declines. Where Kinsey's sample was overweighted with the committed members of the homosexual community, our own is probably much underweighted in this area. Even in Kinsey's view, this group represented only a small minority of the males who had had any

---

*In a personal communiqué, Dr. Bieber adds that he regards the 37-percent overall figure, and the 10 percent said by Kinsey to be "more or less exclusively homosexual," as "grotesque" and "grossly in error."

homosexual experiences or inclinations during their lifetimes; the great bulk of homosexual experiences and inclinations were had by persons within the ostensibly normal heterosexual population. It is this latter population that our survey teams, using conventional sampling techniques, were best able to reach. Many of the members of the homosexual community, on the other hand, live somewhat outside the cultural mainstream and are not adequately reached by such techniques; accordingly, we missed many, if not most, of this special group. As one indication, in our own survey sample only 1 percent of the males and .5 percent of the females rate themselves as "mainly" to "totally" homosexual, which is even smaller than the conservative estimates made by Simon and by Bieber. If we add those who rate themselves as "equally heterosexual and homosexual"—in our interview sample it was clear that most people who made this claim are in fact primarily homosexual—we still find only 2 percent of our males and 1 percent of our females in the category of basically homosexual. This brings the male figure close to—although still below—the Simon and Bieber estimates.

If we missed much or most of the committed homosexual community, by how much do the figures we are about to present understate the case? Obviously we do not know, since the only way to know would be to sample that missing segment of the population. But we can attempt an informed guess. Kinsey's data would suggest that we ought to add about four percentage points to all our incidence figures,[34] but this is undoubtedly too high a correction, for reasons already dealt with. Most of the gay organizations we consulted were not much help, since they use Kinsey's figures as a base from which to make expanded projections consonant with their own wishes, if not reality. But the oldest and perhaps most authoritative of them, the Mattachine Society, advised us that, based on their own national information input and on numerous newspaper accounts and subsamples, they estimate that 1 percent of the adult males in this country are exclusive homosexuals who belong to the openly homosexual community in their own cities, and that if one includes those exclusively homosexual males who avoid the openly homosexual community but are part of the homosexual underground, the figure would be on the order of 2 to 3 percent.[35] This is in good accord with a downward adjustment, based on Kinsey's hundred-percent sample data, of his own

4-percent figure for lifelong exclusive homosexuality in males. We conclude that all our own accumulative-incidence figures for males are too low by something like two percentage points.

With these several qualifications and caveats, here are the comparisons we believe we are warranted in cautiously making:

—A generation ago the total percentage of all American males who ever had any overt homosexual experience beyond the onset of adolescence was 37 percent, according to Kinsey, but for the reasons given above, we feel that a sounder and more credible figure would be one based on Kinsey's own hundred-percent samples, or more on the order of 25 percent.[36] In our sample the most nearly comparable figure is on the order of 17 or 18 percent, but this is not a lifetime accumulative incidence, for a small number of our younger men who have not yet had any such experiences will have at least one before old age. Moreover, it is necessary to make an adjustment for our estimated underrepresentation of the exclusively homosexual individuals. Allowing for these two factors, we think the correct lifetime incidence today is somewhere between 20 and 25 percent. The estimates for a generation ago and today are thus very close and lend no credence to claims that there has been a significant increase, or indeed any increase, in the past generation.

—Accumulative incidences for females are still harder to compare for the reasons already noted. Because Kinsey chose here to compile accumulative incidences of homosexual acts that occurred while his females were single or while they were married, his married sample is in effect robbed of any such experience occurring before marriage, and his single sample is exaggerated by the same amount. The resulting figures contrast oddly with our own. Kinsey gives the accumulative incidence of homosexual acts for married females as only 3 percent, but for single women as 26 percent.[37] In our sample 9 percent of our married women and 15 percent of our single women have had at least one homosexual experience. As with our male data, however, we must project the existing curves to estimate ultimate accumulative incidences; this would give something like 10 to 11 percent for married women, and 20 percent for single women. Even these figures are very unlike Kinsey's, but it is obvious from an analysis of our own data, by age, that the greater part of the homosexual experiences of our married women occurred before they were married. If that portion of female homosexual experience were reassigned to the single category, as in Kinsey, the incidences for both married and single females would be virtually identical with his. Once again, this rather labored comparison suggests that there has been no substantial increase, if any, in the overall incidence of female homosexual activity in recent years.

—Similar conclusions are to be drawn from comparisons of accumulative incidences that exclude adolescent and fleeting experiments. Kinsey asserted that 25 percent of the male population had something more than incidental homosexual experiences or reactions beyond the age of 15,[38] but William Simon, as already noted, thinks the figure is more like 10 percent. In our own sample, only 10 percent of the married males and 11 percent of the single males have had any homosexual experiences after age 15. Some of this, to be sure, may have been merely incidental, but the exaggeration this creates in our figure is offset by our underreporting of the exclusively homosexual males, and by the fact that our incidence has to be projected somewhat to allow for the portion of the young who have not yet but will someday have such experience. All in all, a realistic estimate would be on the order of 12 or 13 percent. Even if we adjusted Kinsey's own figure downward by something between a quarter to a half (in accordance with his hundred-percent sample data), his would still be slightly higher than our own. Once more, therefore, we find no reason to think that there has been an increase in adult male homosexual behavior in the past generation.

—In the female volume, Kinsey did not present accumulative-incidence data for homosexual experience beyond age 15, as he did in the male volume. However, if we subtract from his accumulative-incidence curves those portions that lie below age 20 —a more useful break than 15, in the case of females—we can estimate that something on the order of 15 percent of his single females and 2 to 3 percent of his married females had homosexual experiences beyond the age of 19.[39] In our own sample, 7 percent of single women and 2 percent of married women have had homosexual contact beyond that age, and if we project these figures upward to make them approximately equivalent to life-time accumulative incidences we get something on the order of 10 to 12 percent for single females and 3 percent for married females. These figures are close to his, and once again lend support to our belief that the incidence of homosexuality, if it has not diminished since Kinsey's time, has not demonstrably increased.*

—Kinsey estimated that 10 percent of all males were "more or less exclusively homosexual" for at least three years between the ages of 16 and 55,[40] but William Simon, speaking in roughly similar terms, put the figure at 2 to 3 percent. In our own survey only 1 percent of our males rate themselves as mainly or totally homosexual, but it seems likely, as stated earlier, that the hard-core homosexuals we missed may comprise something like another 2 percent of the adult male population. For single females beyond age 15, Kinsey's data suggest a range of 2 to 6 percent, and for married females something under 1 percent.[41] In our sample, 2 percent of the single females and an insignificant fraction of 1 percent of the married females rated themselves as mainly to completely homosexual. Making the same kinds of allowances as in the previous comparisons—and frankly admitting that in this area we are guessing rather than measuring—we think the incidences are of the same order of magnitude today as a generation ago.

—Comparing active-incidence data poses a different problem: Kinsey defined active incidence as any homosexual experience within a five-year period, while we defined it as any such experience within the past 12 months. Since he cast a net five times as wide, one would expect his figures to be higher than ours, even if the actual extent of homosexual activity were the same then and now; probably they would not be five times as high (since that would only be the case if a wholly different set of individuals were involved in each year), but they would surely be *somewhat* higher. To put it another way, if our figures were nearly as large as his, we would suspect that there had been a notable increase in active incidence. This is not the case. Kinsey reported that anywhere from 1.7 to 8.5 percent of his married males had had at least one homosexual experience in a five-year period, the rate being highest for the 16-to-20 cohort and lowest for the 46-to-50 cohort[42]; in our own sample of married males of all ages, only 1 percent have had any homosexual experience in the

---

*In this comparison we do not assign any of the homosexual experiences of married females to the single contingent, as we did on pp. 311–312, because in taking age 20 as the starting point of this accumulation, we have in effect equated our single and married bases with Kinsey's.

past year. For single males Kinsey's five-year active incidences ranged from 14.5 to 40.2 percent[43]; among our singles the over-all one-year active incidence was 6 percent. These comparisons are of the roughest sort, but they do appear to bear out our contention that there has been no measurable increase in the active incidence of male homosexuality since the 1940s.

—We cannot make a similar comparison between our own and Kinsey's active-incidence data for female homosexuality. Kinsey defined active incidence, for females, as any homosexual act, during a five-year span, that resulted in orgasm.[44] We did not consider orgasm an essential criterion, and therefore did not make it a part of the questions we used to elicit female-homosex-ual-activity data. Elsewhere, and inconsistently, Kinsey used the term "active incidence" to refer to those females who, at any specified age, rated anywhere from 1 to 6 on his heterosexual-homosexual scale, although this included persons who had merely experienced positive psychosexual reactions—feelings of arousal when looking at a sensuous female nude, for example—without overt contact.[45] We did not define homosexual re-sponse this broadly in our questionnaire, but limited it to overt contact. Thus, Kinsey's criteria are sometimes narrower and sometimes broader than our own; accordingly, we do not feel that comparisons between his data and ours would have any validity. Our own findings, however, are as follows: 3 percent of our single females and somewhat less than 1 percent of our married females had at least one overt homosexual contact within the past year. The figures would probably be a percent-age point or two higher (at least for the single females) had we reached the committed homosexual community and under-ground more adequately. Whether the figures represent any increase in the active incidence of female homosexuality since Kinsey's time we cannot say.

To sum up: Wherever we can legitimately compare our findings with Kinsey's, the raw data seem to show a sharp de-cline in homosexual activity in the past generation, both for males and females. But when we manipulate the raw data to correct for differences between Kinsey's sample and methods of reckoning and our own, the decline largely or wholly disappears. In no case, however, do we succeed in producing evidence or even the suggestion of measurable increase in either the ac-cumulative or active incidence of homosexual behavior throughout the married or single populations in our sample. Presumably, this applies to the national populations they represent: married and single people of basically (or ostensibly) heterosexual orientation. A real increase may, however, exist among those committed exclusive homosexuals of the gay community whom we probably failed to reach adequately, and whom Kinsey reached all too well. But if it is true that many secret homosexuals have recently become overt members of the homosexual community, a marked growth may have taken place in that community without indicating any increase in the overall incidence of homosexuality throughout the national population. What appears to be a rise might only be a shift from one sphere of living to another.

If our sample is short of exclusively or primarily homosexual persons, it is nevertheless generally representative of the national population, which includes by far the largest part of all persons who ever have any homosexual experience during their lifetimes. One might suppose that even as sexual liberation has enabled many people to increase the frequency with which they engage in other formerly taboo or forbidden acts, it would have increased the frequency with which basically heterosexual persons engage in homosexual acts. But it does not seem to have done so; homosexual acts by primarily heterosexual persons remain very infrequent, as they were in Kinsey's time. Indeed, Kinsey was struck by the low average frequencies of homosexual contacts among all persons having any current homosexual contacts. Among married males beyond their teens who were having any homosexual activity, he found a median frequency of only some five to six contacts per year.[46] Even for single males having homosexual activity, the median frequency was only about 30 times a year.[47] Kinsey himself remarked several times that these rates were quite low in comparison to heterosexual outlet, and implied that social pressure and fear were the major restraining factors.[48]

Our own sample is too small to permit computing medians for married or single persons separately, or even together. However, of those married and single males who have been at all homosexually active in the past year—singles outweigh the married two to one in this subsample—fully half had three or less homosexual experiences during the year. More than a quarter of these homosexually active males had only one such contact, and only a third had eight or more such contacts during the year. To be sure, had we reached more of the committed exclusive homosexuals, they would have pulled the figures up close to Kinsey's. In our interview sample, indeed, we did succeed in reaching some homosexual males who regularly cruise the gay bars and steam baths, and some who live with homosexual partners, and found that these people have frequencies of sexual activity comparable to those of heterosexuals. But our questionnaire data indicate that sexual liberation has not made it easy for any male other than one who is primarily or exclusively homosexual, and committed to it as a way of life, to incorporate homosexual acts into his sexual repertoire.

Median frequencies for female homosexual behavior, as reported by Kinsey, were on the order of less than one contact every three weeks for married women who had any active homosexual life, and a little more than one every three weeks for homosexually active single women.[49] (The frequencies vary by age group; these are rough summaries of the total sample.) In our own very limited group of homosexually active adult females (lumping married and single together), one-third had 3 or less, and only one-third had 6 or more, homosexual experiences in the past year. Clearly we did not reach as many fully committed female homosexuals as did Kinsey, and our figure represents primarily the level of activity typical of married and single females who are striving to hide their homosexuality or to lead a basically heterosexual life. We can reasonably conclude that even though sexual liberation has freed a number of primarily homosexual females to "come out," or to live thoroughly homosexual lives, it has not freed primarily heterosexual females to seek frequent or regular gratification of any homosexual desires they may feel. Whether the constraints upon these people today are still largely social or chiefly internal is a matter of conjecture. In any event, sexual liberation has removed the constraints only for those females whose orientation is definitely or wholly homosexual, and, we think, only for some of them at that.

Two other measurements confirm our general impression that sexual liberation has made little change in the homosexual behavior of those who are not part of the homosexual world.

Even in Kinsey's sample, despite its overrepresentation of committed homosexuals, half of the males and nearly three-quarters of the females with any homosexual experience had had only one or two homosexual partners[50]; in our sample the same thing is true of two-thirds of the males and four-fifths of the females. Only 22 percent of Kinsey's males and only 4 percent of his females with any homosexual experience had had 11 or more partners[51]; in our sample the percentages were 8 and less than 1 respectively. Granted the differences between Kinsey's sample and ours, these comparisons again suggest that there has been no change in the role homosexuality plays in the life history of most Americans who ever experience it; by and large it remains part of pubertal and adolescent experimentation, being explored briefly and only with one or two close friends, then rejected and set aside in favor of heterosexual behavior. This is further indicated by other relevant data derived from our own sample:

—Forty-five percent of the males and 58 percent of the females in our sample who have had homosexual experiences have had them within a single year or less of their lives, and 58 percent of the males and 71 percent of the females have had them within a two-year span.

—Only 37 percent of the males and 22 percent of the females who have had homosexual experiences have had them for a period extending more than three years. Or in terms of our entire sample: Only 7 percent of all males and 3 percent of all females in our total national sample have had homosexual experiences during more than three years of their lives.

—Half of the males and well over half of the females in our sample who have had homosexual experiences ceased having them before they were 16.

Moreover, although we have seen that sexual liberation has widened the range of the sexual variations sometimes or often employed in heterosexual contacts, it does not seem to have done so in homosexual contacts. Kinsey reported that about 30 percent of all males had been fellated at least once in their lives by another male, and about half as many had themselves been fellators of another male at least once.[52] In our sample the comparable figures are 11 percent and 5 percent, which, even allowing for differences between Kinsey's sample and ours, indicates no growth of freedom to employ this technique.

Much of the homosexual experience in our sample was, however, limited to the adolescent period. It is easier for older and more sophisticated persons to use advanced and variant techniques, and accordingly we find that among those adult males in our sample who are currently having homosexual activity, two-thirds experienced fellatio in the past year as "insertor" and half as "insertee." Yet even these proportions are smaller than one might expect; the literature of homosexuality would lead one to suppose that fellatio is all but universally used. Anal intercourse, also commonly thought to be all but universal among homosexual males, has been experienced as insertor by only 20 percent of all males with any homosexual experience, and by 18 percent as insertee; and even in the currently active adult group, only about half had experienced it either actively or passively, or both, within the past year. Manual masturbation remains the most common activity for all males who have had any homosexual experience (over two-thirds have had it done to them; over half have done it) and even, remarkably, for adult males currently having homosexual contacts (four-fifths have had it done to them, and two-thirds have done it, in the past year).

Kinsey's information on female homosexual techniques is a bit more detailed. Those with little experience, he reported, generally limited their activities to simple kissing and general body contact; the more experienced progressed to breast stimulation and manual-genital techniques; and the most experienced to cunnilingus.[53] Even among the highly sophisticated, however, vaginal penetration by penis substitutes was very rare.

Our own findings show no change. Of all females who have ever had any homosexual experience, less than half have ever touched a partner's breast, and less than half have ever been touched on the breast by a partner. Only a quarter had ever made mouth-breast contact in the active role, and only a quarter had ever experienced mouth-breast contact in the passive role. Manual stimulation of the genitals was by far the most common experience, having been passively experienced by a little over half, and actively by a little under half. Simulated intercourse (body to body) had been experienced by a third, but cunnilingus was relatively rare; fewer than one out of five of the females with any homosexual experience had ever had it done to them, and only one out of eight had ever done it. Only 2 percent had ever employed an artificial penis on another female, and only 2 percent had ever had one used on them.

Once again, of course, adult females who are currently having homosexual activities are much freer in their choice of techniques than the larger group which includes adolescent and teen-age experience. The currently active sample is too small for precise statistical breakdown, but we can report that mouth-breast techniques are employed by a majority, and oral-genital techniques, either as active or passive partner, by about half the group. Even so, this is smaller than the incidence of oral-genital activities among our young heterosexual respondents. It is noteworthy, moreover, that the most popular of all techniques among our active adult female homosexuals is still body-to-body contact; this was used within the past year by four-fifths of the homosexually active sample. The use of an artificial penis, or dildoe, often supposed by "straight" (heterosexual) people to be very common among lesbians, was rather limited; only a few individuals—roughly a sixth of the active sample—had been insertees, or had been insertors, of such a device within the past year. None had used a dildoe for anal intercourse.

There is thus no evidence of great freedom in the use of sexual techniques in homosexual contacts—certainly not on the part of those males and females who have ever had any such contacts, and not even on the part of those males and females who continue to be homosexually active in adult life, although living within a heterosexual society. It may be that for most of these individuals the physical intimacy with another of the same sex is so fraught with fear, tension and excitement that they neither can, nor need to, attend to the refinement of sensuous technique. On the other hand, among the kind of homosexuals we did not reach in our sampling, the range and frequency of the use of sophisticated erotic techniques may well be comparable to those of sexually liberated heterosexuals, although for obvious mechanical reasons there is very likely a particular emphasis on oral-genital techniques by homosexuals of both sexes and on anal intercourse among male homosexuals. But this is conjecture on our part, and not a finding.

In all the earlier chapters of this book we have sought to add experiential immediacy to our data by the use of illustrative

quotations from individual interviews. It is more difficult for us
to find representative material of this kind in connection with
homosexuality than in the preceding areas of discussion. For
one thing, homosexual experience and its various meanings
seem to us more diffuse, less coherently structured and less
amenable to a systematic taxonomy than heterosexual experience and its meanings. For another, among the 200 individuals
in the interview sample, the subsample of persons with homosexual experience was small, and the subsample of persons with
more than incidental adolescent homosexual experience was
still smaller, making the selection of genuinely illustrative
material difficult.

With this by way of apologia, we now offer a handful of interview excerpts that seem to us to exemplify at least some of the
major points made in the preceding discussion.

First, two excerpts that illustrate the fact that fantasies of
one's self engaging in homosexual activity are still thoroughly
alarming to a large number of American men and women, even
when they consider themselves liberal on the subject and are
able to read about it with interest and pleasure. The first speaker
is a young man from a blue-collar background, now completing
training in a professional field. Athletic, vain and obsessed with
the importance of being a superb performer in his sexual relations with women, he has read a good deal of literature about
sexuality in order to improve his own technique, and a number
of issues of gay magazines "just to see what they're all about."

> At one time, when I was a freshman in college, I was having
> constant thoughts about sex, including sex between two
> guys, and I was extremely afraid I was a homosexual. I went
> to a priest and he said, "Read these books about it and fight
> it." Shit! He was putting it on *me*, like I was sick and had
> to cure myself. But as I began to read about it, I found out
> that everybody has feelings and thoughts like that, and here
> I'm worrying and feeling terrible for nothing. Because I'd
> sometimes look at a guy in the gym who was physically
> beautiful, and I'd feel some kind of fascination—and it
> would make me feel really guilty. But now I saw that I didn't
> have to feel guilty just because I had occasional feelings. It
> doesn't bother me anymore since I came to terms with it.
> I figure that even if I ever wanted to know what it was like,

it would cause me a lot of anguish, and emotional problems, and maybe some social problems. So fuck it, I don't
need it. Besides, I dig women.

The second is a comparable comment by a quite different person, a middle-class, Jewish, college-educated woman of 28 who
is currently a full-time homemaker and mother of two preschool
children:

I never did have any actual experience—not unless you call
"looking," at the age of six or seven, an experience. But
there was a time, when I was maybe thirteen or fourteen,
when I had this special feeling about one woman teacher.
I think she was encouraging the feeling in me, and it made
me feel strange and excited, but nervous, and I didn't really
know what it was. And then once, when she had two of us
over at her apartment for tea, she said something about the
poems of Sappho, and I went to the library and read up on
Sappho, and I didn't know whether I was more excited or
more horrified at the whole thought. Sometimes I'd try to
picture it, but actually I could never quite figure out who
did what, or with what, and all that. That whole thing lasted
only a few months, and died out by itself when I got into
dating boys. As an adult, of course, I can read about lesbians or even imagine lesbian activities, and sometimes it
turns me on, but oddly enough when I actually see it done
in a blue movie, it gives me the creeps.

And now two examples of the kind of experimental and inconsequential homosexual experience that is had by sizable
minorities of males and females in adolescence but not thereafter. The principal influence of sexual liberation shown in these
examples is the relative freedom of the individuals to recall their
homosexual experiences in adulthood, and to recognize their
occasional transient fantasy desires without alarm.

First, a 49-year-old biologist, married, from a middle-class,
inactively Protestant background:

When I was twelve my penis suddenly grew a lot, and in a
little while I discovered masturbation, so naturally I told my
closest buddy about it and showed him how, and we would
do it together. Then he got hold of a few dirty magazines
and paperbacks from an older boy, and we pretty much got

the idea of what it is that men and women do. We were crazy to know how it felt, and we talked it over and decided we could get at least some idea by trying it with each other. First, we tried to do it between the thighs, but that was awkward and embarrassing—we didn't really like the face-to-face contact—and anyway, the penis didn't slide around well. So then he suggested that we could stick it in the anus. We tried that, but neither one of us could relax the sphincter sufficiently to let the other one get inside. Finally, we had the brilliant idea of trying sixty-nine, and that worked, it *really* worked! It was the most high-pitched, exciting experience I had ever had in my life. But one minute after I ejaculated, I felt sick and disgusted, and horribly guilty, and I didn't even know why. I came back for more in a few days, but again I felt rotten afterwards. After maybe half a dozen sessions, I told my buddy I wasn't going to do it anymore because I felt wrong about it. He was sore as hell and took it personally, and for a couple of years we hardly saw each other. When we did get together again, neither of us ever mentioned it by so much as one syllable. Later on, as young adults, we would tell each other a lot about how we were making out with women, and sometimes refer jokingly to our early foolishness. . . . I've never had any other such experience, but at times I can recognize a certain appeal in the idea—intellectually, anyhow. But I have never felt the urge to actually seek it, nor would I accept it if I were solicited. It's not something a normal adult man would do. He might *think* about it—but to do it would be a symptom of emotional disorder.

And here is the roughly parallel experience of a young divorcée, currently involved in TV production in Hollywood, who grew up in a well-to-do but relatively liberal community in San Francisco:

When I was only five or six, three of my girl friends and I would play doctor and we'd use bobby pins to take rectal temperatures. We giggled a lot, and knew somehow that it was wrong, but we didn't know why. Sometimes we'd try to turn female cats on by playing with their genitals, and that was exciting mostly because we were doing it together—not that I realized that at the time. I got interested in boys by eight or nine, and sometimes would have crushes, but my first real sexual experience, at around eleven or twelve, was with my best friend, a girl I had known since I was two or three. We started out by saying we had to practice up on kissing so we'd be ready for it when we started to date. So we kissed, and it got very exciting, and after a while we said, "What do they do next?" and took turns pretending that one of us was a boy, and feeling the other one up, and that was even more exciting. And on a later occasion we got to feeling each other's thighs, and finally to genital play, and we were fingering each other's parts and playing with them, both at the same time, and getting carried away, and all of a sudden I had an orgasm. I was petrified. I was scared to death. I didn't know what it was, but I knew it was something very big and important, and that it was very wrong to have it with my best friend. So I found excuses, first one and then another, and never let it happen again. Until I began having sex with boys I often worried about having done it, but then that put an end to the worry. It has never interested me since, except in artistic form—in fiction, or sometimes in movies.

Some of our essentially heterosexual interviewees had had occasional experimental homosexual experiences in adulthood; for the most part these were anxiety-producing and self-limiting, but some of them could never have occurred except within a milieu of sexual ultraliberalism. An example is this experience, narrated by an advertising executive in his thirties:

I guess I'd been as secretly curious, and as generally afraid of it, as most other guys. After my first marriage broke up, I went to a number of swinging parties, and at one of them somebody said, "How come no guy here has the guts to find out what it's like with another guy?" That's usually *verboten* at swinging parties, you know, but somehow we all said, "Let's all try it," so one after another, with a lot of kidding around, the four guys there each sucked another guy's cock. The fact that we were all doing it was what made it kind of all right. I felt very odd; it was both sickening and exciting. I wouldn't let my man come in my mouth, though; that would have been like too much. And the minute I stopped, I started in on one of the girls, to show everybody

—and myself—where I really was at. But I had liked it
enough to do it again at the next two get-togethers of the
same bunch. By the third time, though, it didn't seem like
such a big deal and I could tell it wasn't really my thing,
because I never felt really attracted to the guy, as a person,
but only to his cock. So I stopped doing it.

A young single woman working as a laboratory technician tells
of a somewhat similar experience:

There were two couples of us spending a weekend at the
lake, a year ago, and we got to kidding around about swapping, and after a while we actually did. I had never done it
before, and it was a lark—it was so forbidden, sort of, but
no problem, really, because none of us was hooked on the
other. And then, after a joint or two, we were all nice and
high, and the other girl said, "Why not find out about the
other thing, too?" and I knew what she meant, and felt
scared, but then I thought, "Why not? Once, anyway, in a
lifetime." The guys egged us on, even though they said *they*
wouldn't do it. So she and I went in the other room and she
caressed me and touched me, and finally even ate me, and
I thought it was all very nice, especially because her body
felt so different from a man's. I enjoyed the experience. But
I didn't come; I didn't even get close to it. Afterwards, I felt
quite pleased that I had had the courage to do it, and also
I knew that I didn't want to bother with it ever again.

Some self-styled bisexuals, as we have indicated, are basically
homosexual but seek to minimize their conflicts and sense of
deviance by having occasional heterosexual episodes. Others
have had a bisexual period when, for many reasons, they still
thought or hoped that they were heterosexual, though they
eventually recognized that their real orientation was toward
same-sex partners. Sexual liberation is very likely responsible in
large part for the relative honesty with which some of these
people can think about their experiences, and even convey them
to others. A 45-year-old college professor exemplifies this
behavior pattern and this kind of freedom.

I'd had this brief period of homosexual activity with a
cousin when I was eleven or so, and it came out and was
a scandal in the family. As a result, I put all that behind me,

and in my teens, whenever I saw effeminate or faggy homosexuals, I found their affectations disgusting, and acted
scornful of them. I didn't date girls much until my freshman
year in college, but then I had a couple of big crushes and
thought myself wildly in love both times. But I never did
more than kiss and pet a little, and whenever I got close to
the real thing with any girl I panicked. I had no idea why.
After college I moved to New York and one night stumbled
into a gay bar—and I knew where I was immediately, and
somehow I knew this was it. It was like a revelation. I went
home with one fellow that night, and then dropped right
into the gay life. Sometimes I'd cruise the bars and pick up
someone for a quickie in the john. Sometimes I'd pick up
a guy on the street and take him home for an hour or two.
Sometimes I'd spend the whole night with some fellow I
really liked. One thing developed into a deep friendship—
he was an older man, and very sane and warm—and we
spent many evenings together, and sometimes we'd have
sex, and sometimes we'd just talk all evening.

Right about then, I met a very attractive, somewhat older
woman in business—a divorced woman, very feminine,
very intelligent—and she seemed to like me. I decided I
would try to experience intimacy with a woman, so we went
to dinner, and I gave her the whole *Tea and Sympathy* bit,
and told her what the situation was. Believe it or not, she
responded, and took me to bed, and was a marvelous instructor, and it was a very sensuous, beautiful thing. It
made me feel much more a whole person, made me proud
of myself. It went on for three weeks, but then it got too
emotionally involved for her, and we broke off.

So for the next five years I considered myself bisexual,
and would make it with a girl now and then to keep my
franchise, but the truth was that I was predominantly
homosexual even then. All of my close relationships were
with men, and so was much of my casual sex. I didn't want
to admit it to myself, but fucking a girl really wasn't very
exciting or gratifying to me, except in an intellectual way.
Sexually, the thing I enjoyed most was fucking another man
anally, and second-most was seeing another man get
aroused and enjoy himself fucking me. As time went by, I
gradually gave up the effort to make it with girls, and since

my late twenties I have had almost no sexual experiences with women. And I haven't missed them or wanted them.

But while homosexual sex is my thing, what bothers me is that most homosexual relationships are so often shallow or cruel, or both. I have seen very few good and deep homosexual love relationships. Most of them are brittle and thin, and some are terribly sadomasochistic: I myself almost killed one guy whom I considered my lover. I hate the swishiness and bitchiness of many homosexuals. . . . The truth is that I still regard it as a kind of enslavement, even though today we're all supposed to feel free to be ourselves.

A 23-year-old female graduate student is another example of the technical bisexual who has recently recognized her own thoroughly homosexual orientation; unlike the preceding speaker she is representative of the relatively unconflicted committed homosexual of our time.

When I was only twelve, I had some type of sex play with my girl cousin when we slept in the same bed one night— some genital touching, I remember, which was terrifically stimulating to me. We never did it again, but I often thought about it, especially when I would masturbate. I started going out with boys when I was fifteen, and got into heavy petting by seventeen and would have orgasm quite easily. I was very much turned on by the whole thing. I had intercourse for the first time at eighteen, and for the next three months it was very heavy, with that one fellow. Then he went to graduate school three thousand miles away, and for a while I became promiscuous. I'd go to bed with a new guy the first night, if I liked him, and would have relations with two or three guys concurrently—not simultaneously, you know, but like one night after another. I went through about 25 men in a little over a year. But the peculiar thing was that I would often fantasize sexual acts with a woman while I was in the middle of sex with a man. I don't know why it wasn't clear to me what the real story was. Anyway, one time I met a girl in the park and fell into conversation with her and found her interesting and appealing. We went back to her apartment for a drink, and all of a sudden she was kissing me—and I wasn't shocked, but only excited and scared. Eventually she took off my clothes in a regular seduction scene, and there was a lot of kissing and foreplay —she was doing it all—and touching my thighs, and kissing and stimulating the clitoris. Finally I had an orgasm, and it was marvelous. I didn't reciprocate, though—I wasn't ready for that—and afterwards I felt guilty and hung-up about the whole experience. But a year later I quit fighting; I went to a gay bar and shopped around until I found what I wanted, and went home with her and spent the night. We had sex twice, and this time I was really loose—I did as much as she, and I felt great about it. Well, not all *that* loose —we didn't do cunnilingus that time, but mostly touching of the genitals, and a lot of tenderness, and breast play, and kissing and touching of the hair, and we both had orgasms. But since then I've gotten into the whole thing, and it's *right* for me. I have my preferences, though—I can't stand a real butch who only wants to play the aggressive role and who won't let her partner do anything to her. I've come to feel very easy about cunnilingus, both doing it and having it done. I think females are much better lovers than men— they do more foreplay and show more tenderness. Touch-ing and stroking and kissing and all that sort of thing—a woman will do that much better, and longer and more lovingly, than a man. For the past year I've been trying out as many women as possible, but right now I'm seeing one woman who excites me emotionally. When she calls, I feel just the way I used to when a man I was excited about would call. But I'll still occasionally go to a bar by myself and let some girl buy me drinks and dance with me, and try to talk me into coming home with her, and if I'm excited by her, I will. I'm not ready to come out and openly call myself a homosexual; I still label myself bisexual, even with my inti-mates. But the truth is I'm not having any relationships with men any longer, and have no interest in doing so.

Sadomasochism: Incidence, Frequency, Techniques

In contrast to the foregoing findings about homosexuality, our survey data on sadomasochistic sexual behavior lead us to be-lieve that the incidence of such acts has increased somewhat in the past generation. This seems surprising, for, as we have said, sadism and masochism in connection with sexual relations are not only pathologically deviant but expressive of unhealthy and antihedonistic emotional needs, and thus antipathetic to the central values of sexual liberation. Upon closer inspection, however, it turns out that part of the apparent increase consists of activities more in the nature of teasing and playful roughhousing than true sadomasochism. For the rest, we think that the increase in sadomasochism is indeed a concomitant of, and possibly a side effect of, sexual liberation. In any case the present incidence remains extremely small.

S/M is deviant in a very different sense from homosexuality. It has no social structure or subculture of its own (there are few or no S/M bars or communities, and there is no codified body of S/M manners and mores); rather, it is a genre of individual and frequently idiosyncratic deviancy. Nor is most of it, as in the case of homosexuality, confined to the experimental or developmental phase of sexuality in the immature; on the contrary, S/M is largely an ongoing long-term activity of young adults and adults. In Western civilization it has never been socially acceptable and, as far as one can judge from the historical record, has always been very rare. Even in England, the well-known addiction of Victorian gentlemen to flagellation was limited chiefly to those wealthy enough to have been governess-trained and to have been caned by headmasters and teachers in the schools of the élite. Today, though it is more common than formerly, it is still quite rare and, unlike the various forms of normal deviance and of socially structured deviance with which we have dealt thus far, has won no measure of social approval or acceptance. According to our own data it remains even less common than incest and roughly on a par with bestiality. From our review of the professional literature we would guess that it outranks in accumulative incidence only the most bizarre or incontestably pathological forms of sexual deviance, such as transvestism, pedophilia, exhibitionism, voyeurism, urolagnia, coprophilia and coprophagia and necrophilia.

Before presenting our data, we need to enlarge briefly upon our assertion that sadomasochism is pathologically deviant and expressive of unhealthy emotional needs. Prior to copulating, many species of subhuman animals, mammals in particular, engage in acts vaguely resembling combat, and the males of some species bite the female before or during copulation, inflicting a certain amount of pain. By and large, however, the fighting is only mock combat, and the male's biting of the female is primarily a matter of his seizing the skin or fur of the female's neck in order to maintain a good hold upon her while mounting.[54] Moreover, as we noted earlier, such pain as she feels tends to be biologically functional, causing the release of the egg that is to be fertilized, and with very rare exceptions (the mink being the one known to most people) the pain inflicted is not accompanied by actual trauma.[55] None of this, of course, bears any relationship to S/M in human beings. Our biology does not require mock combat, force or pain to ensure sexual arousal, successful intromission or the release of the egg from the ovary, and we accordingly have no instinctual programing calling for either the infliction or reception of pain as part of the sex act.

It is true, nevertheless, that mildly painful acts have been part of the pattern of sexual behavior in many human societies. But as Ford and Beach point out, this is far from universal, and in any case the human use of such stimuli is quite unlike the nonhuman mammalian use of them.[56] For even in those societies where painful stimuli are a normal or frequent part of sexual relationships, they are usually mild and consist of fundamentally playful acts such as gentle biting, scratching, tugging at the hair, eyebrow-tweaking, pinching and the like. What is even more important, after reviewing the cross-cultural data Ford and Beach conclude that "all human societies that encourage the infliction of mild pain in connection with intercourse take the attitude that such behavior should be bilateral or mutual. If the man bites the woman, she is permitted and expected to bite in return. If the girl scratches her lover, he retaliates."[57] In both respects, therefore, the use of painful stimuli in connection with sexual activity, even where socially acceptable, is totally unlike the practice of S/M as portrayed in the clinical literature or in fiction, magazines and films. Such portrayals emphasize bondage, whipping, beating, cutting, burning and the like, which are neither playfully administered nor mildly painful but savagely performed and torturous—and which, furthermore, are inflicted by the sadistic partner upon the masochistic one without being reciprocated.

Accordingly, most sex authorities—including most of those who are generally very liberal—regard S/M as pathological. An occasional sexual radical such as Albert Ellis takes the position, as quoted earlier in this chapter, that even S/M should not be considered deviant or abnormal as long as it is not the only way in which the individual can obtain sexual pleasure, but this criterion, as we have indicated, strikes us as inadequate, if not absurd.

A more appealing argument in favor of S/M is that offered by many of its practitioners to the effect that as long as the two parties to an S/M encounter are "consenting adults," anything they choose to do is their own business and should therefore be deemed unobjectionable by society. But this distorts the doctrine of consenting adults, for even if society grants people the legal right to behave in a deviant fashion, it need not abrogate its own right to make ethical and scientific judgments of that behavior. Society has no legal or moral right, for instance, to intervene in the life of a hermitlike, friendless and isolated individual, but it has every right to judge his way of life as abnormal and unhealthy, and to seek social remedies for the conditions that produce people like him. Moreover, the doctrine of consenting adults has implicit limits: It applies only to individuals who are truly adult and competent to consent, and extends only to acts which do not directly endanger society by violating the essential social contract prohibiting assault and murder. The issues were well stated by psychiatrist Dr. Warren Gadpaille, a member of the Group for the Advancement of Psychiatry, in a recent communiqué to *Medical Aspects of Human Sexuality*[58]:

> In its extreme forms, actual physical damage, mutilation, and even death may be inflicted upon the masochistic partner. Our cultural values do not permit aggravated assault upon even a "consenting" victim. Such a victim might even be regarded as manifesting such impaired judgment as to be incompetent to give consent. . . . Another concern might be the fear that the primarily sadistic individual could unexpectedly turn the destructive impulse upon an unwilling victim. In the study of sex offenders at the Institute for Sex Research, it was found that sexual aggressors against adults and minors showed the greatest degree of sexual arousal from sadomasochistic "pornographic" materials. No causal relation was demonstrated between sadomasochistic arousal and violent attack. But the speculation certainly

exists that the individual who derives intense pleasure from the fantasied or real inflicting of violence upon another may well be unusually dangerous.

For the foregoing reasons, we classify as nondeviant and normal those forms of pain infliction, connected with sexual behavior, which are playful, mutual and relatively mild. On the other hand, we classify as both deviant and pathological those forms of behavior ordinarily thought of as genuine S/M: serious, malevolent, nonmutual acts involving such practices as painful bondage of all sorts, beatings and whippings, the use of studded or sharp objects, rough or traumatic treatment of the genitals and breasts by means of pincers, tongs and other instruments, burning of the tissues by lighted cigarettes or heated objects, the forcible use of oversized or prickly-surfaced dildoes, fellatio in which the penis is rammed so deep into the throat as to gag the recipient, and so on.

In attempting to measure the changes in such behavior over the past generation, we begin, as in previous parts of this study, with the incidence of the behavior in fantasy life and with the degree to which individuals are sexually aroused by written or other materials dealing with it. There is little information on this in Kinsey, but what there is does help us judge the nature of the change that has taken place. Kinsey reported that only occasionally did sadistic or masochistic fantasies accompany male masturbation, and that only 4 percent of the females who had masturbated had ever fantasized a sadomasochistic situation while doing so.[59] Sadomasochistic stories, although more acceptable to the ego than one's own sadomasochistic fantasies, were interesting or arousing to relatively few males and fewer females: Only 10 percent of Kinsey's males and 3 percent of his females reported having definitely or frequently experienced arousal by such stories, with another 12 percent of the males and 9 percent of the females reporting that they had had at least "some response," at some time.[60]

In recent years there has been a definite increase in the general acceptability of fictional and dramatic presentations of sadomasochistic material. One has only to remember the popularity, several years ago, of the paperback edition of selected works of the Marquis de Sade or of *The Story of O* when changing standards of obscenity made them freely publishable and distributable in this country, or, more recently, the public fascination with the movie *Belle de Jour*. A few years ago, according to *The Report of the Commission on Obscenity and Pornography*, S/M magazines constituted less than 5 percent of the market of sex magazines *per se*[61]; today, a cursory examination of the magazines in any porn shop indicates that S/M has become a part of the general fare offered in a fairly large number of sex magazines not specifically devoted to S/M.

Our own survey indicates an increase in the use of sadistic and masochistic sexual fantasies. We asked our respondents whether, while masturbating, they had ever had thoughts of forcing someone to have sex with them, or of being forced to have sex; this is, of course, only one part of the spectrum of possible S/M fantasies, and perhaps the least bizarre part, but the difference between older respondents and younger ones is indicative of the general trend. Since we were asking not for current use of such fantasies but whether the respondent had ever had them at any time, the contrast between the older group and the younger one is likely to be a fair comparison, and a good indicator of change coming about in the population (see Table 43). The two sets of figures show, first of all, that the traditional tendency of males toward aggressiveness and the corresponding tendency of females toward passivity in the sex act still exist.*
What is far more interesting is that in every comparison in Table

Table 43

Ever Had Thoughts, While Masturbating,
of Forcing Someone to Have Sex:
All Who Ever Masturbated, Percents

Males		Females	
Under 35	35 and over	Under 35	35 and over
18	7	3	2

Ever Had Thoughts, While Masturbating,
of Being Forced to Have Sex:
All Who Ever Masturbated, Percents

Males		Females	
Under 35	35 and over	Under 35	35 and over
14	5	24	12

*The twin tendencies may never wholly vanish, for while both are in large part the product of cultural conditioning, they also owe something to biological factors (see Money and Ehrhardt, chap. 6–8).

43, younger persons have felt freer than older persons of the same sex to employ force fantasies while masturbating. Much the same trend appears in our data on the incidence of force in sex dreams.

The actual infliction or receipt of pain is far less common than the fantasizing of either one, but here, too, the incidences of males and females who have ever experienced either is distinctly larger in the younger half of our sample than in the older half. At least a portion of the total incidences, however, involves not genuine S/M but those acts of playful roughhousing that we spoke of earlier. We base this statement on the fact that a quarter of all males and nearly a third of all females who have ever inflicted or received pain have done *both* things, which suggests that they are reporting mutual mock-painful activities rather than classic S/M. In Tables 44 and 45, therefore, the total percentages of persons who have ever inflicted or received pain as part of sexual activity probably considerably exaggerate the incidences of genuine S/M. Two facts are immediately apparent: First, in our society today very few people have ever intentionally inflicted or received pain in connection with their sexual activities; and second, within these tiny percentages the classic tendency of males to be more often associated with the infliction of pain—and females with its receipt—is still apparent.

But far more interesting is the indication of social change that is revealed when we split the sample into two halves by age and compare the incidences of sadistic and masochistic sexual experience of the older half with those of the younger (see Table 45). Even in the younger age groups the predilection of the American male for the sadistic role and that of the American female for the masochistic role persist. But of much greater interest from the viewpoint of our present inquiry is the fact that, for each sex, both the inflicting and the receiving of pain are distinctly more common for each sex in the younger half of the sample than in the older half.

Table 44

Ever Obtained Sexual Pleasure from Inflicting or Receiving Pain: by Sex, Total National Sample, Percents

	Males	Females
Inflicting pain	4.8	2.1
Receiving pain	2.5	4.6

Table 45

Ever Obtained Sexual Pleasure from Inflicting or Receiving
Pain: by Age and Sex, Total National Sample, Percents

	Males		Females	
	Under 35	35 and over	Under 35	35 and over
Inflicting pain	6.2	2.9	2.5	1.5
Receiving pain	3.7	1.0	5.4	3.5

Even though there are higher incidences of both kinds of behavior in the younger half of our sample, they are not associated with adolescent or youthful sexual experimentation but with the enduring adult behavior patterns of the individuals involved. About two-thirds of our males and females who have ever experienced either sadism or masochism as part of sexual activity did so for the first time at 18 or older, and only a sixth of the males and a fifth of the females with sadistic experiences (and even fewer of those with masochistic experiences) have limited them to three years or less of their lives. Indeed, most of the males and females who have ever engaged in either kind of experience are still actively doing so. Hence, the incidences of current sadistic and masochistic activity given in Table 46, following, are not a great deal smaller than those for total experience given in Table 44.

Small as these active incidences are, they may give an exaggerated notion of the amount of sadistic and masochistic sexual behavior that exists today. The fact is that over half of the active males had three or less sadistic or masochistic experiences in the past year, and nearly half of the active females had fewer than three sadistic or five masochistic experiences. Fewer than one out of five active males had more than ten episodes of either kind of experience in the past year, while only a quarter of the active females had more than ten episodes in which they in-

Table 46

Obtained Sexual Pleasure in Past Year from Inflicting
or Receiving Pain: by Sex, Total National Sample, Percents

	Males	Females
Inflicting pain	3.5	1.3
Receiving pain	1.6	3.1

flicted pain and only a third had more than ten episodes involving the receipt of pain.

Virtually none of the S/M activity reported to us involves homosexual partners, and relatively little involves spouses; in fact, only about a quarter to a third of all males and females with S/M experiences have ever had such experiences with a spouse. S/M is not, however, primarily an extramarital activity of married persons but an activity of single persons (see Table 47). This table, taken in conjunction with our comments on the relatively delayed beginning of S/M experience, suggests that S/M is neither primarily a phase of single sexual development that is given up by married persons, nor an activity that married persons engage in with outside partners; if either were the case, we would expect the married to have total incidences far closer to those of the single. The differences between the single and married incidences are so wide as to require another explanation: They suggest that among S/M practitioners, emotional problems or personality distortions account both for the avoidance of marriage and for the need or taste for S/M experiences.

Nevertheless, the S/M activities engaged in by those who have ever had any such experiences, or who are currently active, are rarely as bizarre as those portrayed in fiction. Kinsey asserted that biting was the most frequent manifestation of S/M responses,[62] but in our sample biting severe enough to inflict serious pain was reported no more often than a number of other forms of pain infliction, except by female masochists, among whom it occupied an important place. This suggests that the latter permit or encourage it in preference to any other form of pain infliction, perhaps because biting appears to be only an extension of the kiss, while slapping and similar acts are more obviously allied to genuinely aggressive behavior. Varying

Table 47

*Ever Obtained Sexual Pleasure from Inflicting or Receiving
Pain: by Marital Status, Total National Sample, Percents*

	Males		Females	
	Single	Married	Single	Married
Inflicting pain	10.3	2.5	5.2	*
Receiving pain	6.3	*	10.0	2.1

*Less than 1 percent

minorities of each sex reported giving or receiving pain through the latter genre of activities, including hitting, punching, slapping, scratching, pinching and the pulling or twisting of the flesh. Interestingly, however, two of the classic S/M activities—spanking, bondage and discipline—were somewhat less common than these more ordinary acts. Finally, a certain amount of what our respondents reported as infliction or receipt of pain turned out, upon inspection of their comments, not to be S/M *per se* but extreme or inconsiderate performance of standard acts, such as unduly hard kissing, anal intercourse, or vaginal intercourse prolonged beyond the point at which one partner's genitals were sore.

Contradicting the mythology of S/M fiction, our respondents reported that orgasm rarely occurred as a direct result of the inflicting or receiving of pain; indeed, it appears that about half of all our sadists and masochists sometimes or always abort the encounter after the S/M activity without proceeding on to other sexual activity or to the achievement of orgasm. In contrast, S/M fiction often portrays either the S/M activity itself or subsequent sexual acts as resulting in stupendous orgasms and extreme satisfaction.

The net impression we get from the data in this part of our survey is that the recent increase in S/M is only indirectly related to the sexual-liberation movement. For the increase consists, in some part, of an expansion of normal, playful, mock-sadistic and mock-masochistic behavior which cannot be categorized as genuine S/M, while the rest of it is attributable to the somewhat greater opportunity that the freer milieu offers to the pathologically deviant to seek and locate partners with whom to turn their fantasies into reality—a reality that has nothing in common with the central meaning or values of sexual liberation.

Incest: Incidence by Relationship to Partner, by Type of Activity and by Sex and Age

We consider next the impact of sexual liberation upon the incidence of incest. This may strike some as a frivolous inquiry and not worthy of serious attention: Surely (they might say) no one can seriously maintain that freedom to have incestuous relationships is part of the meaning of sexual liberation. We do not maintain that it should be part of it; we ask only whether the social changes of the past generation have caused an increase in incestuous behavior. This is a far from frivolous question. There is, at least on the surface, some evidence of greater public tolerance than formerly for the theme of incest in fiction and film. Formerly it appeared only in hard-core pornography or in serious tragic works, but now it is considered suitable for ribald humor *(Candy, Blue Movie)* or even for tender and sympathetic romance *(Murmur of the Heart)*. Where there is such attitudinal change, there may be behavioral change; and if sexual liberation has, in actual fact, caused a rise in the incidence of incestuous behavior, this would be reason for genuine concern. For a wealth of evidence makes it certain that incest, at least within the primary family or between closely related persons, is not only pathologically deviant but very often severely damaging to the individuals involved and seriously disruptive of social order.[63]

Not surprisingly, therefore, incest has always been regarded with horror and strenuously repressed by human societies everywhere. But until a few years ago it was thought that incest avoidance was peculiar to the human species, and zoologists reported that, almost without exception, domestic and wild animals would copulate as readily with their own parents, offspring or siblings as they would with other opposite-sex members of their own species. Among primates, however, something like an incest taboo has lately been observed in certain apes and monkeys. Among the apes, incestuous matings of young males with their mothers are prevented by the fathers—not for moral reasons but because they see the sons as rivals, an explanation which comes close to the Freudian account of the incest taboo.[64] It was thought that in the absence of the father incestuous coupling would take place freely, but Japanese primatologists, after ten years of observing wild monkey groups, have recently reported that they witnessed almost no episodes of mother-son copulation under any circumstances, and confirmation of their reports has come from studies elsewhere. The explanation offered is that during the prolonged infant dependency of higher primates, bonds are created between mother and son that are never forgotten, and that create obstacles to the dominance the male must exert to copulate successfully.[65]

This may well be part of the explanation for the attitude of human beings toward incest—but only in part, since it does not explain the barrier to father-daughter or sibling incest. Yet both kinds of parent-child incest, and sibling incest, have been universally taboo in all known human societies, and behavior deviating from the norm has been viewed with loathing and generally severely punished. In many societies the prohibitions extend much further, barring coitus or marriage with uncles and aunts, nieces and nephews, and cousins. Other societies even rule out sex between any persons with the same family or clan name, as was the case in traditional China and among the Australian aborigines. In a few societies the taboo has been so broad as to exclude, as sexual or marriage partners, half the available population.[66] The essential fact, however, is that in 100 percent of the 250 societies reviewed by anthropologist George P. Murdock in his classic work *Social Structure,* and in 100 percent of the nearly 200 societies summarized by Ford and Beach in *Patterns of Sexual Behavior,* sexual intercourse and marriage are forbidden between parents and children, or brothers and sisters.[67] The only exceptions—and they are extremely rare and apply only to special situations—involve royal or sacred prerogative, as in the brother-sister marriages of the rulers of ancient Egypt or of the Incans, or the ritual father-daughter intercourse permitted an important hunter of the African Thonga tribe before a great hunt.[68]

In American society the incest taboo, as embodied in the laws defining sexual crimes and regulating marriage, extends in all 50 states not only to members of the nuclear family but to uncles and aunts, nieces and nephews, grandparents and grandchildren. In about half of the states the taboo on marriage extends to first cousins and half-siblings, and about a third of the states define sexual intercourse between first cousins as incestuous and make it a crime.[69] Inconsistently, however, in about half of the states there is no ban on cousin marriage, and in some American social circles—among the "proper Bostonians," for instance, and the highlanders of the southeastern states—it has even been rather popular.[70]

Since there is no instinctual basis for the avoidance of incestuous mating in subhuman animals, and since, even if there were, man has far less instinctual specificity than those animals, it is remarkable that human beings regard incest with universal antipathy. But the universality of this antipathy toward parent-child and sibling incest is related to the universality of the family itself. As with the monkeys, the human infant has a long dependent infancy, during which innumerable learnings occur that may well be inhibitory of or incompatible with sexual interaction with the parents. What is probably more important is that, whatever the form of family life in any society, the nuclear portion of that family and to a lesser extent the extended portion have to be protected from the disruptive sexual rivalries, passions and jealousies that incest would create. In addition, the taboo helps to preserve essential parental authority over children, makes for the adjustment of the children to the larger society outside and favors the creation of cohesive interfamily relationships.[71]

Biologically, too, incest within the nuclear family would be hurtful, resulting in more than the usual number of weakened or defective offspring. Even primitive and nonscientific peoples have apparently recognized this fact, though without understanding why it is so. The reason is that by far the largest number of genetic mutations are harmful but recessive, being controlled and overridden by the healthy dominant genes paired with them, but in parent-child or brother-sister matings there is a far greater chance that the offspring will inherit the defective mutant genes from both sides. Such bilateral inheritance results in disorders ranging from severe metabolic malfunctions, generally fatal in childhood or early life, to a variety of minor undiagnosable flaws in organ, nerve or biochemical functions that result in generally poor health or lowered intelligence, or both.[72] It is also true that incestuous matings can occasionally combine excellent traits from both sides to produce extraordinarily gifted human beings, but because of the ratio of harmful to beneficial recessive mutations, the chances of ill effects from incestuous matings vastly outweigh the chances of good ones. The greater the genetic consanguinity of the mating couple, the greater the chance of ill effects, but even between first cousins the effects are distinctly measurable. In Japan, for instance, where cousin marriages are acceptable and fairly common in all classes, the children of such marriages average eight I.Q. points lower than children of comparable noncousin marriages.[73]

But despite the universality and intensity of the incest taboo, there has been some suspicion that incest is far more common than has generally been recognized. Kinsey, who was clearly scornful of this idea, said that it was espoused chiefly by clinicians and social workers, adding that "there are some psychoanalysts who contend that they never had a patient who has not had incestuous relationships." He dismissed this viewpoint as a gross distortion due to the special nature of clinical populations, and wholly out of line with his own survey data.[74] But what his own data were remained a mystery; in the male volume he published only one brief paragraph of general comment about incest, and in the female volume not a single word.

The impression gathered by psychotherapists and other clinicians that incest is fairly common derives, however, not just from the special nature of the patient population but from something far more fundamental. Freud himself first observed the phenomenon, and misunderstood it. His earliest patients included a number of women suffering from symptoms of hysteria, and when he got them to free-associate and to resurrect hidden memories, he was astounded to find that in every case their neuroses had developed as the result of their having been sexually seduced by their own fathers. At first he thought he had made a monumental discovery, but after a while he reluctantly recognized that this explanation of his patients' neuroses was not only thoroughly improbable but that therapy based upon it did not lead to improvement or cure. After an agonizing reconsideration of the problem, he had a monumental (and, later, verified) flash of insight: Young children experience sexual desires, utilize their parents as fantasy material, and then, unable to bear the internal conflicts that this causes, bury those fantasies in the unconscious—from whence, later, they can be resurrected, but with the distinction between fantasy and reality blurred.[75] What is universal or at least very common, therefore, is not child-parent incest but the childish fantasy of child-parent incest. But while Freud recognized his mistake and based some of his most important theoretical and practical work upon the discovery of the repressed sexual desires of children, some less perspicacious therapists have continued to repeat his early error.

Actual incest, according to all other indications, is relatively rare, but we have virtually no data that establish exactly how rare it was a generation ago and with which to compare the data from the present survey. Kinsey either gathered too little information on the subject or began investigating it too late in the survey process to be able to publish any data in either the male or female volume.* We will therefore have to rely on our own sample not only for estimates of the incidence of different forms of incest today but for clues as to the changes, if any, that have taken place in the incidence in the past 20-odd years.

Our first observation is that if we include sexual acts between relatives well outside the nuclear family, and if we define incestuous behavior broadly so as to include not only coitus but light and heavy petting, the overall incidence of incest today is surprisingly high. It is, for instance, definitely higher than that of sadomasochistic acts or of sexual contacts with animals, even though the taboo on incest is far stronger than those on either of the latter. Our figures on the total incidence of any kind of incestuous act ever experienced are given in Table 48.

When we analyze the data in terms of age groupings, we are further surprised by what looks like a major increase in incestuous behavior in the younger half of the sample as compared with the older half. If incest were experienced for the first time in adulthood or late adulthood by any substantial fraction of those who ever experience it, the comparison would understate the increase, but only 4 percent of the males and 2 percent of the females with any incestuous contact had the first such contact after the age of 21. Accordingly, the accumulative incidences for

Table 48

Ever Had Any Sexual Contacts with Relatives:
Total National Sample, by Sex and by Sex of Partner,
Percents

	Males	Females
Heterosexual incestuous acts	13.5	8.1
Homosexual incestuous acts	0.5	1.1
All incestuous acts	14.0	9.2

---

*Years later, Paul Gebhard and three other members of the staff of the Institute for Sex Research presented, as a control group, some data on incest drawn from the Kinsey files in their study *Sex Offenders*. We have chosen not to use these data here for the following reasons: (a) one-fifth of the Gebhard sample of 477 white males was collected in 1959 and 1960, which makes the sample poorly representative of the situation existing in the 1940s; (b) the Gebhard sample is purposely limited to men with high-school education or less, in order to make it reasonably comparable to the convicts being studied in the volume, but this makes it poorly representative of conditions throughout the population, and even poorer as a standard with which to compare present-day data; and (c) Gebhard offers data only on incestuous coitus, although this is only a small part of the totality of incestuous sexual activities.[76]

the younger half of the sample and the older half, presented in Table 49, are quite comparable.

The figures in Table 49 appear to show a significant rise in incestuous activity, if broadly defined to include noncoital acts and contacts with relatives well outside the nuclear family. But there is an ambiguity in our raw data that makes it likely that these figures considerably exaggerate the actual increase. In the older age cohorts, considerable numbers of individuals failed to answer either yes or no to the question—a phenomenon often due in large part to concealment. Since such nonresponses (and the experience concealed within them) are proportionately far more numerous in the older half than in the younger half, the figures probably understate the actual incidence for the older half, thus exaggerating the apparent increase. If only half of the nonresponding individuals of all ages were concealing incestuous experiences, the figures in Table 49 would have to be corrected to read as shown in Table 50. And if more than half of the nonresponding individuals of all ages were concealing incestuous experience, the apparent increase would vanish. A conservative interpretation of the data would therefore be that the increases in the overall incidence of incestuous experience for both males and females are on the order of 25 to 50 percent.

Even so, there is a good deal less to these estimated increases than meets the eye, for most of the incestuous behavior reported to us is actually only marginally deviant and pathological, as the following data indicate:

Table 49

Ever Had Any Sexual Contact with Relatives:
Total National Sample, by Sex and by Age, Percents

	Under 35	35 and over
Males	17.8	10.2
Females	11.4	6.1

Table 50

Ever Had Any Sexual Contact with Relatives:
Corrected to Allow for Experience by Half of Nonrespondents, Percents

	Under 35	35 and over
Males	18.9	13.4
Females	12.6	11.3

—Two-thirds of all the incestuous experience of males, and nearly two-fifths of all the incestuous experience of females, was had with cousins—some of them perhaps not even first cousins.

—Over a quarter of the males and over half the females went no further than light petting in their incestuous contacts, and another quarter of the males and a fifth of the females reported heavy petting but no coitus.

—A third of the males and nearly half of the females had their incestuous experiences before age 12, and most of them ended it within the same year. It is reasonable to assume that most of this experience consisted of childish sex play.

—A fifth of the males and a third of the females had only one incestuous experience of any kind, and three-quarters of the males and over four-fifths of the females had half a dozen or fewer such experiences.

From these indications we conclude that the estimated increases in incestuous activity are far less momentous than they seem at first glance. Apparently, a large part of the incestuous activity reported by our respondents consists of relatively isolated, experimental, noncoital contacts between children or between young adolescents. Since the same kind of early experimental activity has greatly increased between nonrelated persons, due to the general loosening of sexual inhibitions, the increase in incestuous activity of this sort is undoubtedly attributable to the same cause, and of limited psychosocial import. Much of the activity, moreover, is had with cousins, and since half of the states do not ban cousin marriage and the majority do not define sex between cousins as a crime, the increase in this area of incestuous behavior does not seem grounds for alarm. The incidences of incestuous acts with relatives closer than cousins, which are of far greater concern to society, are extremely small, with the sole exception of brother-sister contacts. The latter, of course, can have very grave psychological and social consequences, but most brother-sister incest consists of childish sex play and noncoital adolescent experiments, and is limited to one or a few episodes.

In Table 51 we present a complete summary of the incestuous experience of our total male and female samples. The data are arranged by familial closeness: The first six lines constitute incestuous contacts within the nuclear family; the next six with relatives outside the nuclear family but close enough to be for-

Table 51

Ever Had Any Sexual Contact with Relatives:
Total National Sample, by Sex and by Relationship
of Partner, Percents

		Males	Females
Had incestuous contact with:			
Nuclear family	Father	0	0.5
	Mother	0	0
	Son	0	*
	Daughter	*	0
	Brother	*	3.6
	Sister	3.8	0.7
Other close relatives	Uncle	*	0.6
	Aunt	*	0
	Nephew	0	0
	Niece	*	0
	Grandfather	0	*
	Grandmother	0	0
Marginally consanguineous and nonconsanguineous relatives	Male cousin	*	3.2
	Female cousin	9.2	*
	Brother-in-law	0	*
	Sister-in-law	*	0
	Stepfather	0	*
	Stepmother	0	0

*Less than 0.5 percent..

bidden both by law and social custom in every state; and the last six with relatives remote enough to be of marginal incestuous status. (We arbitrarily include stepparents in the latter category, although it is obvious that in some circumstances the emotional relationship of stepparent and child becomes so much like that of real parent and child that incestuous contact is extremely serious.)

In view of the fact that our national sample is fairly large and reasonably representative, the data in Table 51 lead us to the following conclusions: With the exception of brother-sister contacts, incestuous acts within the nuclear family today remain extremely rare, as do incestuous contacts with close relatives outside the nuclear family; and beyond the boundaries of close blood relationship the only species of incestuous contact of statistical importance is that between cousins. (The disparity between the incidence of cousin contacts reported by males and that reported by females is puzzling. However, a plausible explanation might be that because of the greater tendency of females toward sexual conservatism, far fewer young girls than boys ever dare to indulge in sex play with opposite-sex cousins—but those girls who do so are deviant enough to serve as contact for a number of cousin partners.)

Clearly, the only areas in which the overall increases estimated earlier in this section could have occurred are those of brother-sister contact and heterosexual cousin contact, since these two categories account for some eight-tenths of all incestuous experience of the females and nine-tenths of all incestuous experience of the males in our sample. Because of the limitations of sample size, we cannot determine exactly what portion of the overall increase is due to each of these categories, but generally speaking it appears that each accounts for a share proportionate to its part in Table 51. To put it another way, each category has increased in roughly the proportions suggested earlier for the overall generational change, namely on the order of 25 to 50 percent.

This sounds alarming—at least as concerns brother-sister incest—but we have already pointed out that a major part of all incestuous contacts are childish or adolescent, experimental and relatively trivial. We can get a clearer idea of the present-day magnitude of incest of the more serious sort if we limit our view to the incidence of incestuous contact involving actual coitus. It is true, of course, that the emotional impact of prolonged and advanced heavy petting in an incestuous relationship may be considerable, but most of the noncoital incestuous activity reported by females and half of that reported by males went no further than light petting. In any event, actual coitus, with intromission and orgasm, has far greater psychological impact as incestuous experience than even heavy petting. Table 52 presents our data on incestuous coitus; for the sake of brevity we omit all those categories of relatives—parents, children, nephews, grandparents, brothers-in-law and stepmothers—with whom no such coitus was reported within our sample. It is apparent from the figures in this table that incest of the more

Table 52

Ever Had Heterosexual Coitus with Relatives:
by Sex and by Relationship of Partner, Total National Sample,
Percents

	Males	Females
Had coitus with:		
Sister	1.5	
Aunt	*	
Niece	*	
Sister-in-law	*	
Female cousin	3.9	
Brother		0.8
Uncle		*
Stepfather		*
Male cousin		0.5

Less than 0.5 percent.

serious sort—coitus within the nuclear family, or with close relatives—is extremely rare in our sample and therefore, presumably, in the American population in general. The one category of incestuous coitus that is both serious and significant in incidence is that involving brothers and sisters, but even this is extremely uncommon, and most of those who experience it do so only one or a few times before abandoning it. The actual sample with such experience is so small—14 out of 919 males, and 8 out of 971 females—that a breakdown by age is not statistically warranted, and thus we cannot say whether or not there has been any increase in this genre of incestuous behavior.*

One other finding of interest emerges when we break down our data on incestuous behavior by educational level. Again, because of small sample size, this would not be statistically warranted if we were to limit ourselves to incestuous coitus; it is warranted, however, if we include noncoital incestuous acts. On this broader basis our data seem to challenge a popular and long-held belief that nuclear-family incest is more common at lower social levels than at middle and upper levels, a belief that has long been widespread among social workers and court offi-

*The bases of 919 for males and 971 for females are smaller than the total numbers of males and females in our sample because, as in nearly all of our calculations, we omitted blank responses and others whose meaning was not ascertainable before percentaging.

cers. Lending support to this was the finding by Gebhard *et al*, in their study of convicted male sex offenders, that those who had committed incestuous acts within the nuclear family were generally lower in intelligence and in socioeconomic standing than persons convicted of other kinds of sex offenses.[77] While our sample did not tap the lowest levels of American society, some part of the alleged association between lower socioeconomic status and incest ought to show up in a comparison of our noncollege and college populations, and of our blue-collar and white-collar populations. We find no such association. Indeed, we find the opposite: Incestuous acts are more common among our college-level males and females than among our noncollege males and females, by a ratio of about two to one in the older half of the sample and by a somewhat smaller margin in the younger half. Much the same contrast exists between white-collar and blue-collar males and females of 35 and over, and while the gap between the white-collar and blue-collar people under 35 is small, it is still the former who lead. We suggest that the belief that incestuous coitus is more common at lower socioeconomic levels may be erroneous, and a by-product of differences in the reporting of such activities at different class levels. The poor, the ignorant and the incompetent come to official attention, while people of higher socioeconomic status are either able to keep their incestuous acts hidden or, if discovered, to keep the discovery from becoming part of the official record.

Our conclusion to the inquiry we set out to make in this section is that a fairly substantial increase in the incidence of incestuous contact does appear to be either a result of or a concomitant of sexual liberation. As far as we can see, however, most (and perhaps nearly all) of this increase consists of early, exploratory, noncoital behavior, the greatest part of which takes place between cousins, and much of the rest between siblings. Sibling incest is something which responsible citizens should be concerned about, even though in less than half the male cases and less than one-quarter of the female cases reported to us does the activity include actual coitus. This may or may not represent an increase in sibling coitus over a generation ago, but in any case it points to the need for parents and teachers to be more open, honest and informative in providing early sex education to their children and aiding them in learning to discriminate among various kinds of sexual activity. The danger lies in

passively allowing children to uncritically adopt the values, however archaic, they may encounter among their peers and in their
contacts with hard-core pornography and the writings of irresponsible extremists.

While a number of our interviewees spoke of their incestuous
experiences, nearly all of these involved relatively minor experimental episodes in childhood or early adolescence. What these
interviewees said was not substantially different from what we
have already heard other persons saying about early sex experiences which they recognized as being "wrong" and which, being
troubling, they soon abandoned without further consequence.
Accordingly, we will not quote from any of these accounts of
incestuous behavior.

But three females and one male, out of a total of 200 interviewees, did recount incestuous experiences with close relatives
or members of the nuclear family. The transcripts of their re-
marks unfortunately lose much of the impact of the facial ex-
pressions and body language that accompanied these confessions. One woman, for instance, spoke in a virtual whisper when
she came to this part of her story. Another woman told it with
long pauses, bursts of inappropriate laughter, and a generally
disjointed manner. The man frequently sighed, had spells of
coughing and ended up drenched with perspiration. Equally
unfortunate is the impossibility, without giving lengthy histories, of doing more than suggesting the dismal effects of these
people's incestuous experiences on their lives. In brief: One
woman has had two unsuccessful and sexually hopeless marriages; the second woman has a cool, sexually pallid marriage
(she and her husband, although only in their thirties, have intercourse only once or twice a month, and with almost no variation
or sensuous freedom); the third woman, who is quite young, had
one brief stay in mental hospital, later entered a religious commune but fled from it after a year, and following a period of
sexual promiscuity has been living with a considerably older
divorced man. The male, whose own father seduced him when
the boy was 11, spent his teens as the rejected outcast of his age
group, and two decades of his adult life as a homosexual, hating
it much of the time. Only after eight years of psychotherapy has
he recently been able to abandon homosexuality, develop a

genuinely close relationship with a woman and marry.

Two quotations—with interpolated indications of nonverbal communication—will perhaps give some faint flavor of the actual interviews. First, the ex-commune member:

My mother says she told me about sex, but I don't remember it. My father, God love him—I'm sure he must have thought it was right—he tried to *show* me. And I guess he did it the wrong way [nervous laughter]. He would go to bed with me—I was, like, thirteen—I didn't know how children were created, not really, and my mother was very Catholic and I couldn't talk to her about it, and so he decided—he was a very shy man—and he decided, instead of telling me or saying a man is built this way and a woman this way, and you do this step and the next step, instead he showed me. Not that he actually had intercourse with me —no!—but everything leading up to that [wild giggling]. I was scared, I didn't know what was going on. But I had a great amount of respect for my father, and to me he could do no wrong. So when this happened, I said to myself there has to be a reason why he did it, so I asked him one day— this was after it happened about four times—I said, "Why? Why are you doing this?" And he said, "Well, I went to this parent-teacher conference, and one of the women said to the priest that her daughter wanted to know what a man looks like, and the priest said, 'Show her, don't let her go out and find out for herself.' " Well—[laughter]—he misinterpreted it and did exactly that. So I couldn't blame him. I just said, "Don't ever do it again." I think he really believed that he was teaching me by getting into my bed at night and showing me himself and touching me and all. . . . [Long pause] Oh, who's to say? I don't really know what went on in his mind. Anyway, he didn't do it anymore, but by the time I got to high school I decided he wasn't my idol anymore. Since then, we say very few words to each other. I don't see him, I don't talk to him, I've been completely severed from my family. . . . I must admit that what happened with my father must have had some bearing on me. I was always looking for love, I didn't know where to find it, I had my breakdown, I tried the commune, I've become very bitter against religion. . . . But now I have a very serious, very intimate thing with this one man, and I think I could live with him for the rest of my life.

And now the man who was seduced by his own father:

I was told explicitly about sex when I was nine years old. My parents were both educated people, and my father was prominent in the community. I had developed rather early —when I was only nine, I found that if I would cross my legs and press them together over my penis, it would get erect and I would have an orgasm. Not ejaculate, of course, not that early, but an orgasm anyhow. I suppose that's why my mother talked to me about sex. Well [sighing, squirming] . . . aside from that my first [coughing] . . . my first sexual union was with my father. My father was evidently homosexually oriented [long pause]. . . . I was about eleven. My grandfather had had a heart attack, and my mother was sleeping downstairs to be near him, so I asked could I please sleep in the big double bed with my father? Well, we're in bed [coughing] . . . and he was sleeping with his back to me, and I cuddled up to him and slept that way. And the second night, I awakened and my penis was erect, and he [sighing, long pause] . . . he was attempting to put my penis in his anus. . . . And it took place, and I found it the most fantastic experience of my life.

He felt no conscious guilt at the time, but recognized that what had happened had to be kept strictly secret. He did keep the secret while such episodes occurred repeatedly over a matter of weeks, but then he rashly attempted to make similar contact with an uncle, and the story broke wide open. His mother ordered the father to leave the city permanently that very day, upon pain of being publicly exposed and taken to court. The boy "went through hell," torn between feelings of admiration and hatred for his mother, and longing and utter contempt for his father. The full realization of what he and his father had been doing grew upon him slowly, and at 15 he had a nervous breakdown and required electroshock therapy. Even after recovering, he spent the next 20 years troubled by—and trapped in—his own homosexuality, until prolonged therapy finally repaired the damage of his early incestuous experience.

Bestiality: Incidence, Frequency, Age When Actively Practiced

Sexual contact between a human being and an animal is known in Christian clerical tradition and in Anglo-American law as "bestiality." Because the more common, nonsexual meanings of the word are pejorative and carry extremely negative connotations, some sex researchers have sought to avoid the term. Kinsey himself used the expression "animal contacts," although this is semantically inaccurate, since he was discussing *human-animal* contacts, and he held such activities to be "biologically and psychologically part of the normal mammalian picture."[78] His argument was that cross-species matings among subhuman animals were far more common than biologists had long believed, and hence human-animal contacts, at least between human males and animals, were limited in incidence not by any natural factors but by the unavailability of suitable animals to young nonfarm males.[79]

Here again he was overshooting the mark in his effort to be dispassionate and nonjudgmental about sexual behavior. Both then and now the available evidence of cross-species matings consists of a meager assortment of eyewitness reports of isolated incidents. Ford and Beach, reviewing the zoological literature several years after Kinsey did so, said that such episodes, even if reported for a number of species, are extremely rare for each, and that sexual union in such matings is almost never complete.[80] There are good reasons for this. Quite apart from anatomical difficulties, animals are nearly always sexually attracted by and responsive to an array of stimuli specific to their own species, including odors, visual displays, types of physical contact and movements and sounds that act as "releasers" of preprogramed (gene-controlled) sexual responses. This is truest of the lowest and most instinct-guided creatures; the scent given off by a female gypsy moth, for instance, is so specific that only the molecules of that one pheromone (chemical signal) will trigger off sexual questing and mating behavior in the male— and only of that species—and will do so even if synthetically produced by man and used in traps.[81] The same thing is true, though to a lesser extent, of animals with a more complex neural structure, including the mammals and, among them, even the subhuman primates, despite their considerable capacity for learning and individual adaptation. According to the testimony of ethologists, each species of primate in its natural environment mates exclusively with its own kind.[82] It is largely, or perhaps only, in captivity that cross-species matings are sometimes attempted—but captivity does odd things to animal (and human) behavior, and what occurs in cages or pens can hardly be considered normal mammalian behavior.

Since human beings are so much less rigidly guided by instinct than are subhuman animals, it is at least arguable that sexual contact between human beings and animals is more nearly normal, or at least less violative of inherent patterns of stimulation and response, than are other cross-species matings. But what mankind lacks by way of instinctual control is more than made up for by the conditioning of the long child-rearing and socializing process. During infancy and early childhood the human being is thoroughly imprinted and taught to choose other human beings as love objects and, eventually, as sex objects. Since this is part of the normal and inevitable process of child-rearing in every society, the choice of a human partner is psychologically normal for the human being, the choice of a nonhuman creature abnormal. Over and above these considerations, the sexual connection of human beings with animals is, in general, grossly unsuitable in the anatomical sense, and is universally nonfunctional in the reproductive sense.

It is for such reasons that very few societies have deemed human-animal sexual contacts to be acceptable; almost everywhere, such acts have been either scorned and derided or punished with varying degrees of severity.[83] But fantasies of such contacts are another matter. The mythologies of many primitive societies, and of ancient Greece and Rome, contain numerous tales of such behavior, and similar stories have continued to be part of our own culture down to recent times. Even the most unlettered, though they may never have heard of Leda and the Swan, have seen King Kong on late-night TV, bearing off the frail white person of Fay Wray. More recently and more explicitly, the satirical play *Futz!* told of a man who both spiritually and carnally loved a pig. And the Woody Allen movie *Everything You Always Wanted to Know About Sex* devoted a long sequence to the presumably hilarious idea that a successful young New York physician could fall in love with a sheep and not only woo her but make love to her in a *grande luxe* hotel room.

The official Judeo-Christian view of human-animal contacts has, however, always involved the harshest possible condemnation. Several references in the Old Testament clearly spell out the ancient Hebrew law: A man or woman who "lies with" an animal is to be put to death—and so is the animal.[84] In later centuries the Talmud forbade females even to be left alone with animals because of the danger of sexual contact, and the Catholic code characterized the mere touching of an animal's genitals out of curiosity as a sin, and touching them out of lust as a grave sin.[85] In nearly every state in America the law makes bestiality a crime, and in most states it is subject to severe penalties, although prosecutions have been few in recent years. Even where prosecutions are uncommon, however, social attitudes toward persons who commit such acts have long been extremely hostile. Summing up, for his own time, Kinsey said that probably no type of human sexual behavior was more severely condemned by those in society who had not experienced it.[86]

The questions before us now are whether sexual liberation has modified the severity of such disapproval since Kinsey's time, and, if so, whether it has also resulted in an increase in the incidence of human-sexual contacts. We did not ask our respondents questions concerning their attitudes toward human-animal sexual contact, but it seems indisputable that the subject has become more common of late in pornographic writing, films and sex shows. (In such shows, inexplicably, the spectacle always involves a woman copulating with a male animal such as a pony, donkey or large dog, but never a man copulating with a female animal.) More tellingly, it has recently become somewhat acceptable, as already noted, in satirical and humorous drama and film, and in the cartoons and jokes in certain mass-circulation magazines. The former public horror and indignation at the very thought of human-animal sexual contact have apparently moderated to something more like scorn and amusement.

We find no indication, however, that this has resulted in any increase in the incidence of such activity; on the contrary, our survey data, when compared with Kinsey's, indicate that the percentages of males and of females who ever have any such experience have sharply declined. In this instance, unlike the case of extramarital behavior or that of homosexuality, we think the declines are real. The figures:

—Kinsey estimated that about 8 percent of all white males in the U.S. population had at least some sexual contact with animals in the course of a lifetime.[87]* Our own overall incidence is not a lifetime accumulative projection, but since there is no increase, either in Kinsey's data or ours, beyond age 25, our figure is reasonably comparable to his: It comes to 4.9 percent.

—As for females, Kinsey reported that 3.6 percent of his total sample had sexual contact of some sort with animals after they had become adolescent.[88]** Our own most nearly comparable figure is 1.9 percent.

Before asking why such declines have taken place, let us explain why we think they are real. For we think they are, though quite possibly the indicated magnitude is inexact. First of all, we can exclude the possibility that one important difference between Kinsey's sample and our own, which we have had to deal with in some other calculations, is in any way responsible for this decline—the presence in Kinsey's sample of a small group of males who never went beyond grade school, and the absence of such persons in our own sample. For while we cannot extract them from the overall-incidence figures as given by Kinsey, his own analysis of active incidences and frequencies shows that there is no appreciable difference between them and the high-school males when it comes to human-animal contacts.[89]

On the other hand, Kinsey had a distinctly larger proportion of farm-reared males in his sample than we have in ours, and this difference is definitely a matter of consequence when it comes to calculating the incidence of human-animal contact. Kinsey reported that by far the largest number of all males who ever had sexual contact with animals had been raised on farms: 17 percent of this group had had such experiences, as against somewhere between 2 and 4 percent of city-reared males.[90] (Presumably, the same thing is true today, although our own sample of males who have had sexual contact with animals is too small to permit a breakdown by rural-urban background.) Since rural males made up some 14 percent of Kinsey's male sample,[91] but make up only 9 percent of our own, this difference alone is enough to account for the apparent decline.

---

*Here we are obliged to use Kinsey's "U.S. Corrections," although elsewhere in this study we have generally used his raw data. In the male volume he does not provide an accumulative-incidence curve based on raw data, but only on the U.S. Corrections.

**This is a raw datum; in the female volume Kinsey does not make U.S. Corrections.

But the decline is not only apparent. During the several decades when the males interviewed by Kinsey had been in their teens, the farm population of the United States made up somewhere between a third and a quarter of the national population. In contrast, during the years when the males in our own sample were teen-agers, the farm population was declining from somewhat over a quarter to about a ninth of the population, the average for the whole period being somewhere below the halfway point between these two figures.[92] If no substantial changes took place in the incidences of bestiality among rural-reared males and among city-reared males, this shift alone would yield an overall decline in the incidence for the total population roughly comparable to that which we have found. We therefore think the decline is genuine, and that its principal cause is nothing more arcane or subtle than the shrinkage in the proportion of the U.S. population which lives on farms.*

The decline in the female incidence of bestiality is not so easy to explain. Rural-reared females made up less than 10 percent (and possibly as little as 6.8 percent) of Kinsey's female sample,[94] and make up 6.5 percent of our own. Obviously, the decline owes little to sampling differences in this area. But even if the two samples had adequately reflected the drop in the percentage of farm-reared females in the national population, the decline in the incidence of bestiality would not have been attributable to that fact, for Kinsey found little difference in incidence between farm-reared and city-reared females—so little, indeed, that he felt it unnecessary even to present separate data for the two categories of females. His explanation was that, due to parental control, farm girls were far less likely than farm boys to witness animal mating, and that the kinds of animals with which females do have contact (a matter we will come to in a moment) are no more easily available on a farm than elsewhere.[95]

Thus we cannot account for the decline in the female incidence on the grounds of the decline in the farm-reared popula-

---

*The actual decline in the proportion of the farm population between 1940 and 1970 is much greater than that in the two survey samples. In the 1940 census the farm population was 23.2 percent of the national population, and in the 1970 census, 4.8 percent.[93] But we are comparing the proportions in the periods when persons in the two samples were between 12 and 18 years of age, this being both Kinsey's criterion and our own for classifying individuals as having a rural background.

tion. There is, however, one other difference between the two sample populations that must be considered. Nearly 60 percent of Kinsey's female sample consisted of single (never married) persons,[96] as against 25 percent of our own, and since most instances of sexual contact with animals in Kinsey's sample occurred among single rather than married females, it might seem that this disproportion accounts for the drop in overall incidence. But while it may account for a small part of it, it can scarcely account for all of it, for well over half of the total accumulative incidence in Kinsey's sample had been gathered by age 25 or thereabouts.[97] Accordingly, there should have been nearly as large an accumulative incidence in our sample, since our married women were single long enough, on the average, to have had nearly as much total exposure or potential for such experience.

Nevertheless, this consideration of the single females in both samples leads us to a conjecture, based on what has gone before in this study, as to what accounts for the larger part of the indicated decline. Single females in Kinsey's sample, as we have seen, were generally far more inhibited concerning heterosexual contacts than those in our own sample; we suggest that somewhat more of them occasionally and in desperation turned to experimental contact with animals. To put it another way, today's single females are so much more likely to become involved in petting and coitus before 21 that they are far less likely to turn to the awkward and unsatisfactory expedient of contact with animals. This, we think, accounts for most of the difference in the incidence of female bestiality between Kinsey's sample and our own, and for what we believe to be a comparable decline of the incidence in the national population between his time and our own.

In other respects our data, though scanty, paint much the same picture of human-animal contact as do Kinsey's. In his male sample those individuals who had any animal contacts at all were most likely to have them between the onset of adolescence and age 15, the active incidence dropping off sharply thereafter and becoming negligible among adults.[98] Similarly, in our sample four-fifths of the males with any such experience started having it prior to age 15, such contacts terminating altogether for most of them within a year or less of the first contact, and contacts by adult males being negligible. In Kinsey's female sample, half of those individuals who had had any animal contact after childhood had done so between the onset of adolescence and before age 21, and the amount of such activity during adulthood, while somewhat larger than in the case of males, was very small.[99] In our better-balanced sample the great majority of those females who had any animal contacts had them between late childhood and age 21; beyond that point, only a few individuals had any such contacts whatever.

Thus, the bulk of human-animal sexual contact is only a part of childhood and teen-age sexual experimentation and rarely an important or protracted phase of sexual life. Kinsey reported that at the most active period the median frequency for those males who were engaging in any sexual contact with animals was only about once every ten weeks, and such contacts as did occur were usually limited to two or three years of the individual's life.[100] Our own survey yields an even more conservative portrait: Three-quarters of our males who have ever had contact with animals have had it on six or fewer occasions, and over half of the active males had such contacts during one year or less of their lives. Among females, Kinsey found extremely low frequencies: About half of those with any experience of bestiality had had only one such episode, and less than a quarter had had six or more episodes.[101] In our own sample over two-thirds of the females had only one to three experiences, and only one out of eight had six or more. Kinsey did not say how long such activity continued for his sample, but since half the females had only one such episode, at least that many of them (and probably more) confined such contacts to a single year of their lives. In our own sample, similarly, well over half the females with such experience had it within a single year of their lives.

In mythology, folklore and humor, the most usual form of sexual contact between human being and animal is vaginal coitus. Kinsey found this to be true of the males in his sample: They preferred coitus to other forms of sexual interaction and generally chose calves, sheep, burros and other animals of convenient size and placid temperament. Much less important, in his sample, were fellation of the human male by the animal, masturbation of the animal by the human male, and a kind of quasi-coital masturbation in which the human male rubbed his genitals against the animal's body.[102] Our data show some differences in the pattern: Only a little over a third of our group of males with experience of bestiality have ever had vaginal coitus with an animal. But over a third have had an animal lick or mouth their penises, and similar numbers have masturbated an animal or have masturbated themselves by rubbing their genitals against the animal. Dogs were the chosen species in about half the sample, with farm animals somewhat less often the sexual objects. This change is not surprising, considering the reduction in the farm population since Kinsey's era.

Females, Kinsey reported, nearly always chose household pets rather than barnyard animals for their human-animal contacts; dogs were the partners in nearly three-quarters of all cases, and cats in most of the rest. Over half the episodes involved only general body contact; about a fifth had had the animals lick or mouth their genitals; only a very small number of females had masturbated the animal; and actual coitus with an animal was reported for only two children and one adult in Kinsey's entire sample.[103] We found little change in the choice of household animals over barnyard animals, except that dogs were even more popular than in Kinsey's sample. The choice of techniques, however, again shows a somewhat different pattern from that of Kinsey's females, for nearly all of ours, whatever else they did, had had animals lick or mouth their genitals. Masturbating the animal, and rubbing the genitals against the animal, were the other principal techniques reported, neither of them being anywhere near as common as cunnilingus by the animal. There were no cases in our sample of vaginal coitus between a male animal and a female human being.

Since the data for both our male and female samples indicate notable increases in the use of oral-genital contact with the animal playing the oral role, this finding is unlikely to be either an anomaly of sampling or a statistical error. The increase is probably real, and owes something to sexual liberation; evidently, among those having animal contacts, a technique that previously seemed even more perverse to them than bestiality itself now no longer seems so.

Our net impression is that most human-animal sexual encounters today are isolated or rare experiences of a primarily experimental nature, and are largely confined to the immature years of life. Most of these episodes, therefore, are sociologically deviant but psychologically normal or, at most, marginally pathological. True pathological bestiality consists of repeated animal contacts during the late teens and adult years, when the normal processes of interpersonal growth should have made such sexual activities unnecessary, unrewarding and psychologically repellent. Kinsey found relatively few such individuals in his sample.[104] For our part, none of our females and only one of our males has had more than 20 sexual encounters with animals; only very small percentages of either sex have had any such contacts in adult life; and none of the latter has done so often or over any long period of time. We suspect that those human-animal sexual contacts that can be considered genuinely pathological have shown no increase in incidence or frequency in the generation during which sexual liberation has affected so much else in American sexual behavior.

Similarly, we would guess that those other extremely bizarre and pathological forms of deviance on which we did not gather data have not recently increased in actual incidence, though they have undoubtedly gained in visibility. But at this point our investigation of sexual behavior among American males and females in 1972 has gone as far as our material will take us. We willingly leave it to others, if they think it worth the effort, to explore these curiosa and trivia of sexual behavior which we could not.

Epilogue

The analysis of our questionnaire data shows that profound changes have taken place in American sexual attitudes and behavior in the period of roughly a generation since Alfred Kinsey and his associates did their basic fieldwork—changes often loosely referred to as sexual revolution, but which we have preferred to call sexual liberation. We have seen that these changes add up to a major increase in attitudinal and behavioral liberalism, but not a radical break with those cultural values linking sex to love, marriage and family life.

Sexual liberalism, we conclude, is the emergent ideal upon which the great majority of young Americans—and a substantial minority of older ones—are patterning their beliefs and behavior. Sexual liberalism covers a broad range of possibilities, but essentially combines the spontaneous and guilt-free enjoyment of a wide range of nonpathological sexual acts with a guiding belief in the emotional significance of those acts. It identifies liberated sexuality as the expression, the concomitant or the precursor of monogamous heterosexual love. While this love, when it flourishes, may exist for a while as a consensual and informal alliance, its implicit ultimate goal is the more formal and committed status of marriage. Within marriage, moreover, emotional security permits a still greater development and completion of the sexually liberating process for each partner. Advocates of nonexclusive marriage may argue that the greatest liberation of all comes about when each partner grants the other the right to outside sexual and emotional alliances, but while one may persuasively argue that this should be so, our data show that no more than a tiny minority of Americans have yet attempted such open marriages, and fewer still have made them work.

We thus find the results of our survey contradicting what both the evangelists and the Cassandras of sexual liberation have been saying about what has been happening of late. We find ourselves validating the more balanced (but little heeded) appraisals made by many behavioral scientists, including sociologists Ira Reiss and Erwin Smigel, psychologist Keith Davis and sexologist Isadore Rubin, to the effect that there has been no chaotic and anarchic dissolution of standards, but, rather, a major shift toward a nonpuritanical, hedonistic, and highly organized set of attitudes and behaviors that remain integrated with some of our most important social values and with the institutions of courtship, love, marriage and the family.[105]

This is not to belittle the scope or importance of the changes we have been reporting; it is merely to quantify them. The changes that are taking place are none the less important and profound for taking place within the culture rather than breaking away from it; indeed, they may be more valuable than total sexual radicalism would be. For while they are bringing so much that is pleasurable, healthful and enriching into American life, they are doing so without destroying emotional values we have rightly prized, and without demolishing institutions necessary to the stability of society itself.

Notes on Sources

Most of the sources cited in these notes are identified by author's name only, or author's name and a year, or in a few cases by short title. All these sources can be found in the Bibliography, where they are identified in full.

Certain additional sources, identified fully in these Notes, are not duplicated in the Bibliography.

CHAPTER 1

1. Pomeroy (1972), pp. 10, 298, 361.
2. Edward Sagarin, "Sex Research and Sociology," in Henslin, pp. 397–98.
3. Pomeroy (1972), pp. 172–78; Brecher (1969), pp. 293–94.
4. John J. Honigmann, "A Cultural Theory of Obscenity," *Journal of Criminal Psychopathology*, vol. 5 (1944), pp. 715–33.
5. *Obscenity*, pp. 13–20.
6. Van de Velde, p. 223.
7. Reuben, pp. 52–53.
8. "M," pp. 89–90.
9. "J," pp. 128–29.
10. *The New York Times*, Oct. 29, 1972, p. 1; *Time*, May 14, 1973, p. 72.
11. *Time*, Aug. 21, 1972, p. 36; *Life*, Nov. 20, 1970.
12. For the estimate, Bartell, p. 21. For the demographic characteristics of the swingers, Bartell, pp. 23–38, and Bartell, "Group Sex Among the Mid-Americans," *The Journal of Sex Research*, vol. 6 (May 1970), pp. 113–30.
13. For the estimate, *Time*, Jan. 21, 1974, p. 63. The psychiatric studies were presented at the 1973 meeting of the American Psychiatric Association.
14. Hefner; Rhodes.
15. Kinsey (1948), pp. 57–58.
16. Reiss (1968), p. 27.
17. See, for instance, Stone and Stone, p. 184, and M. Davis, p. 97.
18. Stanton Wheeler, "Sex Offenses: A Sociological Critique," in Gagnon and Simon, pp. 87–90.
19. Reiss (1968), and the entire April 1966 issue of *Journal of Social Issues*.

20. *The New York Times,* Aug. 12, 1973.
21. Wheeler, p. 90 (see Note 18 above).
22. *Obscenity,* p. 190.
23. Same as Note 22.
24. For Kinsey's data on both sexes, see Kinsey (1953), pp. 652–72.
25. Kinsey (1948), chapters 10–13; Kinsey (1953) throughout, but esp. chapters 5–11; Christensen and Gregg; Ehrmann (1957); Reiss (1968).
26. Cannon and Long, p. 44.
27. Kinsey data are in Kinsey (1948), p. 502, and Kinsey (1953), pp. 141–43; detailed comparisons with our own data will be found in Chapter 2 of this book.
28. Kinsey (1948), p. 240, and Kinsey (1953), p. 151; detailed comparisons with our own data will be found in Chapter 2 of this book.
29. Kinsey (1948), p. 241.
30. Same as Note 29.
31. Kinsey (1953), p. 188.
32. Kinsey (1948), p. 550, using the raw data rather than the "U.S. Corrections."
33. Kinsey (1953), p. 333.
34. Kinsey (1953), p. 337.
35. Kinsey (1953), p. 336.
36. Kinsey (1948), p. 368, omitting the 0–8 educational level for better comparability to our own sample, and combining Kinsey's data for the 9–12 and 13–plus levels.
37. Same as Note 36.
38. E.g., even among married men 45 and over in our sample, nearly one-third had been fellated by their wives in just the past year (i.e., with some regularity); in Kinsey's sample, only about a third of college-educated men of 46 and over had had the experience, even once, in their married lives.
39. Kinsey (1948), p. 370.
40. Kinsey (1948), p. 579.

CHAPTER 2

1. Kinsey (1948), p. 512; Kinsey (1953), p. 132.
2. Kinsey was of two minds as to whether this constituted genuine masturbation; cf. Kinsey (1948), p. 163, and Kinsey (1953), pp. 133–34. But most up-to-date informed sources do consider it a form of masturbation: see Spock, p. 372; Stella Chess and Alexander Thomas (eds.), *Annual Progress in Child Psychiatry and Child Development* (New York: Brunner Mazel, 1972), pp. 66–67; Mussen, pp. 281–82.
3. Ford and Beach, pp. 156–59.
4. Detailed citations are in Kinsey (1953), p. 168, n. 46 and n. 47; see also, for a more recent discussion, Cole, pp. 374–75.
5. Same as Note 4.

6. Cole, pp. 374–75.

7. Beigel (1969); Kinsey (1948), p. 513; Kinsey (1953), pp. 166–67; Schwarz.

8. Brecher (1969), pp. 51, 59.

9. Schofield and Vaughan-Jackson, pp. 30–42.

10. Brecher (1969), pp. 65–66; Kinsey (1948), pp. 514–15; Kinsey (1953), pp. 170–71.

11. Stone and Stone, pp. 221–23.

12. Personal communications from several Reichian therapists and patients. The Reichian literature is perhaps intentionally a trifle vague on the subject.

13. Kinsey (1948), pp. 507–8.

14. Kinsey (1953), p. 172.

15. Masters and Johnson (1966), pp. 118, 133.

16. Pomeroy (1968), pp. 53–55; Pomeroy (1969), p. 130.

17. See, for instance, the contributions by Dana Densmore, Anne Koedt and others in Tanner.

18. "J," pp. 38–52.

19. "M," pp. 45–52.

20. Kinsey (1948), pp. 339–43; Kinsey (1953), p. 190. Note, however, that for females, the social taboo seemed to make little difference in either accumulative or active incidence: Kinsey (1953), pp. 182–83.

21. Kinsey (1948), pp. 499–500; Kinsey (1953), pp. 142, 177, 180.

22. Kinsey (1948), p. 500. This is a "U.S. Correction," but even if we use the raw data and exclude the 0–8 educational level for closer comparability to our own sample, the accumulative incidence by age 13 would be only about 50 percent, or considerably lower than our figure.

23. Kinsey (1953), p. 141, (fig. 9).

24. Kinsey (1953), p. 177. Actually, this is the accumulative incidence for the oldest cohort in Kinsey; an overall figure more closely comparable to our own would be on the order of 40 percent or less.

25. Masters and Johnson (1966), p. 118.

26. Kinsey (1948), p. 240.

27. Same as Note 26.

28. Same as Note 26; also Kinsey (1948), p. 270, (fig. 55).

29. Same as Note 26; also Kinsey (1948), p. 271, (fig. 58).

30. Kinsey (1953), p. 178.

31. Same as Note 30.

32. Same as Note 30.

33. Kinsey (1948), p. 241.

34. Kinsey (1953), p. 178.

35. Kinsey (1948), pp. 507–9; Kinsey (1953), pp. 148–58. (N.B.: Overall, parental occupational level was only weakly correlated with the inhibition of masturbation; nonetheless, for some cohorts the correlation is considerable enough to merit inclusion in our list.)

36. Kinsey (1948), p. 482, comparing medians for inactive Jews and inactive Protestants. No medians of marital coitus for inactive Catholics

are included, but in other areas of sexual activity Kinsey's data show inactive Catholic males and inactive Protestant males to have quite similar medians. See Kinsey (1948), pp. 478–81.

37. Kinsey (1948), pp. 240–1, 272–77, 512; Kinsey (1953), pp. 144, 178.
38. Kinsey (1948), pp. 218–21, 238–43; Kinsey (1953), pp. 144–45, 518–19, 528.
39. Freud's views, and the contemporary view, are summarized in Jerome Singer, "The Importance of Daydreaming," *Psychology Today,* April 1968.
40. Hunt (1969), pp. 31–41.
41. Kinsey (1953), pp. 164–65.
42. Kinsey (1953), p. 712.
43. Beigel (1969), p. 98.
44. Sherfey (1966). This is also and more readily available as Sherfey (1973), where her discussion of multiple clitoral orgasms can be found on pp. 104–14.
45. Beigel (1969), p. 99. The same view is expressed by psychiatrist and sex educator Dr. Walter Stokes, "An Appraisal of Erotic Emotion and Autoerotic Behavior," Kirkendall and Whitehurst, pp. 77–84.
46. Same as Note 45; also, Hunt (1966), pp. 150–51.
47. *Über den Nervosen Charakter* (1922), cited in Beigel (1969), p. 102.
48. Beigel (1969), p. 102, but the analogy to alcohol is ours, not his.

CHAPTER 3

1. "Cultural Relativism," *IESS,* vol. 3, pp. 543–47; Clyde Kluckhohn, "Ethical Relativity: Sic et Non," *The Journal of Philosophy,* vol. 52 (1955), pp. 663–77.
2. Same as Note 1, but esp. the entry in *IESS.*
3. Murdock, p. 124; Clyde Kluckhohn, "Universal Categories of Culture," in A. L. Kroeber (ed.), *Anthropology Today* (Chicago: Univ. of Chicago Press, 1953).
4. Murdock, pp. 264–65.
5. These various provisions are to be found in *Deuteronomy* 22; see also discussion in Cole, pp. 235–39.
6. Kinsey (1948), p. 548.
7. All details in the paragraph: Hunt (1959), pp. 233–35.
8. Rhodes.
9. Kinsey (1948), p. 364, using the 46+ group.
10. Same as Note 9, but using the "Adol.–25" group.
11. The minor surveys are cited in Kinsey (1953), p. 309, n. 24; the 89 percent figure is from the same, pp. 314–15, 344.
12. See Chapter 1, Note 18.
13. Reiss (1967), pp. 27, 29, 225.
14. Landis's data are cited as summarized in Smigel and Seiden, p. 12.
15. Reiss (1967), pp. 25–26, 225.
16. Christensen and Gregg, pp. 619–20.

17. Reiss (1968), p. 29.
18. Packard, p. 271.
19. Kinsey (1948), pp. 443, 445.
20. Kinsey (1953), p. 16.
21. Libby and Nass, pp. 230, 233.
22. Athanasiou, p. 49.
23. Chartham, pp. 47, 52–53.
24. Zelnik and Kantner, p. 369.
25. Hunt (1959), pp. 356–59.
26. Kinsey (1953), pp. 231–33, esp. n.7, seeks to show that it has been very common, but he is speaking of petting techniques and not of petting as a long-term behavior pattern within the individual's life cycle. The very sources he cites, plus the evidence summarized in Ford and Beach, indicate that petting was only a brief phase in most societies.
27. Willard Waller, Margaret Mead and Geoffrey Gorer, as summarized in Hunt (1959), p. 358.
28. Kinsey (1948), pp. 407, 409, 537, 539.
29. Kinsey (1953), pp. 239–44, 273–75.
30. Ehrmann (1960), chaps. 5–6; Reiss (1967), throughout; K. Davis; Packard, chaps. 11–12.
31. Reiss (1967), p. 29.
32. Same as Note 31, but lumping together Reiss's male and female responses.
33. Same as Note 31.
34. Kinsey (1948), pp. 245, 539; Kinsey (1953), pp. 235, 238.
35. Kinsey (1953), pp. 236–37.
36. Kinsey (1953), p. 234.
37. Kinsey (1948), p. 534. This is a "U.S. Correction," but even if we use the raw data and exclude the 0–8 educational level for closer comparability to our own sample, the figure would be 92 percent—still somewhat below our own.
38. Kinsey (1948), p. 536. Same comment as Note 37; the raw data, omitting the 0–8 educational level, would yield a figure closer to half—still considerably lower than our own.
39. Kinsey (1953), p. 275, looking at the cohort born between 1920 and 1929.
40. Kinsey (1948), p. 368, using the Adol.−25 cohort and synthesizing a sample without the 0–8 educational level.
41. Kinsey (1953), p. 281.
42. Kinsey (1953), p. 272.
43. Same as Note 42.
44. Kinsey (1948), pp. 379, 541.
45. U.S. Dept. of Health, Education and Welfare: "Marriages: Trends and Characteristics" (DHEW 72–1007), 1971, p. 7, and "Monthly Vital Statistics Reports," esp. vol. 20: 4, 13.
46. Same as Note 45.
47. Kinsey (1948), p. 603.
48. Kinsey (1948), p. 352, combining his 0–8 and 9–12 educational levels.

49. Kinsey (1948), p. 250.
50. Terman (1938), pp. 321–23.
51. Kinsey (1953), p. 339.
52. Kinsey (1948), p. 557; see also Kinsey (1953), pp. 300–1.
53. Summary for both sexes: Kinsey (1953), p. 330.
54. Kinsey (1948), p. 550, synthesizing a sample from his raw data rather than using his "U.S. Corrections"; Kinsey (1953), p. 333.
55. Summarized in Kinsey (1953), p. 331.
56. Kinsey (1948), p. 348.
57. Kinsey (1953), p. 333.
58. Christensen and Gregg, p. 617; Cannon and Long, pp. 39–40.
59. Ira L. Reiss, "The Sexual Renaissance: A Summary and Analysis," *Journal of Social Issues*, vol. 22 (1966), pp. 125–26.
60. Reiss (1973); he stated this conclusion in 1972, in the mimeographed version of this paper.
61. Zelnik and Kantner, p. 360.
62. Kinsey (1948), p. 550.
63. Kinsey (1953), pp. 286, 333.
64. Kinsey (1953), p. 336.
65. The Kinsey data in Table 24 are from Kinsey (1953), p. 336.
66. *The New York Times*, Aug. 29, 1972, p. 38; also, sociologist Roger Libby has kindly sent me a list of nearly a dozen recent or current studies in "premarital living together."
67. Kinsey (1953), p. 345.
68. Christensen and Gregg, p. 626.
69. Kinsey (1953), p. 345.
70. Zelnik and Kantner, p. 371.
71. *Time*, May 22, 1972, p. 34.
72. Kinsey (1953), p. 311.
73. Same as Note 72.
74. Kinsey (1948), p. 580.
75. Kinsey (1948), p. 368, omitting the 0–8 educational level, and collapsing the high-school and college levels.
76. Kinsey (1953), p. 400.
77. Kinsey (1948), p. 248.
78. Kinsey (1953), pp. 289, 334.
79. Kinsey (1953), p. 339.
80. Kinsey (1953), p. 334; the figures given here are median frequencies for the whole active sample rather than just the sample with orgasm.

CHAPTER 4

1. Reiss (1973).
2. On the entire paragraph: Hunt (1959), pp. 114–15.
3. Quoted in H. Ellis, vol. I, part 3, p. 195.
4. H. Ellis, vol. I, part 3, p. 203; Hunt (1959), p. 337.
5. Hunt (1959), pp. 352–53.

6. Kinsey (1953), pp. 397, 403, and see comments in Reiss (1973).

7. Lehrman, p. 109.

8. Albert Ellis, O'Neill and O'Neill, and Lawrence Lipton are only a few of the many who have made such statements; see Bibliography. The Cubers, Virginia Satir, and Ernest van den Haag have made similar, though more qualified, statements; see Hunt (1969), pp. 148–49. See also the collections by Roszak and Roszak, and by Tanner.

9. See, for instance, Harvey J. Locke, *Predicting Adjustment in Marriage* (New York: Henry Holt, 1951), pp. 133–37; Paul Popenoe, "Premarital Experience No Help in Sexual Adjustment After Marriage," *Family Life,* vol. 21 (Aug. 1961); and Ernest W. Burgess and Paul Wallin, *Engagement and Marriage* (Phila.: J. B. Lippincott, 1953), chap. 12. For a brief recent study, see Shope and Broderick (1967).

10. Terman (1938), pp. 324–30; Burgess and Wallin (see Note 9); Kinsey (1953), pp. 328–29, 383. See also Shope and Broderick (1967), p. 424, for other sources. A good summary of the evidence can be found in A. Ellis and A. Abarbanel, vol. I, pp. 80–3.

11. Kinsey (1953), p. 406.

12. Kinsey (1953), pp. 329–30. The largest number of divorces occur in the third year of marriage, but most divorces are preceded by separations; the first and second years are the high point for these. See Hunt (1966), pp. 18–19.

13. *Medical Aspects of Human Sexuality,* Oct. 1971.

14. Ginsberg, et. al., *Archives of General Psychiatry,* vol. 26, no. 3 (March 1972).

15. Sherfey (1973), pp. 14–15, 144.

16. Pearlman and Kobashi.

17. Bell and Bell (1972).

18. Terman (1938), p. 269; Kinsey (1948), p. 571; Kinsey (1953), pp. 349, 353–54; Clark and Wallin (1964); James; Levinger.

19. Kinsey (1953), pp. 74–78.

20. Udry and Morris.

21. Kinsey (1948), p. 252, collapsing his five-year cohorts into ten-year cohorts. In both the Kinsey data and our own, means and medians for marital coitus are calculated on the basis of the total sample, not just the active sample (as in many other calculations), since in this case the social norm is 100 percent participation; the inactives are therefore a significant part of mean and median calculations.

22. Kinsey (1953), p. 394; see discussion in Note 21.

23. Kinsey (1953), pp. 652–54, 670–72; these figures are for single and married samples combined, as are our own.

24. *Obscenity,* pp. 218–22.

25. Gunter Schmidt and Volkmar Sigusch, "Sex Differences in Responses to Psychosexual Stimulation by Films and Slides," *The Journal of Sex Research,* vol. 6 (Nov. 1970).

26. Kinsey (1948), p. 253; Kinsey (1953), p. 353; Masters and Johnson (1966), pp. 223–70; Rubin (1965).

27. Masters and Johnson (1970), chap. 13.

28. Same as Notes 21 and 22.
29. For both male and female: summary in Kinsey (1953), p. 392.
30. Kinsey (1948), p. 482; Kinsey (1953), pp. 359–60.
31. Kinsey (1953), p. 360.
32. Kinsey (1948), pp. 370–73, 571–73.
33. Kinsey (1948), p. 573.
34. Kinsey (1948), p. 368.
35. Cf. the data in Kinsey (1948), p. 368, with those in Kinsey (1953), p. 399.
36. Same as Note 35; these references cover all data in the next four paragraphs.
37. Kinsey (1948), p. 368.
38. Same as Note 37.
39. Same as Note 37.
40. Kinsey (1953), p. 399.
41. The qualification "ever" is part of the wording of Table 93 in Kinsey (1948), p. 368. The qualification "used at least on occasion" appears in Kinsey (1953), p. 361, and pertains to the data found in Table 100 in Kinsey (1953), p. 399.
42. Kinsey (1948), p. 368.
43. Kinsey (1953), p. 399.
44. Kinsey (1953), p. 364.
45. Kinsey (1948), pp. 572–73.
46. Masters and Johnson (1970), chaps. 12, 13; Kaplan and Sager.
47. Comparisons which follow are based on Kinsey (1948), p. 372, and Kinsey (1953), p. 400, assuming that the truth lies somewhere midway between the estimates. Note, however, that table 95 in Kinsey (1948), p. 372, specifies "frequent," but that the discussion, on p. 374, uses the expression "at least occasionally." The reasonable assumption is that "frequent" use, in Kinsey, means something more than "rare" and less than "very often or almost always." We have made our comparisons on the basis of this assumption.
48. Beigel (1953).
49. D. H. Lawrence, *Lady Chatterley's Lover* (New York: Grove Press, Inc., 1957, 1959), pp. 297–98.
50. Kinsey (1948), p. 580.
51. Stone and Stone, p. 188.
52. R. L. Dickinson and L. Beam, *A Thousand Marriages* (Baltimore: Williams & Wilkins Co., 1931), p. 221; Paul Popenoe, *Preparing for Marriage* (Los Angeles: American Institute of Family Relations, 1938), p. 13.
53. Kinsey (1948), p. 580.
54. Terman (1938), p. 295.
55. See, for instance, the discussion of this point in Nimkoff, pp. 501–4, which is typical of much writing on the subject in the 1940s and 1950s. See also Note 76, this chapter.
56. Paul Wallin and Alexander L. Clark, "A Study of Orgasm as a Condition of Woman's Enjoyment of Coitus in the Middle Years of Mar-

riage," *Human Biology,* vol. 35 (May 1963), p. 134; see also Clark and Wallin (1965), which shows the association between wives' orgasm reliability and the quality and duration of marriage.

57. Bell and Bell (1972).
58. Kinsey (1953), pp. 371–72, and many others; see Note 56 above.
59. Masters and Johnson (1966), pp. 119–22.
60. Masters and Johnson (1966), pp. 273–93. The same point had been made, though without all the evidence gathered by Masters and Johnson, in Kinsey (1953), in which see esp. pp. 640–41.
61. Same as Note 4.
62. Same as Note 4.
63. G. V. Hamilton, *A Research in Marriage* (New York: Albert & Charles Boni, 1929); Dickinson (see Dickinson and Beam, Note 52, this chapter), p. 438.
64. Terman (1938), p. 474.
65. Kinsey (1953), p. 408.
66. Kinsey (1953), p. 403.
67. Kinsey (1953), p. 401, collapsing the data for 60–89 percent and 90–100 percent, and collapsing the 13–16 and the 17+ educational levels.
68. Kinsey (1953), pp. 379–80, 402.
69. Kinsey (1953), pp. 381–82, 404.
70. Same as Note 65.
71. Kinsey (1948), p. 579; Kinsey (1953), p. 393.
72. Kaplan and Sager; Masters and Johnson (1970), chap. 12.
73. Robert R. Bell, *Premarital Sex in a Changing Society* (Englewood Cliffs, N.J.: Prentice-Hall, Inc., 1966), p. 137.
74. Kinsey (1948), p. 571, and Kinsey (1953), pp. 353–54.
75. Robert R. Bell, "Some Factors Related to the Sexual Satisfaction of the College Educated Wife," *Family Life Coordinator,* May 1964, pp. 43–47.
76. Terman was one of the principal investigators finding a very low correlation between the sexual adjustment of wives and their marital happiness; see his paper in DeMartino, pp. 197–207 (esp. p. 202), and/or the original and fuller presentation of his study in *The Journal of Psychology,* vol. 32, October 1951, pp. 115–72. See also Note 55, this chapter.

CHAPTER 5

1. Ford and Beach, p. 107.
2. Ford and Beach, pp. 113, 115–16.
3. Ford and Beach, pp. 109–11; Marler and Hamilton, p. 83.
4. Ford and Beach, p. 118.
5. Rhodes.
6. *Historical Statistics* gives 0.3 per 1000 for 1867; *Monthly Vital Statistics Report,* vol. 20, no. 13 (U.S. Dept. of Health, Education and Welfare)

gives 3.7 per 1000 for 1971. Provisional estimates for 1973 indicate that the rate had risen still higher during that year.

7. Bernard (1973), pp. 75–76.

8. This is the overall conclusion of Hunt (1969), and Hunt (1971). Cuber and Harroff found nonexclusive marriages more common and more viable, at least in the upper-middle class, than is generally recognized; tellingly, however, the marriages in which nonexclusivity worked best were not the closest and warmest. For other discussions of the advantages and difficulties of nonexclusive arrangements, see Bartell, Constantine and Constantine, Denfield and Gordon, Libby and Whitehurst (1973), Lipton, Neubeck, Otto (1970), Otto (1971), O'Neill and O'Neill, Packard, and Whitehurst (1969), among others.

9. Gebhard's figures are in Bohannan, pp. 104–5 (Gebhard's study appears as chap. 4 of Bohannan's book).

10. Hunt (1966), p. 143.

11. *Statistical Abstract*, 1972, p. 37; as for their relative inactivity, see DeMartino, chap. 24 (by Gustave Newman and Claude R. Nichols), dealing with the Duke University study of sexual activities of older persons. (The Duke sample was larger than Kinsey's over-60 cohorts, and hence more definitive on this issue.)

12. Assuming, that is, that Kinsey's "postmarital" male sample and "previously married" female sample included widows and widowers in about the same proportions, per cohort, as did the U.S. population in the 1940s (for which see *Statistical Abstract* 1945–1952).

13. Ratios of under-55 divorced males to widowers, and under-55 divorced females to widows, are derived from various issues of *Statistical Abstract* for the 1940s; however, since Kinsey counted long-separated persons as equivalent to divorced, the ratios must be doubled (Hunt, 1966, p. 18). Result: roughly 2 to 1 for males, 3 to 1 for females.

14. Same as Note 9.

15. Kinsey (1948), p. 296.

16. Kinsey (1953), p. 536.

17. Kinsey (1948), p. 280 (using raw data, not "U.S. Corrections").

18. Kinsey (1948), p. 279 (fig. 70).

19. Kinsey (1953), p. 559.

20. Comparing median frequencies of active samples: Kinsey (1953), pp. 394, 559. Even if we use the total sample for the married women (as in chap. 4, note 21), the ratios remain about the same.

21. Same as Note 17.

22. Same as Note 19.

23. Since the tables in Kinsey (1948) give no medians on this point, we have estimated an overall median by taking the midpoint of the postmarital curve in fig. 70, p. 279.

24. Same as Note 19.

25. Kinsey (1948), p. 288, using the raw data.

26. Hunt (1966), esp. pp. 156–59.

27. Same as Note 9, but p. 102.

28. Same as Note 9, but p. 106.

29. Otto (1971), p. 189; Neubeck, p. 21; and Otto (1971), p. 95.
30. Libby and Whitehurst (1973), pp. 134–35: the Christensen data for 1968 are from a direct communication to Libby.
31. Sam Blum, "When Can Adultery Be Justified or Forgiven?" *McCall's,* May 1966.
32. Hunt (1969), pp. 13–14.
33. Kinsey (1948), p. 585.
34. Same as Note 33.
35. Kinsey (1948), p. 284, using raw data.
36. Kinsey (1948), p. 348.
37. Kinsey (1948), pp. 481, 589.
38. Ratio of postmarital to married males in Kinsey is about 1 to 7 (1948, pp. 294, 252); in *Statistical Abstract,* 1940, the ratio is nearly 1 to 11, but doubling the number of divorced (to equate with Kinsey's inclusion of long-separated persons) yields a ratio of 1 to 8.7.
39. Kinsey (1953), p. 32. N.B.: One must subtract the "Ever wid., sep., div." from the "Ever married" to get a figure for the presently married; this is then divided by the "Ever wid., sep., div." to get the ratio. For the U.S. population: *Statistical Abstract,* 1952, p. 37, but doubling the divorced to allow for the separated, in order to make the figure comparable to Kinsey's. See Notes 13 and 38.
40. Same as Note 39.
41. Gebhard's figures are in Bohannan, pp. 96, 309 (Note 6); Kinsey (1953), p. 439.
42. Gebhard's figure: same as Note 41.
43. Kinsey (1953), p. 440.
44. Since Kinsey's accumulative incidences are for all women who are or have ever been married, and since the divorced proved (in Gebhard's analysis) to have higher accumulative incidences of extramarital coitus, the presently married women in Kinsey's sample would have to show lower accumulative incidences than those given in Kinsey (1953), p. 440.
45. Kinsey (1953), p. 440.
46. To factor out the accumulative incidences for presently married and for previously married women from Kinsey's data for ever-married women, we used the formula:

$$a(2\tfrac{1}{2}x) + b(x) = \text{Kinsey's accumulative incidence for ever-married women,}$$

where a is ppn. of sep.+div. within ever-married in Kinsey's sample,

b is ppn. of presently married within ever-married in Kinsey's sample, and

x is the accumulative incidence for presently married women in Kinsey's sample.

Having factored out accumulative incidences for ages 25, 35 and 45, we then synthesized a corrected sample in which the proportions of presently married women to separated-plus-divorced women were those which actually existed in the U.S. population toward the end of the period of Kinsey's field work (1950). We did so by means of the formula:

$$a(2\tfrac{1}{2}x) + b(x) = X,$$

where   a is ppn. of sep.+div. within ever-married in U.S. popula-
            tion, 1950, for ages 25, 35 and 45,

            b is ppn. of presently married within ever-married in U.S.
            population, 1950, for ages 25, 35 and 45,

            x is accumulative incidence for presently married women
            in Kinsey's sample (as derived previously) for ages 25,
            35 and 45, and

            X is corrected accumulative incidence for ever-married
            women in U.S. population, 1950.

47. Kinsey (1953), pp. 423, 442, showing higher rates for the later-born cohorts all along the accumulative incidence curves.

48. Kinsey (1953), p. 439.

49. Kinsey (1948), p. 589.

50. Kinsey (1953), pp. 424, 443.

51. Kinsey (1948), pp. 348, 350, 587.

52. Kinsey (1948), pp. 592–93; Kinsey (1953), pp. 433–34.

53. Kinsey (1953), p. 444.

54. Kinsey (1953), p. 434.

55. Whitehurst (1969), in Neubeck, pp. 137–40, 142–44.

56. *Time*, Jan. 8, 1973, p. 35.

57. Quoted in Bartell, p. 20, and Denfield and Gordon, p. 95.

58. Bartell, p. 21.

59. Kinsey (1953), p. 418; for the married women, Kinsey (1953), p. 408.

60. See Note 8. Carolyn Symonds's study of swinging in southern California was her master's thesis in sociology at the University of California in Riverside, and is discussed briefly in Bartell, p. 21. James and Lynn Smith's article on comarital sex appears in *The Journal of Sex Research*, vol. 6 (May 1970).

CHAPTER 6

1. These themes run throughout. For several examples, however, see Kinsey (1948), p. 574, on oral and anal stimulation among animals, Kinsey (1953), pp. 410–12 on "mammalian origins" of extramarital coitus, and Kinsey (1953), pp. 412–16, on the prevalence of extramarital coitus in human societies.

2. Ford and Beach, pp. 202–7.

3. Ford and Beach, pp. 58–60.

4. R. M. Yerkes, "Sexual Behavior in the Chimpanzee," *Human Biology*, vol. 2 (1939), p. 103.

5. Same as Chapter 3, Note 1.

6. Edward Sagarin, "Sex Research and Sociology," in Henslin, esp. p. 391 (and n. 34), pp. 403–4 (and n. 67, 68).

7. This, at any rate, is the overall impression to be derived from the

professional literature; no one, however, has to our knowledge done a controlled study comparing the psychosocial relationships of pathological deviants with those of normal control groups.

8. Gagnon and Simon, pp. 4–11. The three-part categorization is their own, and appears in their Introduction; however, the sequence of the categories has been changed in our own presentation.

9. Marmor was quoted to this effect in *The New York Times*, Feb. 9, 1973, p. 24, in an article discussing the trend toward reclassification of homosexuality. See also NIMH: *Homosexuality*, pp. 55–57, and Bieber, pp. 15–18. The decision of the American Psychiatric Association to change the diagnostic label of homosexuality was announced on December 15, 1973, and reported in *The New York Times*, Dec. 16, 1973, I, p. 1.

10. Ethologist Erwin DeVore, interviewed and quoted by Karlen, in Karlen, pp. 431–32.

11. Ford and Beach, pp. 129–33.

12. Same as Note 11.

13. Hunt (1959), pp. 20–28, 49–51. Plato's late-life change of mind is documented in Book Eight of his *Laws*.

14. The evidence is reviewed in chapter 6 of Money and Ehrhardt.

15. Kolodny.

16. Karlen, pp. 452–53.

17. Kinsey (1953), p. 501, collapsing the experienced and inexperienced females, and collapsing attitudes toward homosexuality in other females and in males.

18. Same as Note 17, collapsing responses on keeping female friends and keeping male friends.

19. Kinsey (1948), pp. 625, 650; Kinsey (1953), p. 490. For accumulative incidences of response without actual experience: Kinsey (1953), p. 487.

20. Kinsey (1948), pp. 636–41; Kinsey (1953), pp. 469–72.

21. Kinsey (1948), p. 650.

22. Kinsey (1948), p. 650, includes those who rate "2" in his scale among the 25 percent, but see description of the "2s" on his p. 641.

23. Kinsey (1948), p. 651.

24. Pomeroy, pp. 63–64, 133, 139–40.

25. Kinsey (1948), pp. 93–95.

26. Kinsey (1948), p. 100; compare this with data on his pp. 94, 96 and 98.

27. Kinsey (1948), p. 95.

28. Pomeroy, p. 466.

29. Karlen, p. 282.

30. Karlen, p. 456.

31. His recent statement appears in *Medical Aspects of Human Sexuality*, Jan. 1973, p. 32.

32. Kinsey (1953), p. 32. N.B.: The column labeled "Ever married" includes the "Ever wid., sep., div."; thus, total number of females married at time of interview was 1695, or 29.3 percent of the sample (excluding preadolescents).

33. In Kinsey (1953), p. 490, table 126, the headings specify "While single," etc. See also discussion on his pp. 453–54.

34. Kinsey (1948), p. 651.

35. Personal communication from Don Goodwin, president of the Mattachine Society, New York.

36. Using typical ratios of "partial sample" to 100 percent sample from data in Kinsey (1948), p. 100. Kinsey himself believed the partial sample to be more reliable than the 100 percent samples, but clearly his partial sample was nothing like a randomized sample—and he himself admits that he found the best substitute for a randomized sample to be the 100 percent sample; see Kinsey (1948), p. 93.

37. Kinsey (1953), p. 490; see Note 33.

38. Same as Notes 21 and 30.

39. Using figure 83 in Kinsey (1953), p. 453, and the data on his pp. 496, 499.

40. Kinsey (1948), p. 651, and Note 30.

41. Kinsey (1953), p. 499, taking "more or less exclusively homosexual" to be made up of ratings 5 and 6. N.B.: For single females, exclude ratings below age 15.

42. Kinsey (1948), p. 258, using raw data ("Sample Population").

43. Same as Note 42.

44. Kinsey (1953), pp. 496–98, but see p. 499.

45. Kinsey (1953), p. 499.

46. Same as Note 42 above, taking a midpoint of the medians.

47. Same as Note 42 above, taking a midpoint of the medians.

48. Kinsey (1948), pp. 631–33, 636.

49. Kinsey (1953), p. 491, taking a midpoint of the medians.

50. Kinsey (1953), p. 488, for both males and females; also, in more detail for females, p. 492.

51. Same as Note 50.

52. Kinsey (1948), p. 373. This represents a "U.S. Correction," rather than raw data, and includes the 0–8 educational level; however, the raw data that appear on p. 370 suggest that the quoted figures would also be roughly correct for the high-school and college males combined, with the 0–8 cohort omitted.

53. Kinsey (1953), pp. 466–67.

54. Same as Note 3.

55. Same as Note 3.

56. Ford and Beach, pp. 65–67.

57. Ford and Beach, p. 67.

58. *Medical Aspects of Human Sexuality*, Sept. 1972, pp. 155–56.

59. Kinsey (1948), p. 510; Kinsey (1953), p. 164.

60. Kinsey (1953), p. 677.

61. *Obscenity*, pp. 18–19.

62. Kinsey (1953), pp. 677–78.

63. See, for instance, Margaret Mead, "Incest," in *IESS;* the extensive bibliography includes many references attesting the correlation between incest and pathology.

64. Ford and Beach, pp. 118–19.
65. Hewes, pp. 71, 75.
66. For the universality of parent-child and sibling incest: Murdock, p. 12. For broader definitions of incest: Mead (see Note 63 above); Berelson and Steiner, pp. 316–17; Winch, pp. 316–18.
67. Murdock, p. 12; Ford and Beach, pp. 112–13.
68. Murdock, p. 13; Ford and Beach, p. 112.
69. Direct communiqué from Prof. Walter Barnett, Hastings College of Law, San Francisco, Calif.
70. Winch, p. 317.
71. Mead (see Note 63 above); Berelson and Steiner, p. 317.
72. Dobzhansky, pp. 136–37, 148–50.
73. W. J. Schull and J. V. Neel, *The Effects of Inbreeding on Japanese Children* (New York: Harper & Row, 1965), as adapted by Arthur R. Jensen, "How Much Can We Boost IQ and Scholastic Achievement?" in *Environment, Heredity, and Intelligence (Harvard Educational Review*, Reprint Series No. 2, 1969), pp. 55–57.
74. Kinsey (1948), p. 558.
75. Freud (1953), vol. 7, pp. 127–29, 274–75; Freud (1954), pp. 215–18 (letter to Fliess, Sept. 21, 1897).
76. Gebhard (1965), pp. 16, 27.
77. Gebhard (1965), pp. 226, 268, 401, 422.
78. Kinsey (1948), p. 677.
79. Kinsey (1948), pp. 668, 671.
80. Ford and Beach, pp. 148, 151.
81. Ford and Beach, p. 151; Marler and Hamilton, pp. 92–93, 95–100. On the gypsy moth, the artificially manufactured pheromone has even been marketed for the past year or two as the "bait" in traps which attract the male of only this one species.
82. Ford and Beach, p. 150.
83. Ford and Beach, pp. 146–48.
84. *Exodus* 22:19; *Leviticus* 18:23, 20:15.
85. Kinsey (1953), p. 508, n. 12, cites on this H. Davis, *Moral and Pastoral Theology* (New York: Sheed and Ward, 1946), vol. 2, p. 249.
86. Kinsey (1948), p. 677.
87. Kinsey (1948), pp. 670, 672.
88. Kinsey (1953), p. 505. 1.5 percent of his female sample had had some sort of sexual contact with animals in preadolescence, but Kinsey nowhere says whether or not this should be added to the 3.6 percent to make a lifetime accumulative incidence. Since the preadolescent contacts are apparently mostly trivial, we have ignored them in our comparison.
89. Kinsey (1948), p. 672.
90. Kinsey (1948), pp. 461, 671.
91. Kinsey (1948), p. 672, shows 749 rural-reared males; Kinsey (1953), p. 3, states that total male sample of the 1948 study included 5300 persons. See also detailed tables in Kinsey (1948), pp. 686–735.
92. *Statistical Abstract*, 1972, p. 584, assuming Kinsey's males had been aged

12–18 from about 1890 to 1940, according to the cohort, and our own from about 1910 to 1955.

93. Same as Note 92.
94. Kinsey (1953), p. 33 and note on p. 34.
95. Kinsey (1953), pp. 504, 506.
96. Kinsey (1953), p. 32 (omitting the preadolescent sample).
97. Kinsey (1953), p. 506. He does not pinpoint accumulative incidence by age 25, but one can infer it from the material in the first full paragraph on the page.
98. Kinsey (1948), p. 260.
99. Kinsey (1953), pp. 505–6.
100. Same as Note 98, using medians. See also Kinsey (1948), pp. 670–71.
101. Kinsey (1953), p. 506.
102. Kinsey (1948), pp. 675–76.
103. Same as Note 99.
104. Kinsey (1948), p. 673; Kinsey (1953), p. 506.
105. Reiss (1973); Smigel and Seiden, p. 14; K. Davis, p. 142; Rubin, "New Sex Findings: Some Trends and Implications," in Otto (1971), p. 37.

Bibliography

There appear here, for the most part, only those works cited by author's last name or by short title in the Notes, plus works named in brief form in the text. References cited in complete form in the Notes or text are not duplicated here.

The editions listed are those cited in the Notes or in the text. Of those identified as being paperback editions, some are originals, and others are reprints of hardcover books published only a year or two prior to paperback reprinting. Where, however, more than two years elapsed between original publication and reprinting, the original date of publication is also indicated.

Angelino, Henry, and Mech, Edmund. "Some 'First' Sources of Sex Information, as Reported by Sixty-Seven College Women." *Jour. Psychol.*, vol. 39 (1955), pp. 321–324.

Angrist, Shirley. "The Study of Sex Roles." *Jour. Social Issues*, vol. XXV, no. 1 (1969), pp. 215–232.

"An Intimate Revolution" (coeducational dormitory life), *Life*, Nov. 20, 1970.

Athanasiou, Robert, et al. "Sex." *Psychol. Today*, July 1970, pp. 39–52.

Baber, Ray. *Marriage and the Family.* New York: McGraw-Hill Book Co., 1953.

Bartell, Gilbert D. *Group Sex.* New York: New American Library, 1971. Paperback.

Beigel, Hugo. "The Meaning of Coital Postures." *Internat. Jour. of Sexology*, vol. 6 (1953), pp. 136–143.

_____. "Autoeroticism: What It Is and Why It's Misunderstood." *OP: The Osteopathic Physician*, vol. 36, (Sept. 1969).

Bell, Robert R., and Chaskes, Jay B. "Premarital Sexual Experience Among Coeds, 1958 and 1968." *Jour. of Marriage and the Family*, Feb. 1970, pp. 81–84.

Bell, Robert R., and Bell, Phyllis L. "Sexual Satisfaction Among Married Women." *Med. Aspects of Human Sexuality,* Dec. 1972, pp. 136–144.

Berelson, Bernard, and Steiner, Gary. *Human Behavior.* New York: Harcourt, Brace, and World, 1964.

Bergler, Edmund. *Counterfeit-Sex.* New York: Evergreen, 1961. Paperback; original ed. 1951.

Bernard, Jessie. *The Sex Game.* New York: Atheneum, 1972. Paperback.
————. "Infidelity: Some Moral and Social Issues." In Libby and Whitehurst (1973), q.v.

Berne, Eric. *Sex in Human Loving.* New York: Pocket Books, 1971. Paperback.

Bieber, Irving, et al. *Homosexuality: A Psychoanalytic Study.* New York: Basic Books, 1962.

Bohannan, Paul, ed. *Divorce and After.* Garden City: Doubleday Anchor, 1971. Paperback.

Bowman, Claude C. "Social Change as Reflected in the Kinsey Studies." *Social Problems,* July 1954.

Brecher, Edward. *The Sex Researchers.* Boston: Little, Brown, 1969.

Brecher, Edward, and Brecher, Ruth. *An Analysis of Human Sexual Response.* New York: New American Library, 1966. Paperback.

Cannon, Kenneth L., and Long, Richard. "Premarital Sexual Behavior in the Sixties." *Jour. of Marriage and the Family,* Feb. 1971, pp. 36–49.

Caprio, Frank. *The Sexually Adequate Female.* New York: Citadel, 1953. Paperback.

"Change, Yes—Upheaval, No" (sexual behavior of the young). *Life,* Jan. 8, 1971.

Chartham, Robert. *The Sensuous Couple.* London and New York: Penthouse-Ballantine, 1971. Paperback.

Christensen, Harold T., and Gregg, Christina F. "Changing Sex Norms in America and Scandinavia." *Jour. of Marriage and the Family,* Nov. 1970, pp. 616–627.

Clark, Alexander L., and Wallin, Paul. "The Accuracy of Husbands' and Wives' Reports of the Frequency of Marital Coitus." *Population Studies,* vol. 18 (1964), pp. 165–173.
————. "Women's Sexual Responsiveness and the Duration and Quality of their Marriages." *Am. Jour. Sociol.,* vol. 71 (1965), pp. 187–196.

Clark, LeMon. "Sex Life of the Middle Aged." *Marriage and Family Living,* vol. 11 (Spring 1949), pp. 58–60.

Clausen, John. "Biological Bias and Methodological Limitations in the Kinsey Studies." *Social Problems,* Apr. 1954, pp. 126–133.

Cole, William Graham. *Sex and Love in the Bible.* New York: Association Press, 1959.

Comfort, Alex. *Sex in Society.* New York: Citadel, 1966. Paperback.

Commission on Obscenity and Pornography. See *Report of the Commission on Obscenity and Pornography.*

Constantine, Larry L., and Constantine, Joan M. "Sexual Aspects of Multilateral Relations." *Jour. of Sex Research,* vol. 7 (Aug. 1971), pp. 204–225.

Cuber, John F., and Harroff, Peggy B. *The Significant Americans.* New York: Appleton-Century, 1965.

Cutright, Phillips. "The Teenage Sexual Revolution and the Myth of an Abstinent Past." *Family Planning Perspectives,* vol. 4 (Jan. 1972), pp. 24–31.

Davis, Keith E. "Sex on Campus: Is There a Revolution?" *Med. Aspects of Human Sexuality* (Jan. 1971), pp. 128–142.

Davis, Maxine. *The Sexual Responsibility of Woman.* New York: Permabooks, 1959. Paperback.

DeMartino, Manfred, ed. *Sexual Behavior and Personality Characteristics.* New York: Grove, 1963. Paperback.

Denfield, Duane, and Gordon, Michael. "Sociology of Mate Swapping." *Jour. of Sex Research,* vol. 6 (May 1970), pp. 85–100.

De Rougemont, Denis. *Love in the Western World.* New York: Pantheon, 1956.

Dietz, M. L., and Whitehurst, R. N. "Violence in Response to Extramarital Sex." Unpublished: University of Windsor, Ontario. n.d.

Dobzhansky, Theodosius. *Mankind Evolving.* New Haven: Yale University Press, 1962.

Driscoll, Richard H., and Davis, Keith E. "Sexual Restraints." *Jour. of Sex Research,* vol. 7 (Nov. 1971), pp. 253–262.

Edwardes, Allen. *The Jewel in the Lotus.* New York: Julian Press, 1959.

Ehrmann, Winston. "Some Knowns and Unknowns in Research Into Human Sex Behavior." *Jour. of Marriage and the Family,* vol. 19 (Feb. 1957), pp. 16–22.

——————. *Premarital Dating Behavior.* New York: Bantam, 1960. Paperback.

Eichenlaub, John E. *New Approaches to Sex in Marriage.* New York: Dell, 1971. Paperback.

Ellis, Albert. *The American Sexual Tragedy.* New York: Lyle Stuart, 1962.

Ellis, Albert, and Abarbanel, Albert, eds. *The Encyclopedia of Sexual Behavior.* New York: Ace Books, n.d., 5 vols. Paperback; original ed. 1961.

Ellis, Havelock. *Studies in the Psychology of Sex.* New York: Random House, n.d., 2 vols. Hardcover reprint of originals published from 1905–1928.

Fenwick, Henry. "The Law and the Normally Sexed Bachelor (and others)." Unpublished research memorandum, *Playboy* research library.

—————. Untitled summary of sex laws in force, state by state, c.1970, *Playboy* research library.

Fisher, Seymour. *The Female Orgasm*. New York: Basic Books, 1972.

Fleming, Thomas, and Fleming, Alice. "What Kids Still Don't Know About Sex." *Look*, July 28, 1970.

Ford, Clellan S., and Beach, Frank A. *Patterns of Sexual Behavior*. New York: Harper and Hoeber, 1951.

Freud, Sigmund. *The Complete Psychological Works of Sigmund Freud*. Standard Edition. London: Hogarth Press, 1953.

—————. *The Origins of Psychoanalysis: Letters to Wilhelm Fliess*. New York: Basic Books, 1954.

Gagnon, John, and Simon, William, eds. *Sexual Deviance*. New York: Harper & Row, 1967. Paperback.

Gebhard, Paul, et al. *Pregnancy, Birth and Abortion*. New York: Harper and Hoeber, 1958.

Gebhard, Paul, et al. *Sex Offenders*. New York: Harper and Hoeber, 1965.

Gecas, Viktor, and Libby, Roger. "Sexual Behavior as Symbolic Interaction." Paper presented at 1972 annual meeting of the National Council of Family Relations.

Gesell, Arnold, and Ilg, Frances L. *Child Development*. New York: Harper & Brothers, 1949.

Gilman, Richard. "The Femlib Case Against Sigmund Freud." *The New York Times Sunday Magazine*, Jan. 31, 1971.

Ginsberg, G. L.; Frisch, W. A.; and Shapiro, Theodore. "The New Impotence." *Archives of General Psychiatry*, March 1972.

Glick, Paul C., and Norton, Arthur J. "Perspectives on the Recent Upturn in Divorce and Remarriage." Mimeographed. (Published by U.S. Bureau of the Census.) Revised version of a paper presented at the 1972 annual meeting of the Population Association of America.

Gordon, Michael, and Shankweiler, Penelope J. "Different Equals Less." *Jour. of Marriage and the Family*, vol. 33 (Aug. 1971), pp. 459–467.

Grant, Igor. "Anxiety About Orgasm." *Med. Aspects of Human Sexuality*, March 1972, pp. 14–45.

Greer, Germaine. *The Female Eunuch*. New York: Bantam, 1972. Paperback.

Group for the Advancement of Psychiatry. *Sex and the College Student*. New York: Fawcett, 1966.

Hamilton, Eleanor. *Sex Before Marriage*. New York: Bantam, 1970. Paperback.

Hefner, Hugh M. "The Legal Enforcement of Morality." *University of Colorado Law Rev.*, vol. 40 (1968), pp. 199–221.

Henslin, James, ed. *Studies in the Sociology of Sex.* New York: Appleton-Century-Crofts, 1971.

Hessellund, Hans. "On Some Sociosexual Sex Differences." *Jour. of Sex Research*, vol. 7 (Nov. 1971), pp. 263–273.

Hewes, Gordon W. "Communication of Sexual Interest: An Anthropological View." *Med. Aspects of Human Sexuality*, Jan. 1973, pp. 66–92.

Historical Statistics. See U. S. Bureau of the Census.

Hollender, Mark H. "Women's Fantasies During Sexual Intercourse." *Archives of Gen. Psychiatry*, vol. 8 (1963), pp. 86–90.

Humphreys, Laud. "Tearoom Trade." *Trans-Action*, Jan. 1970.

Hunt, Morton. *The Natural History of Love.* New York: Knopf, 1959.

—————. *Her Infinite Variety.* New York: Harper & Row, 1962.

—————. *The World of the Formerly Married.* New York: McGraw-Hill, 1966.

—————. *The Affair.* New York: World, 1969.

—————. "The Future of Marriage." *Playboy,* Aug. 1971.

Hyde, H. Montgomery. *A History of Pornography.* New York: Farrar, Straus & Giroux, 1965.

IESS. See *International Encyclopedia of the Social Sciences.*

International Encyclopedia of the Social Sciences. The Macmillan Company and The Free Press, 1968.

"J." *The Sensuous Woman.* New York: Dell, 1971. Paperback.

James, William H. "The Reliability of the Reporting of Coital Frequency." *Jour. of Sex Research*, vol. 7 (Nov. 1971), pp. 312–314.

Johnson, Ralph E. "Some Correlates of Extramarital Coitus." *Jour. of Marriage and the Family*, vol. 32 (Aug. 1970), pp. 449–455.

Journal of Social Issues. April 1966, special issue: "The Sexual Renaissance in America" edited by Ira L. Reiss.

Kaats, Gilbert R., and Davis, Keith E. "Effects of Volunteer Biases in Studies of Sexual Behavior and Attitudes." *Jour. of Sex Research*, vol. 7 (Feb. 1971), pp. 219–227.

Kalyana Malla. *The Ananga Ranga, or Hindu Art of Love.* New York: Lancer, 1969. Paperback; a 19th-Century translation of the 16th-Century original.

Kaplan, Helen S., and Sager, Clifford J. "Sexual Patterns at Different Ages." *Med. Aspects of Human Sexuality*, June 1971, pp. 10–23.

Karlen, Arno. *Sexuality and Homosexuality.* New York: Norton, 1971.

Key, Ellen, et al. *The Woman Question*, ed. by T. R. Smith. New York: Modern Library, n.d. (c. 1918).

Kinsey, Alfred; Pomeroy, Wardell B.; and Martin, Clyde E. *Sexual Be-*

havior in the Human Male. Philadelphia and London: W. B. Saunders Company, 1948.

Kinsey, Alfred; Pomeroy, Wardell B.; Martin, Clyde E.; and Gebhard, Paul H. *Sexual Behavior in the Human Female.* Philadelphia and London: W. B. Saunders Company, 1953.

Kirkendall, Lester, and Whitehurst, Robert N., eds. *The New Sexual Revolution.* New York: Donald W. Brown, 1971. Paperback.

Kokkoka. *The Koka Shastra.* New York: Stein and Day, 1965. Paperback; a contemporary translation of the 12th-Century original.

Kolodny, Robert C., et el. "Plasma Testosterone and Semen Analysis in Male Homosexuals." *New England Jour. of Med.,* vol. 285 (Nov. 18, 1971), pp. 1170–1174.

Kramer, Heinrich, and Sprenger, James. *The Malleus Maleficarum.* New York: Dover, 1971. Paperback republication of 1928 translation of the 15th-Century original.

Laws, Judith Long. "A Feminist Review of Marital Adjustment Literature: The Rape of the Locke." *Jour. of Marriage and the Family,* vol. 37 (1971), pp. 483–517.

Lehrman, Nat, ed. *Masters and Johnson Explained.* Chicago: Playboy Press, 1970. Paperback.

Levinger, George. "Systematic Distortion in Spouses' Reports of Preferred and Actual Sexual Behavior." *Sociometry,* vol. 29 (1966), pp. 291–299.

Libby, Roger W., and Nass, Gilbert D. "Parental Views on Teenage Sexual Behavior." *Jour. of Sex Research,* vol. 7 (Aug. 1971), pp. 226–236.

Libby, Roger W., and Whitehurst, Robert N., eds. *Renovating Marriage: Toward New Sexual Life-Styles.* Danville, Calif.: Consensus Publishers, Inc., 1973.

Life. Nov. 20, 1970. "An Intimate Revolution."

Life. Jan. 8, 1971. "Change, Yes—Upheaval, No" (sexual behavior of the young).

Lipton, Lawrence. *The Erotic Revolution.* New York: Pocket Books, 1966. Paperback.

"M." *The Sensuous Man.* New York: Dell, 1972.

"Mademoiselle's Modest Little Sex Survey." *Mademoiselle,* Feb. 1970.

Maranell, Gary M., et al. "Social Class and Premarital Sexual Permissiveness." *Jour. of Marriage and the Family,* vol. 32 (Feb. 1970), pp. 85–88.

Marler, Peter, and Hamilton, William. *Mechanisms of Animal Behavior.* New York: John Wiley & Sons, 1968.

Masters, William H., and Johnson, Virginia E. *Human Sexual Response.* Boston: Little, Brown, 1966.

————. *Human Sexual Inadequacy.* Boston: Little, Brown, 1970.

May, Rollo. *Love and Will.* New York: W. W. Norton, 1969.

Mead, Margaret. *Male and Female.* New York: New American Library, 1955. Paperback.

Middendorp, C. P., et al. "Determinants of Premarital Sexual Permissiveness." *Jour. of Marriage and the Family,* vol. 32 (Aug. 1970), pp. 369–380.

Millett, Kate. *Sexual Politics.* New York: Equinox Books (Avon Books), 1971.

Money, John, and Ehrhardt, Anke. *Man & Woman, Boy & Girl.* Baltimore: Johns Hopkins University Press, 1972.

Murdock, George P. *Social Structure.* New York: The Macmillan Co., 1949.

Mussen, Paul Henry, et al. *Child Development and Personality.* New York: Harper & Row, 1963.

Nefzawi, the Shaykh. *The Perfumed Garden.* New York: Castle Books, 1964. Hardcover reprint of 19th-Century translation of 16th-Century original.

Neubeck, Gerhard, ed. *Extramarital Relations.* Englewood Cliffs: Prentice-Hall, 1969. Paperback.

"The New Woman." *Time,* special issue, Mar. 20, 1972, esp. pp. 25–80.

NIMH: *Homosexuality.* See U.S. Department of Health, Education, and Welfare.

Nimkoff, Meyer. *Marriage and the Family.* New York: Houghton Mifflin, 1947.

Obscenity. See *Report of the Commission on Obscenity and Pornography.*

O'Neill, Nena, and O'Neill, George. *Open Marriage.* New York: M. Evans, 1972.

Otto, Herbert, ed. *The Family in Search of a Future.* New York: Appleton-Century-Crofts, 1970. Paperback.

——————. *The New Sexuality.* Palo Alto: Science and Behavior Books, 1971.

Packard, Vance. *The Sexual Wilderness.* New York: David McKay, 1968.

Pearlman, Carl K., and Kobashi, L. I. "Frequency of Intercourse in Men." *Jour. of Urology,* vol. 107 (Feb. 1972), p. 298f.

Pomeroy, Wardell B. *Boys and Sex.* New York: Delacorte Press, 1968.

——————. *Girls and Sex.* New York: Delacorte Press, 1969.

——————. *Dr. Kinsey and the Institute for Sex Research.* New York: Harper & Row, 1972.

Reiss, Ira L. *The Social Context of Premarital Sexual Permissiveness.* New York: Holt, Rinehart and Winston, 1967.

——————. "How and Why America's Sex Standards are Changing." *Trans-Action,* vol. 5 (Mar. 1968), pp. 26–32.

——————. *Hetero-sexual Relationships: Inside and Outside of Marriage.* Morristown, N.J.: General Learning Press, 1973.

Report of the Commission on Obscenity and Pornography. New York: Bantam, 1970. Paperback reprint of the official final report.

Reuben, David R. *Everything You Always Wanted to Know About Sex—But Were Afraid to Ask.* New York: David McKay Company, Inc., 1969.

Rhodes, Richard. "Sex & Sin in Sheboygan." *Playboy,* Aug. 1972.

Roszak, Betty, and Roszak, Theodore, eds. *Masculine/Feminine.* New York: Harper Colophon Books, 1969.

Rubin, Isadore, ed. *Sexual Freedom in Marriage.* New York: New American Library, 1969. Paperback.

Rubin, Isadore. *Sexual Life After Sixty,* New York: Basic Books, 1965.

Schmidt, Gunter, and Sigusch, Volkmar. "Patterns of Sexual Behavior in West German Workers and Students." *Jour. of Sex Research,* vol. 7 (May 1971), pp. 89–106.

Schofield, A. T., and Vaughan-Jackson, Percy. *What a Boy Should Know.* London and New York: Cassell and Company, 1913.

Schwarz, Gerhart S. "Devices to Prevent Masturbation." *Medical Aspects of Human Sexuality,* May 1973, pp. 141–153.

"The Sexual Renaissance in America." See *Jour. of Social Issues.*

Sherfey, Mary Jane. "The Evolution and Nature of Female Sexuality in Relation to Psychoanalytic Theory." *Jour. of the American Psychoanalytic Association,* vol. 14 (Jan. 1966), pp. 28–128.

—————. *The Nature and Evolution of Female Sexuality.* New York: Vintage Books, 1973. Paperback.

Shope, David F. "The Orgastic Responsiveness of Selected College Females." *Jour. of Sex Research,* vol. 4 (Aug. 1968), pp. 206–219.

Shope, David F., and Broderick, Carlfred B. "Level of Sexual Experience and Predicted Adjustment in Marriage." *Jour. of Marriage and the Family,* vol. 29 (Aug. 1967), pp. 424–427.

Singer, Jerome. "The Importance of Daydreaming." *Psychol. Today,* April 1968.

Smigel, Erwin O., and Seiden, Rita. "The Decline and Fall of the Double Standards." *Annals of the American Academy,* March 1968, pp. 6–17.

Somerville, Rose M. "Family Life and Sex Education in the Turbulent Sixties." *Jour. of Marriage and the Family,* vol. 33 (Feb. 1971), pp. 11–35.

Sorenson, Robert C. *Adolescent Sexuality in Contemporary America.* New York: World Publishing Co., 1973.

Spock, Benjamin. *Baby and Child Care.* New York: Pocket Books, 1973. Paperback revised ed.; original ed. 1946.

Statistical Abstract. See U.S. Bureau of the Census.

Stephens, William, ed. *Reflections on Marriage.* New York: Crowell, 1968.

Stone, Hannah, and Stone, Abraham. *A Marriage Manual.* New York: Simon and Schuster, 1952. Revised edition; original ed. 1935.

Tanner, Leslie B., ed. *Voices from Women's Liberation.* New York: New American Library, 1970. Paperback.

Taylor, G. Rattray. *Sex in History.* New York: Thames and Hudson, dist. by Vanguard, n.d. (post 1954).

Terman, L. M., et al. *Psychological Factors in Marital Happiness.* New York: McGraw-Hill Book Co., 1938.

Time, March 20, 1972. Special issue, "The New Woman," esp. pp. 25–80.

Udry, J. Richard, and Morris, Naomi M. "A Method for Validation of Reported Sexual Data." *Jour. of Marriage and the Family,* vol. 29 (1967), p. 442.

—————. "Frequency of Intercourse by Day of the Week." *Jour. of Sex Research,* vol. 6 (Aug. 1970), pp. 229–234.

U.S. Bureau of the Census. *Historical Statistics of the United States,* 1789–1945.

—————. 16th Census Report. *Population,* vol. IV, pt. I; and *Characteristics of the Non-White Population by Race.*

—————. *Statistical Abstract of the United States,* 1940, 1946, 1950, 1952, 1972.

—————. "Current Population Reports, Series P-20," various dates.

U.S. Commission on Population Growth and the American Future. *Demographic and Social Aspects of Population Growth* (vol. 1 of Commission Research Reports), Charles F. Westoff and Robert Parke, Jr., eds. Washington, D.C.: Government Printing Office, 1972.

U.S. Department of Health, Education, and Welfare. National Center for Health Statistics. "Vital Statistics of the United States, 1968: Vol. III—Marriage and Divorce."

—————. "Marriages: Trends and Characteristics, United States." Vital and Health Statistics, Series 21, Number 21. DHEW Publication No. (HSM) 72-1007.

—————. "Monthly Vital Statistics Report" for years 1970 through 1972, and "Annual Summary" of same for years 1970 through 1972.

—————. National Institute of Mental Health. *Homosexuality: Final Report and Background Papers* of the Task Force on Homosexuality, John M. Livingood, ed.

Van de Velde, Theodor H. *Ideal Marriage, Its Physiology and Technique.* New York: Random House, 1930. Original published in 1926.

Vatsyayana. *Kama Sutra.* New York: Castle, 1963. Hardcover reprint of 19th-Century translation of 3rd-Century original.

Wallin, Paul, and Clark, Alexander L. "A Study of Orgasm as a Condi-

tion of Women's Enjoyment in the Middle Years of Marriage."
Human Biology, vol. 35 (May 1963), p. 131f.

Weinberg, Martin S. "The Male Homosexual." *Social Problems,* vol. 17
(Spring 1970), pp. 527–537.

——————. "Homosexual Samples: Differences and Similarities."
Jour. of Sex Research, vol. 6 (Nov. 1970), pp. 312–325.

Whitehurst, Robert N. "Extra-marital Sex: Alienation or Extension of
Normal Behavior," (1969), in Neubeck, q.v.

——————. "Swinging into the Future." Paper presented at 1972
annual meeting of the Midwest Sociological Society.

——————. "Sex in and out of Marriage: A North American Perspective." In Libby and Whitehurst (1973), q.v.

Winch, Robert. *The Modern Family.* New York: Holt, Rinehart, and
Winston, 1965.

Zelnik, Melvin, and Kantner, John. "Sexuality, Contraception and
Pregnancy Among Young Unwed Females in the United
States." In U.S. Commission on Population Growth and the
American Future, *Demographic and Social Aspects of Population
Growth* (1972), q.v.

Index